The Rise of an African M

The Rise of an African Middle Class

Colonial Zimbabwe, 1898–1965

Michael O. West

INDIANA
University Press

Bloomington & Indianapolis

This book is a publication of

Indiana University Press
601 North Morton Street
Bloomington, IN 47404-3797 USA

http://iupress.indiana.edu

Telephone orders   800-842-6796
Fax orders   812-855-7931
Orders by e-mail   iuporder@indiana.edu

© 2002 by Michael O. West

The paper used in this publication meets the minimum
requirements of American National Standard for Information
Sciences—Permanence of Paper for Printed Library Materials,
ANSI Z39.48-1984.

Manufactured in the United States of America

Library of Congress Cataloging-in-Publication Data

West, Michael O. (Michael Oliver)
   The rise of an African middle class : colonial Zimbabwe,
1898-1965 / Michael O. West.
      p.   cm.
Includes bibliographical references and index.
   ISBN 0-253-34085-3 (cloth : alk. paper) — ISBN 0-253-21524-2
(pbk. : alk. paper)
   1. Middle class—Zimbabwe—History. 2. Zimbabwe—Colonial
influence. 3. Zimbabwe—Politics and government—1890-1965.
I. Title.
   HT690.Z55 W46 2002
   305.5'5'096891—dc21

                                                2001008304

1 2 3 4 5   07 06 05 04 03 02

For Gloria Martha Waite
in life, and death, our shining glory

Contents

Acknowledgments

MANY INDIVIDUALS and institutions have contributed to this project. As the footnotes bear witness, it is based on sources located in archives and libraries in Zimbabwe, South Africa, Great Britain, and the United States. I am greatly indebted to the staffs and custodians of these institutions for their generosity, patience, and forbearance. A number of other institutions—including Harvard University, Macalester College, Northwestern University, the University of Illinois at Urbana-Champaign, and the University of North Carolina at Chapel Hill—offered space, fellowships, grants, and employment along the way.

Various scholars have generously given of themselves and their time, sharing knowledge and expertise—even though I may have failed, in whole or in part, to absorb the lessons and instructions provided. Foremost among such teachers and instructors is the late Hazen Leroy Vail, under whose supervision (as a doctoral advisor) the initial draft of this book was written. Martin Kilson, contrarious intellectual, sui generis, has been a mentor and source of inspiration for some two decades.

With exemplary timeliness, the readers for the press, John Higginson and Elizabeth Schmidt, offered very constructive comments and helpful suggestions. My editor at Indiana, Dee Mortensen, also gave wise counsel, even as she rendered the process of production smooth and seamless. Other members of the press's fine staff, including Jane Lyle, played their part. Kathryn Gohl provided sharp-eyed copy-editing. Leslie Bessant and Allison Shutt have been generous friends and colleagues over the years. I am thankful, too, to Gerald Horne, Barbara Moss, Sheila Ndlovu, Godfrey Mpofu, Sam Njovana, Terence Ranger, George Shepperson, Kenneth Vickery, and Luise White.

For encouragement and support, spiritual and material, over many moons I am indebted to Tajudeen Abdul-Raheem, Sara Abraham, Kwame Alford, Barbara Ballard, Dawn Callender, James I. Clark, Veronica Colon, Afua Cooper, Jacques Depelchin, Curline Dorham, Karen Fields, Beverly Grier, Sheila Harding, Mae Henderson, Catherine Higgs, Winston James, Catherine John, Wilma Jones, Vasant Kaiwar, Haile Larebo, Sakui Malapka, Sucheta Mazumdar, Micere Mugo, Tiffany Patterson, Minoca Pinto, Peter Rachleff, Brian Thomas,

Chandra Thomas, Juliet Walker, Bobby West, Komozi Woodard, and Assata Zerai.

At the very lowest moment of my life, Jeanne Penvenne demonstrated that generosity of spirit for which she is so well known, and deservedly so. Amid those same dreary clouds, Judi Byfield supplied music that helped to soothe the soul. Ann Dunbar, Julius Nyang'oro, Bereket Selassie, Debby Crowder, Robin Vander, and other members of the Carolina crew have been enormously kind and generous. Carla DiScala and Al Cramer helped to anchor the Boston end, providing hospitality, conviviality, and humor. Jim Hijiya, in Dartmouth, Massachusetts, played his part with much dedication. Grace Waite Jones kindly offered her services at a particularly crucial moment, while Paul Waite made a number of equally critical interventions. Mike Mcethe and Betty Mcethe have been firm in their support.

Ibrahim Abdullah has excelled as friend, co-worker, and role model, teaching by both precept and example. Fanon Wilkins, a promising laborer of whom much is expected, has been a source of strength, personal and intellectual. I thank Marcus Rediker for his friendship as well as for his advocation and practice of historical reconstructing from below. Horace Campbell has been a true keeper of the flame. His unrelenting and infectious optimism, together with his liberality and giving spirit, anchor many of our hopes and aspirations. I have benefited from Makini Roy-Campbell's hospitality and learned from her fierce, if quiet, determination.

I thank Keletso Atkins for friendship and intellectual commerce, both of which have enriched my life and work. Al Kagan, faithful friend and principled comrade, has gone through many a storm with me. Joye Bowman has been a great blessing to me and mine, and I deeply appreciate her wise counsel and hospitality. Three cheers for John Higginson for lending his broad shoulders and for being a fount in so many ways, not least in making gumbo for Gloria. Merle Bowens's thoughtful and considerate ways, her caring and loving spirit, have helped to sustain me in ways great and small. Carol Thomas, too, has been a willing worker, assuming many offices—brother, counsel, spiritual advisor, among others—all of them with love, sensitivity, and panache.

I am enormously grateful to Sandra Jackson-Opoku, whose friendship, affection, and encouragement have been consistent and unceasing over the years. Selinah Aisam has been a most caring friend and wonderful resource, and I am very pleased to acknowledge her support of this project.

David Johnson has withstood the test of time and circumstances, proving himself a steadfast and unfaltering soulmate, as solid as the Rock of Gibraltar —an analogy I trust he will allow me to make. Bill Martin, an indefatigable laborer if ever there was one, certainly makes his home on the rock. As a friend, comrade, and co-worker, Bill is simply unrivaled; his willingness to give of himself seemingly knowing no bounds. Then there is rock-steady Savi

Horne. If, in fact, there is a better friend and ally than Savi, she has yet to appear in the flesh.

Marjorie (Brenda) Thomas constitutes a rock unto herself. Consistent and dependable, sure-footed and steady-handed, Brenda is a sister by both consanguinity and choice, blood and bond. Which brings me to the mother of all rocks—my mother, Avis West, whose succor and support, it is sufficient to say, have been unwavering and unceasing. It is my earnest hope and fervent supplication that Shannon Mariama Houston will, in the fullness of time, plant her feet on the rock.

I have saved the best for last: Gloria Martha Waite. Stripped, quite literally, of her robe of flesh by the rapacious forces of breast cancer, Gloria now makes her stand on the rock of ages, having retreated from this life on July 29, 2000. While she walked among us, Gloria chose to assume a good many roles —wife, mother, sister, friend, confidant, scholar, teacher, and partisan—all of which she fulfilled with characteristic determination, conviction, and gusto. Her aversion to declamation and commitment to action will forever be her song of praise. She remains in death, as she was in life, my shining glory—nay, our shining glory.

Abbreviations

TEXT

AME	African Methodist Episcopal
ATA	African Teachers Association
BSAC	British South Africa Company
CAS	Capricorn Africa Society
FAWC	Federation of African Women's Clubs
ICU	Industrial and Commercial Workers Union of Africa
IRA	Inter-Racial Association of Southern Rhodesia
NCW	National Council of Women of Southern Rhodesia
NDP	National Democratic Party
PCC	People's Caretaker Council
RBVA	Rhodesia Bantu Voters Association
RICU	Reformed Industrial and Commercial Workers Union of Africa
SRBC	Southern Rhodesia Bantu Congress
SRNA	Southern Rhodesia Native Association
UNIA	Universal Negro Improvement Association
ZANU	Zimbabwe African National Union
ZAPU	Zimbabwe African People's Union

NOTES

BIHR	Borthwick Institute of Historical Research (University of York)
CHS	Chicago Historical Society
HL	Houghton Library (Harvard University)
ICS	Institute of Commonwealth Studies (University of London)
LC	Library of Congress (Washington, D.C.)
NA	National Archives (Washington, D.C.)
NAZ	National Archives of Zimbabwe (Harare)
NAZ (Byo)	National Archives of Zimbabwe (Bulawayo)

PRO	Public Record Office (London)
PTL	Pitts Theology Library (Emory University)
RAC	Rockefeller Archive Center (North Tarrytown, N.Y.)
RHL	Rhodes House Library (University of Oxford)
SAA	Salvation Army Archives, International Headquarters (London)
SOAS	School of Oriental and African Studies (University of London)
SA	State Archives (Pretoria)
UWA	University of the Witwatersrand Archives

Colonial and Postcolonial Place Names

Colonial	Postcolonial
Fort Victoria	Masvingo
Gatooma	Kadoma
Gwelo	Gweru
Hartley	Chegutu
Que Que	Kwekwe
Salisbury	Harare
Selukwe	Shurugwi
Shabani	Zvishavane
Sinoia	Chinhoyi
Umtali	Mutare
Wankie	Hwange

The Rise of an African Middle Class

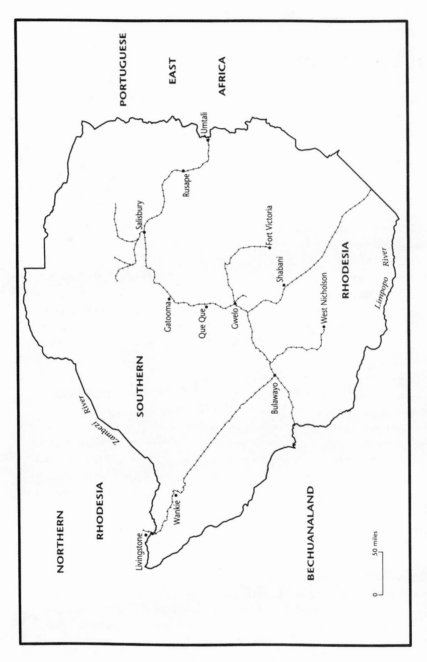

Colonial Zimbabwe, major cities, towns, and railroads, 1955

Introduction

THIS BOOK TELLS the story of the rise of an African middle class in colonial
Zimbabwe (Southern Rhodesia) over three generations, from 1898 to its full
emergence as a self-conscious class in 1965.[1] As a group, the African middle
class constituted a singular corporate entity; it was distinguishable from the
other major social strata in the society—the dominant European settlers (who
were themselves internally differentiated) on the one hand and the African
peasants and workers on the other.

The design of the colonial project in Africa was such that this book
should not have been possible, that is, the rise of an African middle class simply was not part of the scheme of the European colonizers. On the contrary,
public policy in colonial Africa, and even more so in white-settler-dominated
territories like Southern Rhodesia, vitiated the process of social mobility
among the colonized. Consistent with the dominant trend among colonial administrations in Africa, Rhodesian policy emphasized the mobilization of labor for the dominant industries: mining, commercial agriculture, and domestic service. In this political economy, the vast majority of the wage workers
were destined to join the ranks of the unskilled, semiskilled, and low-paid laboring class. The peasants, who formed the majority of the population, fared
no better; the seizure of the best land by the government and the white settlers it encouraged to "develop" the colony also condemned the peasantry to
a life of drudgery. The peasants' toil included reproducing the labor force for
the colonial economy, both physically and socially, as well as providing a social
security net for retired and injured workers from the dominant industries.

For the African population, this arrangement was hardly conducive to
upward social mobility. Yet a small minority of Africans managed to defy the
odds. By exploiting the few alternate social spaces available to the colonized,
these individuals were able to achieve a certain degree of upward social mobility. Elite Africans in colonial Zimbabwe envisaged a lifestyle, and endeavored to attain a lifestyle, that was quite different from the one their colonial
rulers thought suitable for "natives." By its very existence, the African middle
class—a group whose social prominence and political importance amply off-
set its relatively small number—stood as a protest against the colonial politi-

cal economy's tendency toward social leveling. Indeed, the aspirations and achievements of elite Africans amounted to a subversion of the colonial will.[2]

To say that elite Africans subverted the colonial will is not, however, to say that the process by which they became a class unfolded in accordance with some elaborate blueprint or grand design, or that it was smooth and uninterrupted. Though purposeful and persistent, elite Africans' protestations of colonialism were, until quite late in the process, neither fulsome nor frontal, their subversion of the colonial will more covert than overt. For most of the period under consideration, the class strategy of the African middle class emphasized reforming colonialism rather than overthrowing it, as the members of this group sought, ever so gingerly and gently, to overcome the structural barriers that impeded their aspirations for social mobility, individual and collective.

The members of the African middle class—clerks, teachers, preachers, social workers, journalists, businessmen, nurses, lawyers, and doctors, among others—shared similar personal and social experiences in the areas of education, occupations, family life, consumption habits, residential patterns, and organizational affiliations. Despite their privileged position in relation to the mass of the colonized peasants and workers, however, elite Africans were not, for the most part, wealthy, especially when compared with most white settlers. As much as anything else, the African middle class in colonial Zimbabwe was held together by a unity of purpose: its members had interests, aspirations, and ideas that set them apart from other social classes, and they were conscious of these differences.

This book, then, assumes a definition of class that is as much ideological (consciousness) as it is material (economic). Class, in the first instance, is determined by a person's relationship to the means by which wealth is produced, distributed, and appropriated. Traditionally, the middle class is a social category consisting of those who stand between the owners and controllers of the major means of production—that is, the upper, ruling, or governing class—and those who are most directly involved in producing wealth—that is, the working class and other lower ranking social strata, including the peasantry. The members of the middle class are usually distinguished by their professional standing—which generally presupposes a level of educational attainment above the societal average—and the white-collar nature of their work.

Yet one's relationship to the means of production and distribution is merely the starting point of class ranking; it is not the ending point or sole determinant. Ideology, or the consciousness of class, is no less important than the material reality of class. Far from being a static phenomenon, class is a social, which is to say a historical, process. Ultimately, class is determined by the overall experiences of individuals and groups—experiences that are cultural, social, and political as well as economic. These feelings of shared experience and destiny assume even greater urgency in a situation in which the aspirations for social mobility are negated by the imposition of colonialism and racial stigma, as was the case in Southern Rhodesia.

This study is bounded in time by two events—the first in 1898 and the second in 1965. Although the colony of Southern Rhodesia had been established eight years earlier as part of the British empire, the year 1898 marked a new beginning in the colonial project. Throughout colonial Africa, the initial process of expropriation—land enclosure, cattle confiscation, and forced labor, along with the terror that accompanied them—provoked violent resistance by the newly colonized populations. Two such uprisings occurred in Southern Rhodesia, in 1893 and again in 1896–97. In 1898, a year after the second revolt, which was bloodier and more destructive than the first, the imperial power took a series of drastic steps. Circumventing the local colonial administration, which they regarded as politically inept, the authorities in London significantly rearranged the colony's governmental structure. The Reform of 1898 had two aims: to establish more systematic and predictable methods of subjugating and controlling the colonized people and to increase the power of the white settlers in relation to the British South Africa Company, the privately owned business that also governed the colony.

The linchpin of the reform was the institutionalization of oppression. Although brutal and repressive in its treatment of the Africans, the British South Africa Company—at once Southern Rhodesia's government and its biggest investor, owning the railways, most of the mines, and much of the best arable land—did not have a methodical and well-ordered "native policy." To bring more systematic planning and greater efficiency to the task of ruling the subject population, which also meant attenuating the colonial nexus of business and politics that the British South Africa Company so crudely exemplified, the imperial authorities created the Native Affairs Department. A sprawling bureaucracy with authoritarian, even arbitrary, powers—administrative, legislative, and judicial—the Native Affairs Department was charged with forestalling further rebellion and reconciling the Africans to their status as hewers of wood and drawers of water in the colonial order. This mandate did not, it stands to reason, include fostering social mobility among the Africans. In fact, the Native Affairs Department regarded an African middle class as a bane of colonialism and attempted to frustrate its emergence in ways large and small.

The Native Affairs Department's antagonism to the African middle class was rooted in both its mission and its philosophy of African culture. Native affairs officials were preoccupied with tradition and custom, which they regarded as agencies for social cohesion and political stability. These officials, accordingly, focused on the countryside, the hub of their notions of tradition and custom, which they largely imagined and invented. Native affairs officials also attempted to build up the stature of what they considered the traditional authorities, that is, African chiefs and headmen, who they regarded as the guardians of custom and tradition and who served at the pleasure of the government. This ideological stance amounted to a formal disavowal of the African middle class and all it stood for. In the first instance, the identification of elite Africans with urban life and ways raised the suspicion of the rural-centered Native Affairs Department. More substantively, native affairs officials resented the fact that, implicitly or explicitly, elite Africans constituted an alternative leadership cadre to the traditional authorities. The African middle class apparently had rejected tradition and custom in favor of modernity and progress, values the native affairs officials saw as tending toward social dissolution and political instability.

In addition to creating the Native Affairs Department, the Reform of 1898 included certain concessions to the white settlers, a move that had far-reaching, if unforeseen, consequences for the rise of the African middle class. The settlers, like the imperial authorities, blamed the British South Africa Company for the uprisings and demanded a say in the governance of the colony. Central to the empowerment of the settlers was the introduction of the Legislative Council, a partially elected body that curbed the authority of the company, which previously had ruled unchecked. With the Legislative Council came a voting system that was notably color-blind and nonracial, even if the franchise was restricted to males and determined by property and literacy qualifications.

Although color-blind, the franchise was not introduced with Africans in mind. Few if any African men indigenous to Southern Rhodesia could meet the criteria for voting at the time of the Reform of 1898. This state of affairs, however, was only momentary. In less than a generation, the strivings of an emerging cadre of colonial subjects, the vanguard of the African middle class, came to center on the nonracial franchise and the potential it seemed to hold out for political and social equality with the white settlers. In this way, the Reform of 1898 became a double-edged sword for elite Africans, producing at once a major instrument for fettering their rise as a social category—the Native Affairs Department—as well as a noted formula for advancing their class aspirations—the nonracial franchise.

The substantive and symbolic importance of the nonracial franchise to the emerging African elite soon caused a backlash by white settlers, who saw a self-conscious colonized black middle class as a threat to their racially determined privileges and, ultimately, to the entire colonial project itself. Politically, the attack on the African elite took the form of opposition to the nonracial franchise, as the settlers and their elected representatives began a decades-long campaign to strip all Africans, regardless of social standing, of the right to vote.

Predictably, and in direct response to the settlers' agitation against it, some of the first attempts at political mobilization by elite Africans centered on preserving the nonracial franchise. The mantra associated with these efforts, "equal rights for all civilized men"—words, paradoxically, first uttered by Cecil Rhodes, founder of the British South Africa Company and the man for whom the colony was named—became the rallying cry of the African middle class, a veritable theme song of its struggle for a color-blind meritocracy in which careers would be open to talented and educated individuals on a nonracial basis.

The study ends with 1965, the year in which the race-neutral meritocratic formula and all that it entailed were formally, and violently, repudiated by the colonial regime. Here, the defining event was a constitutional rebellion by the white-settler-run government. Although ostensibly directed at the British imperial overlords—whose Reform of 1898, including introduction of the Legislative Council, laid the foundation for the development of settler political culture—the rebellion of 1965 fundamentally was an attack on the African middle class. At the root of the revolt stood the African elite's changing political strategy, itself a reaction to the settler rejection of the equal-rights-for-all-civilized-men principle.

Beginning in the late 1950s, members of the African middle class, which had now fully evolved, became increasingly convinced that the white ruling race would not accede to their call for a nonracial equalitarian society. Ideologically, this conviction was expressed in the rise of African nationalism among the black middle class. Politically, the embrace of African nationalism meant that the black elite would abandon its historic quest for an alliance with the white settlers—fellow "civilized" people—and seek instead to forge a coalition with the mass of African peasants and workers, groups from which elite Africans had long maintained social distance. The new all-African compact was cemented by one overriding demand: universal franchise.

The demand for universal franchise meant that all Africans, not just the "civilized" middle-class minority, should be given the vote, without regard to property and literacy (women had been accorded the franchise, with the same qualifications as men, in 1919). Instead of striving to share power with the settlers, as previously, the African middle class would now seek to take power on behalf of an African nation, over which it claimed leadership. The old trope of equality among civilized men was consigned to the dustbin of history; in its place came a new mantra—majority rule.

The settler rebellion of 1965 sought to nullify the central claim of African nationalism, the demand for universal franchise. Politically, rebellion was a white-supremacist dagger in the heart of majority rule. The rebellion was directed against the imperial power only to the extent that Britain—under pressure from the independent African states, which supported the Zimbabwean African nationalists—refused to grant Rhodesia independence until it made provisions for eventual universal franchise, effectively, majority rule. The white-settler regime rejected this condition and unilaterally declared independence from Britain. The rebellion marked the end of an era. If the Reform of 1898 offered colonized subjects a political and social opening, albeit one with a concomitant tendency toward closure, then the settler rebellion of 1965 was an unqualified historic setback for the self-conscious African middle class. Africans, led by the middle-class nationalists, would subsequently forsake the ballot in favor of the bullet, resorting to armed struggle to achieve majority rule.

As already indicated, elite formation among Africans in Southern Rhodesia had a strong urban bias. The more highly educated and technically proficient individuals whose social and political strivings are charted in these pages worked and lived in disproportionate numbers in the colonial cities and towns. These same urban areas generally doubled as the centers of gravity for the various voluntary associations—social, cultural, religious, professional, political—that were among the most salient factors in the rise of the African middle class. Similarly, the news organs in which elite Africans expressed their grievances and aspirations, a stream of evidence in which this study is partially grounded, were virtually all based in the metropolitan areas.

Of course, not all members of the African middle class resided in the urban centers or made their living there. Elite Africans—preachers, teachers, clerks, and medical workers, among others—also could be found in the rural areas, most conspicuously on Christian mission stations. More significant still, socially if not numerically, were the Purchase Area farmers—that is, Africans with the means to acquire farm land on a freehold basis, in contrast to the communal tenure that existed in the Reserves, where the peasants lived. In one prominent case, that of the Samkange family, Terence Ranger maintains that Purchase Area holdings helped to lay the socioeconomic foundation of an elite dynasty.[3] Allison Shutt argues even more broadly along the same lines, seeing the Purchase Areas as a template for many elite Africans, who formed a rural middle class.[4]

Yet whatever their rustic charm and social significance, the Purchase Areas remained, for the most part, appendages to the urban centers. Actually, many of these Purchase Area landowners had no intrinsic interest in farming. Rather, for those Africans with the desire and ability to own land privately, the Purchase Areas, which were racially segregated, offered the only option. Africans were denied freehold tenure not just in the Reserves—where, according to the colonial regime, communal ownership protected the peasantry from speculation and the resulting potential for landlessness—but also in the cities, which were designated as white areas, making African urban dwellers mere temporary sojourners. Allison Shutt's research shows that Purchase Area farms ordinarily were acquired with capital accumulated from paid employment, usually in the cities. Having secured the property, few owners could afford to retire to their farms. Denied the subsidies and extension services that white farmers took for granted, most Purchase Area landowners were compelled to keep their jobs to subsidize their farms.[5] Even for the putative rural African middle class, then, the urban centers retained their centrality—not just socially, culturally, and politically, as was the case for the black elite as a whole, but economically as well.

From the standpoint of civic prominence and public pronouncements, the rise of the African middle class in colonial Zimbabwe was, to a very large extent, a male-dominated affair. This is not to say, however, that the actual process by which the elite emerged as a distinct social category was delimited solely by men. The women of the elite, which in the patriarchal society that was Southern Rhodesia usually meant the wives and daughters of the men of the elite—along with other women, some of them far removed from elite status—significantly determined the strategy of middle-class formation, directly and indirectly. Thus the story told here is by no means exclusively male. African women are neither silent nor absent. Although perhaps muted overall, their voices can still be heard above the din of male utterances, and women become rather vocal at some points in the narrative. To be sure, most elite women agreed, in principle if not always in practice, that they should concede the public sphere to the men of their class, even as the women sought satisfaction and fulfillment in the more private domains of life, beginning with home and hearth. Yet even when women were silent, the female presence, always a major consideration in male actions and decisions, made itself felt, often exercising a decisive influence on the political and social undertakings of the men.

Internationalism, a search for connections beyond the borders of Southern Rhodesia, was an important factor in the rise of the African middle class. In their struggles against the economic, social, and political disabilities that fettered their desire for upward social mobility, elite colonial Zimbabweans looked abroad for succor, inspiration, and models of emancipation. Especially noteworthy were the interconnections and interrelationships they developed with other colonized and oppressed Africans on the southern African subcontinent, in Africa more generally, and in the transatlantic African diaspora. In this way, elite colonial Zimbabweans became participants in a wider ideological commerce, most conspicuously a pan-African ideological commerce, that shaped their collective outlook and worldview in significant ways.

As a narrative in the rise of an African middle class in Southern Rhodesia, this study is a synthesis of social and political history. From a historiographical standpoint, it departs most sharply from the scholarship on labor, particularly migrant labor, that has defined much of Zimbabwean (and more generally southern African) historical research over the past quarter century or so. Charles van Onselen and David Johnson are, respectively, among the earliest and latest contributors to this body of literature.[6]

In contrast to the scholarship on the proletariat, my research focuses on another group of colonial subjects, individuals whose relatively paltry numbers belie their historical importance. Terence Ranger has adroitly illuminated this process of African middle-class formation among the Samkange family, focusing on the patriarch Thompson and his sons Stanlake and Sketchley.[7] Other published, major studies also shed considerable light on various aspects of the rise of the African middle class. Ngwabi Bhebe's biography of Benjamin Burombo offers a highly unconventional view of an important, even pivotal, figure in elite African politics from the early post–World War II era until his death in 1958.[8] Although not primarily concerned with elite formation, Elizabeth Schmidt and Teresa Barnes provide vivid and arresting accounts of African women and their struggles for personal and gender autonomy from both colonial rule and patriarchal authority, black as well as white.[9] Carol Summers's work on social ideals and social control enhances our understanding of education, the major avenue to social mobility for the colonized, while Timothy Burke's imaginative research on the making of a consumer culture draws attention to an emphasis on purity, hygiene, and cleanliness, issues that historically resonated strongly among female members of the African middle class.[10]

Although building on the extant literature concerning various aspects of social differentiation and class formation among Africans in Southern Rhodesia, my work also differs from this earlier research—topically, geographically, and chronologically. Focusing on social and political factors, I chart, over a period spanning three generations, the rise of an African middle class—as a *national* project of the social category as a whole, not just sections of it. I further situate the African middle class in relation to the white settlers and the African masses, the two groups against which elite Africans came to define themselves. In addition to being an exercise in historical investigation, this study can also be read as a sociopolitical introduction to postcolonial Zimbabwe.

The book is in two parts, each consisting of four chapters. Part 1 charts the social construction of the African middle class, with an emphasis on mobility and identity, education, family, and housing. Chapter 1 discusses the structural and ideological obstacles to African social mobility, along with attempts by elite Africans to assert their own identity in opposition to the colonial project. Chapter 2 deals with education, the gateway to social mobility, focusing on a three-way struggle between the state, the missionaries, and elite Africans to determine the parameters within which colonial subjects would be able to rise to a higher level. In chapter 3 we move to the realm of homemakers and households, with the discussion centering on notions of domestic ideal, marriage, bridewealth, and the wedding ceremony. Chapter 4 is concerned with another aspect of the domestic ideal: the struggle of elite Africans for housing commensurate with their self-perceived status and social aspirations as well as their desire to flee the racially segregated urban townships or ghettoes, thereby gaining spatial distance from the working class.

Part 2 deals with the political construction of the African middle class. This part of the story begins in chapter 5, with the origins of elite African political mobilization, including efforts to define an agenda, with respect to both the white settlers and the African masses. Chapter 6 focuses on the depression years, World War II, and its immediate aftermath, when an elite-led search for political consensus with African workers ended in disastrous failure. Chapter 7 looks at renewed attempts in the 1950s to create "racial partnership" and, in so doing, finally to realize the African elite's foundational dream of equality with the white settlers. The consequences of the failure of these attempts form the subject of chapter 8, which concentrates on the rise of African nationalism and its repression, a process that culminated in the settler rebellion of 1965.

PART I

The Social Construction of the African Middle Class

1

Running against the Wind
African Social Mobility and Identity in
a Settler Colonial Society

IN 1915, a high police official in Bulawayo, responding to repeated entreaties by various African organizations, appealed to the top colonial administrator to establish a housing scheme "for the more respectable class of natives who form part of the labour supply of the town, and who shun the location [or African ghetto] as a dwelling place for their wives and families."[1] Shortly thereafter the chief native commissioner, the head civil servant in charge of the colonized people, announced that the government had purchased land outside the city for such a scheme, asserting further that the move was aimed at accommodating the "wishes of the better class of natives . . . who desire to remove their women and children from the contaminating influences inseparable from town native locations."[2] Yet despite such statements by officials acknowledging the existence of a "more respectable" and "better" stratum among the colonized population, the preponderant tendency of government policy, and certainly the general tenor of Southern Rhodesian settler society, vitiated the process of African middle-class formation. In the case of the housing scheme, for instance, it took two decades for the colonial regime actually to fulfill its promise, and even then the project fell so short of minimal expectations that it was initially boycotted by elite Africans in Bulawayo, their abhorrence of ghetto living notwithstanding. In this, as in almost all respects, the rise of a black petty bourgeoisie in Southern Rhodesia was largely a tale of running against the wind.

Succinctly stated, the Rhodesian settlers and their political leaders opposed the rise of an African middle class because they believed such a social stratum posed a threat to white colonial domination. The colonialists were especially fearful that a politicized black elite, its aspirations frustrated by racial barriers, would seek to mobilize the African masses against settler rule. These concerns, previously expressed only inchoately, began to crystallize in the immediate post–World War I era, hard on the heels of a vast upsurge in African political consciousness, agitation, and organization.

THE NEGATION OF AFRICAN SOCIAL MOBILITY

The first target of the postwar attack on African middle-class formation was education, the principal avenue of social mobility in colonial Africa.[3]
Blaming their problems on the missionaries, who at that time provided practically all the formal schooling Africans received, colonial officials opened a
major critique of African education, focusing on what they considered an over-
emphasis on literary development. The missionaries, these officials sneered,
had sown a patch of book learning, leaving white society to reap the bitter fruit of deracinated and frustrated school-leavers who existed in a social
netherworld: alienated from the African masses, these striving blacks were rebuffed by the ruling race as well. But mission natives, as Africans with formal schooling were derisively called, did not just threaten white domination.
They also were seen as a menace to the colonially constructed conception of
"tribal" society, an imagined community of pristine Africans whom the authorities jealously sought to protect from the baneful influences of "civilization," especially if those professing to be the bearers of civilization were
black.[4]

Missionary education, then, had produced the Dangerous Native, a figure portrayed—and caricatured—in settler lore as a miseducated, urbanized
male agitator, his lips dripping with wild and imperfectly understood rhetoric
about rights. Juxtaposed against the Dangerous Native was the Good Native.[5]
Equally idealized and masculinist as his sinister opposite number, the Good
Native was "properly" trained and respectful of authority, deferring to white
Native Affairs bureaucrats and their African underlings (chiefs) as he moved
about the countryside, tools in hand, making himself useful to his neighbors.
As the image suggests, the Good Native was, fundamentally, a product of in-
dustrial education.

Lauded as a social alchemy, an antidote to the Dangerous Native, industrial education occupied pride of place in the "retribalization" campaign
launched by the colonial regime in the post–World War I era. Dubbed "native
development" in official parlance, retribalization had as one of its main objectives a full-scale reorientation of African education, with academic pursuits, if
they figured at all, occupying a decidedly inferior position to industrial training in the curriculum.

Retribalization also privileged chiefs and other so-called traditional authorities over the emerging African middle class, a sociopolitical assault much
resented by elite blacks. The resentment was especially strong in the rural areas, where elite Africans were far less concentrated than in the urban centers
and where, conversely, the traditional authorities and their Native Affairs De-

partment patrons were strongest. T. Joseph Magore Chitenene, a teacher in
Gutu, an area notorious (and celebrated) for its rebellious ways, vented the
feelings of the rural, educated black elite: "There are two divisions of people
to-day, the cultured division and the division of the illiterate. Cultured people
are finding it hard to be ruled over by the illiterate, simply because the illiterate swallow things unchewed, that is they get anything from the authorities
and they do not bother to ask why it is like this or who has made this thing.
Cultured people like to do things when they understand why they should
do them."[6] Retribalization was directed against self-described cultured and
civilized Africans like Chitenene. As envisaged by officials, the recipients of
industrial training, a major plank in the retribalization project, would be rus-
ticated. Thus discharged into the Reserves—the official name for the unpro-
ductive rural areas to which Africans were consigned under the system of racial segregation—educated Africans would develop "along their own lines,"
instead of being allowed to migrate to the white urban centers to compete
directly with European settlers.

The leading strategist in the campaign to undermine the foundation of
African middle-class formation was Herbert S. Keigwin, a roving British imperial bureaucrat. "The policy of raising the mass ever so little is infinitely preferred to any scheme for the advancement of the few," Keigwin announced in
a landmark report submitted to the Southern Rhodesian Legislative Council
in 1920.[7] Such a high-profile rebuke of missionary education for its alleged
elitism and bookish propensity—a gross exaggeration of the missionary enterprise as it actually operated, as we shall see—was not altogether unprecedented. A decade earlier the colony's first general commission on native policy,
using similar language, had "greatly deprecate[d] any scheme of education
that aims at the development of the exceptional, while advocating with all
their power the steady enlightenment and upliftment of the mass."[8] Now, with
the full and enthusiastic backing of officials at the highest level, and under the
guise of "raising the mass," Keigwin offered a comprehensive plan to retard
the development of a cadre of modern-educated Africans.

The notion of raising the mass was an integral part of the project to
checkmate the Dangerous Native. In his report to the Legislative Council,
Keigwin outlined the goal of the policy of native development and its linchpin, industrial training. He conceded that "talented men will from time to
time emerge" among the Africans, individuals whose desire for "advanced
education" could not easily be frustrated. Instead, the regime should seek to
"minimise the dangers arising from over-education," that is, literary training,
by reducing "the gap between these [educated men] and the mass" through
what amounted to universal industrial education. If the "general standard of
intelligence will be raised," Keigwin reasoned, more Africans would "become

capable of a correct appreciation of values, political and economical. The educated agitator will not have the same ignorant populace to work upon, and his
inflammatory doctrines will have less chance of success."[9]

Keigwin's plan both expressed and reinforced widespread settler fear
and loathing of Africans with any kind of book learning. It had long been considered axiomatic by officials and ordinary whites alike that missionary education virtually rendered Africans useless. Indeed, the colonialists were never
more rhapsodic than when holding forth on the virtues of "raw natives" as
compared with educated "boys" (educated "girls" were much more rare). In
evidence presented to the South African Native Affairs Commission of 1903–
1905, which included Southern Rhodesia, one native commissioner exclaimed:
"The majority of educated Natives I have met usually turned out to be idle
and in a great measure dishonest. . . . I don't think the State should support
Native education beyond what is required to make him a good workman; he
should not be educated until he fancies himself a fine gentleman too good to
undertake ordinary work."[10] Literate Africans, another official informed the
commission, faced open discrimination in employment: "Many employers of
labour will not engage a boy who is a 'Mission boy.' "[11]

The vilification, effectively a disinformation campaign against the aspiring African elite, became more intense and widespread over time. Appearing
before another commission in 1925, this one investigating the concerns about
black education so prominently publicized by Keigwin, a "kind and justly employer" with more than two thousand Africans in his service declared: "if you
want to spoil a good nigger send him to a mission. He is casual and approaches
you as an equal."[12] Nor was the animus gender-specific. The 1925 education
commission also heard testimony that white women shared the views of their
husbands: "A clear majority of Rhodesian women, a large number of whom
are fair and indulgent mistresses, have the opinion that mission-trained Natives are self-assertive and impudent. It is also said that mission Natives are
not as honest as 'raw' Natives."[13]

The Rhodesian settlers were in no doubt as to why the colony had been
established, and they generally regarded pursuit of their individual and group
interests as mutually exclusive of whatever aspirations toward mobility the
colonized majority might hold. "The white people came here primarily not to
uplift the native," Godfrey Huggins, then leader of the opposition, announced
bluntly in the Legislative Assembly in 1931.[14] "They came here for commercial reasons."[15] Little wonder, then, that the negation of African aspirations
reached its high point under Huggins, who became prime minister in 1933, a
position he retained for two decades before moving up to head the government of the newly created Federation of Rhodesia and Nyasaland, a union of
Southern Rhodesia, Northern Rhodesia (Zambia), and Nyasaland (Malawi).
Huggins, his sympathetic biographers affirm, "dreaded the idea of producing

[African] *babus* who could not find jobs but would read or write revolutionary pamphlets instead."[16]

Huggins's eventual political ascendancy reaffirmed the preeminence of settler over African interests in Southern Rhodesia, both in substance and symbol. Yet the prime minister's policy of segregation, called parallel development—a formulation inspired by the American doctrine of separate but equal —involved no radical disjunction; it was more a refinement of, rather than a sharp departure from, past segregationist practices. The major pillars of Rhodesian segregation—territorial, juridical, educational, and occupational—had been established under the British South Africa Company (BSAC), which governed the colony from its inception in 1890 until 1923. In 1923, when company rule gave way to self-government, chosen by the almost exclusively white electorate in preference to incorporation into the Union of South Africa, the system of segregation underwent additional fine-tuning.[17]

Self-government, a British imperial arrangement stopping just short of independence, greatly enhanced the political power of the settlers. The new dispensation spawned increasingly shrill demands to "make Rhodesia white," that is, to enshrine settler privileges by closing all major avenues of social mobility to Africans and, concomitantly, guarding against Indian (South Asian) "penetration."[18] Especially eager for protection against black advancement, present and future, were the national bourgeoisie (that is, settler businessmen who had chafed under the BSAC, which they considered an agent of international capital) and organized white labor, composed mainly of artisans and other skilled workers.[19]

The Rhodesia Party—which ruled the colony for a decade, from the advent of self-government in 1923 to Huggins's assumption of power in 1933— did not betray the confidence of the settler electorate; indeed, it strengthened the barriers against African aspirations in two crucial areas—land and education. In the history of colonialism in Southern Rhodesia, no issue was more vexatious than land, and the crowning achievement of the Rhodesia Party government was codification of territorial segregation. The racial division of the land, legally and formally, commenced with the appointment of a blueribbon commission, in good British imperial fashion. The commission's report, presented in 1925, culminated five years later in the Land Apportionment Act.[20] Hailed as a settlers' Magna Carta, this legislation designated the colony's best farm land, as well as its mines and urban centers, as exclusive white preserves—areas from which Africans were barred, except as temporary sojourners in the employment of Europeans.[21] The Land Apportionment Act thus forbade Africans from owning real property in the urban centers, dashing the dreams of aspiring black homeowners as well as crippling the accumulation prospects of black would-be entrepreneurs.

In yet another blow to black social mobility, the Rhodesia Party government sought to further limit the aspirations of the colonized people by expanding the BSAC policy of undermining African education.[22] Toward this end, a commission on African education was appointed, with the commission presenting its report in 1925, the same year—and not coincidentally—that the land commission tabled its findings. The report of the education commission repeated the stereotypes of educated Africans and came out in favor of industrial training over academic learning. Extolling the virtues of raising the mass instead of advancing the few, it advocated a broad approach to native development and industrial training.[23] In line with the commission's recommendations, the government eventually established a new agency, the Department of Native Development, ostensibly to promote social and economic progress in the Reserves. The department's name, however, belied its mission: it promoted underdevelopment rather than development.[24] Using its admittedly limited funds, and more importantly the coercive capacity of the state to bend the missionaries to its will, the Department of Native Development and allied agencies funneled scarce resources into the cul-de-sac of industrial training, which they regarded as the counteragent of African middle-class formation.

The efforts of the Rhodesia Party government to consolidate white supremacy did not, however, impress Godfrey Huggins and his Reform Party. As leader of the opposition in the Legislative Assembly, Huggins—the most prominent to date in a long line of alpha-champions of white Rhodesia—attacked the government's initiatives as insufficient, sounding a note of settler populism as he thundered against the economic threat allegedly posed by Africans. The Rhodesia Party, reputedly beholden to the settler national bourgeoisie, had not done enough to protect white labor and small settler shopkeepers, Huggins objected. He thought it "absolutely wrong from the white man's point of view if you are going to allow and to place these educated natives, preachers, parsons and skilled people of every description, to throw them back on the white civilisation," that is, to allow them to take up residence in the urban areas where they would compete with the settlers.[25] To guard fully against the economic black peril, Huggins advocated influx control, a rigorous screening of Africans in the urban centers to weed out those considered undesirable, coupled with greater control over the ones allowed to remain.

On coming to power, Huggins was forced to swallow much of his fire-eating rhetoric: the indispensable role of African labor in the colonial economy —agrarian, mining, and urban—ruled out the more drastic measures he had advocated while in the opposition.[26] But although unable to expel Africans en mass from the cities, Huggins's government maintained and intensified the regime of segregation it inherited from the BSAC and the Rhodesia Party, including in the crucial areas of land and education. Further, Huggins's unremitting hostility to African entrepreneurship in the urban business districts, his even deeper aversion to anything remotely smacking of social equality between the races, and his repeated attempts to disfranchise the small number of African voters—all measurably solidified the edifice against African social mobility.[27]

THE ASSERTION OF AFRICAN SOCIAL MOBILITY

The elaboration of white supremacy and its corollary, the denial of African aspirations, did not go unchallenged. Elite Africans, rallying behind their famous mantra, "equal rights for all civilized men," stood firmly on the classical bourgeois principle that careers should be open to those with talent, in this case on a nonracial basis. Armed with that conviction, they used all available peaceful means vigorously to contest the project to circumscribe or liquidate them as a social category. These efforts included passing resolutions at organizations they controlled, making representations directly to the authorities and the missionaries, and waging a public crusade in the white-controlled, African-oriented press, thereby demonstrating their belief in the British colonial shibboleth that the pen is mightier than the sword.

In 1933, a few months before Huggins took power, J. H. Sobantu, in a newspaper article, had eloquently drawn attention to the plight of the emerging African middle class. Sobantu began by posing a series of questions: "Why is it that natives think that they have no opportunities in the country? Why is it that they think good things are for Europeans only?"[28] Sobantu, with a foot on the social-mobility ladder himself, had no doubt about the answer. "It is because civilised natives are being unfairly treated," he declared emphatically. Aspiring Africans, he protested in words that provide the inspiration for the title of this book, were not "given a better chance of rising to a higher level so that those who are backward may see what a civilised man deserves."[29]

The dearth of elite black role models, Sobantu complained, negated the "civilizing mission," a highly ambiguous conception invoked endlessly by the colonialists, even as their behavior made a mockery of their braggadocio. When the "clean and well-dressed native is chased away from the sidewalk," he continued, the "backward" African could only conclude that education "means nothing because he sees no difference" in the treatment accorded blacks, regardless of social standing. Indeed, Sobantu's own career objectives had been thwarted by racial exclusion. Although desiring to join the police force, he refused, as a "civilised man," to submit to the indignities meted out daily to "native police boys," such as being forced to wear "short trousers and walk barefooted."[30] Emblematic of the process of African middle-class formation in Southern Rhodesia, Sobantu, in a triumph at once personal and collective, overcame the odds and rose to a higher level. His dream of entering law enforcement dashed, he set his sights instead on business, going on to become a proponent of African cooperative economics, a prominent entrepreneur in his own right, and chairman of the residents' association at Pelandaba, an elite African community built in Bulawayo in the 1950s.[31]

Sobantu was hardly alone in attacking the barriers against African social mobility and in agitating for a race-neutral meritocracy. Although the occasional one-person virtuoso added color to the performance, the struggle to rise to a higher level was really a symphonic composition of the black elite as a whole. A few months before Sobantu's broadside, the Rev. Matthew Rusike, a leading African minister, had used another important forum to launch an appeal for upgrading "the lot of the educated Native." One of the first Africans to address the Advisory Board for Native Development, a body composed of government officials and missionaries, Rusike pleaded for more opportunities and better pay for Africans with "qualifications and ability." Turning to the issue of respectability, a touchstone for members of his class, he urged the government to upgrade the segregated black hospitals, including providing facilities for patients desiring greater personal privacy. Rusike also entreated the authorities to discourage the use of Kitchen Kaffir, long a source of irritation to the emerging black petty bourgeoisie.[32] Elite Africans objected to this bastardized English-based vernacular because many whites, assuming that colonial subjects could never fully master the language of Shakespeare and Milton, insisted on addressing all blacks in Kitchen Kaffir.

If anything, the "almost pathological objection most of the settlers had to being spoken to in English by a black person," as Lawrence Vambe expressed it, only fueled the determination of elite Africans to flaunt their command of the language, often in "jaw-breaking" ways.[33] The penchant for big words when using the language of the oppressor, a form of lexical amplification not specific to colonial Zimbabweans, was most publicly displayed in the African-oriented press. The tone was set in the earliest issues of the *Native Mirror,* the first in a series of white-run publications intended for an African audience. Typical of the genre in question is the following report, submitted by Charlton Ngcebetsha, a South African immigrant and noted public intellectual among the emerging black middle class:

> Wednesday, the 20th May [1931] was a red-letter day at Ntbasenduna Mission, the occasion being the breaking up of the school for winter vacation and departure of the Rev. J. C. Mills, who has been principal for the last eighteen months, and has during the period of his residence rendered such yeoman service in an endeavour to restore and enhance the prestige of the Mission that his name will remain always ineffaceable in the minds of those who enjoyed to the full the benefits of his sage counsels and instructions."[34]

Bradfield Mnyanda, Ngcebetsha's good friend and fellow South African immigrant, also reportedly did "not seek to simplify his English and has a good vocabulary."[35]

Such malapropism did not escape commentary by elite Africans themselves. P. C. Taperesa Dube, a teacher, urged contributors to the African-oriented press to use simple English, lest they discourage the less well educated from reading the paper. Dube was particularly critical of two recent offenders. He quipped: "I think these two gentlemen forgot that their articles were to be read by their Bantu fellow-men whose knowledge is shallow, and who cannot manage properly the long rolls of sonorous words or scientific terms."[36]

As indicated by their angst over the use of Kitchen Kaffir, along with the compensatory lexical indulgences, elite Africans desired more than just material betterment. They also coveted public affirmation of their social standing by the settlers, whose ranks they ultimately hoped to join. In a society in which both the policies of the government and the private actions of the dominant race promoted a social leveling of the entire colonized population, without regard to class, elite Africans scanned the horizon for any sign of settler recognition of their claim to a common citizenship and mutual standards of cultural refinement. Thus it was considered a social breakthrough and a major breach of Rhodesian racial etiquette when, at a Wayfarer (the African equivalent of Girl Guides or Girl Scouts) meeting in 1935, "Native ministers were also provided with chairs; this was the first time on which African ministers were provided with chairs at a gathering of Europeans and Natives." Then, in a commentary pregnant with pathos, the reporter who covered the story added: "We, the ordinary Africans, do not wish to be recognized. We desire that our ministers and leaders should be given that respect which we believe they are entitled to as leaders of the African people of the Colony."[37] In any event, such gestures in colonial noblesse oblige were few. Ultimately, the quest for respectability, a notion central to the process of middle-class formation everywhere, eluded the African petty bourgeoisie in Southern Rhodesia.[38] If anything, many settlers took delight in humiliating these striving Africans.

Take an incident involving Lennox Njokweni, which happened in 1931. A clerk at the London Missionary Society's school at Inyati, Njokweni was described by the school's white principal as a "well educated Native" and a "very courteous and well behaved young man." He had attended secondary school in South Africa, a rare achievement for an African (and one not so common among Europeans) in Southern Rhodesia at that time, and held "splendid testimonials" from his alma mater.[39] Nattily attired in his hat, Njokweni would easily have conformed to Sobantu's portrait of the "clean and well-dressed native," a solid and self-respecting member of the emerging African elite seeking to rise to a higher level. Precisely for this reason, however, he would also have been viewed with a mixture of scorn and suspicion by many a settler, who might even be tempted to publicly demean him, should the opportunity arise.

Njokweni had the misfortune of running afoul of such an individual, a settler willing, even eager, to provoke a casus belli for the express purpose of demonstrating contempt for aspiring Africans. Njokweni, no doubt conspicuous by his attire, was leaving the office of the local native commissioner, where he had gone on business, when a white man emerged from an automobile. Then, as Njokweni described it:

> This man came round the spot where I was standing, and just when I was making a turn to go he passed near me and asked who I was. I told him that I am Lennox Njokweni. Then he said, "Well! Lennox Njokweni you must take off your hat when I pass you." I asked the reason for this order, and in response he said, "'You take it off now,'" and he came and grabbed it and threw it right over the Post Office hut, and it fell on the stones beyond. I went quietly to take it and left feeling that I had been treated uncivilly.[40]

Leaving the scene of his humiliation with, perhaps quite literally, hat in hand, Njokweni ran a gauntlet of onlookers consisting of students who had accompanied him on his mission and Africans employed in the native commissioner's office—a piece of settler-colonial theatrics staged in good measure for the benefit of the audience. The lead actor in this, an all-too-typical and farcical performance in Rhodesian white hostility and aggression toward elite Africans, turned out to be none other than an assistant native commissioner, a senior official in the Native Affairs Department.

An aggrieved Njokweni reported the matter to his employer, the principal of the Inyati school, a white missionary and himself no coddler of "natives"; the principal, in turn, protested strongly to the chief native commissioner.[41] After investigating, the chief native commissioner determined that the assistant native commissioner's conduct had been "ill advised" and recommended to the prime minister, who doubled as minister of native affairs, that he be censured. The son of a pioneering Southern Rhodesian missionary, the prime minister, H. U. Moffat, was regarded in settler circles as "a friend of the natives."

Moffat agreed with the chief native commissioner that the "knocking off of the boy's hat was reprehensible and a lowering of the status of a highly placed official of the Native [Affairs] Department." But, in an apparent reference to Njokweni's disputation of the order to remove his hat, the prime minister adjudged that the assistant native commissioner "had been greatly provoked by the Native." Given the extenuation, censure, as recommended by the chief native commissioner, would be too severe a punishment, a "Black Mark." Instead, the prime minister merely required that the assistant native commissioner formally submit "an expression of his regret for his conduct which I recognize was the result of natural annoyance at the general attitude of the Native." Njokweni's employer was informed of the disposition of the case.[42]

The hapless complainant, meanwhile, was totally ignored, his sense of violation and abasement having played no part in the official deliberations. Njokweni's feeling that he had, in his own words, been "treated uncivilly"— delicate language worthy of the civilizationist discourse of the African elite— amounted to naught in the eyes of the chief native commissioner and the prime minister and minister of native affairs, the top two Native Affairs officials. Far from being punished for attacking Njokweni, the assistant native commissioner received a mere slap on the wrist, and that allegedly for lowering his personal status and, presumably, the "prestige" of the colonial regime and the white race as a whole. Africans in Southern Rhodesia seemingly had few rights, and even fewer feelings, that the majority of settlers, including those who ruled over them, deemed worthy of respect.

To members of the black elite, who were far more likely than African peasants or workers to formally complain or publicly protest, the quest for social mobility often seemed like an endless nightmare. The slights, indignities, and rejections appeared interminable. Although transformed in ways large and small during the period between the depression of the 1930s and the boom of the 1950s, Southern Rhodesia seemed enmeshed in a time warp when it came to the public treatment of striving Africans. A quarter century after Njokweni's demeaning ordeal, racial debarment remained alive and well.

Consider the agony of three middle-class African men during the Christmas holiday of 1958. The trio—a university graduate, a headmaster, and a schoolteacher—visited the ruins of Great Zimbabwe, the remarkable, mortarless series of stone buildings, perhaps the most noted architectural wonderment in precolonial Africa outside of Egypt. On arrival, the men's request to sign the visitors' log was rejected, the black attendant explaining that this was not a courtesy extended to Africans. Long-suffering and forbearing—hard lessons learned from both personal experiences and three generations of collective wisdom accumulated under the colonial yoke—the visitors proceeded to the ruins. The color bar, mercifully, did not extend to gazing upon their ancestral legacy. After taking in the sights, they retired to the tearoom, a sure sign of (British) bourgeois respectability. But racial exclusion beckoned again, service being rendered "only with difficulty."[43] In sum, the yearning of elite Africans for treatment commensurate with their level of "civilization," as defined by the colonialists themselves, would remain unfulfilled in Rhodesian settler society.

Indeed, few words fell off the tongues of elite Africans more easily than "civilization" and its derivatives, as will already have been noticeable. African teachers demanding higher salaries argued that their pay was inadequate to enable them "to live on the simplest civilised standard."[44] Lawrence Vambe, then a student at mission school, urged that girls be educated as an imperative in the march toward civilization: "We must also remember that if we only take care of the boys' education and not of girls' as well, we shall never be properly civilized."[45] Elite Africans even took it upon themselves to lecture the settlers and the colonial regime about civilization. For instance, political activists Solomon Maviyane and Charles Mzingeli attacked the Subversive Activities Bill of 1950, a piece of legislation aimed at stifling African labor, as "an infringement on the principle of human rights and it definitely cannot be treated in any way as an accepted precept of Western civilisation, if that civilisation refers to the British civilisation, as we understand it."[46]

The civilizationist rhetoric was, however, occasionally tempered. Some elite Africans worried that members of their class were confusing civilization with Europeanization, with a consequent rejection of their Africanness. Thus the biblically named Enoch Dumbutshena, without bothering to reflect on the paradox, worried aloud that "Educated Africans who have pride in their names will find that most [educated] people are foolishly neglecting their Native names the reason being that we are now civilized." Dumbutshena believed that colonial Zimbabweans were "doing what the American Negroes did after the years of bondage. The Negroes gave themselves names so as to denote that they were free." Africans in Southern Rhodesia, he complained, also were giving "their children names so as to indicate that they are civilized and educated." Assuming the mantle of defender of African cultural integrity, at least at the nomenclatorial level, Dumbutshena urged his fellow educated Africans "to encourage all the people not to neglect those beautiful Native names. If this can be done, it will stand as a badge of clear pride to our nation."[47]

To Dumbutshena's emphasis on nation, Gerald Mtimkulu, another champion of African cultural integrity, added the element of race. Mtimkulu regarded the aversion of petty bourgeois blacks to things African, or things identified as African, as an exercise in self-loathing. "The African," he stated emphatically, "does not respect himself." Continuing, he accused the oppressed of being complicit in their own oppression, blaming the Africans for the problems of white supremacy and racial discrimination:

> I say that the fault lies entirely with the African because the African, unlike other races of mankind, is oblivious to that great secret of national greatness, racial prosperity and general advancement, namely race consciousness. You probably know that race consciousness implies Pride of Race. Now some of our African intelligentsia will refute or oppose the above statement —namely that we are not proud of the fact that we are black-skinned Africans born of [the] most noble black-skinned mothers that this dear black

African soil has ever produced. I say that some of us, in the presence of Europeans, seem to apologise for the tremendous fact that we are black![48]

To individuals like Dumbutshena and Mtimkulu, with their emphasis on preserving African cultural heritage, civilization was a process, not a finished work, the varnished gift of Europe to Africa through the agency of colonialism. The African genius, they believed, had a special contribution to make to humankind, a contribution that would have as its point of departure an affirmation of Africanness, both in its cultural and "racial" manifestations.

A QUESTION OF IDENTITY: ASSUMING THE POWER TO NAME

The question of identity, individual and collective, was central to the rise of the African middle class in Southern Rhodesia. Thus, there was no issue more basic than that of name: What should the indigenous inhabitants of the colony, the Shona and the Ndebele, be called? As with much else, the white settlers and the colonial regime that represented them assumed the power to name—in effect, to impose an identity on the colonized people, nomenclatorially speaking, at least. For the colonialists, the question was: What shall we call them? The Africans, in a quest for self-identity, which involved nothing less than a subversion of the colonial will, responded with a question of their own: What shall we call ourselves? The resulting "names controversy," as it has been dubbed in the African American context, provoked a bitter polemic against the government and the settlers by members of the emerging black middle class, especially between the 1930s and the 1950s, when a peculiarly Zimbabwean African national consciousness was being forged.[49]

The European colonialists, many of whom came from or by way of South Africa, especially the Cape Province, had definite ideas about who Africans were and what they should be called. To many, perhaps most white settlers, the indigenous people were Kaffirs (also spelled Kafir and Caffre), a word of Arabic derivation meaning infidel or nonbeliever in the Muslim religion. The Portuguese, arriving on the East African coast in the sixteenth century, adopted the term and used it to refer to Africans in general. The Kaffir designation was subsequently embraced by the Dutch, who began establishing a colonial outpost at the southern tip of Africa, the so-called Cape of Good Hope, in the mid-seventeenth century. The Dutch, one historian has speculated, "possibly acquired [the Kaffir designation] . . . during their contacts with the Portuguese throughout the Indian Ocean region."[50]

The British, in turn, appropriated the term on their arrival on the southern African subcontinent in the nineteenth century, applying it specifically to the Xhosa and other Bantu-speaking Africans in the Cape. Hence such laws as the Kaffir Employment Act and the Kaffir Pass Act, both of which came into force in 1857. A series of British-instigated military conflicts on the "frontier" with the Xhosa-speakers, who naturally resided in "Kaffraria," became known as the Kaffir Wars.[51] Similarly, in the colonial jargon the sorghum grown by the Africans was Kaffir corn, whereas their alcoholic beverages were Kaffir beer. It followed, too, that the Kaffirs themselves, incapable as they were deemed to be of fully grasping the language of their colonial masters, had to be addressed in Kitchen Kaffir, as we have already seen.

Yet in southern Africa, at least, it seems that until approximately the latter part of the nineteenth century, Kaffir was more a descriptive than a disparaging designation. Besides the colonial administration, the missionaries who came in the wake of the British occupation also used it. The first mission-run, African-oriented newspaper in the Cape was called *Kaffir Express,* and one missionary created a Kaffir almanac in an attempt to bridge the different conceptions of time between Europeans and Africans, between the solar and lunar months.[52] Moreover, the first generation of mission-educated Africans appears not to have objected to the use of Kaffir. Nor was the term necessarily restricted to Africans, as indicated by the existence of white Kaffrarians, that is, Europeans who settled in the newly created Cape colony.[53] The neighboring British colony of Natal also had its share of European Kaffir farmers—large-scale white landholders, some of them based in London—who exacted rent from African "squatters."[54]

However, by the closing decades of the nineteenth century, the word Kaffir increasingly acquired derogatory as well as race-specific connotations, the southern African equivalent of the word nigger, that most notorious term of anti-black opprobrium. This transformation was, in all likelihood, a by-product of the intensification of the colonial project in the southern African interior after the discovery of precious minerals and metals, notably diamonds and gold. In particular, the mineral revolution fundamentally altered the relationship between Europeans and Africans, placing the labor question at the center of the colonial project. Under the new dispensation, European imaginings of Africans came to be refracted primarily through the employer–employee or, to use the colonial formulation, the master–servant nexus. And as Keletso Atkins has so skillfully demonstrated in the case of Natal, at the core of the labor problem in southern Africa—the recruiting and disciplining of African wage workers—stood the question of Kaffir time. As Atkins notes: "No sooner was a work agreement made than confusion arose from the disparate notion of the white employer and his African employee regarding the computation of time. In other words, the record of persistent desertions from service was in very many instances related to the fact that the terms of master–servant contracts, which were based on European units of measure, did not accord with the African mode of temporal reckoning."[55] It appears that the European contempt for Kaffir time proceeded in tandem with and, indeed, powerfully determined increasingly negative images of Africans—images that, of course, had a history dating back to the era of the Atlantic slave trade and African slavery in the Americas. Eventually, it seems, the colonial disdain for African time reckoning, for Kaffir time, was transferred to the so-called Kaffirs themselves, which then became a racialized term.

What is clear, at any rate, is that the white settlers who established the Southern Rhodesian colony in the 1890s applied the word Kaffir exclusively to Africans, and then in a negative sense. It is perhaps a measure of the generalized dishonor in which the term was understood, both among colonizer and colonized, that with one exception—the Kaffir Beer Ordinance of 1909—the term never attained the status of an official designation for Africans in the colony. It was, however, widely used by the settlers, especially those most flamboyant with their anti-black animus. Certainly no word elicited greater indignation among elite Africans in Southern Rhodesia than the opprobrious "Kaffir."

The more respectable alternative to "Kaffir" was "native," the official designation for Africans in Southern Rhodesia until the 1960s. The natives, as already noted, were governed under a separate legal regime by a special government agency, the Native Affairs Department. Founded in 1898, after two anticolonial uprisings, the department came to acquire its own corps of "experts" who specialized in issues as varied as land, labor, law, education, and agriculture. It was a unique fiefdom within the colonial regime, distinct from the other agencies of the state, which dealt with "general" affairs, that is, matters pertaining to Europeans (as well as Indians and coloureds).

Integral to the making of the native, which is to say, to the depersonalization of the colonized, was the denial of individuality. The individual native had no distinctive feature, no personalized quality or characteristic. In fact, the native had no name. As represented by the colonized male—whose physical proximity to settlers, employers, officials, and missionaries alike made him a more familiar object of white commentary than was his female counterpart—the individual native was simply a generic species called Tom, Jim, or some other popular English name that came to mind.[56] Mostly, though, the male native was known as "boy." This term spawned others, such as "police boy," "houseboy," "boys' kia" (a shack for houseboys), "boss-boy" (an African foreman), and "boys' meat" (the left-over scraps). Consistent with the Europeans' history of interaction with Africans and other colonized peoples, the less conspicuous female native was most commonly known to white settlers as "girl." In the 1940s and 1950s, as more women joined the urban-based wage-labor force, especially as domestic workers—a form of employment hitherto dominated by men—"nanny" often became a substitute for "girl."

Africans, as might be expected, objected strongly to being called by names
other than their own, and particularly to being called boy or girl. Black teachers, the predominantly male African Teachers Association protested in the
late 1940s, were "not 'boys' but men who have given their lives to a higher calling."[57] "What," inquired A. M. Shoniwa Ziyambi, writing as late as 1961, "does
the word 'boy' mean when used by certain Europeans referring to Africans?
What effect is it intended to have on an African? What is it intended to make
an African think about himself?"[58] The intention, of course, was to rob the
Africans of their dignity, their humanity, and their reason for being. "In hear-
ing this word [boy] used to address an African man of between 50 and 60 years
of age," S. B. Nxumalo confessed, "I always feel very small." This psychological warfare constantly undermined his sense of worth and self, causing him to
question his very existence. "Under these circumstances I even feel I should
not have been born because I personally do not want to be called boy till I
die."[59] Others struck a more hopeful and defiant chord. "These words are insults," warned Richard D. Makoni, referring to "boy," among other pejora-
tives, "and I do not think Africans will tolerate these insults forever."[60]

By this time—the 1950s and early 1960s—African women too began to
publicly and strenuously object to being called girl. To most whites, an un-
attributed article in the African-oriented press noted, "an African woman
never grows [up]. She remains a girl until she dies." African women, however,
had become "conscious of this and are no longer prepared to be addressed by
all sorts of names. They say that if any person does not want to know their
names he or she should not bother about addressing them."[61] Among the newly
assertive African women was Mrs. A. Mhlanga, who flew to London first class
in 1960. She recalled that from the moment she boarded the plane, "I was
'Madam,' until I got back home to be 'Nanny' once more! In all my stay [in
Britain], I was treated with kindness and respect. . . . My colour did not matter
for the first time in all my life."[62] Betty Mtero, who visited Germany (West
and East) around the same time, also returned home with a sense of restored
humanity. "My 3 months stay in Germany," she exulted, "has given me the
impression that above all, I am a human being. While there, I felt I was a human being with the human rights of freedom of movement and freedom of
happiness."[63]

Terms like boy, girl, and nanny, along with that of native, from which they
ultimately derived, denoted a profound otherness. To the colonial mind, use of
"native" was a concrete manifestation of the wide, even unbridgeable chasm
between colonizer and colonized, white and black, Christianity and fetishism,
civilization and barbarism, reason and emotion.[64] The natives, certainly when
left to their own devices, were deemed incapable of material, cultural, and intellectual growth. As one Southern Rhodesian official commented, "the na-

tive in his present state is but a child."[65] This was an acute case of arrested development. In the opinion of one settler, whose nomenclatorial choice attested to his scorn for the colonized people, the dichotomy between European and African extended to bodily excretions. Objecting to a proposal to build a housing scheme for elite Africans in an area adjoining his farm, he asserted, from all indications with a straight face, that the site was "quite unsuited for the purposes in view, as the surface consists of a stiff clay which will not absorb kaffir excrement like sand veld will do. In the selection of an area for the settlement of natives, the question of the nature of the soil should be very seriously considered."[66] For whatever reason, the government eventually found another site for the native village settlement.

A QUESTION OF SELF-IDENTITY: CLAIMING
THE RIGHT TO NAME

Despite its dubious etymological beginnings, "native" as a term of self-designation was accepted initially by Africans. This might have been partly the result of their own internalization of the devaluation of Africanness and blackness inherent in the colonial project, the infamous colonial mentality. This argument, however, should not be pushed too far; it is certainly undermined by the Africans' rejection of Kaffir. It seems more likely that Africans in Southern Rhodesia and elsewhere on the continent began calling themselves natives for want of a better word to designate people of different linguistic, ethnic, and cultural backgrounds who suddenly found themselves in similar political and social circumstances as a result of the colonial imposition.

At any rate, the word native appears in most of the political and other associations formed by Africans in Southern Rhodesia up to around the mid-1930s. Hence the Union Native Vigilance Organization, which was founded before the onset of World War I. A body representing the small but relatively influential group of black South African immigrants, the Union Native Vigilance Organization apparently was the first modernist attempt at political self-organization by Africans in Southern Rhodesia. In the immediate post–World War I era there emerged the Southern Rhodesia Native Association, which served as the political voice of a reconstituted black elite that now included both South African immigrants and Africans indigenous to the colony. The Southern Rhodesia Native Missionary Conference, established by ministers and church workers in 1930, was perhaps the last major African organization to use the word native in its name.

By the mid-1930s, elite Africans began to voice objection to the designation of native. The initial motivating factor appears to have been resentment of the honorific used by the Native Affairs Department and allied agencies to

address Africans, a practice bearing directly on the sensitive issue of treatment or respectability. Instead of the customary Mr., Mrs., or Miss, Africans
were addressed simply as "Native So-and-So" in official correspondence.

The battle was joined publicly in 1934 when the Native Missionary Conference passed a resolution "humbly requesting" the government "to discard
the use of the word 'Native' in their communications with Africans, as its appearance on envelopes tends to offend."[67] The response was dismissive. "It is
considered that there is nothing whatever offensive in the use of the term native," the chief native commissioner retorted, "and the need for this resolution
is not understood."[68] Two years later the Native Missionary Conference, noting that it represented "Christian leaders who desire co-operation between
the two races," reiterated the objection more forcefully, warning that continued use of the Native honorific would "create ill-feeling towards Europeans
by Africans."[69] The authorities, however, remained unfazed. "A change to the
use of 'Mr.' on envelopes is a matter of social etiquette, not of enforcement,"
came the disdainful rejoinder.[70] The protestation continued, increasing in frequency and vociferousness over time, but it was only in 1956 that the objectionable practice finally ceased.

Meanwhile, an alternate self-designation, Bantu, had gained increasing
currency among elite Africans. Bantu was not a new nomenclature. Strictly
speaking a linguistic rather than an ethnic, racial, or cultural category, it had
been used for decades in various parts of southern Africa by scholars, colonial
officials, and Africans alike. In Southern Rhodesia, for instance, the Union
Native Vigilance Organization had replaced the word Native in its name with
Bantu as early as the era of World War I.[71] Then in 1923 came the Rhodesia
Bantu Voters Association, which represented a political synthesis of the black
South African immigrants and the indigenous African elite—just like its contemporary and rival, the Southern Rhodesia Native Association. Yet while not
new, "Bantu" ran a distant second to "native" in terms of popularity among
the African petty bourgeoisie, up to the mid-1930s.

The subsequent rise of Bantu as the preferred self-designation coincided
with, and can be directly attributed to, the black elite's struggles with the colonial regime over the issue of honorifics, which evidently spawned a generalized rejection of the appellation "native." The transition occurred quite rapidly. The venerable Native Missionary Conference—which emerged as the
most authoritative voice of African protest with the onset of the depression
and took the lead on the honorific issue, among others—officially dropped the
word Native in its name in favor Bantu in 1936.[72] When, in that same year, a
new political organization was formed, with the support of top officials of the
renamed Bantu Missionary Conference, it was called the Southern Rhodesia
Bantu Congress.

The growing acceptance of Bantu is well illustrated by a contest that took place, again in 1936, the year the *Native Mirror,* a government-subsidized, white-run monthly newspaper moved to a weekly format under titular African editorship. Seeking to generate interest in the reconstituted venture, the paper invited readers to suggest possible new names, with the result that suggestions bearing the Bantu label were easily the most popular.[73] Thus did the *Bantu Mirror,* the most famous African-oriented newspaper in Southern Rhodesia and an important stream of evidence for this book, come into existence. Two years later there emerged the Bantu Co-operative Society, the latest and most successful (relatively speaking) in a series of organizations seeking to promote African capitalism. Africans in Southern Rhodesia, then, entered World War II with what appeared to be a firmly fixed Bantu self-designation.

No sooner had the internal debate about nomenclature and identity ended, however, than it began all over again. The Bantu, it was now claimed, were really Africans who had been robbed of their true cultural and historical designation. So rapidly did the new term African gain acceptance that by 1944, one writer could assert that it is "absolutely and categorically untrue that educated Africans like the name 'Bantu.'" To explain the seeming confusion over this issue, the writer invoked the notion of the stolen legacy, an intellectual device dear to the hearts of culture brokers and identity makers among the dispossessed everywhere. "We Africans," he allowed, "know full well that all the names Europeans call us are abusive, we are robbed of our original name 'Africans,' which is substituted with abusive names."[74] Another writer, although conceding that there was "nothing bad with the word 'Native' so long as it is used in the right sense," asserted that it had "long been used or misused in such a way as to give it a bearing of an insult, and, to the Bantu, it has become as disagreeable as the word 'boer,' in spite of its meaning, to the Dutch Farmer," that is, an Afrikaans-speaking white. Consequently, "every right-thinking Bantu would not oppose but welcome the change" to African.[75] Having entered the war as Bantu, Southern Rhodesia's elite indigenous denizens left it as African.

Actually, the African appellation, like the Bantu one before it, was not altogether new. Already in the early 1920s Southern Rhodesian Africans resident in Cape Town had formed the African Universal Benefit Society, which, despite its name, turned out to be an Ndebele ethnic-specific formation. A few years later, an organization initially called the Gwelo Native Welfare Association underwent a series of nomenclatorial changes, one of them being to the African Native Welfare Association. It is hardly accidental that the founders of the latter organization, like those who comprised the misnamed African Universal Benefit Society, had done stints of employment in South Africa, and more specifically in Cape Town, then the center of black political activism on the southern African subcontinent. South Africa's indigenous people, who also experienced their own names controversy, had more or less settled on the

African self-designation by the mid-1920s, a move perhaps best signaled by the renaming of the South African Native National Congress to the African National Congress of South Africa. In this, as in other respects, the Southern Rhodesian Africans were likely influenced by their South African sojourns. Indeed, a number of those urging a changeover from Bantu to African in the era of World War II wrote to the Rhodesian African-oriented press from South Africa.

In Southern Rhodesia, the supporters of the new terminology demanded a change in the names of "such societies as the Native Welfare Society, to the African Welfare Society, etc."[76] Yet, by one account, five years earlier the African members of the Native Welfare Society, which maintained separate white and black branches, had spurned that idea. According to the Rev. Percy Ibbotson, the group's national leader, as late as 1939 many among the black middle class resisted being called African, because they did not wish to be confused "with 'Africaaners' which is often used to describe the Dutch people." But, asserted Ibbotson, a noted white paternalist and key authority on the "Native problem," by 1944 such reservations had largely been abandoned and African was "becoming popular."[77] Two years later the Bantu Congress, now more vigorous and assertive than ever, changed its name to the African National Congress.[78] Henceforth all new black organizations of any significance, political or otherwise, would proudly display the African insignia.

The leading white-run organizations concerned with the "welfare" of the colonized people soon fell in line with the latest self-designation, changing their names accordingly. In 1946, with the full backing of its segregated black branches, the Native Welfare Society, organized nationally into an umbrella formation called the Federation of Native Welfare Societies, formally went African. In any case, Ibbotson had been using the new term in the organization's official documents for some time.[79] Meanwhile, two years earlier, a South African–owned media trust had gained control of the Rhodesian black-oriented press, creating a second organ, the *African Weekly,* alongside the *Bantu Mirror* (which, however, retained its name).

The colonial regime was far less sensitive to questions of African self-identity than were business interests and "liberals" such as Ibbotson. Thus, although government-appointed commissions in the era of World War II tended to accept the new usage,[80] "native" remained the Rhodesian state's official designation for the colonized people, with the intransigence most poignantly symbolized by the crusty old Native Affairs Department. Indeed, it was only in 1952 that the authorities decided, "out of deference to the wishes of the native people," to formally change the Kaffir Beer Act to the Native Beer Act. "Why not 'African beer,'" one legislator objected, as the government's outdated nomenclatorial concession, now twice removed from black reality, was introduced in the Legislative Assembly. African, the unreconstructed minister of native affairs shot back, "is too wide a term. 'Native' is the accepted term."[81] And "native" it would remain in official parlance for another decade.

The obduracy of the authorities, along with most white settlers, led one exasperated black observer to suggest, not altogether in jest, that the only way to induce the colonizers to make the desired nomenclatorial transition was for the Africans themselves to revert to the word native. "The more we protest the more they enjoy using" the word native, he asserted. Following inverted white Rhodesian logic, therefore, "if we [Africans] accept this name [native], forsaking the meaning which the users want it to convey, taking it to mean the owners of the land, and become very proud of it, even claiming to be so-called, they will not enjoy using it. They will feel that they are exalting us which is what they do not like."[82]

The Rev. Esau Nemapare, who had made his own nomenclatorial declaration in 1947 when he left the Wesleyan (British) Methodist Church to form an independent denomination, the African Methodist Church, joined the debate by proposing a transracial definition of the term African. "We have chosen 'African' for our name and we must not be expected to bow our shoulders before anybody to load over us any name that person may choose to give us," he announced defiantly. Nevertheless, Nemapare continued, African identity was not racially exclusive: "If the White men . . . want to call themselves 'Africans,' let them join us in this name."[83] Ernest Mhlanga, a frequent contributor to the African-oriented press, agreed: "The African being an aborigine of Africa has all the right to be called by the name connected with his birthplace. If the other races want to be called African, that is alright."[84]

Few whites, however, would agree to a shared identity across racial lines, or even to adopt the African nomenclature in reference to the colonized people. Consequently when, in 1956, Nathan Shamuyarira, then a prominent journalist, gave the "green light" for generalized use of the term, most whites remained stalled at the intersection. The resistance, according to Shamuyarira, stemmed from the settler belief that the African designation was "too general. A European born in Africa is also, correctly speaking, an African. Furthermore, the word 'African' raises the clarion cry 'Africa for the Africans,'" a cry long associated with the quest for global African self-assertion against European imposition.[85] Indeed, the call for democratic governance, or majority rule, seen by the bulk of the white settlers as a threat to the Rhodesian way of life and to Western civilization itself, was precisely the demand that the African nationalist movement would soon begin to make.

The emergence of an African identity specific to Southern Rhodesia, which is to say a Zimbabwean African national consciousness, as evidenced by the rise of anticolonial nationalism in the late 1950s, had been a long time in the making. The "nationalizing" of the African elite took an important turn in the mid-1930s, culminating in the establishment of the Bantu Congress, the first political formation that could credibly claim to represent Africans throughout the colony, albeit largely in the urban centers. Even when they had the will, the quest for national representativity had eluded earlier protest groups, which essentially were organized on a regional or ethnic basis.

An important aspect of the new exercise in African self-organization and self-consciousness nationally was the increasing political salience of the anthem "Nkosi Sikelel' iAfrika" (God Bless Africa). This song, like a number of other cultural and ideological practices adopted by Africans in Southern Rhodesia, was imported from South Africa. Initially composed in 1897, "Nkosi Sikelel' iAfrika" was later popularized by various choral groups, including the Ohlange Zulu Choir, an important fundraising arm of the Ohlange Institute, a school founded by John L. Dube and modeled on Booker T. Washington's Tuskegee Institute in the United States. With the formation in 1912 of the South African Native National Congress, under Dube's presidency, "Nkosi Sikelel' iAfrika" became its unofficial theme song.[86] In time, the anthem was diffused throughout the southern African subcontinent by migrant workers, students, travelers, and newspapers.

Sung in the original Xhosa in the Ndebele-speaking areas of Southern Rhodesia, "Nkosi Sikelel' iAfrika" was translated eventually into the Shona language as "Ishe Komborera Afrika." This translated version was sung at the close of the inaugural meeting of the Bantu Congress.[87] Four days earlier, a regional branch of the Southern Rhodesia Native Association, one of the constituent organizations of the Bantu Congress, had commenced its proceedings with a rendition of the same song.[88] By the time of the momentous general strike of 1948, "Nkosi Sikelel' iAfrika"/"Ishe Komborera Africa" had become an integral part of African political culture in Southern Rhodesia.[89] Rural protesters joined their urban counterparts in singing it. A year after the 1948 general strike, agrarian producers took to the streets of Bulawayo, bellowing the anthem as they protested plans to evict them from parts of the Matopos Hills that had been slated for a national park, that is, a home for wild animals and a playground for white tourists.[90] The "Nkosi Sikelel' iAfrika" refrain could be heard not just at political events, narrowly defined, but also at gatherings as varied as those of the African Teachers Association and the Advisory Boards, institutions established after World War II to give Africans an input into the running of the urban ghettoes.[91]

The growing national consciousness of the black elite—as exemplified by the adoption of a national anthem, among other things—had become fully crystallized by the early 1960s. An important outward sign of this crystallization was the emergence of the term Zimbabwean, which marked the denouement of the names controversy. The origin of this latest self-designation was, of course, no mystery. It derived from the ruins of Great Zimbabwe. Although the structures had been built by Shona-speaking Africans between the twelfth and fourteenth centuries A.D., the Europeans refused to believe that the ancestors of their lowly colonial charges could have achieved such an amazing feat, claiming instead that Great Zimbabwe was the handiwork of various non-Africans, such as Phoenicians, Arabs, or Jews. It was therefore only natural that a reawakened African nation, whose leaders were then demanding a formal transfer of political power from colonizer to colonized, would seek to claim a glorious patrimony, especially one their oppressors had sought to deny them. In their attempt to fuse historical legacy and political power, the colonial Zimbabweans were much inspired by similar processes then taking place in other parts of Africa, most conspicuously in the Gold Coast turned Ghana, named after the famous medieval West African empire.

The term Zimbabwe (initially sometimes also spelled Zimbagwe) began to gain currency in the early 1960s. As far as can be ascertained, the first organization to formally embrace the appellation was the Zimbabwe National Party. Formed in June 1961, the Zimbabwe National Party was first in more ways than one; it also inaugurated the political schisms that came to characterize Zimbabwean African nationalism. Its founders accused the National Democratic Party, the mainline nationalist formation from which they split, of having sold out the cause of African majority rule and of "treacherously leading us into a gas chamber."[92] Despite heady rhetoric about replacing the National Democratic Party as the vanguard of African nationalism in Southern Rhodesia, however, the Zimbabwe National Party made little headway politically.

Although deeply unpopular itself, the Zimbabwe National Party helped to popularize the new nomenclature, which began to spread like wildfire. No sooner had the group been formed than critics began accusing it variously of betraying the "sons and daughters of Zimbabwe," the "people of Zimbabwe," and the "majority of Africans in Zimbabwe" by shattering national unity through its secession from the National Democratic Party.[93] It was thus all but inevitable that when, in December 1961, the National Democratic Party was banned by an increasingly repressive settler regime, its successor, which appeared nine days later, would be called the Zimbabwe African People's Union. Outmaneuvered politically and nomenclatorially, the Zimbabwe National Party soon disappeared from the stage, its place later to be claimed by other schismatic formations.

"Zimbabwe," more than any previous self-designation, would become a politically loaded and oppositional term, one counterpoised against "Rhodesia," which then became a byword in African nationalist circles, a synonym for racist oppression. The journey from native to Zimbabwean was now complete. The story of the rise of the Zimbabwean African middle class is the story, writ large, of the social and political consequences of this nomenclatorial odyssey.

2

Courting "Miss Education"
The Love Affair with Social Mobility

SINCE THE ADVENT of the bourgeois epoch, an era marked by the industrial revolution and the consequent rationalization of production, distribution, and consumption, education has been a major avenue for social mobility.[1] In the empires established by the industrializing European powers in the second half of the nineteenth century, education played an even more decisive role in facilitating personal advancement than it did in the metropoles. Specifically, in the African territories, characterized as they were by massive economic and social deformities, colonial subjects quickly realized that Western-type education offered one of the few means of rising to a level higher than the one envisaged for them by the European architects of the new social order.

Social mobility, however, was an unintended consequence of colonial education. The missionary societies that pioneered formal schooling in Southern Rhodesia and elsewhere in colonial Africa saw education primarily as a handmaiden to Christianity: literacy enabled converts independently to read the bible and other religious literature. In 1925, a leading Rhodesian Anglican churchman declared that he "would rather the Native remained uneducated than he should get education without Christianity."[2] This credo transcended both time and denominational boundaries. As late as 1955 the moderator of the Presbyterian Church remained wedded to the view that without Christianity, "the foundation of all good education," attending school "was of little value."[3]

Those colonized Africans fortunate enough actually to attend school also tended to take a functionalist view of education. Their goal, however, differed markedly from that of the missionaries. The majority of mission-educated Africans, except perhaps for a small group of pious converts, such as Stephen Sithole, regarded education primarily as an agency for social mobility.[4] In 1942 William T. Madeya, a high school student and no hedonist, then or later, wrote on essay titled "Why I Want to Be Well Educated."[5] Education, he announced, "is the passport to success; it is the provision for old age; hence we get from it knowledge, which is power." In the end, a mesmerized Madeya exclaimed: "I love 'Miss Education' with all my heart."[6] Consider, too, Nicodemus Gombedza, another seeker of the passport to success and suitor of Miss Education. Hardscrabble, unlike his exalted biblical namesake,[7] Gombedza, whose parents were "as poor as a church mouse," persevered in his academic pursuits despite numerous hardships because he "wanted very much to be literate, educated and civilized."[8] The quest for literacy, education, and civilization—translated into a better life, materially and socially—was the driving force behind the rise of an African middle class in Southern Rhodesia.

CHRISTIAN MISSIONS AND THE FOUNDATIONS OF AFRICAN EDUCATION

The educational institutions that provided the structural scaffolding for African elite formation were an integral part of the colonial enterprise. Although missionary activity in what would become Southern Rhodesia commenced in the 1860s, Christian religious and educational work only gained a firm footing after 1890.[9] Like other white "pioneers," the various missionary societies that arrived after the advent of colonial rule received parcels of land from the government, a total of some 325,000 acres.[10] The mission stations, the name given to the religious-cum-educational fiefdoms established by the missionaries on their land grants, were spread out over the colony—a spatial disaggregation promoted by the government to limit denominational rivalry in the rush to save African souls. The authorities, concerned about social stability, were afraid that Christian sectarianism, fueled by arcane doctrinal disputations, would wreak havoc on the mind of the bewildered native.

In its mature form, the mission station consisted of a church, a boarding school, and housing for the white missionaries and their so-called assistants, actually African teachers and preachers who did much, often most, of the work. The more elaborate mission stations would also have a farm, a clinic, or perhaps even a small hospital. In addition to preachers, teachers, and students, mission stations attracted an assortment of deracinated and disaffected individuals, including refugees, landless converts, and young women fleeing arranged marriages, usually to older men.

From their base on the mission station, the missionaries moved out into surrounding communities, establishing subsidiary churches and schools. In time, the subsidiary schools came to be divided into two categories: second class and third class; these schools, unlike the first-class school on the mission station, were nonboarding. Second-class schools, like first-class ones, were usually under the direct supervision of white missionaries, whereas third-class or kraal schools, the most downscale of the three categories, were run on a day-to-day basis entirely by African teachers.

The religious and educational activities of most missionary societies were underwritten by sponsoring bodies outside of Southern Rhodesia, typically in Europe or the United States, as well as by school fees and donations by African converts. Unpaid labor performed by students and members of local communities, not always voluntarily, constituted another important, though often overlooked, source of support for the missions. Unpaid labor was especially crucial in the construction of schools and churches and in the operation of mission farms. After a decade of budgetary disengagement, the colonial state also began providing limited subventions for African education, purportedly because of a newfound desire in the wake of the uprisings of 1896–97 to "civilize" the Africans.[11] If so, this was civilization on the cheap. Ever niggardly when it came to anything beneficial to the colonized, the regime made only a minimal investment in African education, and that as part of an attempt to effect control by imposing its will on the missionaries rather than as a sincere desire to implement the "civilizing mission."[12]

Official parsimony contrasted sharply with increasing African demands for education, demands that were already beginning to outstrip the supply by the second decade of colonial rule. In 1910–11, an official commission found that educational resources had become so scarce that many missionary societies could no longer open new schools.[13] Fifteen years later, another commission, this one expressly charged with inquiring into African education, found the system in crisis: Africans everywhere clamored, largely in vain, for more schools and better-qualified teachers to staff them.[14]

There was no greater testament to the desire for education than the emergence in the urban centers of night schools, dubbed "the Cinderella of Native education" by the 1925 Commission on Native Education. In these makeshift schools, laborers and domestic servants, mostly men but also a few women—exhausted from a long and hard day's work yet determined to rise to a higher level—would gather "in a gloomy and badly ventilated room, lit only by one smoking oil lamp, round which a circle of earnest students pore vainly over books of exceedingly small print." White madams, too, frowned on such incipient essays in personal betterment, bewailing servants "who study books at odd intervals, often to the detriment of their tasks."[15]

The beleaguered missionaries—faced with a rising tide of demand from below for education, but operating under perennial financial constraints—readily conceded their helplessness and pleaded for more substantive state support. No such support, however, would be forthcoming. Fiscal stinginess, combined with the regime's long-standing policy of interdicting black middle-class formation, ruled out any dramatic budgetary increase for African education. Indeed, by the time the Commission on Native Education issued its report in 1925, the government and the missionaries had become locked in a simmering dispute, the commission having been appointed largely as a result of the dispute and, more precisely, the policy issues that provoked it.

Up to the end of World War I, the relations between church and state, although fraught with contradictions and constant official sniping at the missionaries, had been more cooperative than conflictual.[16] With the end of the war, however, officials ratcheted up their attacks on mission education, the disapproval centering on that most vexing and intractable of Rhodesian public policies—black advancement. The question of African social mobility had received some attention before the war, but it acquired much greater urgency in the postwar period, as popular discontent erupted and as an indigenous, mission-educated black elite announced its emergence by, among other things, forming political associations to advance its group interests.[17] Dismayed, officials attributed the growing discontent to overeducation, charging that the missionaries, in their supposed preoccupation with cultivating the intellect, had neglected to instruct Africans in more practical and useful endeavors.

Yet the stereotypical mission-educated African, a racial leveler who shirked manual labor while surreptitiously poring over political treatises and plotting to bring about social equality between black and white, existed only in the imagination of the settlers and their government officials. Actually the missionaries, many of whom shared the racist views of the settlers and often were no less demeaning and cruel in their personal relations with Africans, differed considerably in pedagogical approach and social philosophy.[18]

Some missionary societies maintained that African converts should be completely refashioned, culturally and spiritually, in preparation for integration into society, although whether on an equal basis with whites remained unclear. Among the most prominent exponents of the integrationist ideal were two United States–based denominations: the American Methodist Episcopal Church and the American Board of Commissioners for Foreign Missions, a Congregational body. The way to refashion Africans and make them ready for integration into settler-dominated society, an American Board missionary asserted in 1900, was to "'denationalize' the people,—change their whole ideas and purposes of life, by teaching them a 'Christian civilization.'"[19]

From an educational standpoint, Christian civilization meant instruction in literary and industrial subjects as well as religious training. The convert's head as well as hands had to be educated, but more attention was paid to the latter than the former. Thus by 1920 students at Mt. Silinda Institute, the American Board's flagship school, received daily between five and ten hours of industrial instruction, both theoretical and practical, compared with just three hours of literary education.[20] Indeed, the best African craftsmen—against whom white artisans began establishing an industrial color bar as early as the turn of the century—graduated from schools associated with the integrationist or civilizationist thrust within the missionary enterprise.[21]

Not all missionary societies, however, subscribed to the civilizationist philosophy. Other religious bodies, holding a much lower estimation of African potential, maintained that integrating the colonized people into the dominant culture was neither possible nor desirable. The African "is not equal to us [whites] and we cannot make him so," a representative of the Dutch Reform Church, one of the most illiberal missionary societies, informed the Commission on Native Education. Although rejecting integration and racial equality, both in principle and in practice, Dutch Reformers believed Africans had "souls to be saved" and occupied themselves in working toward that end. From a pedagogical standpoint, the Dutch Reform Church and like-minded denominations concentrated on "simple home industries,"—meaning that students received sufficient instruction to enable them to develop "along their own lines" in the Reserves, but not enough to make them competitive with settler craftsmen in the white towns.[22]

Elite Africans, ever attuned to the connection between education and personal advancement, were acutely aware of the divergent pedagogical approaches and social philosophies of the various missionary societies. In 1956 Enoch Dumbutshena, then a leading spokesman on African education and later chief justice of independent Zimbabwe, summarized the concerted opinion of middle-class blacks on mission schools. Whereas the American Methodists "were interested in developing a Christian character to enable the African to play a full part in the economic, political and social life of the country," Dumbutshena averred, the Dutch Reformers historically had opposed "giving an education that would go towards making Africans and Europeans equal."[23]

THE COLONIAL STATE AND AFRICAN EDUCATION

The specter of racial equality, and all that it conjured up in the settler mind, was precisely what state intervention in African education sought to avoid. Beginning in 1899, when the first Education Ordinance was promulgated, government policy formalized the development of two distinct, separate and unequal educational tracks for whites and blacks. Official policy offered the settlers' children an academic education commensurate with their predetermined status as members of the ruling race, whereas young Africans, condemned by the colonial political economy to a life of drudgery, would receive industrial training to make them more tractable laborers and docile subjects. This arrangement made no provision for an African middle class and, indeed, was antithetical to the emergence of such a social formation. The settler state, in short, would spurn the African elite's beloved Miss Education.

The Education Ordinance of 1899 established an Education Department, mainly to promote the development of white education. An ancillary order to the ordinance provided for annual grants of ten shillings per student to mission-run African schools, with a maximum of £50 to any one school. To actually obtain the grant, schools were required to offer daily at least four hours of instruction, no less than two of which had to be devoted to industrial training. The Education Ordinance was amended in 1903 and again in 1907 to add more conditions to government grants, including an increase from two to four in the number of hours devoted to industrial training. Furthermore, schools desiring official funding were required to instruct students in "cleanliness and discipline" as well as basic spoken English, the better to facilitate communication between master and servant. As a means of recruiting female domestic servants, thereby releasing male household labor for more "useful" tasks, the amended Education Ordinance also offered financial incentives for instructing African girls and young women in sewing, cooking, washing, ironing, and general housework.

In 1903, as part of its campaign to make industrial training the centerpiece of all African education, the colonial regime invited Booker T. Washington to visit Southern Rhodesia, ostensibly to solicit his advice but more likely for the potential propaganda value attendant on such a visit. After serious consideration, Washington, the chief apostle of industrial training for African Americans and other dependent peoples worldwide, declined the invitation.[24] However, the Tuskegean's name and legacy would be invoked for decades to come by the main participants in the debate over African education—notably the government, the missionaries, and the black elite.

Consistent with the introduction of the Education Ordinance of 1899 and the invitation to Washington, the colonial regime intensified its attack on mission education. In evidence presented to the South African Native Affairs Commission of 1903–1905, Rhodesian officials unanimously condemned the book learning they imagined Africans were receiving from the missionaries. Far from acquiring steady habits of industry and respect for the duly constituted authority of the white man, these officials charged, mission-educated Africans were noteworthy for their slothfulness and chicanery.[25]

Some officials, arguing that the African condition was immutable and did not lend itself to social amelioration, seemed willing to dispense with education altogether, whether literary or industrial. J. W. Posselt, for instance, had "not seen any institution which has effected a marked improvement among Natives. All such efforts are, I fear, foredoomed to disappointment." It seemed patently absurd to this minor colonial potentate that the Africans over whom he lorded in his capacity as native commissioner could produce a college graduate, much less a lawyer. "It would be ludicrous," Posselt blurted out, "to imagine a Mashona holding a University degree, or being called to the Bar;—and yet, it is hardly an exaggeration to say that some such dream of the future enters into the schemes of many who profess to have the social welfare of the Natives at heart."[26]

The actions of the government belied such gloomy assessments of the colonized people's potential: African education, and related concerns about social mobility, remained a burning issue in official circles. Thus the Native

Affairs Committee of 1910–11, appointed to inquire into the general status of Africans, inevitably became enmeshed in the education debate. The committee supported giving Africans "some small amount" of academic instruction to produce the clerks, teachers, and interpreters demanded by the colonial political economy; mostly, however, it favored industrial training, for which it recommended increased government expenditure, including the establishment of an institute. The settlers, though, were deeply divided over providing industrial training to Africans, a rift that ran along class lines. Whereas employers generally supported industrial training as a way to produce "a better workman and a more useful servant to the European," white artisans opposed it or, at best, insisted that it should be severely circumscribed.[27]

Yet opposition to industrial education, at least of the kind officials had in mind, was not limited to white artisans. The Native Affairs Committee also was "informed that unless there is offered at the same time a measure of literary teaching, the native will not submit to industrial instruction."[28] Africans in Southern Rhodesia, barely a generation under colonial rule, had developed very clear ideas about education. They welcomed industrial training, which had always been a major component of mission education, but insisted that literary instruction also should form a central part of the curriculum. The Africans, in sum, demanded a balanced education that would enable them to rise to their highest potential, individually and collectively, in the colonial political economy. Such aspirations were, however, anathema to the settlers, a sentiment well reflected in official policy. Where the Africans demanded education for elevation, the colonial state envisaged only training for thralldom.

Still, officials realized that it would be virtually impossible to completely deny Africans access to academic education; "do what we may, the native will get it," the Native Affairs Committee observed. Rather than denial, the guiding principle would be control, a word that appeared repeatedly in the committee's report and in subsequent debates in the Legislative Council. Concerning literary training for Africans, the committee urged officials to "take every means of retaining the control of this class of education, so that it may be directed into paths which we can approve of." Concretely, this meant state control over the establishment of schools, the instruction they offered, and most importantly, the African teaching staff, a potential vehicle for the introduction into the classroom of "undesirable political propaganda." As a means of stanching such ideological subversion, then most readily associated with Ethiopianism or African religious independency, the committee recommended that blacks should not be allowed to teach unless they were under white supervision.[29]

These proposals formed the basis of the Native Schools Ordinance of 1912. The ordinance required government permission to open schools, a measure aimed directly at the Ethiopian movement, because a church without schools would be unattractive to those in search of education as a pathway to social mobility. The ordinance also compelled all African schools, not just those receiving official financial aid, as before, to submit to government inspection, including the qualification of the teaching staff and the nature of the instruction. Schools that did not meet the requirements could be closed. "The whole idea was to regulate and control the basis of education as applied to the native," the attorney general admitted in introducing the ordinance. "It was a new departure, and a very big one; but . . . the advantages to be gained" by both blacks and whites made it justifiable, he concluded.[30]

Thus, from the Education Ordinance of 1899 to the Native Schools Ordinance of 1912, the colonial regime gradually outlined its policy on African education and constructed the machinery to implement it. Dangling financial incentives before the cash-starved missionaries, the state attempted to reconstitute African education by turning mission schools into industrial-training centers, with little in the way of literary instruction. But the authorities did not only offer carrots; they also took care to arm themselves with sticks. Under the law, officials had wide latitude to authorize the opening or closing of schools at will, and government inspectors were empowered to order changes in matters ranging from the curriculum to the qualification of teachers and their demeanor. The system, however, did not always work as envisaged. As in other areas, the vaunted colonial Leviathan proved to be less than all powerful. Some schools evaded aspects of state control, such as the mandate on industrial training, by declining the limited government grants, whereas the inspectors were too few and spread too thin to fully impose the official will on the missions.

From an official standpoint, the most important indication of the failure to fully control the development of African education was the emergence in the years immediately following World War I of a relatively significant group of mission-educated blacks. Increasingly, the ranks of this aspiring middle class, which were slowly but constantly expanding, consisted of Africans indigenous to Southern Rhodesia, marking a major shift from the prewar years when the bulk of the colony's black petty bourgeoisie consisted of immigrants from South Africa.[31] The emerging black elite, officials believed, constituted a cancer in the body politic, a threat to the stability of settler society and the system of white domination. To guard against the coming onslaught, the government would have to act, and act affirmatively and decisively, to more securely foreclose the avenues to African social mobility by further restricting academic training and employment opportunities.

The principal exponent of the harder line was the now-familiar Herbert S. Keigwin, whom we met in the previous chapter and whose 1920 report to the Legislative Council offered the most thoroughgoing blueprint for arresting African middle-class formation to date, going well beyond anything previously envisaged. Although commending their "good work," Keigwin attacked the missionaries as "short-sighted and unpractical. Their zeal for the spiritual and the literary has been too little tempered with regard for the material and industrial."[32] In a private memo to his superiors, although not in his public report, Keigwin proposed a radical solution to the problem created by the missionaries: notably, abolishing the mission schools and dismissing the African teaching staff, the single most important group of elite blacks. In their place would come "a comprehensive system of State Education" run entirely by white teachers.[33]

Under Keigwin's secret plan, "mental education" would be restricted to simple English lessons, "as the root of all trouble between master and servant is due to the want of mutual understanding." But literary instruction past puberty would be futile, he pronounced, since "at this age the [African] intellect is arrested by the closing up of the sutures." With the African youngster no longer capable of cognitive development, industrial training would begin and continue through adolescence. As part of the training, students would be required to secure employment for at least six months out of the year, failing which they would be forcibly indentured. "Surely it is our duty as the ruling race, and for the honour of our great Empire, to take the native in hand and save him from himself, even if we have to resort to compulsory means," Keigwin exhorted his superiors. Refusal to do so, he intoned, would be a sure sign that "we are ourselves degenerating."[34]

These suggestions apparently met with official approval at the highest level, and the British South Africa Company regime, over strong missionary objection, appointed Keigwin to the newly created position of director of native development.[35] As an initial installment on the Keigwin plan, in 1920 the regime established an industrial-training center at Domboshawa in Mashonaland, the first public school for Africans. The following year, a second government-run industrial center was opened at Tjolotjo in Matabeleland. Presently, it appeared as if the regime was moving seriously to implement Keigwin's grand scheme of supplanting mission education with public industrial schools. This, however, was not to be. The machinery of state-sponsored industrial training soon ground to an inglorious halt, another victim of official parsimony. The government, after all, would not assume direct control of African education.

Although forced to retreat, the state had seized the political initiative by the early 1920s, making industrial training the buzzword of African education and relegating critics in the missionary community and among the African elite to a reactive role. The movement for industrial education received a major boost in 1925 with the publication of the report of the Commission on Native Education, which repeated the indictment of mission education. But this time around the critique was less searing, tempered by the stark reality that the mission schools were not about to be replaced by a system of state education. Still, the commission endorsed industrial training as well as other measures to frustrate African social mobility.[36]

In a move aimed at deepening de jure segregation, the Commission on Native Education recommended severing all formal links between the education of black and white youngsters. Accordingly, the Education Department, entrusted with responsibility for all education under the Education Ordinance of 1899, would now become entirely white, with African education fobbed off to the Native Affairs Department and its ancillaries. The commission also proposed to impede the career objectives of educated Africans by "encouraging" them "to engage in work in purely Native areas," that is, in the Reserves as opposed to the urban centers, even as it hypocritically proclaimed that "there should be no repression of Native aspirations."[37] The Commission on Native Education, in sum, was yet another layer in the construction of what Godfrey Huggins, the future prime minister, would call "parallel development," a term apparently coined by F. L. Hadfield, the commission's chairman and a former missionary, legislator, and champion of white labor.[38]

The Rhodesian authorities were hardly unique in using industrial training as a foil to attack African social mobility and, more especially, what they regarded as its attendant potential for political subversion. In fact, the campaign for industrial education in the post–World War I era stood at the center of an international crusade by colonial officials, especially in the British empire, to contain a widening chain of rebellion ranging from resurgent nationalism in India and Egypt to strikes, riots, trade unionism, and other forms of agitation throughout the dependencies.[39]

The search for solutions to the colonial dilemma led to the former Confederate States of America, where a remarkable experiment in nonracial democracy after the American Civil War had been violently suppressed in a white supremacist counterrevolution, resulting in a purging of blacks from public life in the southern United States. The subsequent "redemption" ushered in Jim Crow, a major hallmark of which was industrial education as exemplified by Booker T. Washington's Tuskegee Institute and its sister institutions, including Hampton Institute, Washington's alma mater.[40] The Tuskegee model of black development placed as much emphasis on inculcating respect among African Americans for the color line and established (white) authority as it did on instruction in craft and mechanical subjects.[41]

To many defenders of empire in the post–World War I era, the American New South offered numerous lessons on how to deal with wayward colonial subjects. The subsequent attempt to adapt the Tuskegee model to the conditions of dependent territories, especially (although not exclusively) the British ones, was enthusiastically supported by various U.S. foundations.[42] Chief among these was the Phelps-Stokes Fund, which conducted much of the research for this latest experiment in colonial social engineering. Significantly, Thomas Jesse Jones, the Phelps-Stokes Fund's leading "expert" on African American education, also headed its research projects in Africa.[43]

As elsewhere on the African continent, the Phelps-Stokes intervention gave an aura of international legitimacy to, and helped frame the debate on, industrial education in Southern Rhodesia. It is hardly coincidental, for instance, that the Commission on Native Education was appointed two months after a visit to the colony in 1924 by Jones and his team of investigators.[44] Jones strongly supported the commission's appointment, lauding it as "a statesmanlike measure which should result in great good," while the commission, not to be outdone, repaid the compliment by quoting Jones authoritatively.[45]

Not surprisingly, the defenders of empire everywhere were delighted with the work of the Phelps-Stokes Fund. Jones, basking in his role as chief apostle of the international networks championing industrial education in Africa, made no attempt to disguise the purpose of his research, which, he asserted, was aimed at preventing the Indianization of Africa. Indian nationalism, he argued, was attributable to an educational system that "too exclusively prepared the young Indians for literary and clerical occupations to the neglect of the activities that are more fundamental in the economic and social development of their great country."[46] Consequently, the colonial authorities, using the blueprint provided by the Phelps-Stokes Fund, would seek to erect a political cordon sanitaire against the anticolonial contagion then raging through India, principally by introducing industrial education and retarding the growth of an indigenous intelligentsia. The campaign for industrial education in Africa was further boosted by an official British imperial commission, a panel on which J. H. Oldham, a leading missionary statesman and close associate of Jones and the Phelps-Stokes Fund, exercised a dominant influence.[47]

Although suspicious of the overall project, members of the African elite in Southern Rhodesia were especially captivated by one individual associated with the international industrial-education campaign—notably James E. K. Aggrey, a United States–based Gold Coast national and the sole black member of the Phelps-Stokes group. In 1924, while visiting Southern Rhodesia in his capacity as a Phelps-Stokes investigator, Aggrey addressed a group of Africans in Bulawayo, a near epiphanic moment for many in the audience. Almost seven decades after the event, Esau Nemapare, the future Methodist minister and champion of Ethiopianism who served as a translator at the Bulawayo meeting, distinctly remembered Aggrey's electrifying effect.[48] Aggrey, who later earned the sobriquet "Booker T. Washington of Africa" on account of his advocacy of the Tuskegee model of development throughout the continent, also would have gratified the Rhodesian authorities by decrying political agitation and lauding interracial cooperation within the colonial framework, his favorite subjects.[49]

The Rhodesian government had good reasons to be pleased with Aggrey, his Phelps-Stokes colleagues, and their worldwide network of interlocking alliances. Collectively, these external agencies bolstered the case for industrial education and helped to disarm its critics among the missionaries and the emerging African elite. And yet, for all its bluster, the ideological hegemony of the state came at a minimal cost to the public treasury. In 1923, for instance, official grants to mission schools amounted to just over £19,000, an amount that had more than doubled over the three-year period since 1920. By comparison, the Commission on Native Education estimated that in 1923, seven of the leading missionary societies contributed close to £50,000 in direct expenditure and voluntary work on African education. No figures were available for seven other denominations. Nor did the commission offer figures on the amount of money Africans paid in school fees, although it estimated "Native contributions to general missionary work" at nearly £7,000. This amount, however, did not include unpaid African labor.[50]

Seeking at once to further institutionalize segregation and raise the barrier to African social mobility, the government in 1927 created a separate Native Education Department, a move long urged by the advocates of industrial training, most recently by the Commission on Native Education. Then, two years later, and in an ongoing refinement of the industrial education campaign, itself a reflection of the deepening segregationist impulse, the Native Education Department was superseded by an expanded agency, the Department of Native Development. In addition to education, the new agency was responsible for agriculture, community welfare, and other aspects of "native development." Domestic science, which the defunct Native Education Department had championed—hiring a white woman as "organizing instructress"— received even greater attention under the Department of Native Development. With funding from the Carnegie Foundation of New York, the new department dispatched male "Jeanes teachers" and female "home demonstrators" to effect "improvement" in the underdeveloped Reserves.[51]

Inevitably, the Department of Native Development, with its broad mandate, came into conflict with the Native Affairs Department, which viewed the newer and more dynamic agency as intruding on its domain as the premier agency for Native Affairs. In 1934 the Department of Native Development was bested in the ensuing bureaucratic infighting, prompting its routed director, Harold Jowitt, to resign and leave for Uganda to continue his peripatetic career as a British imperial bureaucrat. Jowitt was replaced by George Stark, an aide he had brought along from South Africa upon assuming his position in Southern Rhodesia.[52] Finally, in 1935 the Native Education Department was resurrected, but this time as a subunit of the triumphant Native Affairs Department rather than as a freestanding agency. Collectively, the various Native Affairs units dutifully carried out the policies of Godfrey Huggins, who had been elected prime minister in 1933 on a platform that promised to intensify the assault on Africans' prospects for social mobility.

THE STATE AND AFRICAN EDUCATION
IN THE ERA OF WORLD WAR II

World War II, a momentous event in the history of European colonialism in Africa, led to a reassessment of state policy on education, among other areas of African life. This reassessment, to be sure, presaged no wholesale reversal of the settler regime's historic hostility to the rise of an African middle class, a disposition that remained intact and, indeed, continued to be expressed in various ways, including a highly publicized attempt in 1945 to disfranchise the small number of black voters. The wartime and postwar reassessment, in brief, fell well short of an embracement of Miss Education. Even so, there was a gradual loosening of the state-imposed strictures on African education, a process driven by socioeconomic and political forces set in motion by the war.

The most striking indicator of the reassessment of African education was a huge expansion in school enrollment, financed largely by a dramatic increase in government expenditure, albeit from a low base. The number of students more than doubled between 1940 and 1950, while government grants to mission schools, which continued to educate all but a handful of Africans, rose more than sevenfold during the same period, as shown in table 2.1. Yet even with these increases, African education accounted for only about 3.5 percent of the state education budget, the rest going to white schools.[53] The bulk of the new African educational resources went toward salaries, the government having undertaken in 1947 to pay all "approved" teachers, that is, those who had gone beyond standard VI, the highest level in primary school.[54] The amount of public funds devoted to African education continued to rise over the next fifteen years, reaching close to £2 million by 1958 and more than £6 million by 1965.[55] As a part of the reassessment, the Native Education Department, a subsidiary unit of the Native Affairs Department for over two decades, once again became an independent although still racially separate government agency in 1956. African activists had long urged such a transfer of authority, although to an integrated and nonracial ministry in charge of all education.

The expansion of the school system at the primary level led to a proportional increase in the demand for secondary education. Africans—barred from the Rhodesian white schools and concerned about the costs and logistical

Table 2.1. Government Grants to Mission Schools for Africans

Year	Amount	No. of Schools	No. of Students	Expenditure per Student
1901	£133	3	265	£.50
1910	£2,780	115	9,873	£.28
1920	£9,467	750	43,094	£.22
1930	£48,426	1,422	107,122	£.45
1940	£72,655	1,392	111,686	£.65
1950	£527,088	2,232	232,689	£2.26

Source: *Report of the Native Education Inquiry Commission, 1951.*

problems associated with postprimary training in South Africa—had been agitating for the creation locally of secondary educational facilities since the 1930s.[56] In response the Anglican Church, eager to gain an advantage over its denominational rivals in the contest for membership, opened the first secondary school for Africans in 1939 at St. Augustine's mission outside Salisbury. The government, in line with its evolving policy, followed suit in 1946 by establishing a public high school for Africans at Goromonzi, also outside Salisbury. By 1953, when the Federation of Rhodesia and Nyasaland came into being, the number of African secondary schools had increased to twelve. Goromonzi, still the lone government-run high school, had 314 students, 82 of them female, while the remaining eleven mission schools boasted a total enrollment of 771, including 91 females.[57] Subsequently, the number of secondary school students increased along with the overall school enrollment. In 1961, high schoolers accounted for 5,069 of the more than 500,000 students at all levels. By 1965, there were 75 secondary schools for Africans—61 of them run by missionaries and the remaining 14 by the government—with an aggregate enrollment of 11,495.[58]

Yet, despite the rapid expansion, the demand for primary and secondary schooling continued to run far ahead of the supply, as in the pre–World War II era. As late as 1964, secondary education remained an elusive goal for most African primary-school graduates, with only one in five finding a place in the regular high schools, although many others continued their studies through correspondence courses.[59] What is more, only a tiny fraction of African students who began primary school managed to graduate, the figures being less than one seventh of one percent in 1946. This was the consequence of a huge bottleneck at the lowest rungs of the educational system, resulting in a precipitous decline in the number of students remaining in school after only three years of instruction, as shown in table 2.2. The massive dropout rate, in turn, was caused by an acute shortage of both schools and teachers, especially at the upper primary (post–standard III) level. Thus the base from which the

Table 2.2. Students Continuing from Standards I–VI

	1936	1941	1946
Total enrollment	88,211	97,829	152,323
Percentage of total enrollment by grade:			
Below standard I	92.235	79.784	69.246
Standard I	5.506	13.409	15.508
Standard II	1.691	4.800	9.059
Standard III	.486	1.732	4.948
Standard IV	.082	.237	.797
Standard V	—	.038	.131
Standard VI	—	—	.014

Source: *Report of the Director of Native Education for the Year 1947.*

wartime and postwar increases in government funding began was too low, and per capita expenditure remained too small, to reverse the endemic crisis in African education, which deepened after 1965.[60] In the final analysis the settler regime, although abandoning the overt hostility it had shown during the interwar years, continued to demur on African education and, with it, the prospects of the colonized people for social mobility.

Still, it is certainly the case that in the postwar years, the fortunes of the emerging African middle class improved, quite considerably in some instances, compared with that of the pre–World War II era. Some observers, then and later, attributed much of this relative educational and occupational mobility to the efforts of Garfield Todd, the missionary-educator turned politician who succeeded the arch-segregationist Godfrey Huggins as prime minister of Southern Rhodesia upon the establishment of the Federation of Rhodesia and Nyasaland.[61] Among other feats, Todd removed education from the control of the much-despised Native Affairs Department, reconstituted the Native Education Department as an independent government ministry, and personally assumed the new portfolio—events described by Enoch Dumbutshena, the noted African point man on the subject, as "the biggest reform ever" in black education.[62] And indeed Todd, a quintessential racial paternalist impatient with any sign of restiveness on the part of the beneficiaries of his altruism, genuinely desired some measure of advancement for elite Africans, although certainly not equality between black and white.[63] In the end, though, the bulk of the reforms for which Todd has been credited, including the increases in educational expenditures, began well before he came to power and continued after his ouster in 1958.

The reassessment of the regime's so-called native policy in the post–World War II era, then, had little to do with personalities; the process was driven by economic and political transformations beyond the control of any single individual, no matter how powerful. In particular, the rapid wartime and postwar industrial growth that made increased public expenditures on African education possible also required a better-educated labor force. Although all but a few managerial and technical positions continued to be filled by whites (many of them recent immigrants), capital and state looked to Africans to perform increasingly skilled tasks.[64] It was these systemic changes, rather than the prime minister's personal concerns, that forced a reconsideration in official African educational policy, thereby widening the scope for black social mobility.

As a function of increasing industrialization and urbanization, the expansion of African education also enhanced the utility of schools as an agency for training and, more to the point, disciplining the next generation of workers. Thus social control, an enduring theme in the history of African education in Southern Rhodesia, became even more pronounced in the post–World War II era.[65] With fathers, and increasingly mothers, away at work during the day, more and more schools came to be seen as a means of keeping young people off the streets and out of trouble. As the director of native education noted pointedly in 1949: "In large urban areas where conditions may be such as to encourage delinquency on the part of the young, training in discipline is a matter of major importance."[66]

The idea of controlling and disciplining young urbanized Africans through the school system continued to gain currency, reaching a high point in the late 1950s and 1960s, a period that coincided with the emergence of mature African nationalism. The nationalists were accused by officials of exploiting the educational crisis by instigating "disturbances," including encouraging students to enroll in schools outside the areas in which they lived, an act contrary to government regulations.[67] As part of its attack on African nationalism, the settler regime introduced a new Native Education Act in 1959, the year it banned the Southern Rhodesian African National Congress, the first full-throated nationalist group. Among other provisions, the Native Education Act forbade teachers, now designated civil servants, from "taking an active part in political matters," meaning African nationalist matters.[68] In this way, the colonial authorities hoped to detach teachers, traditionally an important leadership element within the African elite, from the nationalist locomotive.

THE AFRICAN EDUCATIONAL AGENDA

The mature African nationalists, whose appearance testified eloquently to elite black disillusionment with the entire process of social mobility, readily seized on education as a potent symbol of colonial perfidy. Far from breaking new ground, however, the nationalists were treading well-worn paths. As part of the project of personal betterment and collective advancement, Africans had been centrally involved in the education debate since the 1920s, the sum total of their claims adding up to a methodical and systematic agenda. The African educational agenda, as initially elaborated by various organizations and individuals between the two world wars, a period of such unrelenting attacks on black aspirations, emphasized both entitlement and self-help. Demands on the state and the missions, although foundational, were counterbalanced by attempts to initiate private ventures ranging from independent schools to scholarship programs.[69] The Tuskegee model of development, used by the authorities to promote industrial training and interdict African advancement, assumed an entirely different incarnation in the eyes of proponents of the African educational agenda. In the alternate, African view, Tuskegee and all it represented became a symbol of black achievement, a yardstick by which the colonized could measure their own endeavors in educational self-help.

From the outset, African dissatisfaction with education was directed as much against the missionaries as the state. African unhappiness with mission education, however, was motivated by entirely different concerns from those that exercised the minds of colonial officials. Elite Africans, themselves the products of mission schools and professed Christians, resented the rivalries between the various missionary societies—conflicts which, they believed, retarded educational progress and created unnecessary divisions among converts. Even the eminently moderate Southern Rhodesia Native Missionary Conference, a body consisting of African ministers and church leaders, felt compelled to attack "certain irresponsible persons in different denominations [who] are perpetuating denominational animosity" among African Christians.[70]

Unable to curb the interdenominational feuding, elite Africans called for nonsectarian public education, although again for reasons quite different from Keigwin, the bête noire of black social mobility who sought to replace the mission schools with government-run industrial centers. African claims to education, rather, centered on compulsory, literary-based public schooling at the primary level, with a gradual introduction of secondary education. As if to underline the interconnectedness of education and elevation, proponents of the African educational agenda insisted that English should replace the local languages as the medium of instruction in African schools as soon as practicable—an insistence that sometimes infuriated even missionaries of a "civilizationist" bent.[71] It is a measure of the determination to master the colonial tongue that the principal association representing African teachers went so far as to make English its official language.[72]

Appropriately, the first concerted attempts to define an African educational agenda were made by the political associations that emerged in the post–World War I era, that is, the social processes that provoked the state-sponsored backlash against the emerging black middle class in the interwar years. The Rhodesia Bantu Voters Association, one of the more assertive of these groups, also became one of the most active on the education issue. Indeed, as Terence Ranger has noted, in a situation in which (English) literacy was one of the qualifications for voting, the Bantu Voters Association naturally took a special interest in education.[73] In 1925—nine years after an official commission recommended the same for white children, and ten years before that recommendation went into effect—the Bantu Voters Association called for free and compulsory public education for African youngsters up to the primary-school level.[74] Citing the squabbling between the missionary societies so greatly deplored by elite Africans, the association later presented its proposal to the prime minister, claiming that a member of one church attending a school sponsored by a rival denomination "is not a popular pupil and is constantly the object of attempts to convert him." The prime minister, however, rejected the idea of universal African education as too costly, explaining that "too many schools would be necessary." Repeated lobbying by the Bantu Voters Association again was rebuffed on financial grounds.[75]

The cold shoulder of officialdom, however, did not deter the suitors of Miss Education. In 1930, commissions investigating African living conditions in Salisbury and Bulawayo, the two major urban centers, were confronted with the African educational agenda. Whatever their other differences, the Africans who gave evidence to the commissions were united on the need to expand this crucial entree to social mobility. Noting the on-going denominational rivalry, and arguing for greater efficiency and higher standards, African activists again called for universal primary education. The Bulawayo-based Masotsha Ndhlovu, head of the populist-leaning Industrial and Commercial Workers Union of Africa (ICU), summarized the African position with customary forthrightness: "We ask for an undenominational school with professional teachers of high educational qualifications. The teachers in mission schools at present are not sufficiently highly qualified to teach anyone whatsoever. We would welcome the introduction of compulsory education amongst the children of the Location [or segregated ghetto]. We favour primary education being in English."[76] In Salisbury, the Southern Rhodesia Native Association, a group regularly denounced by Ndhlovu's ICU as collaborationist, made similar demands.[77] African clergymen, too, agreed that the mission schools in the urban centers should be replaced with a state-run system.[78] The all-white commissions, dominated by the usual coterie of native affairs "experts," including the ubiquitous F. L. Hadfield, head of the 1925 Commission on Native Education, concluded that the African educational claims had merit.[79] The government, however, offered only more sermonizing on fiscal constraints, even as it intensified the project to vitiate and dissipate African social mobility through industrial training.

As the depression descended over Southern Rhodesia in the 1930s, the political associations that had championed the African educational agenda up to that point ceased to function. By default, leadership on issues of national importance to Africans, including education, devolved to the Southern Rhodesia Native Missionary Conference. Beginning in 1932, when it formally endorsed the call for public schools in the urban areas, the conference became the foremost promoter of African educational claims.[80] In 1936, a year after the introduction of universal primary education for white children, the conference requested parity for African youngsters. Anticipating the government's familiar refrain about budgetary woes, the conference suggested that universal African education could be gradually phased in, first in the urban areas and mining centers, with their relatively small African populations, then later in the Reserves, where the majority of Africans lived. But the authorities, tongue in cheek, pronounced themselves unwilling to discriminate among the colonized by favoring urban over rural residents. The regime was "not convinced as to the wisdom of introducing compulsory education for one section of the Native population only," read the disingenuous reply.[81]

As with the government, so too with its African antagonists: the advent of World War II brought about a significant shift on the educational front, with the African Teachers Association (ATA) emerging as the principal lobbying group, replacing the Southern Rhodesia Bantu Congress, a broad-based movement which itself had supplanted the Southern Rhodesia Native (now Bantu) Missionary Conference as the leading black political vehicle nationally. Teachers, who loomed so large in the rise of the African middle class, had always been highly visible in the education debate, both individually and as members of various political associations and professional groups, including the Bantu Missionary Conference and the Bantu Congress. However, the founding of the ATA in 1941, capping a decade-long organizational drive, resulted at once in a national movement of black teachers qua teachers, the first of its kind, and a new claimant to leadership of the African educational agenda.[82]

The ATA's first objective, as spelled out in its constitution, was to "further the education and general advancement of the African people and to consider all questions that may bear upon the educational interest of the African people." By contrast, promoting the interests of its members earned last place in the ATA's statement of its three cardinal principles.[83] In reality, the ATA made little distinction between the general good of Africans and the collective welfare of teachers. Whether reiterating the call for universal primary education and expanded secondary school facilities on the one hand, or demanding higher teacher salaries and the appointment of blacks as school principals on the other, the ATA justified its stance as a defense of the African commonweal. This position, although transparently self-serving, was not without merit. By challenging the racially determined pay scales and the equally racist occupational ceilings that continually drove many of the best qualified blacks from the teaching profession, the ATA both promoted the careers of its members and more generally helped to break down the barriers that impeded African mobility.[84]

Indeed, in the post–World War II era, the ATA launched a full-scale assault on the entire racist educational structure, buoyed by a general upsurge in defiance on the part of the colonized people, a mood characterized by strikes in the urban centers, unrest in the Reserves, and greater restiveness among the petty bourgeoisie.[85] In 1948, hard on the heels of a general strike, the ATA called for a commission on African education.[86] Outlining its position in advance, the ATA declared that "democracy cannot be saved by 'separation,'" attacked the "repressive" Native Affairs Department and its segregationist educational arm, and demanded a single, nonracial ministry of education. Moving beyond the fixation on primary and secondary schooling, the ATA expanded the list of educational claims by urging the government to build kindergartens for black preschoolers and establish a university to which Africans would be admitted "as full members."[87]

While privileging demands on the state and, to a lesser extent, the missions, the African educational agenda also focused on independent ventures by the colonized people themselves. This self-help and self-improvement tradition, as manifested in the realm of education, emerged primarily in response to the racially bound constraints of settler colonialism and as an integral part of the self-enabling agency of the African elite. Paradoxically, the indigenous self-help tradition was reinforced by the campaign for industrial education, which, in the drive to produce the so-called Good Native, heavily promoted a body of autobiographical and biographical literature centered on Booker T. Washington and James Aggrey, among others. Such writings, however, proved to be a double-edged sword. Instead of submission to colonial dictates, as intended, some readers learned an entirely different lesson from the lives and work of Washington and Aggrey. In a kind of pan-African counterinterpretation, both men, scripted in colonial apologia as supermodels of collaboration, were transposed into Machiavellian characters who had triumphed over white supremacy, thereby vindicating the capacity of Africans everywhere to rise in the scales of Western civilization.[88]

In Southern Rhodesia, as elsewhere in Africa, Washington's Tuskegee Institute became a bellwether of autonomous black achievement, casting a long shadow over self-help initiatives in education and other areas.[89] In 1931 Job Dumbutshena—vice chairman of the ICU and father of Enoch Dumbutshena, the African education point man—raised the specter of Tuskegee in the context of a proposal to help finance African education. The Bulawayo-based Job Dumbutshena harshly criticized the beer hall, a city-run facility that served as the major recreational venue for African workers as well as the source of much of the revenues that sustained the system of urban segregation.[90] Instead of the profits accruing to the municipality, Dumbutshena suggested that Africans "should be allowed to hire the Beer Hall, sell our own beer there, and devote the proceeds to the education of our children. We could get teachers from America."[91]

Self-help ventures became especially popular in the era of World War II, as the ATA assumed leadership of the African educational agenda. Aidan Mwamuka, in his presidential address to the annual ATA conference in 1944, made a strong appeal for self-help, arguing that the "Government's effort will not succeed unless we ourselves are prepared to shoulder the responsibility of raising the masses of our people. We cannot afford to wait for Government assistance. We must have self determination to organize and educate our people."[92] At the next annual meeting Ndabaningi Sithole, then a prominent ATA member, rose to the challenge by proposing "a national fund for African education," a project broached as far back as 1933.[93] Sithole's proposal received the warm endorsement of the ATA, which formed a three-member committee, including Sithole himself, to formulate a program of action for submission to "all recognised" African organizations.[94]

The ATA initiative apparently bore no fruit, but the idea of a national educational fund quickly became something of a cause célèbre. One of the more elaborate proposals came from Ernest Mhlanga, who praised self-help, urging Africans to maintain the "vision and unity of purpose" they had shown during World War II (which had ended only weeks earlier), when they voluntarily contributed more than £28,000 toward the government's war effort. Mhlanga proposed a trust for education and health, to be called the Southern Rhodesia African National Fund, and offered to contribute the first £10, challenging other "ambitious Africans" to match his beneficence.[95] The proposal was strongly supported by N. M. J. Patsika, who went beyond Mhlanga's elitist appeal to "ambitious Africans" and implored "all loafers and workers. Sell your grain and contribute a little."[96] Delighted by the effusive response, Mhlanga called for the formation of a planning committee, an idea that quickly became an agenda item for an upcoming meeting (early 1946) of the Bantu Congress, now renamed the Southern Rhodesia African National Congress (not to be confused with the previously mentioned Southern *Rhodesian* African National Congress) to reflect the evolving consciousness and sense of collective identity. To Mhlanga's bitter disappointment, however, no concrete action was forthcoming.[97] Years later Mhlanga, blaming organizational infighting for the failure to act on his earlier proposal, reiterated his call—again unsuccessfully—for an African National Fund.[98]

As an exercise in African educational self-help, the Tennyson Hlabangana National Bursary Fund had a somewhat more auspicious outcome than did Mhlanga's ill-fated African National Fund. The Hlabangana Bursary was established in honor of Tennyson Hlabangana, who died prematurely in 1948, just a few years into a promising career as a teacher and public intellectual. The aim of the bursary, according to Charlton Ngcebetsha, its secretary and a former teacher of Hlabangana, was to "help educate some of our indigent African scholars who without it might not be able to pursue their studies."[99] With a committee consisting of prominent Africans and a white treasurer, the Hlabangana Bursary managed to collect almost £75 by 1950, a year after its formation.[100] Almost from the outset, however, the Bulawayo-based bursary was bedeviled by latent ethnic tensions, even though its initiators included members of the colony's two major African ethnic groups and attempts were made to publicize its activities nationally.[101] Critics charged that the constitution "had not made it appear as though the Memorial Fund concerned all Africans in S[outhern] Rhodesia,"[102] meaning that it favored the Ndebele over the majority Shona-speakers. In any event, the Hlabangana Bursary subsequently lost its prominence, although reportedly it was still in existence as late as the mid-1970s.[103]

By far, the most ambitious and successful educational venture initiated by Africans in Southern Rhodesia was Nyatsime College, a technical school that opened in 1962. The absence of a technical college (as opposed to a craft-style industrial institute) for Africans had long concerned the ATA and other champions of the African educational agenda.[104] Then, in 1951, Stanlake Samkange formed a committee to raise the funds to build such a college. An active member of the ATA, Samkange had been one of the founders of the bursary named for Tennyson Hlabangana, a friend he would later describe in a book dedication as a "worthy scion of an Ndebele nobleman."[105]

The Nyatsime College scheme may have stood out for its bold vision, but it was refracted through a familiar lens. Samkange, who resigned his teaching post to become its full-time organizing secretary, described Nyatsime as a project patterned "on the lines of the Tuskegee Institute."[106] As if on cue, supporters of Nyatsime took to the stump, appealing to the Tuskegee model in the customary language of racial pride and pan-African solidarity. One fundraiser, the Rev. Oswald Ramushu, regaled his listeners with stories of how "self-help had helped Negroes in America," exhorting them to support Nyatsime, which he claimed would be beneficial "not only to themselves and their children but to the whole African race in this continent."[107] Many Africans, both in the rural and urban areas, rallied to the cause. Native Councils, compliant political bodies established by the government in the Reserves, offered modest contributions. In the cities, Nyatsime fundraisers held street collections, organized boxing matches, and sponsored concerts, the most notable of which was an event featuring the Manhattan Brothers, a famous African musical group from South Africa.[108]

As a scheme based on self-improvement and self-upliftment, fund-raising for Nyatsime initially was limited to Africans. After a three-year campaign, however, the organizers had failed to meet their goal of £10,000, forcing them to turn to non-African donors.[109] A group of Indian businessmen pledged £4,000, a philanthropic gesture that infuriated Prime Minister Garfield Todd, reflecting both an old settler aversion to Indians and new fears of a possible African-led, anticolonial alliance bankrolled by Indian money.[110] Todd was much less perturbed when the U.S. consul general, seeking to increase American influence, persuaded the Rockefeller Brothers Fund to donate US$10,000 (£3,571) to Nyatsime.[111] Meanwhile, though, repeated delays had sent the initial construction costs skyrocketing, causing constant shifts in the fundraising goal post. Ultimately the government, in a move calculated largely to blunt attacks on its educational policy by African nationalists demanding black majority rule, contributed £20,000 to the Nyatsime fund, the single largest donation to date and the pivotal one in the eventual establishment of the college.[112]

The Nyatsime scheme, conceived as a purely African initiative, had taught its organizers a sober lesson, namely, that self-help is not always synonymous with self-financing, a lesson only too familiar to the founders of the much-heralded Tuskegee Institute. Booker T. Washington, called "the wizard" on account of his shrewdness, was legendary for his ability to leverage resources, financial and political, from American philanthropy and the United States government alike.[113] It was therefore entirely appropriate that L. H. Foster, the president of Tuskegee Institute, should have been present at the dedication of Nyatsime College in 1962. Foster, who opened a dormitory named Tuskegee Hall during his visit, later helped to obtain a second Rockefeller Brothers Fund grant of $15,000 for Nyatsime. Foster's immediate predecessor, F. D. Patterson, also visited Nyatsime.[114] The Tuskegee presidents, past and present, were welcomed by their Nyatsime counterpart Stanlake Samkange, who himself had done a stint in the United States, where he had obtained a master's degree in education from Indiana University in 1958 to "prepare myself to take charge of the school."[115]

The opening of Nyatsime College marked a milestone in the life of the African educational agenda, a mixture of demands and wishes to which many groups contributed. The contributors included students, who, situated as they were on the frontline of the struggle for social mobility through education, occasionally resorted to drastic measures, such as striking. Already in 1921, and again in 1922, African students protesting insufficient literary instruction had gone on strike at Domboshawa, the school established by the government as part of its industrial-training campaign. Citing grievances as varied as dissatisfaction with manual work assignments, bad food, and poor treatment, students continued to use the strike weapon, which was deployed with increasing frequency and effectiveness after World War II.[116] By the late 1950s, student grievances became fused with the African nationalist demand for an end to settler rule, resulting in the most serious wave of school disturbances yet. It was only with the illegal declaration of independence and the introduction of permanent emergency measures in 1965 that the colonial regime began to regain control over African schools.[117]

EDUCATION, CHRISTIANITY, AND SOCIAL MOBILITY

The racial inequities exposed by protesting students and other supporters of the African educational agenda had, of course, been put in place precisely to impede black advancement. For Africans in Southern Rhodesia, upward social mobility through education required tremendous personal initiative and unbending collective will, along with much good fortune. And in the rise of the African middle class, those whose forebears readily accepted the colonial order, converting to Christianity and becoming fully integrated into the capitalist political economy, had a clear advantage over the offspring of nonconverts or individuals who were only marginally involved in the cash nexus.[118]

The importance of intergenerational mobility in achieving elite status can be gauged from the composition of the 1940–41 standard VI class at the American Board's Mt. Silinda Institute. According to one (female) missionary-teacher, "Almost half of the class" of thirty-two (twenty-four boys and eight girls) at this civilizationist-inclined institution "come from Christian homes and all but one get some financial help from their relatives."[119] Advancement across multiple generations seemed especially important in facilitating social mobility for women. The same missionary-teacher also reported that all seven of the female students enrolled in a new teacher-training course at Mt. Silinda in 1940 came "from older Christian homes of this vicinity. These older Christians are willing to make sacrifices so that their daughters may become teachers."[120]

Unlike some areas of colonial Africa, where the displaced traditional elite managed to parlay admittedly diminished authority and social standing into an educational investment in its scions,[121] the descendants of Southern Rhodesia's precolonial Shona and Ndebele rulers generally enjoyed no such advantage.[122] To be sure, inherited cultural capital played a decisive role in the rise of the colonial Zimbabwean middle class, but that capital consisted more of a Christian, bourgeois, achievement-oriented background than of lineal ties to the precolonial rulers.

The importance of Christianity, and all that it implied in the colonial context, as an agency for social mobility can be gleaned from the biographies of the first group of Africans in Southern Rhodesia to be educated up to the university level. Cephas Hlabangana, who graduated from the University College of Fort Hare in 1939, was the first African in Southern Rhodesia to earn a bachelor's degree.[123] His younger brother Tennyson, whose early death resulted in the formation of the Tennyson Hlabangana National Bursary Fund, also was among the first handful of colonial Zimbabweans to graduate from college.[124] Although reputed to be descendants of precolonial Ndebele "noblemen," the Hlabangana brothers owed their achievements more to a Christian-bourgeois upbringing than to noble origins. Their father, the Rev. Sitjenkwa Hlabangana, began the deeds of "first" continued by his sons; a leading member of the London Missionary Society, the elder Hlabangana also was one of the first Africans in the colony to join the Christian ministry.[125]

Similarly, Stanlake Samkange, who earned his B.A. in 1948, thereby becoming the first Shona-speaking college graduate, came from a family firmly rooted in the social interstices of the colonial order.[126] His father, the Rev. Thompson Samkange of the Wesleyan (British) Methodist Church, was a veritable poster figure of the emerging African middle class.[127] Joshua Nkomo, who also earned a bachelor's degree in social work in 1948, grew up in a "strictly Christian" household. His father, a successful farmer, teacher, and lay preacher, was among the first Africans in the district to own an animal-drawn vehicle.[128] Abel Muzorewa, the colony's first African bishop and prime minister of the short-lived Zimbabwe/Rhodesia (1978–79), asserted that Christianity was "one of the common denominators which brought my parents together," and he too grew up in a "devout Christian home."[129] Robert Mugabe, who succeeded Muzorewa as prime minister of independent Zimbabwe, likewise was raised in a "Christian village" on a Catholic mission station, and his mother thought he would join the priesthood.[130] Gideon Mhlanga, president of the African Teachers Association for many years, is an exception that proves the rule. He was a 1944 Fort Hare graduate whose "illiterate, poor and non-Christian" parents "strongly opposed" his conversion to Christianity.[131]

Until the 1950s, the majority of college-educated Africans in Southern Rhodesia attended the University College at Fort Hare. Founded in 1916 as a black South African college, Fort Hare soon became something of a pan-African institution, albeit one under colonial control, training several generations of Africans from southern, central, and East Africa. In the post–World War II era, a number of colonial Zimbabweans, mainly medical and law students, were allowed to attend the white, English-language South African universities—notably Witwatersrand, Cape Town, and Natal. Other Africans from Southern Rhodesia pursued higher education at the University College at Roma (now University of Lesotho).[132] The establishment in 1957 of the University College of Rhodesia and Nyasaland (now University of Zimbabwe) brightened the prospects for colonial Zimbabweans in search of higher education. Although far from being "a non-racial island of learning" in a racist society, as some have claimed, the University College did accept Africans, who comprised a fourth of the student body of 477 in 1964.[133]

Numerous Africans in Southern Rhodesia, unable to pursue education through the regular channels, continued their studies by correspondence.[134] One of the more popular correspondence schools was the Johannesburg-based Union College, which began placing advertisements in the Rhodesian African-oriented press in the 1930s, offering everything from primary-school instruction to college courses.[135] After World War II, the Central African Correspondence College, a Rhodesian institution, superseded the Union College as the foremost school of distance learning, boasting an enrollment of nearly twenty thousand in 1962, mainly at the secondary level.[136] For distant learners in search of post-secondary education, the school of choice was the University of South Africa (UNISA), the crown jewel of correspondence studies in southern Africa and the alma mater of many Africans unable to attend residential institutions of higher learning, including political prisoners.[137]

FINANCING SECONDARY AND HIGHER EDUCATION

The fact that so many were forced to resort to distance learning was emblematic of a major dilemma faced by all but a handful of Africans in search of education: a lack of money. Those fortunate enough to get to the upper-primary-school level and beyond generally financed their studies by drawing on a combination of resources, including personal savings, family contributions, freelance gifts, and scholarships. The indigence of many a suitor made courting Miss Education a very quixotic affair indeed.

Most aspiring students turned first to personal and family resources, an area in which intergenerational social mobility privileged individuals whose parents had some prior claim, no matter how tenuous, to elite standing. For instance, Joshua Nkomo, with £25 of his own money, a personal nest egg unimaginable for most young Africans, received an additional £17 from his relatively prosperous Christian parents when he left home for school in South Africa in 1942.[138] Similarly, the family of Fort Hare graduate Stanlake Samkange financed much of his education. "It is true he [Stanlake] was educated on monkey nuts," the Rev. Samkange recalled. "My wife grew crops at the farm, and I struggled on the other hand, and pooled our resources to keep our son at school."[139]

Few Africans, however, could count on consistent family support up to the college level. Indeed, many would-be students themselves were forced to defer their plans, or even drop out of school, to support family members. The case of Maxwell Dzwowa is instructive. In 1947 Dzwowa, desperate for a personal loan to continue his education in South Africa, sought the assistance of the Rev. Arthur Cripps, a renegade Anglican missionary, Fabian socialist, and confidant of African political activists.[140] Dzwowa, who had already spent more than £28 from his meager earnings finishing primary school and taking lessons in shorthand and writing, saw his dream of higher education vanishing, partly because he had to support an elderly aunt who "can't help herself."[141] Others, such as the African Teachers Association's Gideon Mhlanga and Ndabaningi Sithole, also postponed their educational plans to assist poorer family members.[142]

Many students, bereft of personal or family resources, relied heavily on the generosity of individual benefactors. In some cases, such freelance grants —which varied widely, ranging from the insignificant to the substantial— formed part of a diverse financial portfolio. The latter point is well illustrated in the case of Joshua Nkomo, who, as we have seen, went off to South Africa in 1942 with a total of £42 in personal and family funds. In South Africa, Nkomo enrolled at Adams College, an American Board high school in Natal attended by many Africans from Southern Rhodesia, among other southern Africans. In 1945, as Nkomo prepared to leave Adams College for Jan Hofmeyer School of Social Work in Johannesburg, he received a gift of £180 from a former employer, enough to underwrite the cost of his bachelor's degree. With his tuition paid in full, Nkomo, ever resourceful and thrifty, continued his studies uninterrupted, meeting his living expenses with the £40 he had saved from making tools at Adams College.[143]

Some students depended more consistently and completely on freelance gifts than did others. John Shoniwa was among those most reliant on charity and the kindness of strangers for academic and, indeed, personal survival. A graduate of the University of Cape Town, Shoniwa arrived in England to attend Exeter University Law School in 1956. Unable to obtain scholarships or loans, he threw himself on the mercy of British fellow members of the Capricorn Africa Society, a white-dominated multiracial organization that had contributed £350 toward his studies before he left Southern Rhodesia.[144] Five years after arriving in England, Shoniwa's financial status seemed to have changed little. "Apart from his wife's earnings as a nurse which cover his lodgings,"[145] explained Jonathan Lewis, a leader of the metropolitan branch of the Capricorn Africa Society and Shoniwa's principal British benefactor, "he has no source of funds to meet his University expenses and seems entirely dependent on what we can find for him, and for pocket money on what I personally have been able to send him."[146] The prolonged dependence prompted another Shoniwa benefactor, in a fit of exasperation, to suggest that a "sharp threat of no further assistance might be salutary."[147] It is unclear if this threat was carried out. In any case, Shoniwa eventually finished his studies and returned home to establish a successful legal practice.

Shoniwa's predicament bespoke the scarcity, or in many cases, total absence, of organized grants available to African students, especially at the college level and above. Besides personal savings, family contributions, and freelance gifts, scholarships were another way some students financed their education. As with much else, the missions took the lead in establishing scholarship schemes for Africans, many of which were rather informal to begin with, consisting primarily of tuition waivers for selected students attending upper-primary and teacher-training schools. In some instances, Rhodesian-based missions would secure full or partial scholarships for students at affiliated South African institutions with more advanced training facilities.

The American Methodist Episcopal Church was among the first missionary societies formally to offer financial aid to African students, establishing "crusade" or religious scholarships for high school and college students in 1946 and 1947, respectively.[148] This program opened the door to higher education and professional mobility to individuals like Matthew Wakatama. One of the first recipients of a crusade scholarship, Wakatama went on to become headmaster of a secondary school in 1957, the first colonial Zimbabwean to achieve that distinction.[149] In the late 1950s the American Methodists obtained additional scholarships for more than one hundred Africans at United States and British universities. These individuals, who returned to Southern Rhodesia with bachelor's and master's degrees, would go on to form the core group of African school inspectors by the mid-1960s.[150]

Outside the missionary orbit, the South African–based, mining-capital-financed Beit Trust was the first organization to offer financial assistance on a formal and organized basis to Africans in Southern Rhodesia. Beit Bursaries, inaugurated in 1937, provided annual grants of £10 to students enrolled in teacher-training institutions. No doubt because of ignorance of their existence, only fifteen of thirty available awards were made in the first year.[151] But this was an anomaly, and competition became much keener in later years, with the bursaries going to top students like Ndabaningi Sithole, a 1939 recipient who graduated at the head of his primary-school class.[152] In 1941, 109 applicants competed for the thirty grants.[153] Subsequently, as the Beit Trust made more funds available, the number of bursaries and the amount of the individual awards increased accordingly. In 1948, the Beit Trust also instituted annual grants of £8 each to a fixed proportion of the students attending Goromonzi, the government-run high school.[154]

Some Africans were aided in their educational pursuits by the Native (later African) Welfare Society, a white-controlled body initially founded to organize "controlled" recreation for urban workers but which subsequently acquired broader interests. The Welfare Society established a scholarship fund in 1944, when it made sixteen awards of between £5 and £25 to a variety of applicants, ranging from individuals taking correspondence courses to university students. Matthew Wakatama, the future headmaster who was then a student at Adams College, received £10. Joshua Nkomo, apparently completing his studies at Adams College before entering Jan Hofmeyer School of Social Work, also received £20. William Madeya, with a grant of £25, emerged as one of the highest Welfare Society awardees in 1944. Still smitten, Madeya, author of the Miss Education trope used in this chapter, was then pursuing a B.S. at Fort Hare.[155]

In the post–World War II era, the potential sources of funds for lovers of education expanded beyond the private charities, the reassessment of official policy on African education having resulted in additional scholarships. The first state expenditures in this area consisted of supplementing the private charities in the form of annual contributions to the Beit Bursaries. Subsequently, the government began to provide grants of £5 to up to 20 percent of the students at Goromonzi.[156] The state also instituted a program that awarded between £25 and £80 to individual students enrolled in advanced teacher-training institutions and universities, the number of recipients annually ranging from nineteen to thirty between 1949 and 1953.[157] Then, in an innovative move, public funds were earmarked for Africans desiring to pursue a medical career, although it was not until 1951, four years after the initial appropriation, that the first award of £250 was made to an unnamed second-year medical student at the University of the Witwatersrand Medical School. A second such medical scholarship was awarded in 1952.[158]

With the establishment of the Federation of Rhodesia and Nyasaland, state support for African higher education passed from the territorial to the federal government. Under the new political dispensation, the education of whites (as well as coloureds and Indians) at all levels became a federal responsibility, whereas the education of Africans at the primary and secondary school levels devolved to the territorial (i.e., Southern Rhodesian) government. The federation, however, took charge of higher education for Africans. Although deepening existing racially determined educational disparities, and devoting only a fraction of its resources to Africans, the federal government made university and professional training available to scores of Africans from the two Rhodesias and Nyasaland.[159]

The first federal grants to Africans were announced in 1954, and they continued in subsequent years. In 1954, twenty-five undergraduate and graduate students received awards of £60 and £100 each. In a classic colonial dialectic, the recipients included several individuals destined for fame, a distinction earned partly through opposition to the very federation that funded their studies. The Trojan horses in formation included Samuel Parirenyatwa, the first colonial Zimbabwean to earn a medical degree and a future vice president of the nationalist Zimbabwe African People's Union. It is highly likely that Parirenyatwa was the above-mentioned, unnamed second-year medical student who received a grant of £250 from the Southern Rhodesian government in 1951. Herbert Ushewokunze, another aspiring medical doctor and emerging subversive, also received a federal scholarship in 1954. Ushewokunze went on to become the medical corps commander of one of the two guerrilla armies that eventually ended white rule, and then independent Zimbabwe's first minister of health, among other cabinet posts. Also among the bumper crop of alpha-ingrates granted federal financial aid in 1954 was Walter Kamba, the first African in Southern Rhodesia to earn the LL.B. and,[160] after independence in 1980, the first vice chancellor of the University of Zimbabwe.[161]

All of the students who received federal scholarships in 1954 were enrolled at South African institutions of higher learning. Unlike Africans from other parts of the continent, including South Africa, very few colonial Zimbabweans were trained overseas in the pre–World War II era.[162] This exclusion was due primarily to a lack of opportunity, although as far back as 1910–11 a Rhodesian government–appointed commission, seeking to halt the development of the so-called Dangerous Native, had recommended discouraging Africans from attending school overseas, lest they return "filled with a spirit of unrest and dissatisfaction."[163] Such sentiments amounted to little more than wishful thinking. After World War II, no amount of official discouragement could prevent colonial Zimbabweans from accepting the scholarship offers they began to receive from various institutions in the United States, Great Britain, and India, among other countries.[164]

Before World War II, Africans who had completed primary school almost automatically would have been placed in the ranks of the educated, although even this number was never very considerable. In 1962, when such statistics first became available, the African population of approximately 3.6 million included a mere 18,640 individuals, among them 5,980 females, who had gone beyond primary school.[165] The definition of "educated" became more strict in the 1950s, as the number of Africans with a secondary, and even a college, education increased. The number of college graduates went from as few as 6 in 1948 to perhaps 45 in 1954.[166] These figures would rise dramatically over the next decade, at the end of which some 660 Africans were reported to be pursuing higher education—locally and abroad, in residential institutions and through correspondence.[167] Extrapolating from these trends, perhaps as many as 1,000 colonial Zimbabweans actually held or were on the verge of obtaining college degrees by 1965. A much smaller number of Africans also boasted advanced degrees in various fields, including about 30 medical doctors and somewhat fewer lawyers.[168]

Although not the sole measure, education played an extraordinarily large role in determining social standing in Southern Rhodesia, as it did in other rigidly segregated white-supremacist societies.[169] The relatively high incomes commanded by members of the educated elite, along with their attendant higher living standards, constituted the most obvious manifestation of petty bourgeois ranking among Africans in Rhodesia by 1965.[170] Educated blacks also derived social benefits from their status. Although still despised and re-viled by many white settlers, they were admired and revered by lesser-educated Africans. However, as the black middle class became fully formed in the 1950s and 1960s, with a highly educated elite at its core, social and political conflicts among Africans sharpened markedly. Educated blacks, especially the younger university-trained men, became the targets of increasingly sharp criticism, castigated for selfish behavior and an abdication of leadership responsibility. The critics included older members of the elite more firmly grounded in the self-improvement tradition and possessed of a greater sense of mission, such as the Rev. Thompson Samkange.[171] One critic lamented that although there were "men who have attained a high standard of education, . . . they have done nothing to uplift their people," choosing instead "to content themselves with attaching the initials 'B.A.' after their signatures only and no more."[172]

Few among the most educated colonial Zimbabweans attempted to live up to such lofty expectations. Far from endeavoring to uplift the masses, in the 1950s the leading lights among the black middle class embraced "racial part-nership," a new incarnation of the long-envisaged race-neutral alliance of "civilized men." Predictably, racial partnership—which was little more than a fig leaf adorned by the settler leadership to win British imperial approval for creating the Federation of Rhodesia and Nyasaland—foundered on the bed-rock of white opposition, despite the best efforts of many elite blacks and a small group of like-minded white liberals.[173] The failure of racial partnership, like all previous attempts at nonracial meritocracy, eventually forced the frus-trated black middle class into an African nationalist coalition with the masses of the colonized people, with the aim of ending white rule.

Nationalist politics, however, was merely a marriage of convenience for the black petty bourgeoisie, which viewed the coalition with African peasants and workers largely as a means of achieving its historic goal of rising to a higher level unimpeded by the racist barriers of settler colonialism. In 1962, three officials of a local branch of the Zimbabwe African People's Union, then the leading nationalist movement, assayed the colonial problem from the standpoint of the black elite. "The present government," they fumed, "has made the tragic mistake of treating all Africans as one, forgetting that some are educated and civilised and therefore need better treatment than that meted to farmboys. That is why we are determined to take-over the government. We want to change all this."[174] There is scant hint here of social revolution, only a manifesto encapsulating the unmitigated self-interest of an educated colonized middle class. In this vision of the future, the colonial conflation of race and class would most assuredly end. However, farm boys—and notice the use of the socially diminutive "boy," redeployed as a class weapon against the agrarian proletariat, despite the African elite's own angst about it—would remain excluded from the company of civilized men. Similarly, maids ("house-boys" and, increasingly, "housegirls") would continue to serve afternoon tea to madams, who in turn would remain subordinate to the men of their class.[175] In the envisaged new Zimbabwe, things would certainly change, but just as certainly they would also remain the same. All Africans, to be sure, were in love with social mobility; only a small minority, however, had succeeded in courting Miss Education. This distinction constituted the principal starting point in the rise of the African middle class.

3

The Quest for Bourgeois Domesticity
On Homemakers and Households

THE SCHOLARSHIP ON the North Atlantic world has demonstrated the decisive role of the family in forging the new social formations that accompanied the transition from an agrarian to an industrial mode of life. These studies have shown how, in the late eighteenth and nineteenth centuries, the middle classes gradually evolved a domestic ideology that stressed the sexual division of labor and new family practices, with a special emphasis on the role of women as wives and mothers. Under the new dispensation, women were valued more for their reproductive than their productive capacity.[1]

In Southern Rhodesia and elsewhere in colonial Africa, similarly, the economic and social order imposed by European rulers brought about major changes in society, including family life. For those colonized Africans who had assimilated most thoroughly the values of Western bourgeois domesticity, notably the emerging middle class, the nuclear family became the principal institution for the physical and social reproduction of their social stratum. At the center of the search for the bourgeois domestic ideal stood the colonized elite woman, striving mightily to become a good wife and mother, the perfect homemaker of her household.

In family life, as in other spheres, colonized Africans were not blank slates upon which the colonizers—whether officials, missionaries, employers, or settlers—wrote uninhibited. Rather, there was a process of articulation between the modes of life and cultures of colonizer and colonized. Nowhere did this process produce a happier synthesis than on the "woman question," where precolonial African customs and colonial European bourgeois traditions united to uphold the subordination of women. Thus in Southern Rhodesia the question of equality in the relations between husband and wife in elite African households hardly arose, and there were few direct attempts to challenge this concept of gender relations. This state of affairs was stoutly defended by, among others, those African women—many of them wives, daughters, and mothers of elite African men—who had moved from, or, to be more precise, who articulated between, African tradition and colonial modernity.

Ultimately, these women sought personal satisfaction and fulfillment in the calling of homemaker and within the confines of the household.

THE BOURGEOIS DOMESTIC IDEAL: CHURCH AND STATE

The bourgeois domestic ideal, as elaborated in the North Atlantic world, especially Victorian England, was introduced to Africans in Southern Rhodesia primarily through the agency of Christian missionary societies. Good representatives of this ideology that they were, the missionaries left little to chance, carefully grooming and cultivating their African converts for all aspects of life, public and private, including training women for their envisaged role in society.[2] The missionaries were particularly eager to groom proper Christian wives for the African ministers and teachers on whom the success of the missionary enterprise, both in its religious and educational expressions, ultimately depended. The wage-earning husband and the dutiful homemaker, the latter supreme in the domestic sphere and devoted to the care of her husband and children, were held up as models of family life for African converts.

Founded in 1915 by the London Missionary Society, the Hope Fountain Girls Boarding School was one of the earliest and most successful centers for promoting the colonized version of the bourgeois domestic ideal. The administrators of the school were very specific about their objective. "We desire, first and foremost," one report announced, "to produce Christian womanhood, to make our girls good wives and mothers, and all our efforts are directed to this end."[3] The regimen was demanding, with a steady stream of academic, domestic, and recreational activities that began when the students arose at 5:30 A.M. and continued until they retired at 9:00 P.M. Students were instructed in reading, composition, arithmetic, English, and music, plus sewing, cooking, laundry work, gardening, and games. In all of these activities, a premium was placed on discipline, order, and cleanliness. The official school inspector, who visited the institution in 1922, was particularly impressed by this aspect of the curriculum, asserting that Hope Fountain had "set a higher standard and achieved a higher result than any Rhodesian Mission."[4]

Where Hope Fountain led, others followed. Never a missionary society to lag behind, the American Board of Commissioners for Foreign Missions wholeheartedly agreed that "if we are to build up a community of progressive and civilized homes it is necessary for the girls to be educated as well as the boys."[5] Indeed, virtually all of the missionary societies had schools to train girls to be good Christian wives and mothers. Outside the regular educational system, some missions offered domestic science courses in what amounted to finishing schools. The Salvation Army, which established one of the first such schools, reported great interest: "many African prospective husbands . . . sent their brides-to-be . . . and many husbands . . . sent their wives."[6] Even after

World War II, when the permanent entrance of relatively large numbers of mission-educated women into the work force began seriously to undermine the foundation of the bourgeois domestic ideal, leading missionaries continued to insist that the principal aim of female education was to produce Christian wives and mothers.[7]

The missionaries did more than just construct the institutional and ideological scaffolding for promoting the bourgeois domestic ideal; they also sought to maintain an ongoing role in African family life. Thus in 1944 one missionary began collecting information from the various denominations on "what they were doing to teach the African the way of Christian living in their homes."[8] A decade later, in 1954, the Southern Rhodesia Missionary Conference instituted an annual Christian Home and Family Week as a way of showcasing and celebrating the bourgeois domestic ideal.[9] During this period, eventually fixed as the last full week in July, lectures, discussions, and rallies were organized in various public venues. Speakers and discussion groups were encouraged to concentrate on such themes as the responsibilities of Christian couples to one another and to their children, the meaning and purpose of the home, the upbringing of children, the use of leisure time and, for young people, the selection of a spouse. Christian Home and Family Week organizers emphasized that the home should be "a place where there is happiness, where God is given His rightful place, where our children love to be, and where they may 'grow in wisdom and stature and in favour with God and man.' "[10]

The biggest celebrations took place in 1956 when the Christian Home and Family Week, hitherto confined to churches, schools, and halls, became a huge public affair featuring speeches by leading personalities, black and white, as well as bands and choirs. The single largest event took place in Bulawayo, where a crowd of fifteen thousand men, women, and children, a third more than the organizers expected, turned out to hear a variety of speakers, including the prime minister, the mayor, the president of the Southern Rhodesia Christian Conference, Herbert Chitepo, the colony's first black lawyer and later a top African nationalist, and Mrs. T. Z. Lesabe, a teacher and prominent African homecraft personality.[11] Music was provided by school choirs and professional bands.[12] After 1957, however, the Christian Home and Family Week declined in importance as a public event.[13] This probably was the result of changing political conditions, notably the removal from power of one of its chief sponsors, Prime Minister Garfield Todd, a former missionary, and the concomitant rise of African nationalism, which made it less likely that someone like Chitepo would share the same platform with Todd's successors.

Within the mission schools, the ideology of domesticity was reinforced by various subsidiary agencies, chief among which was the Wayfarer movement.[14] Established in 1926 after a visit to the colony by Lady Baden Powell, the in-

ternational Girl Guide leader, Wayfaring was a segregated black version of
the real thing, "a sort of half-way house to Guiding," its missionary organizers
having "reluctantly come to the conclusion that the time for native girl guides
was not yet." In 1935, there were some 600 Wayfarers and 300 Sunbeams (the
African equivalent of Brownies) in Southern Rhodesia.[15] Emphasizing the
usual Girl Guide topics of character building, self-control, and deference to
authority, Wayfaring was hailed as the basis of a new conception of African
womanhood. Mrs. H. Jowitt, its white superintendent, saw Wayfaring as a social cure-all:

> It is going to bring the Native women of Rhodesia together in mutual inter-
> est, and social intercourse, and what can be more valuable to them. It imme-
> diately becomes a national question, for when the Rhodesian native woman
> begins to stir, to take interest, to open herself to being taught, disciplined
> and raised; when she realises she is here to be a help and an intelligent
> mother to generations yet to come; when she begins to realise responsibility;
> and when she is no longer regarded as native cattle; then surely our native
> question will begin to be solved, and the solution lies with the women.[16]

The colonial state, which provided limited subventions to the Wayfarer
movement, also helped buttress the new domestic ideal, beginning in the
1920s. The timing was crucial. Official interest in promoting a particular kind
of domesticity among the colonized population coincided with, and indeed
was central to, a broader project aimed at thwarting the rise of an urban-
based African middle class: notably, the policy of native development, with its
emphasis on territorial segregation, industrial training, and rusticating educated blacks.

From a bureaucratic standpoint, a major step in elaborating the native development policy was the establishment in 1927 of the Native Education Department, the final act in a long drama of educational segregation, as we saw
in the previous chapter. As one of its first acts, the Native Education Department hired a white woman, Mary Waters, as "organizing instructress." Defining her task as nothing less than the transformation of African society, Waters
announced that the colonized woman would be made "worthy of the sacred
term, The Home-maker." Her work, Waters went on, "is symbolised by the letter H. Humanity, Homes, Husbands, Housewives, Hygiene, Happiness and
lastly Heaven. May I say these things will be achieved by women. It is they who
must guide the man!"[17] The settler state's offer of heavenly bliss, however, was
valid only in the countryside: African women would have to guide their men
in the Reserves, far from the white cities and the havens of the much-resented
emerging black middle class.

The means by which the government hoped to encourage a rural version
of the bourgeois domestic ideal was the Jeanes system, a program funded by
the Carnegie Corporation of New York. Hope Fountain, with its highly touted

girls' school, was selected as the site for training home demonstrators, the name given to the Jeanes graduates who would actually promote the new lifestyle in the countryside, most importantly by example. The ideal candidate for home demonstrator, according to the principal of Hope Fountain, was "a girl who has passed Standard VI in one of our missionary institutions, and is engaged to be married to a man of some recognized standing, such as a minister, teacher or Jeanes supervisor."[18] After completing a training program that largely duplicated her earlier education, the home demonstrator would be equipped with medical and nursing kits and sent back to her original place of residence. From there, paid by the government and supervised by local missionaries, she would move out into surrounding communities to provide various services, such as treating minor medical problems and attending to maternity cases. The home demonstrator's greatest service, however, was to teach by example—that is, to establish a model home, one her neighbors could emulate.[19]

The training of home demonstrators with Carnegie funds ended in 1934, but the program was revived after World War II with money provided by the Beit Foundation. Based on a model established by a female missionary working on her own, the new homecraft centers, like the Jeanes program, offered a two-year course.[20] Unlike the Jeanes program, however, women who completed the homecraft course were neither required nor expected to perform community service, its sole objective being to "fit them to be better homemakers."[21] Competition for admission to the homecraft centers was keen, and the number of applicants quickly surpassed the available places.[22] The popularity of the course, according to the director of native education, was "shown by letters received by the heads of schools from husbands and other relatives of some of the women who have attended the schools."[23] The increasing enrollment in homecraft schools resulted in a great demand for domestic science instructors, which the two institutions that trained such teachers were unable to meet.[24]

The prototypical individual to emerge from the girls' school, the Jeanes program, and the homecraft training center was a woman at peace with her God, herself, and her station in life. If not already a wife and mother, she would soon become one, striving mightily to realize within the confines of her own home the bourgeois domestic ideal, deferring to her husband in matters public and political while devoting herself to his happiness and that of their offspring, always bearing in mind that the man's standing in society depended to a large extent on how she comported herself.

In 1934 H. B. Mashengele, a male Jeanes teacher in training (they were mostly male), offered an idealized portrait of "Native leaders' wives." Such women, he wrote, should possess four core qualities: "Self-respect, self-control, self-knowledge and self-reverence. These alone lead life to sovereign power."

Mashengele exhorted wives to become active helpmates, encouraging the men in all of their endeavors: "Be helpful to your husbands, and respect yourselves, so that others and your husbands may respect you. . . . Be clean and quiet in your ways. Be true and just in all your dealings." Gossiping and rumormongering were strictly taboo: "Do not tell tales about others, particularly unkind tales, that give pain to others and spoil the work of your husband." The home and the children, too, should be kept "clean and tidy." Nor should the wives of leading men neglect their personal appearances. Rather, Mashengele advised, "keep yourselves clean, smart and neat as you were before you were married." Most importantly, wives should "Obey the laws of your husbands, and ever bear in mind the words of the Prophet Samuel to King Saul when he disobeyed a command from God, that, 'To obey is better than sacrifice.' "[25] Few elite Africans, male or female, would have disagreed, in principle, with this description of appropriate wifely behavior.

THE AFRICAN AGENCY AND THE BOURGEOIS DOMESTIC IDEAL

As the above admonition indicates, the bourgeois domestic ideal was not simply an imported concept imposed on a credulous people by a culturally alien church and a politically repressive state. Rather, Africans in Southern Rhodesia were active agents in the acculturation process, and both female and male members of the emerging middle class voluntarily accepted the ideology of domesticity. Accordingly African women, either independently or in conjunction with African men or whites, formed various associations, clubs, and societies to facilitate their efforts to become good wives and mothers along the lines of the Victorian model they had internalized. In the last analysis, these self-enabling agencies were even more important than were the missionary-run and state-supported institutions in forging new conceptions of gender roles among elite Africans.

The Manyano-Ruwadzano movement was the first significant African-initiated attempt to promote the bourgeois domestic ideal. Manyano was a direct outgrowth of the Women's Prayer Union of the Wesleyan Methodist Church, an organization that later spread to the American Methodist Episcopal Church, where it became known as Ruwadzano, meaning "fellowship" in the Shona language. Although African women had taken the lead in organizing the prayer groups that evolved into Manyano, the missionaries sought to impose control from above by placing the wives of leading white religious figures in positions of authority.[26] The resulting resentment by the Africans came to a head in 1927 when the Rev. Moses Mfazi, a black South African immigrant and staunch defender of African rights within and outside the church, publicly attacked white leadership of the Manyano movement. Mfazi is reported to have opposed the appointment of "a European organising Secretary" and to have preached a sermon urging his fellow black Wesleyans to reject "those who were trying to take for themselves from the natives, the glory which was theirs in the Manyano work." Mfazi's insubordination landed him before an ecclesiastical tribunal, which found him guilty of attempting to lead an African rebellion against the white Wesleyan hierarchy, whereupon he dramatically resigned in protest and declared for Ethiopianism or African religious independency.[27]

Less ostentatious in their defiance, the Manyano-Ruwadzano women remained within the missionary fold, outwardly accepting the titular leadership of white female missionaries while actually retaining considerable autonomy within their local branches. The Manyano-Ruwadzano movement offered innovative resolutions to the dilemma faced by women who, in Mary Waters's locution, desired to be worthy of the sacred calling of homemaker but whose household resources in the form of their husbands' incomes generally were inadequate to support the domestic ideal to which they aspired. As Barbara Moss, a leading authority on Manyano-Ruwadzano, has noted:

> Christian women, especially ministers' and evangelists' wives, bore a heavy burden. By accepting the standards of the Christian church they were forced into a life of economic dependency. And by rejecting the lifestyle of non-Christian society, they were cut off from familiar sources of support and dwindling resources. Yet family ties and obligations continued to bind them to traditional responsibilities. They were between a rock and a hard place and in desperation, turned to each other for help. Their weekly prayer meetings, set up by the Methodist Church, took on greater importance as they sought solutions to their problems within a context that was meaningful to them as African Christians.[28]

Such women craved fellowship and a sense of community, but they also desired solutions to mundane problems relating to household management. Manyano-Ruwadzano offered a way out, effectively forming a perfect union of the divine and the domestic. Resplendent in their distinctive clothing and headgear, Manyano women gathered to pray and read the bible together. Prayer time, however, doubled as preparation time, an opportunity to exchange recipes and trade tips on any number of other homemaking chores, such as child care, home remedies, and sewing. It is hardly accidental, for instance, that Manyano-Ruwadzano women were renowned seamstresses; such skills were needed to make and mend clothing—a crucial indicator of social standing—for themselves, their husbands, and their children.[29] Indeed, the ingenuity of these women often formed a thin line between the respectable lifestyles elite blacks sought to lead and what these same elite blacks, in their elusive quest for equality with the whites, decried as the roguish existence of the African rabble.

A central concern of the elite African homemaker was purity—spiritual, moral, and physical.[30] In an unsanitary and impure society, characterized by a collapse of traditional mores and a breakdown of the old social order on the one hand and a rising incidence of tuberculosis, venereal diseases, and drunkenness on the other, there was much need for purity. Manyano-Ruwadzano met that need by, among other things, requiring each member to pledge "to love and serve God," "to live nicely and to speak the truth," "to keep my thoughts pure," "to protect my body from all impurities," "to abstain from intoxicating liquor," "to care for my children and to train them in the way of God," and, not least, "to keep my marriage vow."[31]

Manyano-Ruwadzano women also were among the most effective agents of Christianity and bourgeois family values, actively recruiting converts for the church as well as members for their movement. In an essay that won second prize in a contest organized by the *Bantu Mirror* in 1943, Edith Mothlabane ruminated on the advantages of Manyano-Ruwadzano. The movement's emphasis on sanctification within and sanitation without, she explained, encouraged women to lead "good lives thus enabling them to bring up good children physically and spiritually." By opposing "evil things such as beer drinking, immorality, smoking of tobacco and quarreling among people," Manyano-Ruwadzano helped to "spread the gospel of Christ in the most primitive places and naturally builds up the whole of our African Nation," Mothlabane concluded.[32] The Manyano women, like other proponents of African self-help, had become adept at couching their appeals in the language of African solidarity and racial uplift.

Prayer unions, and with them the Manyano-Ruwadzano phenomenon, spread beyond the Methodist community to African women in other denominations, sometimes against the wishes of their missionary patrons. Such was the case with the American Board of Commissioners for Foreign Missions, where a missionary reported in 1940 that the annual women's meeting had assumed the character of "a sort of Camp Meeting. They have taken over some of the methods used by the African Christians of the Methodist Church." Though stern New England Congregationalists who looked askance on such "emotional extravagance," the American Board missionaries were reluctant "to take too strong an attitude toward them, partly for fear of quenching something which does have unquestionably helpful elements and partly because we do not wish to shape their religious ways and habits by outside force but rather through an inner appreciation and development." This was an admission of impotence, and the formal organization of Ruwadzano groups within the American Board soon followed.[33]

Up to the end of World War II, church-based movements like Manyano-Ruwadzano were the main self-enabling agencies for promoting bourgeois domesticity among African women.[34] After the war, however, the incidence of group formation among Africans, including women, increased markedly. Most dramatic of all was the emergence of homecraft clubs, both in the rural and urban areas.[35] These clubs were generally organized and led by graduates of the homecraft schools or the wives of notable men—ministers, teachers, and the more successful businessmen and Purchase Area farmers—who were often the same individuals.[36]

Homecraft leaders included the likes of Anna Dube, the highly energetic founder and "chairman" (the original term) of the Sigombe Women's Club in Matabeleland's Gwanda Reserve and the wife of a "prosperous businessman." Founded in 1955 as a forum for women to "meet on their own to discuss matters of general interest and also hold lessons in various subjects on homecraft," the Sigombe Women's Club within a year had constructed a meeting hall, the funds for which had been raised entirely by its twenty-six members. Mrs. Dube herself became a tribune for bourgeois domesticity throughout the surrounding countryside. Traveling by bicycle, she "covered many hundreds of miles visiting the homes of many women in the Reserve advising them how to run their homes and also telling them to join the Club which is intended to improve their general knowledge in matters affecting their homes."[37]

In the urban centers, leadership of the homecraft movement fell to female members of the emerging black elite, individuals like Mrs. S. Maisiri, who was married to "an enlightened and popular taxi-cab proprietor." A tireless advocate of homecraft, Mrs. Maisiri practiced what she preached, winning prizes for her homemaking skills, including gardening and sewing, in various competitions in her native Bulawayo and representing Matabeleland in national contests.[38] One of the more prominent women's groups in Bulawayo was Vukani M'Afrika Cultural Club, which was founded in 1955 by thirty African women as "a means of teaching each other" and providing guidance to others in matters of the home.[39] The leadership of Vukani M'Afrika, meaning "Africans Awake" in Sindebele, included a number of "leading church women," such as its founding chairman, Mrs. T. Z. Lesabe. Unlike most homecrafters, the South African–born Lesabe worked outside the home as a teacher, having come to Southern Rhodesia with her husband, the Rev. Samuel Lesabe, as a missionary for the black-run African Methodist Episcopal Church.[40]

In Salisbury, the most well-known African women's group was the Helping Hand Club. Formed in 1953, the Helping Hand Club distinguished itself from other homecraft organizations by its emphasis on guarding the morality of female migrants and other women visiting the city, providing them with food and shelter and raising funds to build a house for unmarried pregnant women. Its leaders included women who were securely ensconced in the African middle class, such as Emma Chigoma, organizing secretary of the Harare Helping Hand Club, who in 1957 visited the United States, where she was the guest of black and white women's organizations.[41]

At the national level, homecraft leaders were drawn from the ranks of the wives of the most prominent African men. These included individuals like Maroma Hove, wife of Masotha Mike Hove, the African representative for Matabeleland in the parliament of the Federation of Rhodesia and Nyasaland. Homecraft, Mrs. Hove explained, using the language of uplift so popular during this period, contributed to African advancement by enlightening wives and mothers, thereby allowing them to take "their places alongside their men, as [among] other races."[42]

Undoubtedly, the most famous representative of the homecraft movement in Southern Rhodesia was Helen Mangwende, who had been educated in South Africa and was married to a modernist chief. Mangwende's crowning achievement was the establishment in 1953 of the Federation of African Women's Clubs (FAWC) as a national coordinating body for "the various African women's and girls' clubs, providing them with a common meeting ground where matters affecting their mutual welfare and interests can be discussed."[43] The FAWC held annual conferences and other meetings at which women could exchange ideas on child care and home improvement. In 1957, it had 147 affiliated clubs with a total membership of 7,273 women. By 1959, more than 200 individual clubs belonged to the FAWC.[44]

The colonial state, continuing its qualified, rural-oriented support of bourgeois domesticity among Africans, aided the development of the homecraft movement. The government-run Southern Rhodesia African Literature Bureau published books on the subject in Shona and Sindebele, while officially produced films, shown by a mobile cinema unit, encouraged the establishment of women's clubs, especially in the Reserves.[45] Even more important were the activities of the Radio Homecraft Club, which reached a much wider audience. Established in 1954, the Radio Homecraft Club was geared toward an African female audience. With an all-male staff, it was broadcast in the local languages twice a week, featuring, among other things, visits from a radio doctor, housekeeping tips, knitting and sewing instructions, cooking, shopping, gardening, skits on domestic problems, letters from listeners, visits to women's clubs, music, and stories.[46]

The Radio Homecraft Club was an immediate success, generating more fan mail than any other African-oriented radio program. It sponsored annual sewing, knitting, and jam-making competitions, for which there was no shortage of entrants, most of whom were members of the clubs that had organized around the program. In 1956 there were 322 entries, and prizes included radios and sewing machines. The importance of such occasions was not lost on the captains of Rhodesian commerce, and the meetings of the radio clubs soon became a point of contact between homecraft and merchandising, another opening for the advancing consumer culture.[47] With such impressive sewing talent gathered in one place, representatives of the Singer Sewing Ma-

1. Helen Mangwende, who in 1953 founded the Federation of African Women's Clubs, a national coordinating body for various African women's and girls' clubs. Courtesy of the National Archives of Zimbabwe.

chine Company, which as far back as 1925 had reported doing 40 percent of its business with Africans, eagerly displayed the latest models and took orders.[48]

White female members of the settler ruling and governing classes also played an important role in the homecraft movement. These women, who in many respects embodied the domestic ideal toward which mission-educated and elite African women aspired, assumed leadership functions, at least in a nominal sense, in many African women's organizations, national and local. Yet it bears emphasizing that, as with Manyano-Ruwadzano, there was not necessarily a neat convergence between office-holding and actual responsibility in the homecraft movement. The wives of various white officials—native commissioners, municipal directors of African administration, and at the national level, prime ministers, governors, and others of high rank—were invited to assume positions on account of their superior education and access to those with power and money.[49] Many of the functions performed by upper-class white women were ceremonial, advisory, or adjudicatory in nature, such as opening meetings, giving speeches, and serving as judges in sewing, gardening, and other homemaking contests.[50] The white women themselves often took care to emphasize this point. Thus at its first annual conference in 1954, Lady Tredgold, the Federation of African Women's Clubs chairman and wife of the chief justice, pointed out that white women were involved in the organization largely in an advisory capacity, an assertion also underlined by the white organizing secretary.[51]

The National Council of Women of Southern Rhodesia (NCW), which came into being at around the same time as the FAWC, was another organization that linked African women, mainly those of elite orientation, with the upper crust of female settler society. The formation of the NCW appears to have been inspired by the Rhodes Centenary Exhibition of 1953, which, significantly, coincided with the establishment of the Federation of Rhodesia and Nyasaland and the expansion of Southern Rhodesian settler power.

As a celebration of the one hundredth anniversary of the birth of Cecil Rhodes, the Centenary Exhibition was the most grandiose and momentous social event in the annals of settler rule in Southern Rhodesia. Amid much pomp, swagger, and braggadocio, British settlers from East, central, and southern Africa came together, their assemblage graced by royalty in the person of the queen mother, who performed the ceremonial inauguration. Among the exhibition's many features was the Rhodes Centenary Women's Congress, an ingathering of some of the most prominent women claiming British descent in Africa, a kind of female pan-Britannia, including the presidents of the Federation of Women's Institutes of Southern Rhodesia, the East African Women's League, and the South African National Council of Women. A good deal of the discussion at the Rhodes Centenary Women's Congress centered on how white women could "train" and "work with" African women, reputedly to lift the latter out of ignorance and idleness.[52]

The NCW aimed to do for the various women's groups—welfare, religious, and professional—what the FAWC did for homecraft: provide a national organizational umbrella to promote "sympathy of thought and purpose among the women of S. Rhodesia, Black and White."[53] But this was sympathy on a segregated basis. Black and white members of the NCW were organized into separate branches at the local level, while nationally the organization was dominated by white women. Meanwhile, groups like the Federation of Women's Institutes of Southern Rhodesia—an older white formation perhaps best known for spearheading a campaign in the 1930s to eject African male servants from white homes and replace them with African females, allegedly to protect the purity of white womanhood from a sexual "black peril"[54]—continued to exclude African women from membership, belatedly forming a segregated black wing instead.

There was considerable overlap between the African memberships of the NCW and the homecraft groups, although leadership of the former tended to be concentrated more solidly in the hands of higher-status elite black women, such as Mrs. Hove and Mrs. Lesabe. As befitting their social standing, these women evinced considerable interest in other-serving benevolence, placing more emphasis "on what could be done for the less fortunate African women" than on homecraft, narrowly defined.[55] One NCW branch, headed by Mrs. Hove, who was praised by one male government official for her "wise guidance in things feminine," took up the issue of malnutrition among African children, forming a committee to conduct research on improving the African diet and recommending better methods of cooking.[56] It was perhaps a measure of the widening social chasm among Africans that Mrs. Hove, speaking about juvenile delinquency, could upbraid working-class African women for leaving their children at home unattended. Working mothers, she declared blithely and with complete disregard for the economics of child care, should either get "a good nanny" or send their children to the day nursery.[57]

Despite the organizational linkages, the relationship between black and white women in no way implied sisterhood. This was hardly possible in a society based on racial hierarchy, where white privileges, including those enjoyed by white women, were based on the exploitation of Africans as a whole, male and female, elite and non-elite. Black and white women were separated by a deep racial, social, and (in many cases) linguistic chasm. Consequently, the relations between black and white within the FAWC and the NCW, which were among the most significant points of contact outside the missionary orbit, were largely maternalistic and one-sided. White women provided assistance, advice, and adjudication but assumed that they had little to learn from the recipients of their charity. Equality, social or otherwise, was never a consideration. As late as 1959 it was considered a major breach of the color line when a group of white women in Gwelo invited two black fellow members of the NCW to tea. "This was the first time such an invitation had been extended to African women," crowed a leading African-oriented weekly, which thought the event important enough to merit front-page coverage.[58] Not all white women, however, were willing to concede even that level of social equality. Thus, again in 1959, the older and more stodgy Federation of Women's Institutes of Southern Rhodesia caused a serious racial row when, at a joint meeting with its segregated African wing, the color bar was imposed at mealtime. The offended Africans, who complained about being called "uneducated girls," withdrew and joined the nonracial Radio Homecraft Club. For this act of defiance, the protestors were punished by being forbidden to use the Women's Institute's hall for their sewing activities.[59]

CHRISTIAN MARRIAGE AND THE RISE OF MIDDLE-CLASS HOUSEHOLDS

At the 1959 annual FAWC conference, the following resolution was passed: "We African women feel that it is high time all African men were married to only one wife." The conferees further suggested that legislative action toward

this end would be welcomed, an idea quickly squashed by a government official who addressed the meeting.[60] For the mission-educated, church-going,
and club-joining African women who supported this resolution, monogamous
marriage by Christian rites was the only acceptable form of matrimony, providing the sole foundation for the bourgeois domestic ideal.[61] The alternative
to a Christian union under civil law was marriage under what colonial officials
termed native custom, which sanctioned multiple unions by African men. By
the late colonial period, however, black women in groups such as the FAWC
had come to view polygyny not merely as personally offensive but also as an
affront to African womanhood as a whole.

Legally speaking, the civil and native custom, or customary, forms of marriage were completely separate, neatly complementing the colonial binary op-
posites: European and African, civilized and barbaric, Christian and heathen.
As could be expected, elite Africans, with their vociferous claims to Western
civilization and Christianity, insisted on marrying by civil law—that is, under
the white (if formally color-blind) legal system. Marriage by civil law prohibited other unions while the first marriage remained in effect; violators could
be charged under the bigamy statues. Customary unions, by contrast, were
contracted under so-called native law—that is, the codification by colonial officials of what they regarded as indigenous customs and traditions. The reform
package of 1898 that provided the starting point for this study, along with the
Native Marriages Ordinance of 1901, sanctioned indigenous marital customs,
including polygyny, with the proviso that the consent of the woman was necessary for a valid marriage and that the marriage must be legally registered.

Civil marriages—mainly by Christian rites, more popularly known as
church weddings—remained a small proportion of all unions contracted by
Africans throughout the period covered by this study. The figures in table 3.1,
although in no way accurately reflecting the number of customary unions,
many of which went unregistered in violation of the law, give an indication of
the trends over a fifty-year period. Few non-Christian Africans married by
civil law, and not all black Christians did. Some church members celebrated
their nuptials under native custom, in a union that may or may not have been
monogamous. In other instances Christians, especially female converts, found
themselves in previously contracted polygynous unions.

The emergence of a system of Christian marriage among colonized Africans, backed by the force of law, was a difficult process in Southern Rhodesia,
as in medieval Europe.[62] Most difficult of all, both for church and state, was
the problem of monogamous recidivism—that is, men taking additional wives
after marrying by civil law, usually in a church wedding. The reasons for monogamous recidivism, and the related question of how to deal with the offenders, were much debated by missionaries, African church leaders, and government officials.

Table 3.1. Registered African Marriages, Civil/Christian and Customary

Year	Civil/Christian	Customary	
		Indigenous Africans	Non-Indigenous Africans
1913	460	5,921	—
1921	706	6,895	66
1925	1,819	9,883	224
1930	979	10,092	329
1935	956	7,811	348
1945	—	7,437	1,138
1954	—	10,286	2,608
1963	2,548	7,107	—

Source: *Report of the Chief Native Commissioner* for the years concerned, except the figures for 1963, which are taken from the *Report of the Secretary for Internal Affairs.*

Most missionary societies took the view that monogamous recidivism was a deliberate act of backsliding by individual converts, a subversion of Christianity "by the subtle forces of darkness fighting for their existence," as one white churchman expressed it.[63] The Wesleyan Methodist John White, perhaps the colony's most revered white missionary, made the same point in less flowery language when he attributed the African converts' marital backsliding to "the weakness of their Christian character," noting that there was not "one per cent of those who present themselves for [Christian] Marriage who do not understand what . . . the contract involves."[64]

African church leaders fully concurred in the view that monogamous recidivism was a matter of conscious choice rather than blissful ignorance. Thus the Southern Rhodesia Native Missionary Conference, assuming full knowledge on the part of the violators, demanded strict enforcement of the law against bigamy.[65] Its secretary, the Rev. Thompson Samkange, insisted that monogamous recidivists should be held accountable for their behavior, rejecting as "unfounded and untrue" allegations that Africans were not fully cognizant of the meaning of marriage by civil law and Christian rites.[66]

Such allegations were made by government officials who, as they often did, blamed the missionaries by attributing monogamous recidivism to the practice of force-feeding "civilization" to the gullible "natives."[67] According to this line of reasoning, African converts, with their thin veneer of Western culture, were incapable of either comprehending or honoring monogamous marital vows. As the chief native commissioner opined, "There is great danger attending the solemnization of marriages by Christian or Civil Rites between natives who profess to adopt the Christian faith, but who in reality are not sufficiently advanced to understand the meaning of Christianity."[68]

That there was a certain amount of confusion among some Africans married by Christian rites and civil law is undeniable. In 1939, for example, Henry Mahachi wrote the chief native commissioner explaining that he had celebrated a church wedding three years earlier but wanted "to get two wives at present if possible."[69] Mahachi's, however, was hardly a typical case.

Much more representative of the phenomenon of monogamous recidivism was the story of an unnamed but "very well-known" court interpreter, as told by the native commissioner in whose office he worked. In 1927, the interpreter, a man already married by Christian rites and civil law, decided to take additional wives. Many men in a similar predicament would simply have married again under native custom, but without registering the subsequent union(s)—the technical act that made a marriage legally valid. However, the court interpreter, perhaps because of his occupation, opted to follow the letter of the law. He would first divorce his wife and remarry, but this time under native custom, which allowed polygyny. Accordingly, the native commissioner reported, the interpreter "threw his wife—and I say this with all deliberation —into a position where she must almost inevitably commit adultery." His Christian/civil marriage dissolved on grounds of infidelity, the interpreter then proceeded to celebrate six nuptials under native custom. Far from illustrating the "large number of natives entering into Christian marriage without thoroughly appreciating exactly what they are doing," as the native commissioner who told the story thought, this case demonstrated all too well the shrewdness with which Africans often manipulated the colonial legal system to their own advantage.[70]

The debate over monogamous recidivism was of more than just academic interest, for causation and solution were directly related. If monogamous recidivism amounted to conscious and willful disregard of a legally binding marriage contract, as claimed by the church representatives both white and black, then the obvious solution was vigorous enforcement of the law against bigamy. The colonial state, by contrast, insisted that the problem was more moral than legal, thereby placing the onus back on the church. Government officials maintained that men who took additional wives after first marrying by Christian rites and civil law did so out of ignorance, an indication, they believed, of the church's failure properly to instruct converts in their obligations. In any case, some officials, taking the view that African men were naturally polygynous, if not promiscuous, claimed that few of them were capable of keeping monogamous marriage vows, Christianity or no Christianity.

In counterpoint to the official view, most missionaries insisted on the malicious intent of the individual transgressor and demanded criminal punishment for monogamous recidivism. Thus in 1915 the Southern Rhodesia Missionary Conference called for legislation against the practice, "the penalty to be the same as in bigamy."[71] In fact, there was no need for new legislation, for two years earlier the attorney general had found that native custom did not apply to Africans married by civil law.[72] But enforcement of the law was quite another matter. Government officials, given their fatalistic views of the sexual proclivities of African men, and the concomitant futility of marriage by civil law and Christian rites, were unwilling either to introduce new legislation or to enforce the existing bigamy laws against monogamous recidivists.

Yet African men who engaged in monogamous recidivism violated not only civil law. More important from the official standpoint, most of them also refused to register their additional unions, as required by the Native Marriages Ordinance. The reason for this refusal was not far to seek: registration, which validated a marriage under native custom, was tantamount to self-admission of guilt, an official announcement that the civil law had been violated and an act of bigamy committed. With the impotence of the state exposed by its inability to enforce the Native Marriages Ordinance, the authorities decided to change the law to accommodate reality, amending it in 1917 to make a marriage valid only upon registration. This legal sleight of hand rendered unregistered unions mere cohabitation, but it made little difference to Africans married under native custom, including monogamous recidivists. By their actions, these individuals rejected as an alien cultural imposition the notion of concubinage (and its corollary, illegitimacy) that the amended ordinance introduced.[73] Nonregistration of marriage, in fact, had its virtues: unlike the taxes that had to be paid for taking a wife, no taxes had to be paid for "concubines."

In 1929 the Native Marriages Act, as it was now called, once again was amended to remove the self-incriminating clause. Under the amended law, a customary marriage became legally valid at the moment it was contracted, with the husband having the obligation to register the union "at the earliest possible moment." Now the monogamous recidivist was guilty of bigamy the instant he took another wife, whether or not the marriage was registered. Indeed, failure to register the other marriage made him liable for a second offense.[74]

Still the government continued to resist demands for stern action against monogamous recidivists, seemingly prosecuting only those cases brought by aggrieved wives or missionaries. For example, a certain Nyarambi, who was convicted of bigamy and served a sentence of undetermined length, blamed a Salvation Army officer for bringing charges against him.[75] Even when prosecution resulted in conviction, the native commissioners, who had legal jurisdiction, were often unwilling to impose stiff penalties. In a famous case in

1935, a convicted bigamist was sentenced to seven days of hard labor, with the option of paying a fine of just five shillings. The light penalty provoked the righteous indignation of the Rev. Thompson Samkange, who, affirming the rights as well as the responsibilities of African Christians, strongly attacked the lax manner in which the bigamy law was being enforced.[76]

The reluctance of the colonial state to enforce the bigamy law against monogamous recidivists was based partly on the time-honored conservative dictum that morality cannot be legislated, with one official noting that the legal system "does not penalize immorality, that the function of the law, in short, is not to make people virtuous."[77] Another reason for reticence was the official tendency to discourage the rise of an African middle class by treating the entire colonized population as one undifferentiated whole. Thus the chief native commissioner, responding to a resolution by the Missionary Conference demanding the criminalization of concubinage, asserted that such a move "would mean that a certain class of natives would be subject to penalties for an act which, if performed by any other member of the community, would not entail any penal liabilities."[78] Mostly, however, the government did not attempt to stamp out monogamous recidivism because it could not. Despite its imposing pretensions, there were real limits on the coercive capability of the colonial state, especially in matters of personal choice. When it came to issues like marriage and bridewealth, the authorities were ever mindful of the "danger of attempting unenforceable legislation generally."[79]

THE BATTLE OVER BRIDEWEALTH

For the emerging African middle class, the articulation between tradition and modernity, the precolonial culture and the colonial system, is perhaps best demonstrated by bridewealth, or *roora* and *lobola* as it is known, respectively, in Shona and Sindebele. Under the precolonial regime, bridewealth, which in southern Africa was usually paid in cattle, legitimated a marriage by transferring to the husband control over the offspring of the union and cementing the alliance between the two families.[80] The debate among elite Africans in Southern Rhodesia, as well as between them and the missionaries and government officials, centered on the place of such a practice—particularly in its transmuted and commercialized form—within a self-described Christian and civilized community. Unlike monogamous recidivism, an issue on which the missionaries and the African elite lined up against the government, all three forces staked out differing positions on bridewealth, with the Africans, furthermore, being seriously divided among themselves.

The authorities, concerned as always with procuring a regular supply of labor, collecting taxes, and maintaining order, sought merely to regulate the payment of bridewealth in a manner consistent with these larger objectives. Most missionary societies, by contrast, opposed bridewealth as a slavish and degrading form of wife buying, and the rules of some churches prohibited members from making or accepting payment for the marriage of their daughters.[81] But of all the precolonial customs (even in the deformed incarnation they often assumed under colonialism) that the missionaries tried to uproot, bridewealth arguably was the area in which they were least successful. Significantly, the greatest resistance came not from "heathen" Africans but from members of the emerging black middle class, including leading churchmen, many of whom stoutly defended bridewealth as a practice fully compatible with the illuminating glow of Christianity and Western civilization. However, other elite Africans, especially younger, unmarried men and women, joined the missionaries in labeling bridewealth a commercial transaction and denounced it as unchristian and uncivilized.

Although vociferous, the elite African opponents of bridewealth were outnumbered by its supporters, who also were more influential and enduring. The missionaries, faced with massive noncompliance among African Christians, eventually modified the strictures against bridewealth, and even withdrew them entirely in some cases. Take the following exchange, which occurred in 1923 at a Wesleyan Methodist Native Evangelists and Teachers Convention, where bridewealth was one of the most controversial issues on the agenda:

> The Chairman [apparently an African] asked the speaker [a white missionary] if [the Church's policy of] total prohibition [of bridewealth] amongst Christians was meant? (Laughter). The Speaker said yes, I mean that Lobola should be reduced to a reasonable limit. No! said the Chairman, don't say a little. (Continued laughter). Lobola is a chain around women's necks which they cannot break off, which makes her a slave to her husband [continued the speaker, Mr. Brown]. Mr. Brown said Christians should not receive Lobola for their daughters.

An African clergyman, evangelist (later Rev.) Matthew Rusike, objected, claiming that whites also paid a form of bridewealth in that money changed hands when a marriage took place. "Mr. Brown replied that the white people don't pay or receive Lobola for their daughters. What they do is for the parents of the boy & of the girl to give something to the young people to start the new life with."[82] But the Africans remained unconvinced, and it was the missionaries who finally yielded, unofficially in most cases but officially in others.[83]

The colonial state, always more flexible than the missionaries when it came to so-called native customs, actually accorded bridewealth legal recognition. A 1901 ordinance limited the bridal consideration to four head of cattle (five in the case of a chief's daughter) or the equivalent in cash, but the law proved impossible to enforce and was repealed on the recommendation of an official committee that tabled its report in 1911.[84] Yet the issue could not be legislated into oblivion, and it remained a hotly debated topic in official circles in subsequent years.[85] Then, in 1950 the government, noting that payment of up to £25 in cash and between ten and fifteen head of cattle had become the norm, introduced an entirely new Native Marriages Act, which capped bridewealth at £20.[86]

Up to this point, the state had sided with rural male notables and older men in general by refraining from setting a limit on the bridal consideration, a move traditionally favored by younger men and, it seems, younger women as well. The political realignment signaled by the Native Marriages Act of 1950 was motivated by changing economic conditions in the postwar years, notably increasing industrialization and urbanization and the attendant necessity for a more stable (as opposed to a transient or migrant) work force.[87] As the minister of native affairs explained in introducing the legislation, a city man "is unable to meet the demands made on him by the bride's guardian" and at the same time give his wife "what she thinks is her due." This situation was rife with the potential for marital breakdown and, in the long run, social instability in the urban centers. By imposing a legal ceiling on bridewealth, the state effectively decided to resolve this contradiction in favor of the younger males on whose labor future economic growth depended.[88]

The authorities, however, had underestimated the political potency of bridewealth, and reaction to the Native Marriages Act of 1950 was swift and furious. Chiefs and other rural notables, normally loyal servants and allies of the colonial state, their paymaster, vied with the generally more assertive urban-based political movements and activists in denouncing the law. The authorities were accused of usurping parental authority and of interfering in African family matters. "The price of lobola is purely a domestic affair as far as the African people are concerned," scoffed the would-be Ethiopianist Mischek Zwimba, who two decades earlier had left the Wesleyan Methodist Church and attempted unsuccessfully to establish an independent congregation. Younger activists, too, felt compelled to defend African tradition against settler cultural imperialism. George Nyandoro, a nationalist-in-formation, offered a riposte steeped in the language of supply and demand, a response that betrayed his own class orientation even as it served as something of an allegory to the commodification of bridewealth. The African male, Nyandoro asserted, "paid less lobola in the past because he had less, but now he was materially well-off and was perfectly justified to pay more, especially in view of the fact that it was more expensive to bring up a daughter."[89]

Under fire, the government retreated. The £20 limit specified in the law, the minister of native affairs declared retroactively, referred only to the maximum amount legally recoverable in case of a divorce and a successful suit for return of the bridewealth. The government had no desire, the minister swore, to dictate the bridal consideration parents could demand from their daughters' suitors.[90]

THE DEBATE OVER BRIDEWEALTH: CHRISTIANITY OR COMMERCE?

The controversy surrounding the Native Marriages Act of 1950 was merely the latest episode in a decades-long debate on bridewealth among the African elite, primarily although not exclusively among the men. The first major exchange in the *Native* (later *Bantu*) *Mirror,* the white-run, African-oriented newspaper that was founded in 1931, centered on bridewealth. Bridewealth also emerged as the focus of the newspaper's first essay competition for women. Indeed, the subject became so popular among letter writers that from time to time the *Mirror* would declare a moratorium on it.

No sooner had the *Mirror* appeared than Nsele S. Hlabangana, a scion of the upwardly mobile Hlabangana family we met in the previous chapter, weighed in with an attack on bridewealth, which he described as "almost a process of buying and selling." Although stopping short of saying that lobola is altogether wrong, Hlabangana dismissed it as a backward and heathen custom inconsistent with Christianity. "Life is a struggle upward into the light of civilisation," he concluded, using language so beloved of the emerging African middle class, "and so I think the safest way is to do away with lobola entirely."[91]

The idea of ending bridewealth was warmly endorsed by other writers, one of whom condemned it as "a drawback to every native young man."[92] Bridewealth seemed to be especially unpopular with male students at mission schools, that is, young men thinking about their future, including marriage. Abdull Chama, besieged by students asking, "Teacher, how can we overcome Lobola," appealed for state intervention. Asserting that the bridal consideration was as high as £40 plus cattle in some areas, Chama called for a drastic reduction, recommending a ceiling of £8, which he asserted would be "greatly appreciated by Mashona young men."[93]

The defenders of bridewealth were not unequal to the challenge. They found an eloquent spokesman in Titus J. Hlazo, a descendant of prominent black South African immigrants, who set out to refute the critics and to "enlighten my friend [Nsele Hlabangana] that Lobola is not a process of buying and selling."[94] Bridewealth, Hlazo countered, was no different from the rings and other gifts exchanged by people in "civilised nations." Speaking the language of both African tradition and colonial modernity, he continued: "Cattle are a value. They are a token of love. They are a security as well as a promise to both parents and the intended wife." Ultimately, though, it was the language of colonial modernity, which is to say the language of commerce and the consumer culture, that Hlazo knew best. By insisting on a high bridal consideration, he posited, parents "get their daughters married to well-to-do people, hence their daughter's future comfort." Furthermore, bridewealth helped to inculcate steady habits of industry: "Where will loafers get plenty of cattle for Lobola? Thus loafers are easily checked, which is a very good thing," Hlazo asserted, apparently confident that he had clinched his argument.[95]

Nsele Hlabangana did not, however, find this line of reasoning enlightening or convincing, claiming rather that Hlazo's assertions actually supported the case against bridewealth. In "forcing their daughters to get married to people who own many cattle," Hlabangana retorted, parents only exposed the "weakness and brutality of this custom." Instead, of selfishness and greed, he urged the parents of young women to "try the Christian way of love, and be more eager to give than get, more ready for self-sacrifice for their children."[96]

Women entered the debate through a special essay competition on bridewealth sponsored by the *Mirror*. The paper reported receiving "some excellent letters and essays," including one "10 pages closely written," but only published the two that shared the winning prize of ten shillings. The competition showed that women also were divided on the subject and that, as among the men, the division seemed to be based largely on marital status. It was hardly coincidental, therefore, that the essay supporting bridewealth was written by a married woman, whereas her opponent was unmarried. Both women deployed arguments similar to those of their male counterparts, the one extolling bridewealth as a hallowed African custom that protected women and the other rejecting it as an outmoded practice that imposed a great burden on young people, male as well as female.

Sarah Sanehwe, writing in defense, described bridewealth "as an emblem of introducing the new relationship between the son-in-law and the father-in-law." Invoking tradition, as its defenders were wont to do, she declared that "young women of yore" regarded bridewealth as a guarantee of their rights and "objected to being given away for nothing. Such expressions were often heard when mistreated: 'How many cattle were paid to my father? Why should I be treated as a slave?' If no better steps were taken by the husband she consequently left him and went back to her father." Those who branded bridewealth as wife-buying, Sanehwe allowed, had the "wrong idea—not even a thousand pounds can possibly buy a human being." Even so, Sanehwe also spoke the language of the market. Parents, she added, rightly expected to recoup a "small fraction" of the cost of raising a daughter, both as a form of compensation and as an "expression of love" by her suitor. Sanehwe similarly endorsed the notion that bridewealth spurred the young African man to industry: "If he were to be given his wife for nothing he would lie idly and do nothing to help himself," she concluded with satisfaction.[97]

Joan M. Kawonza, who shared the winning prize with Sanehwe, disagreed. Like her male fellow critics, Kawonza regarded bridewealth as a straightforward commercial transaction. As such, it should be regulated to control parents who believed that "when their daughters get married they will get rich." Greedy parents, Kawonza argued, placed a heavy burden on a young couple, especially the wife. "If a woman tries to ask money from her husband he will say, 'Where do you think I can get money from: am I a white man who has a bank of money? And yet I spent all the money paying for you.' Now is the time of wearing rags and then there will be a famine in your house." Kawonza also suggested that parental greed could backfire, possibly leading to tragic results. In desperation, parents unable to return the bridewealth in the event of their daughter's premature death might resort to suicide, she warned.[98]

Ultimately, then, differences over bridewealth were based more on marital status than gender, creating a generational split on the issue. Younger unmarried people, women and men, especially in the urban centers and on mission stations, tended to favor limiting the bridal consideration or abolishing it altogether. By contrast, older married people of both sexes loudly proclaimed their devotion to bridewealth, hailing it as an ancient African custom fully compatible with a Christian and civilized lifestyle and one that, furthermore, stood as a bulwark against indolence and sloth. This linkage of bridewealth and industry, or for that matter Christianity and civilization, was not just rhetorical; it was grounded in material reality. In the colonial political economy, bridewealth was a means of transferring wealth from younger male workers in the cities and other centers of employment to elders, especially older men, whether in the Reserves or elsewhere.

The positions taken in a debate in 1953 between students at the Salvation Army's Howard Institute and members of the Bindura Cultural Society illustrate well the lines of division over bridewealth. In an exercise that was of more than mere academic interest, the male students supported the resolution "Lobola should be abolished," whereas their opponents, all of them older (and probably married) men, took the other side. Making an argument that had become well-worn by then, one member of the Howard debating team asserted that the commercialization of bridewealth had made it impossible for newlyweds "to start life on the right footing." The other side countered with an equally axiomatic formulation, claiming that "African women could only have a sense of security if they were paid for." Without bridewealth, the reasoning went, the incidence of "immorality among the African people" would increase greatly, as wives would become unfaithful to their husbands.[99] Male defenders of bridewealth had long commended it as tending toward the promotion of virtue, a means of controlling the sexuality of women, because no conscientious daughter would risk an extramarital affair that might result in divorce and a demand for return of the bridal consideration, disgracing her parents and possibly leading to their financial ruin as well.[100] Indeed, the higher the bridewealth, the greater its effectiveness as a control mechanism.

Elite men even cited the need to control the sexuality of women, an objective supported by the colonial state, to oppose the government's policy of forcing rural African producers to "destock," that is, to sell off their cattle, allegedly as a conservation measure. Thus in 1948 the Southern Rhodesia Native Association, a political bastion of the male elite since its foundation some two decades earlier, noted that "Destocking is highly dangerous in that we are already facing a very difficult problem of loose women." Bridewealth, the association argued, "has been and still is the only means of checking this looseness of women. Our greatest fear is that the less cattle Africans possess, the more the lobola custom will diminish, and the more prostitution will increase."[101]

Attitudes toward bridewealth could also be determined by the gender of one's children. One writer, using the pseudonym Srutator, observed cynically:

> fathers of future bridegrooms are boldly out for the total abolition of lobola while fathers of the opposite sex give several reasons even quoting the Bible to prove that lobola is indispensable and a most hallowed custom. They also contend that before the white man came into the country lobola was dearer than it is today. They contend that a prospective son-in-law used to work hard for many seasons before he was allowed to have his future wife; they say that the value of that labor far exceeds what we today call a commercialising of human beings.[102]

Earlier, a government official had noticed a similar tendency, pointing out that "the older men, many of whom are fathers of marriageable daughters, are in favour of a comparatively high lobola, whereas the younger men, many of them poor, are anxious to secure a reduction."[103] But most of these young men and women, even if they remained poor, would eventually marry and establish families. As parents, they would gradually mellow, developing a more positive view of the bridal consideration, especially, it seemed, if they had girls. Thus the opposition to bridewealth, far from comprising a permanent constituency, remained largely ephemeral in character and subject to cross-generational attitudinal shifts.

The commodification of the bridal consideration was more pronounced among what one official called "the Educated and Christian Community than the older Heathen Element." Consequently, bridewealth was highest in the urban centers and on mission stations, areas where educated and Christian Africans could be found in relatively large numbers.[104] This was hardly accidental, because the transmutation from custom to commodity had been driven by the same social processes that resulted in the rise of an African middle class, notably, the erosion of traditional norms, including family and social obligations, and the accompanying creation of new wants, particularly education and the consumer goods that complemented elite African lifestyles.

To be sure, certain procedures traditionally associated with bridewealth, such as the suitor using an intermediary to negotiate with the parents of his fiancée, were preserved. The essential character of the custom, however, had been transformed by the cash nexus. Where formerly it had been infused with rich familial and social meanings, the relationship between the contracting parties now was reduced to naked self-interest.

Returning there in 1957, one urban resident from the Zwimba Reserve called attention to the use value of bridewealth in language that would have been familiar to denizens of that area, with its relatively large crop of "progressive" farmers and other signs of the new order. Parents in the Reserve, the visitor noted, were "driving towards the formation of a 'Daughters Marketing Board,'" because there were rumors of meetings being held to fix the price of bridewealth.[105] Although there was no generalized conspiracy to inflate bridewealth, the increasing monetary demands on suitors stood as an eloquent testimony to its metamorphosis under the impact of colonialism and capitalism, the values and lifestyles of which had been adopted most widely by the emerging African middle class. Nsele Hlabangana had urged parents of brides to put aside their greed and practice true Christianity. To most members of the black elite, however, the commodification of bridewealth *was* the Christian *and* civilized way.

WHITE WEDDING

No less Christian and civilized, in the eyes of members of the emerging African middle class, was the "white" wedding. Indeed, by the 1930s elite African weddings had become elaborate affairs, with the church ceremony, complete with white bridal gown and wedding ring, followed by a reception for family members and friends. A white wedding was one of the most conspicuous expressions of one's adherence to the social norms of bourgeois family life, as introduced by the missionaries. The white wedding, insisted N. J. Malikongwe, a male teacher at the Wesleyan Methodist Tegwani Institute, was not just for Europeans, "but is for all educated and civilised people."[106] The African-oriented press helped to publicize and encourage white weddings; from its inception, the *Mirror* included wedding pictures in its society page and sponsored photo competitions of newlyweds.[107]

The wedding of Hope Kumalo and Mzimuni Masuku, who were united at Hope Fountain mission in 1935, illustrated well the new elite-style marriage ceremony. The bride was the daughter of a notable minister, whereas the groom, a mission-school graduate, had succeeded to his father's chieftaincy. He was, according to Priscilla Moyo, the Hope Fountain teacher who acted as wedding reporter, only the third Ndebele chief to marry by Christian rites. Following a pattern that had become fixed by this time, the newlyweds had two receptions, hosted in turn by the parents of the bride and groom. There was much merriment at the first reception, with singing and dancing, the place having been whitewashed and appropriately decorated for the occasion. Each table contained a vase of flowers and a wedding cake, and the guests were treated to tea and buns, after which dinner was served. The festivities continued the following day at a second reception given by the parents of the groom.[108]

On the whole, elite weddings in the urban centers were more elaborate than those on mission stations or in the Reserves. Take the wedding of Effa David and Benjamin Dhliwayo, which occurred at the Presbyterian Church in Salisbury in January 1947 and was described as one of the most popular ever in the African township. The groom was the brother of Philemon and John Dhliwayo, well-known furniture-makers in the capital. The bride, who was given away by her father, wore a gown of "white moss crepe and a coronet of orange blossom held her embroidered veil in place. She held a bouquet of a beautiful shower of lilies." Her bridesmaid, the daughter of a minister, "also held a similar bouquet while two other girls held the train of her veil." After the church ceremony the guests, who numbered more than five hundred, were driven to the reception at the bride's home; there, to the accompaniment of music, dancing, and acting, they were served a meal of rice, meat, cakes, buns, ice cream, tea, and cold drinks. The menu was not without significance. For instance, the presence of rice instead of maize, the staple of the masses, was a definite indication of class orientation. The same likely was true of tea, the consumption of which appears not to have been widespread among the African masses at that time. "The popularity of the wedding was proved," we are assured, by gifts totaling £20 in cash as well as kitchenwares and other household items.[109]

It is uncertain if there was a second reception for the Dhliwayos, but by the 1940s it had become customary for newlywed elite couples to have two receptions, hosted in turn by the families of the bride and groom. Thus the first reception of a typical elite wedding in October 1947—an event at which Rev. Sitjenkwa Hlabangana, patriarch of the Hlabangana clan, presided—was held at the home of the bride's parents, while the groom's family hosted a second reception for the couple the following day.[110] George Kahari (later to become a distinguished scholar of Shona literature) and Dorothy Sihwamhi, both highly trained teachers, also had two receptions after their church ceremony in March 1955 in Salisbury.[111] Similarly, when the well-known journalist Kingsley Dube and Gledinah Sikupa, a nurse, were married in Bulawayo in

January 1957, the first reception was held at her parents' home on the day of the wedding. On the next day the couple and its wedding party traveled to the residence of the groom's parents, where they were given a "delirious welcome and reception. Excitement mounted to fever-pitch, and there was singing and dancing in the customary way." Reception speakers hailed both bride and groom as the first from their areas or origin to attain, respectively, the highest training in nursing and a university degree.[112]

Speechifying was a central feature of elite African wedding receptions, and speakers vied with each other in heaping adulation on the newlyweds and their families. Usually there would be several speakers at a reception, athough only one person would be selected to toast the couple. For example, at a reception organized in late 1948 by the Harari Choral Society for Mr. and Mrs. Enoch Dumbutshena, the toast was given by the groom's good friend, Stanlake Samkange, while other speakers included the white principal of an African school and Charles Mzingeli, the political activist and businessman.[113]

Generally, reception speeches were confined to reminiscences, small talk about the couple's accomplishments, and words of advice from older people. But occasionally a speaker would dispense with the customary "few well chosen words" and use the opportunity presented by a wedding reception to expound on weightier matters. Thus in 1958 the Rev. Leonard Sagonda, speaking at one of the receptions for Julius Shava and Evelyn Samkange—daughter of the Rev. Thompson Samkange, who had died a year and a half earlier, and Stanlake's sister—spoke at length about the qualities that made for a lasting marriage. "There was no time in the African marriage history," the distinguished Anglican divine assured his auditors, which included some of the most prominent members of the African middle class, "when marriage had such intricate and psychological abnormalities as the present time." These problems, Sagonda went on, stemmed from an excessive emphasis on the level of formal schooling attained. If the educational gap between the bride and groom was perceived as too wide, there would be much loose talk about whether they were "fit" for each other. In the case of Julius Shava and Evelyn Samkange, however, there was no doubt: both partners were teachers, and the groom was a university graduate. Yet it was not so much educational attainment as courtesy, mutual understanding, and tolerance that made a couple compatible, Sagonda noted, no doubt coming down off his toes and resting the heels of his shoes on the floor as he concluded his discourse.[114]

Urban residents often returned to their parents' homes in the Reserves to get married, and others journeyed there for receptions after the church ceremony in the city. But whether in the city or country, most receptions were held in private homes. By the era of World War II, however, there was a noticeable tendency among certain members of the urban-based petty bourgeoisie to go against this trend. For wedding receptions and similar events, these elite blacks wanted a substitute for the home, the physical openness of which served as a beacon to all and sundry, attracting unwanted guests in the segregated townships they were forced to share with the African masses. Excluded from the ballrooms of the white hotels in town by the color bar, elite blacks resorted to renting the township community centers—such as Recreation Hall in Salisbury and Stanley Hall in Bulawayo—for wedding receptions and similar functions. Often, a professional band would be engaged.

With the new spatial setting, the invitation card began to appear more and more, functioning as a social curtain against intrusion by the uninvited. This retreat into formality was an unmistakable demonstration of the desire of elite Africans, most notably in the urban centers, to limit interaction with the masses and to confine their socialization to members of their own class— an imperative made even more acute by the generally cramped circumstances in which even the black middle class lived. Thus, with the possible exception of poorer and lesser educated relations, the guest lists for wedding receptions in rented halls increasingly came to consist of "business people, professional people, limelight socialites and so on," as the social columnist, Naomi, observed.[115] The removal of wedding receptions from the home indicated a growing insistence on the part of the African petty bourgeoisie to make a sharper distinction between the public and private spheres in the realm of social relations.

The bellwether of the emerging trend in wedding receptions was the marriage of Patrick Makoni, a flamboyant bandsman turned businessman, and Gladys Carlsons, a coloured woman.[116] The wedding took place in Bulawayo, in August 1943, and was widely publicized in that city and beyond, Makoni having sent invitations to acquaintances in England, the United States, the Soviet Union, "everywhere." Makoni, who almost five decades after the event claimed to have been "an equal to the whites" on account of his wealth and fame, did not pay bridewealth, since "the whites don't charge lobola" (the bride's father was white and her mother coloured). This marriage also differed from the general run of elite black matrimonial unions in that there was no church wedding; instead, the couple were married in a civil ceremony in the magistrate's court.

The merriment began in the courthouse immediately after the ceremony. Makoni's own band, the Black and White, supplied the music, although it had to play without its leader, who had to escort his bride and who remembered that he "was too smart on that day." Indeed, according to Makoni, "that was the first time a band was allowed to play in court. Even the whites had never been allowed. They allowed that because that was my band and it played very well."[117]

From the courthouse the wedding party proceeded along the city's crowd-lined thoroughfares to the reception at Stanley Hall, which turned out to be

2. Identified only as "Dube's wedding," Tegwani Institute, April 20, 1935. Courtesy of the Borthwick Institute of Historical Research.

too small for all the guests. Evidently Makoni, despite his "equality" with the whites, had been unable to find more spacious and upscale facilities in town, forcing him to repair to the African township. A contemporary account described the scene at Stanley Hall:

> The hall was decorated with carnations on the tables and as time rolled away the troupes entered amidst high excitement and cheers of wellwishers; the band playing "Happy Days are Here Again" made the occasion very inspiring. Gradually after this the band kept going while others danced for the couple, others offered gifts of parcels, and others offered cash, some gifts came from as far away as Salisbury from friends who wish Mr. and Mrs. Makoni a happy, peaceful married life.[118]

With a flashy groom, a coloured bride, an absence of bridewealth, and no church ceremony, this was hardly emblematic of elite black marriages. Yet, although unconventional in so many respects, the wedding of Patrick Makoni and Gladys Carlsons highlighted an important new trend in the patterns of matrimonial celebrations of an emerging social stratum.[119] Henceforth public halls in the African townships, rented especially for the occasion, increasingly

3. Joshua and Johanna Nkomo
at their wedding, 1949. Joshua
Nkomo became a foremost
African nationalist leader.
Courtesy of the National
Archives of Zimbabwe.

would be converted into private clubs for the wedding receptions of the black
middle class.

The removal of wedding receptions from the home was part of a more
general separation of the public from the private sphere among elite Africans.
In the 1950s, the home became increasingly privatized, with the removal not
just of special celebrations like wedding receptions but also of ordinary male
socialization, especially with the emergence of upscale shebeens serving illicit
"European" liquor, which Africans were legally prohibited from drinking, and
of multiracial "tea drinking" involving mainly white liberals and elite black
men.[120] Indeed, by this point many elite men apparently were spending few of
their waking hours at home, a dilemma that exercised the minds of both social
columnists and aggrieved wives, who discussed at length ways to keep husbands closer to the family hearth. All the proffered solutions centered on unilateral initiatives by the women, with wives being urged to keep clean houses,
cook appetizing meals, and pay attention to their personal appearances.

Other women, however, dismissed as absurd and impractical any talk about binding men to the home, or, as one woman put it bluntly, "how to keep your man to yourself." According to this line of reasoning—which, however unintended, was consistent with the argument advanced by the colonial officials in their refusal to crack down on monogamous recidivism—"African women who really know their men are sure that not a single woman has an entire hold on her man for man is, by nature polygamous, and is, by all means, to be tolerated by a woman who wishes to keep her home."[121] Thus, another African woman added, wives "should not at all be discouraged by the evil deeds of their husbands about which they learn from the talk of other people. Husbands can say whatever they like to their wives, but women should stick to their good behaviour and show them that they can achieve something great."[122] That something was, of course, excelling in the domestic realm by being ideal wives and mothers, a lesson well learned and deeply internalized in the mission schools, the homecraft training centers, and most important of all, the African self-enabling agencies, notably the Manyano-Ruwadzano movement, the women's clubs, and various other organizations. For such women, steeped as they were in the ideology of bourgeois domesticity, self-fulfillment became synonymous with homemaking, the sacred calling of home and hearth.

4

The Best of All Homes
Housing and Security of Tenure

IN 1934 Knox J. Tsolo, speaking at the annual conference of the Southern
Rhodesia Native Missionary Conference, presented the case for better housing for the African middle class, then already a two-decades-old struggle. The
appeal, characteristically, was founded on the black elite's claim to superior
standing in the scales of European civilization, as compared with the mass of
Africans. Tsolo's argument, carefully phrased in the respectable and deferential language favored by the Native Missionary Conference, was nothing less
than a condensation of elite African achievements, grievances, and aspirations:

> All over Southern Africa where Europeans are able to live and employ
> Native labour there exists a class of Natives . . . whose lives have been im-
> mensely enlarged. [This elite African] has learned while he has laboured;
> his intelligence has been broadened through acquaintance with the ideas
> and activities of a wider world of which he has been made a part. Especially
> is this the experience of Africans who have worked in the larger towns, and
> have had the privilege of such educational uplift as the Mission schools have
> been able to provide through the help of a liberal and sympathetic govern-
> ment. He has entered into a new life and, if he is progressive, he finds it no
> longer possible to live the restricted live of his fellows in the Reserves from
> which he came.[1]

There were fewer areas in which the "progressive" urbanized African in
Southern Rhodesia felt more restricted than in choice of housing. Indeed,
housing was a touchstone of the ability of the African middle class to control
its own destiny. Thus the quest for decent accommodation began as early as
any struggle waged by the black elite and was no less protracted. In particular,
the members of the urbanized African middle class demanded housing outside of the municipal townships to which all Africans, regardless of social
standing, were consigned under the system of residential segregation. Their
objective was spatial separation from the African workers with whom they
had been forced to live. They sought removal to a place—suburbia—where
they could build homes, both physically and culturally, that would become the
basis of a settled family life; in short, the members of the emerging African

petty bourgeoisie desired a place to work out the middle-class domestic ideal as it had been transmitted to and transformed by them.

THE QUEST FOR MIDDLE-CLASS HOUSING

The members of the African middle class had always been unhappy campers in the municipal township, which was a most unsuitable venue for working out anything approximating a bourgeois domestic ideal. As early as 1915, elite Africans had been clamoring for the establishment of separate residential communities that would be restricted to members of their class. The authorities conceded that the townships were dreadful places, admitting that they "offer few attractions to any native with well-regulated habits, and are inimical to domestic and family welfare."[2] Accordingly, the government acquired land in the two major urban centers, Salisbury and Bulawayo, to rectify this state of affairs.

In Bulawayo, where the call for separate elite African housing was particularly urgent, the authorities pledged that the proposed housing scheme would be "a model" and that it would not be allowed to become a "native kraal," because "the object is to try and uplift the native and give him an opportunity to live as [much] like the white race as possible." Residency in the proposed black suburbs would thus be confined to "bona fide married men" living in nuclear families, with polygynous households "strictly" barred. The residents, who would have to be recommended by an official or some other prominent white person, would be responsible for building their own houses according to municipal specifications.[3]

The idea of "uplifting" the emergent African middle class in this manner was warmly endorsed by the high-level Land Commission of 1925. Asserting that elite Africans "will feel it a grievance if they are not able to acquire sites for residential purposes apart from the Native working classes," the commission considered "it most advisable that an area should be set aside now by the Municipality on each of the township commonages as a residential suburb for the more well-to-do Native of the future."[4] This recommendation was eventually incorporated into the Land Apportionment Act of 1930, itself the outcome of the Land Commission, in the form of a provision for a government-run village scheme for the urban African middle class. Presently, it seemed that a few select Africans would be allowed to approach white standards and enjoy the rustic ambiance of suburbia, that distinctive bourgeois solution to life in the inner city, with its pollution, noise, dirt, crime, and immorality—all of which were associated with the laboring classes.[5]

In fact, things would not be that simple. Proposals for an elite African housing scheme were rejected by white municipal officials as a threat to the existing system of urban segregation, which was administered by the municipalities and financed by the revenues they derived from renting housing, leasing plots, and operating beer halls in the African townships. The rejection was especially vehement in Bulawayo, where the city fathers, in violation of edicts and laws requiring that the money be devoted to "native welfare," routinely diverted township revenues to finance projects earmarked for the exclusive benefit of white residents and municipal employees.[6]

Instead of a separate housing scheme, the city fathers of Bulawayo and Salisbury proposed to accommodate the African elite in specially designed "married quarters" within the existing municipal townships. Elite Africans, however, were unimpressed by the proffered alternative. From Salisbury came complaints that the cottages in the married quarters were "not confined to the respectable class for whom they were designed, and that undesirable women" —that is, purveyors of sexual services and other females who were not "properly" married—could easily gain access to them by bribing African "police boys" and other municipal officials.[7] Similar allegations were made in Bulawayo.[8]

The residents of the Bulawayo township married quarters further complained about a lack of privacy owing to flaws in the design and construction of the cottages. In particular, they objected to the fact that the two-room cottages were divided by a wall that did not extend to the top of the ceiling and that there was no back door, forcing the occupants of the inner room to enter and exit through the outer one. Thompson Samkange, the ubiquitous Wesleyan Methodist minister, appeared before the 1930 municipal commission to protest the inadequate partitioning, which, he asserted, caused children to hear "the quarrels and other conversations of their elders." Giving evidence to the same commission, Zachariah Makgatho, another prominent member of the emerging African elite, condemned the absence of a back door in the married quarters as contrary to "public" morals. The Industrial and Commercial Workers Union of Africa (ICU), with which Makgatho was loosely affiliated, also sought to exploit the back-door grievance, prompting the white location superintendent to attack the organization for "working up feeling[s] about the lack of privacy and the absence of a second door."[9] Clearly, the municipal married quarters were no substitute for a separate community inhabited exclusively by the African middle class.

INSIDE THE TOWNSHIP

The African elite had good reasons for despising the municipal townships, which posed a threat not just to middle-class family life but to life itself. Characterized by confusion, disorganization, and an utter contempt for planning, the townships were little more than an assorted collection of people drawn from all over Southern Rhodesia and southern Africa as a whole.

Rudely thrown together in the same physical space, they lived, quite literally in some cases, on top of one another, sharing the same communal (and largely unsanitary) toilets and washing facilities. "One can scarcely find a clean space in which to tread," a leading African churchman observed of the toilets in the Bulawayo municipal township. Some people relieved themselves in the bushes or in the back of their residences rather than use the communal conveniences.[10]

The municipalities, officially in charge of "native welfare," as the task of controlling urban Africans outside the point of production was euphemistically called, initially paid scant attention to sanitation, public health, or recreation. The city fathers as well as the central colonial administration watched with studious indifference as the black ghettoes, which were denied access to the municipal sewage systems, wallowed in a sea of filth, grime, and disease (especially tuberculosis and venereal diseases). No wonder the Manyano-Ruwadzano women wailed for purity. No wonder, too, that elite African spokesmen denounced the municipal township as a "cesspool of drunken[n]ess and immorality, a place and a home to house wanderers," unfit for the habitation of "decent Natives," who shunned it for "fear of spoiling their families."[11]

By 1930, when commissions were appointed to investigate the living conditions of Africans in Salisbury and Bulawayo, township life had already acquired its defining characteristics. The reports of the commissions put the population of Salisbury's African township at 3,488 and Bulawayo's at 5,550.[12] However, only a minority of the Africans in these two cities actually lived in the municipal townships. Nor do these figures take account of the townships' unregistered population, which may well have been greater than the registered. According to official figures, in 1931, a year of widespread unemployment caused by the depression, there were, respectively, 16,150 and 15,112 Africans, nearly all of them men, formally employed in the legitimate economy in the Bulawayo and Salisbury metropolitan areas.[13] Thus taken as a whole, the African population of each metropolitan area—men, women, and children, within and outside the municipal townships—easily would have been in the tens of thousands.

The municipal township expanded in direct proportion to urban development and the migration it spawned. In the early years of colonial rule, African migrants to the white city were compelled to find their own accommodation, for which neither employers nor the state made any provision. The principal exceptions were domestic workers, who generally slept on their employers' premises, usually in the kitchen or in a shack in the yard, the so-called boy's kia.

The haphazard settlement of urban-dwelling Africans inevitably resulted in the emergence of shantytowns on the outskirts of the city. The unsightly scene, but even more importantly the unsanitary conditions—which threatened general public health, including that of the white population—eventually forced state intervention. Accordingly, in 1907 the Salisbury municipality, acting under new powers granted by the Native Urban Locations Ordinance that had been introduced the previous year, dismantled the city's makeshift settlement and moved its inhabitants to a newly established township well beyond the central business district.[14]

In contrast to Salisbury, the Bulawayo municipal township was built on the site originally staked out by that city's earliest African residents. This is because the township was accorded legal status in 1895, only a year after Bulawayo's foundation as a white urban settlement and well before it could develop the characteristics that so unsettled white Salisbury. Moreover, because it was already in existence when the ordinance took effect, the Bulawayo African township did not come under the jurisdiction of the Native Urban Locations Ordinance. Therefore, from the legal and operational standpoint, the Bulawayo city council was less accountable to the central administration in the governance of its township than were the other municipalities, an anomaly that was only rectified in 1946 with the introduction of the Urban Areas Act, which mandated greater municipal intrusion in the lives of urban Africans right across the board.

The accordance of "location" or township status to an urban area involved municipal acceptance of responsibility for "native welfare." Accordingly, after the establishment of the Salisbury township, the city began building Kaytor huts, one-room circular structures made of corrugated iron and measuring twelve feet in diameter. Construction of these units was discontinued in 1921, when the Kaytor huts were gradually replaced by four-room brick dwellings, a colonial version of the notorious "back-to-back" structures in which the nineteenth-century English working class lived. By 1930, a majority of the township's residents were accommodated in such dwellings.[15]

Bulawayo, by comparison, took a more laissez-faire approach to housing. Indeed, it was not until the 1920s that the municipality launched a housing development program. Prior to this time most Africans in Bulawayo, as in many of the smaller towns, lived in privately owned cottages (that is, brick structures) or huts (structures made of materials other than bricks), built on stands leased from the municipality. The cost of leasing a stand varied, ranging from a monthly rate of five shillings in Bulawayo, Que Que, and Gatooma to two shillings in Fort Victoria and Bindura. There was no charge for stands in Gwelo, although there, as in other centers, occupants of privately owned dwellings were assessed a monthly charge for services, mainly water and waste removal.[16]

The majority of those compelled to provide their own accommodation simply constructed crude and rudimentary huts. The builders resorted to the architectural style they were most familiar with, using whatever materials were available, which usually resulted in round huts made of mud and thatch. In time, the mud-and-thatch structures were replaced by dwellings made from flattened paraffin or petrol cans, augmented with bits and pieces of corrugated iron. These structures, which acquired a deep brown color as the building material rusted, remained standard housing for many Africans, especially in the smaller towns, until well past World War II.[17]

Standing in stark contrast to the crude shacks were the comparatively sturdier and more spacious brick cottages built by a small minority of Africans. In Bulawayo, where the incidence of African homeownership among the municipalities was highest, the construction of private cottages was encouraged by building codes, instituted in 1921, aimed at eliminating the huts. The 1930 commission made a sharp distinction between the two types of dwellings. Where the huts tended to "be small, old, unsightly and unsuitable," the commission found that the cottages "were often a source of pride to their owners," a view confirmed by the missionary in charge of the township's Wesleyan Methodist Church.[18] One such proud homeowner was Presbyterian preacher W. M. G. Tshiminya, who, after buying a four-room cottage for £35, added two more rooms at an additional cost of £18.[19]

In 1930, Africans owned more than a third of the detached cottages in the Bulawayo township, 202 out of a total of 578. Most of the African-owned cottages were family residences, but others were rental properties. Some landlords owned several properties, earning their living entirely from rental incomes. Women were well represented in the ranks of Bulawayo's African homeowners, although on the whole they were less well-off than their male counterparts. Evidently cottage rental, as a business, was dominated by men, whereas female landlords seem mainly to have taken lodgers into their own homes or else rented out huts.[20]

Precisely because of their greater insecurity, women homeowners were foremost among those protesting when, in 1929, the Bulawayo city council banned the construction of new private dwellings and began demolishing existing ones that were in disrepair. One protester, describing herself as "one of Lobengula's queens," charged the city fathers with going back on their promise to replace demolished structures with comparable housing. Her two three-room cottages, which had been torn down by the city, were replaced by only one two-room house. Another landlady emphasized that the women were committed urbanites who were entirely dependent on rental incomes for their livelihood. "We have lived in the towns for many years and we have now no desire to live in the native reserves far from the towns. We are de-tribalised and urbanised," she declaimed. Representing themselves as champions of the African common good, the landladies argued that the demolition of old houses was a serious disservice to the township's predominantly male working-class residents, who would be unable to afford the higher rents for the newer properties, whether they belonged to the municipality or were individually owned.[21]

Desperate, the women appealed to the central government to reverse the municipal decision. But the central authorities, who in any case had limited jurisdiction over the Bulawayo township, as noted, were reluctant to interfere in municipal affairs at that level.[22] Still, some African homeowners managed to keep their properties long after the ban on new private dwellings had gone into effect. A 1939 investigation by the Native Welfare Society noted the existence of African-owned (as well as Indian-owned) buildings in the Bulawayo township, although they were mainly in a "deplorable state." Evidently, these structures subsequently became completely uninhabitable, for another inquiry by the Welfare Society four years later made no mention of private houses in the township.[23]

The living conditions inside the municipal townships may have been bad, but they were even worse in the "private locations," that is, the numerous compounds in and around the urban centers, where many Africans lived beyond the control of the municipal authorities. Many employers—public and private, large and small—housed their employees in such compounds, which increased in direct proportion to the growth of the urban African population and the consequent scarcity of housing in the municipal townships. Families with children were often required to share living space with single men in the employer-operated private locations, some of which had no bathing or sanitary facilities at all. In 1939 the railway compound in Bulawayo, a "model" private location, housed up to three couples and nine single men in a single room. Even the white-run Native Welfare Society, notorious for its deference to the colony's employers, whom it counted among its leading lights and financial backers, was moved to denounce the scandal.[24]

Some urban-dwelling Africans sought to avoid both the municipal townships and the private locations by renting or leasing stands on white-owned (or Indian-owned) property. One such alternate place was Kaufman's plot in Salisbury, a parcel of land outside the city center where many Africans lived and ran businesses until 1946, when the Urban Areas Act removed this black spot from the white city.

For residential freelancers in Bulawayo, the place of choice was Hyde Park, a private estate outside the city. In 1937, when the government threatened an official takeover, charging that it had become an illicit brewery for the Bulawayo municipal township, Hyde Park's population was conservatively estimated at one thousand. Seeking to forestall the threat, some of Hyde Park's more stalwart residents formed the Hyde Park Self-Improvement Association "to deal mercilessly with those men and women who persist in selling beer contrary to the wishes of the powers that be."[25] Eventually, the authorities decided against a takeover, not so much because of the activities of the Hyde Park Self-Improvement Association but because they realized that the estate served "a useful purpose in providing accommodation" for many Africans who could not be housed in the municipal township.[26] The reprieve was temporary, however, for Hyde Park became a township under the control of the Bulawayo municipality in the postwar years as a result of the consolidation mandated by the Urban Areas Act.

Although offering residents exemption from municipal intrusion into their daily lives and providing a relatively wider scope for entrepreneurship, places like Kaufman's plot and Hyde Park were no more suitable than were the municipal townships for most members of the emerging African middle class. Indeed they were, in some respects, even worse. The townships, despite their many drawbacks, at least had some rudimentary facilities, such as schools, churches, recreation centers, regular water supplies, and streetlights, few of which existed in the alternative residential areas. For the African elite, the campaign for respectable housing commensurate with a petty bourgeois lifestyle, ideally with freehold tenure, would go on.

THE CONTINUING STRUGGLE FOR MIDDLE-CLASS HOUSING

By the early 1930s the African elite had grown extremely anxious about the housing issue, which became linked to several other important concerns, the most politically explosive of which was "joint drinking," that is, women and men drinking together in the municipal beer halls. Elite African men viewed joint drinking as a sexual threat and heavily lobbied the municipalities to end the practice. The city fathers, however, rejected the entreaties, fearing that the working-class males who made up the bulk of the beer halls' clientele would retaliate by transferring their patronage to the "skokiaan queens" or illicit women beer brewers. The majority of these workers were either bachelors or married men who had left their families behind in the countryside, often in neighboring colonies, and they tended to support joint drinking. And although few elite wives would have visited the beer halls—these women abhorred liquor and cherished their monogamous Christian marriages—their husbands were nevertheless deeply suspicious of the male workers' wanderlust. Aside from the grime, filth, and lack of privacy, then, the fear of elite African men that they might not be able to control the sexuality of their wives was another powerful reason to seek housing away from the townships.[27]

In any case, elite wives and other upwardly mobile women were no less eager than their husbands and other male counterparts to leave the townships. Although not as conspicuous as the men in the public campaign, some African women also lobbied for respectable middle-class housing. Thus in 1933, aggrieved at the delay in starting the long-promised housing scheme, a delegation of Bulawayo's African women met with officials to protest "the hardships of life in the Location and [express] their earnest wish that land should be set aside" for Africans who wished to live outside the township.[28]

A major aspect of the quest for better accommodation was that any new housing scheme should be made available on a freehold basis, an issue to which elite Africans in Bulawayo were especially attentive. The freehold issue had been mentioned prominently by Bulawayo's Knox J. Tsolo in his speech on housing at the 1934 annual meeting of the Southern Rhodesia Native Missionary Conference.[29] Previously Bradfield Mnyanda, a leading figure in the campaign to end joint drinking and one of the most high-profile elite African spokesmen in Bulawayo, also had held forth at length on the freehold issue in an appearance before a joint meeting of the black and white sections of the Native Welfare Society.[30]

Inevitably, freehold became an important concern of the Bantu Community of Bulawayo, an umbrella body for the city's various elite African organizations. In 1935 the Bantu Community, under the auspices of Zachariah Makgatho, its chairman and a longtime housing activist, held a "well represented meeting" to discuss the proposed government housing scheme. The meeting passed a resolution requesting the government to amend the Land Apportionment Act to make it possible for "detribalised natives to purchase land at the [proposed] Village Settlement."[31] The Bulawayo black elite also called on the central government to assume control of the housing scheme, expressing the desire that the municipalities "should have nothing to do with" it, because the city fathers ignored the Africans, elite and non-elite alike, caring only for "those who put them in power."[32]

THE LENGTHENING SHADOW OF SEGREGATION

The spate of demands for freehold tenure had been prompted by renewed government interest in the elusive housing scheme. Far from heralding a newfound willingness to accede to the aspirations of elite Africans, however, this interest was motivated by legal and political imperatives. Specifically, the Land Apportionment Act of 1930 required Africans living in "European" areas to move within seven years of its enactment, a deadline the settler regime was under pressure to meet. Consequently, provision had to be made for those affected by the law, including urban residents. Many of the latter, an official in charge of land policy for Africans noted, "are of what may be termed the more advanced type of Natives, who desire and look for something more than can be found" in the townships. More to the point, these "advanced natives" were "particularly anxious concerning their womenfolk." The envisaged housing scheme, the official concluded, would thus "provide strictly for the better classes of married Natives and will not be allowed to harbour the flotsam and jetsam of the detribalized Native population."[33]

The emphasis on the elite character of the proposed housing scheme was, of course, merely a restatement of a view that had been repeatedly expressed by officials and government-appointed commissions. However, by this point, 1934, a new government had come to power on a platform even more hostile to the rise of an African middle class than its predecessors.

Led by Godfrey Huggins, the new government had assumed office toward the end of 1933. In his previous role as opposition leader, Huggins had forcefully attacked the allegedly soft segregationist line of the governing party, demanding, among other things, more rigorous control of African urban migration. On coming to power, Huggins attempted to remake the proposed African housing scheme in the image of his more hard-line segregationist vision.

Instead of a suburban development for the "better class of natives," as long promised, Huggins saw the housing scheme as a means to "control the further urbanisation of the native people . . . by interposing a barrier between the white and black races." He was especially concerned about the urban-born Africans, "a generation of natives who have never seen a Reserve, . . . and who if they were ever compelled by law to live in a Reserve would not know how to fend for themselves." These Africans were encroaching "on the white labour market," thereby reducing employment opportunities for Europeans, and that in the midst of the depression. Meanwhile, unemployed "detribalized" Africans constituted "an ever growing menace in the neighbourhood of white towns." No less important than the economic menace was the health menace, namely, the many "avenues of contact between the white community and a large native population living under improperly supervised conditions and without adequate medical attention." Here, Huggins was more concerned about servants living in "miserable conditions" in their employers' backyards than he was with residents of the African townships. To the economic and health threat posed by African urbanization, Huggins added yet another danger, the dreaded "black peril": "the irksome conditions of lack of freedom" felt by white women and children at night owing to the presence of African men on the streets.[34]

Huggins believed that the housing scheme, "properly organised and properly controlled," would address "these unnecessary evils by breaking the contact between black and white at the point where urbanisation commences."[35] Rather than exclusive middle-class communities, therefore, the proposed villages would become urban Reserves, places to send domestic servants at night and to consign African artisans and budding entrepreneurs who competed with Europeans. In this way, there would be both urban territorial and economic segregation, which Huggins had accused the previous government of failing to implement.

The decision to proceed with the housing scheme under the control of the central government, instead of the municipalities, as previously envisaged, caused the city fathers of the two major urban centers to redouble their opposition to the project. The mayor of Salisbury gave Huggins a guided tour of the African township to show off its "married quarters," all the while suggesting "that it would be a pity to start a [new] village which would be competing" with the city's existing housing offerings.[36]

The Bulawayo city fathers took a more apocalyptic view. One member of the city council, who also served as a national parliamentary representative of the Southern Rhodesia Labour Party—which championed the cause of white artisans and smaller merchants—introduced a motion in the Legislative Assembly declaring that the housing scheme would result in "the disappearance of the white population from Southern Rhodesia."[37] Another member of the Bulawayo city council suggested that the African villages would result in increased miscegenation.[38] Bulawayo's white merchants, too, added their objections. Fearing "a serious loss of the big native trade," they rejected any housing scheme that would "be in direct competition with the efficiently run [municipal] native location." White commercial capital was particularly concerned about proposals, consistent with Huggins's policy of economic segregation, to grant African shopkeepers a monopoly within the new villages, predicting that opportunities for settler shopkeepers "must disappear when an adjacent native town is set up in which natives will be allowed to do their own trading."[39] The die, however, had been cast, and no amount of overblown rhetoric would alter that political reality.

FROM HUTS TO HOUSES?

Huggins's village scheme was completed in 1936. The two villages, one in Salisbury and the other in Bulawayo, consisted of two- and three-room cottages, each with a kitchen and a washing place outside. The houses were built on individual plots of land that were much larger than anything available in the municipal townships. As in the townships, however, water had to be obtained from standpipes in the unpaved streets.[40] Although the villages were an improvement in many respects, they were hardly the basis for building suburban dream homes.

Elite Africans in Salisbury and Bulawayo reacted differently to the new housing scheme. The cottages at Highfield, as the village in Salisbury was called, were taken immediately. The reception was much less enthusiastic at Bulawayo's Luveve village, which was named after C. L. Carbutt, the chief native commissioner (the Africans called him Luveve, or "butterfly" in Sindebele). Unimpressed by the description offered by the city's leading white daily, which hailed Luveve as a major exercise in "transplanting natives from huts to homes," Bulawayo's African elite initially boycotted the village.[41]

The ranking official charged with governing Africans in Bulawayo argued that the boycott was the result of high rent and the unwillingness of residents at Hyde Park, the "private location" outside the city, to move to Luveve, because they would "have to submit to regulations and proper control."[42] Actually, the boycott was an expression of disappointment in the government's refusal to amend the Land Apportionment Act, as requested by the Bantu Community of Bulawayo, and make the houses available on a freehold basis. The inability to purchase the cottages or at least lease them on a long-term basis was acutely felt by the black elite in Bulawayo, where, as we have seen, Africans had an earlier tradition of homeownership and where the campaign for freehold tenure was centered.

Alarmed at the boycott, the Bulawayo superintendent of natives resurrected an old proposal to set aside land near the boycotted village where Africans could build their own houses according to government specifications. This idea, however, was rejected by his more unflappable superior.[43] The latter's patience proved virtuous, for a shortage of housing, along with the strong desire of elite Africans to leave the township, made the boycott unsustainable. Soon, it was reported that the "rate at which cottages have been taken has improved considerably," and the authorities were busy building additional rental units at Luveve.[44] The stand for freehold tenure would have to be made at another time and place.

THE CAMPAIGN FOR FREEHOLD TENURE, 1940–65

In 1940 the Southern Rhodesia Bantu Congress passed a resolution in favor of freehold tenure for urban Africans, so they "may enjoy the privileges which are extended to other races," a position reaffirmed at subsequent meetings.[45] Then in 1946 the Bantu Congress, the premier African political movement nationally since its establishment a decade earlier, boldly pronounced segregation a failure and called for repealing the sections of the Land Apportionment Act forbidding Africans from trading in the urban areas.[46]

As these actions suggest, the issue of security of tenure had risen to the top of the elite African political agenda by the era of World War II. After wages, which had been eroded by wartime inflation, housing was the most important concern of the individuals who gave evidence to an influential 1944 commission on the role of Africans in the urban economy.[47] The following year, Jasper Savanhu, one of the most politically savvy members of the African middle class, returned to this issue. In a pamphlet that quickly attained

the status of an elite African manifesto, Savanhu linked economic development and harmonious race relations to security of tenure:

> At present, the African is afraid that he will not be able to support his fam-
> ily or provide for his old age if he loses touch with his reserve. Remove these
> fears by giving the African his OWN HOME in the urban area, and he will pro-
> vide the efficient worker which is so valuable to industry and the future de-
> velopment of Southern Rhodesia for the common good of both Europeans
> and Africans. Equal opportunities for all civilised men and homes for the
> people were two ideals towards which Mr. Rhodes was always working.[48]

Bradfield Mnyanda, whose activism on the housing issue went back to the
1930s, subsequently developed this theme in another paean to the black elite.
"Those who completely break away from rural, tribal or reserve life to become part of the European industrial system cannot be expected to remain
perpetual rent-payers," Mnyanda insisted. "After all, one's own house is the
best of all houses, and none loves his country but he who loves his home," he
concluded with customary rhetorical flourish.[49] For the first time in the history of the colony, elite Africans were beginning to attach conditions to their
political loyalty.

It is a testament to its increasing political urgency that the demand of
elite blacks for their own homes became a recurring theme in the most important document on Africans affairs published by the government on a regular
basis, notably the annual reports of the chief native commissioner. In 1948 the
report acknowledged considerable "dissatisfaction among the Native intelligentsia" over several issues; however, "the main cause of complaint, and [one]
for which every sympathy is felt, is the lamentable lack of housing, and the
feeling of insecurity of tenure."[50]

Indeed, so explosive did the issue become that in 1954, when the minister
of native affairs made a serious political faux pas by publicly rejecting the
idea of African freehold tenure, a major uproar ensued. The All-African Convention, an umbrella movement that had been formed to oppose the establishment of the Federation of Rhodesia and Nyasaland, attacked the comment
as "damaging to healthy race relations."[51] Seeking to control the damage, the
government issued a statement accepting the proposition that "as far as possible the African should be afforded an opportunity of security of tenure in
certain areas."[52] Although not quite a complete reversal in that "security of
tenure" did not necessarily mean freehold tenure, the statement signaled a
perceptible shift in official policy.

This shift was caused by important economic and political changes in the
postwar period. Already in the midst of the war, the 1944 commission on urban African workers had made the case for employers to break the decades-

long reliance on migrant labor. Dismissing the "vagrant bachelor" as an obstacle to economic development, the commission lauded the advantage of the fully proletarianized worker leading a normal family life, noting that without the "married man," Rhodesian industry would be unable to compete effectively on the regional, let alone the world, market.[53] And the married man, as those who spoke for the African elite were quick to add, demanded security, if not outright freehold tenure, as the price for an unequivocal commitment to the country's economic development.

The new willingness to entertain the possibility of black freehold tenure also resulted from a series of postwar developments that increased African political bargaining power. This enhanced empowerment was manifested in various ways, including a bolder challenge to the government on issues like housing and voting rights, and most dramatically, in a strike by railway workers and an even more sweeping general strike in 1945 and 1948, respectively. Africans in Southern Rhodesia, led by the elite, also joined their colonized counterparts north of the Zambezi in opposing the creation of the Federation of Rhodesia and Nyasaland. The federation came into being anyway, but only after its architects promised to work for "racial partnership" between colonizer and colonized. Although the proffered partnership was a diversionary tactic by the settler ruling class to win British imperial approval for the federation scheme, it gave the Africans a yardstick by which to judge official behavior.

Lawrence Vambe, a prominent journalist, listed "security of tenure in the urban areas" as the most pressing objective under the new dispensation. Speaking primarily about members of his class, Vambe continued:

> This is a very sore point with the African of Southern Rhodesia. The denial of the right to own his home where he earns his living—which is in the interests of the employer and therefore the European as a whole—has no justification whatsoever to the African. He regards the enforced confinement to the location as a soul-destroying system as those who know location conditions will admit. Were this grievance to be removed and the African was encouraged and assisted to own his own home the country will have gone a very long way to making the African feel a sense of dignity and responsibility.[54]

The colonial regime, seeking to keep the myth of racial partnership alive and to take the wind out of the incipient African nationalist sail, needed to placate those elite blacks like Vambe who, despite their previous reservations or even outright opposition to federation, had began to warm to the new multiracialist rhetoric.

It was in this context that the Southern Rhodesian government approved a new African housing development plan. In announcing the plan, the authorities admitted, as elite African representatives had insisted all along, that "satisfactory housing, with satisfactory tenure, lies at the very basis of healthy race relations and that only on a foundation of good living conditions can industry and commerce be soundly established."[55] Backed by the British Colonial Development Corporation, the plan called for building five thousand four-room cottages with indoor plumbing, to be divided equally between Salisbury and Bulawayo. The houses would be made available on a ninety-nine-year leasehold basis. As a means of helping leaseholders pay their mortgages, a room specially designed for lodgers would be added to each house.[56]

This plan represented a definite improvement over the first government-run housing development, whether in terms of space, facilities, or security; still, it was not freehold tenure. For that reason, the announcement of the scheme received only a lukewarm reception from elite Africans in Bulawayo. J. Wilson Vera, a prominent social worker and member of the township Advisory Board, welcomed it as "a great step forward" but expressed reservations that the lodger system "might make the whole area a slum." The qualms of Bulawayo's black middle class was well captured by Masotha Mike Hove, the African representative for Matabeleland (which included Bulawayo) in the parliament of the Federation of Rhodesia and Nyasaland. Although "commendable," Hove asserted, "freehold tenure would have been better. It is to be regretted that while these schemes were being planned nothing should be heard about freehold tenure."[57]

There was no such second-guessing in the capital, where Jasper Savanhu, Hove's parliamentary opposite for Mashonaland (which included Salisbury), unequivocally endorsed the scheme. Savanhu, who had written so eloquently on the housing issue in his 1945 pamphlet, lauded the new initiative as "an answer to the aspirations of the better class of urbanised Africans and a demonstration of the Government's intention to implement [racial] partnership."[58] His enthusiasm was exceeded by a group of black, Salisbury-based editors of African-oriented publications. Confessing that they could "hardly restrain" themselves, the editors pronounced the leasing scheme "the greatest thing that has happened to the African in the history of Southern Rhodesia." The government, they gushed, had "raised the dignity of the African people in full keeping with human and Christian standards, and in so doing have amply demonstrated your sincerity in the foundation of a Central African nation of black and white, living together in peace and mutual respect, and according to the best British traditions of justice and fair play."[59]

In 1956, the leaseholders began moving into the new villages, named New Highfield in Salisbury (so called to differentiate it from the first government village, which now became known as Old Highfield) and Mpopoma in Bulawayo. But once again, all was not well in suburbia. Leaseholders complained bitterly that the monthly payment was too high. In Bulawayo, Gibson Fraser, a fiery African nationalist and member of the Western Commonage

Advisory Board, virtually earned his political spurs attacking "high rent" at Mpopoma.[60]

The most earnest complaints about the new villages, however, centered on their "moral tone" and the lodger system. Even though the payment of many a mortgage depended on the incomes they brought in, the mostly working-class male lodgers were much resented by their own landlords as well as other leaseholders. The lodgers were accused of numerous transgressions, including disrespect, theft, desertion, nonpayment of rent, showing sexual interest in the lady of the house, holding rowdy parties, and singing and making noise in the streets.[61]

Conspicuous among the critics was Nathan Shamuyarira, one of the above-mentioned editors who initially had praised the housing scheme in such a fawning display of rhetorical extravagance. Yet Shamuyarira, oblivious to the fact that he was not among the original naysayers, now asserted that in the "African community there was little enthusiasm [for the scheme] at the start, and some quarters had reservations." Instead of the envisaged middle-class haven of respectability, Salisbury's New Highfield, then not quite two years old, was fast becoming another urban slum, a "lowering of moral standards" Shamuyarira attributed to the presence in the village of skokiaan queens and, even worse, lodgers.[62]

Echoing elite African complaints that went back to the 1920s, Shamuyarira faulted the authorities for attaching little or "no importance to character in the sale of houses; the main requirement was just the applicant's ability to raise his deposit and rentals." Consequently skokiaan queens, many of them from Salisbury's old municipal township, had relocated to New Highfield, where they continued holding "tea parties" and serving "heavy Coca-Cola" to their many customers. Meanwhile, Shamuyarira continued—betraying a hint of the nativism that helped shape Zimbabwean African national conscious-ness, particularly of the elite male variety—the lodger system had brought into the village "a large, rootless, mobile singlemen population, some of them immigrants from neighbouring territories." Many of these men were unem-ployed and made their livelihoods by gambling and stealing. As a solution to these problems, Shamuyarira urged the authorities to return to the principle of middle-class respectability by carefully screening prospective leaseholders, phasing out the lodger system, and increasing police patrols.[63]

But although a desirable ideal, getting rid of the lodgers, whose rent often amounted to more than half of the monthly house payment, was not a realistic option for many leaseholders. At the beginning, the mortgage and other ex-penses (that is, taxes, water, and sewage disposal) averaged around £3 7s. in Salisbury and slightly higher in Bulawayo. Leaseholders could legally take in up to two lodgers (and most of them appear to have exercised the option), with each lodger paying as much as £1 per month. Despite the added incomes, many leaseholders were still unable to make the monthly payments. In mid-1961, for instance, almost one thousand leaseholders in both villages were in arrears; of these, more than half were three months or more behind.[64] The highly racialized political economy ensured that the material basis of many, if not most, elite Africans was slender in the extreme. Indeed, there are indications that some of the partying blamed on lodgers was really surreptitious fundraising by desperate leaseholders.[65]

Normally, leaseholders in arrears were given written or verbal warnings; in extreme cases, the leasing agreement would be canceled and the account turned over to collection agencies. In at least one instance, though, the white superintendent at Bulawayo's Mpopoma, declaring that leaseholders "allowed themselves to be in arrears for several months for no apparent convincing reasons,"[66] resorted to more highhanded methods. He roused the delinquents from their sleep and marched them to his office for an explanation, leaving the aggrieved leaseholders feeling they had been treated "like prisoners."[67]

This was hardly the manner in which self-respecting elite Africans expected to be treated. By the late 1950s and early 1960s, no longer content to make polite protests, such frontal assaults to their personal dignity only helped drive them into the arms of the nationalist movement, which was now demanding African—a shorthand for black middle-class—rule. Thus both Salisbury's New Highfield and Bulawayo's Mpopoma became important nationalist strongholds, with the anticolonial forces gaining control of the leaseholders' associations.

The Southern Rhodesian African National Congress, the first mature Zimbabwean African nationalist movement, had its headquarters at New Highfield. In 1959, after the banning of the African National Congress, one member of the still all-white Legislative Council alleged that "a sort of Hyde Park corner has been set up [in New Highfield] where demagogues can harangue the crowds."[68] A few years later, the security minister described the village as a political "trouble spot of the worst possible order."[69] A good many of the troublemakers, such as Frank Ziyambe of Mpopoma,[70] and even Joshua Nkomo, president of the African National Congress,[71] had come up through the leaseholders' associations.

Yet Nkomo and Ziyambe, although both residents of Bulawayo, belonged to different leaseholders' associations. Almost two years before the central government announced its intention to build Mpopoma and New Highfield, the Bulawayo municipality, using funds from beer hall profits, had introduced a similar program for the city's African elite, although on a thirty-year leasehold basis. Nkomo was among the first individuals to take advantage of this offer, moving into the village of Pelandaba, which quickly became the address of choice for Bulawayo's black entrepreneurs and higher-income professionals.

From the standpoint of urban African life, the Bulawayo plan was the most significant breach of the Land Apportionment Act since its promulgation in 1930. The construction of Pelandaba and other villages by the Bulawayo municipality was an implicit renunciation of the segregationist fiction that Africans were temporary sojourners in the imaginary white city, thereby laying the basis for the central government's more ambitious ninety-nine-year leasehold scheme. Indeed, the latter's chilly reception by Bulawayo's elite Africans can be explained largely by the existing municipal alternative. To Africans in the colony's second city, another leasehold scheme, albeit one with a longer lease, was still leasing; it was no substitute for freehold tenure.

In fact, the Bulawayo municipal plan also was frowned on initially by the city's black middle class, one member of the township Advisory Board explaining that "many Africans were afraid of building only for 30 years because when the lease expired they would lose money."[72] As with the government-built village of Luveve almost two decades earlier, however, an acute housing shortage, along with the historic quest of elite Africans to leave the township, made a long-term boycott untenable.

Soon, Africans with more sophisticated architectural tastes, as well as the means to back them up, began complaining about the drabness and monotony of the houses built by the municipality. The result was the establishment of two new villages, Nkomo's Pelandaba and Pumula, where Africans were allowed to erect houses on plots leased from the city.[73] This was the first time since 1930 that Africans had been granted such a right, and it amounted to a return to the situation that existed before that time, but on a much grander scale.

Pelandaba proved especially attractive, emerging as the trendiest black community in Bulawayo, a place where wealthier Africans competed with one another to build the plushest and most lavishly furnished homes. By 1957, it had "attracted most of the City's leading [black] businessmen who have erected houses which compare favourably with any other houses in the poshest European suburbs of Bulawayo. Leading Africans too who are not businessmen have built their own houses there which have turned this township into one of the most beautiful African suburbs of Bulawayo."[74] In 1958, one couple built a ten-room house in Pelandaba, a far cry indeed from the usual way Africans were accommodated in the old municipal townships.[75]

Good suburbanites that they were, the residents of Pelandaba quickly developed a sense of social exclusiveness about their community. In 1960 they formed a "strong and determined" body of some three hundred souls to protect their property and community when rioting broke out in Bulawayo's poorer neighborhoods.[76] Earlier the village association—whose chairman boasted that there was no juvenile delinquency in Pelandaba and that even the police there were friendly—opposed the construction of beer halls on the grounds that it "would bring many undesirables to the Village who would start making mischief."[77] For some middle-class Africans, the joys of suburbia, along with its snobbishness, finally were becoming real.

In the early 1960s, the Pelandaba model was adopted by Salisbury, which established a similar municipal leaseholding scheme. The Salisbury village, called Mufakosi, had become a community of 2,290 homes by 1963.[78] With an average mortgage was £5 3s. 6d., it attracted only Africans of means. In addition to Mufakosi, two other leaseholding schemes were initiated in Salisbury in the years leading up to 1965, namely, Kambuzuma and Marimba Park, both run by the central government rather than the municipality.

Conceived with the economically weakest sections of the African middle class in mind, the houses at Kambuzuma were built in such a way as to easily facilitate the addition of new rooms. This feature, and the relatively low cost (£275 cash or £10 down payment and £1 16s. 8d. per month), ensured the rapid growth of this particular village, which mushroomed into a community of 1,464 dwelling units between 1963 and 1965. During this same period, only 182 new houses went up in the more upscale municipal village of Mufakosi, in sharp contrast to Kambuzuma.[79]

Within the Salisbury area, Mufakosi was eventually exceeded in exclusiveness by Marimba Park, the second government-run elite African housing scheme to be initiated in the 1960s. Established as a place where the most prosperous Africans could build their own houses on parcels of land varying in size from one to three acres, Marimba Park quickly became the poshest black community nationally. The houses in Marimba Park, one visiting British supporter of the 1965 rebellion declaimed, were "the most luxurious types of bungalows comparing very favourably with the best that can be found in England anywhere."[80] This was an exaggeration. Still, by this time Marimba Park had acquired a reputation as the sole African "luxury suburb" that was not surrounded by less fastidious communities and that, consequently, was the only place where the black middle class could "establish its own style of living."[81]

Thus by 1965, between the various national and municipal schemes, relatively decent housing had come within the grasp of most middle-class Africans in Salisbury and Bulawayo as well as in some of the smaller towns. In a few cases, the accommodations could even be described as luxurious. These new communities, most of which were located some distance away from what now became known as the "old townships," offered elite blacks a good deal of the spatial distance from the African working class they had so long craved. Increasingly, the middle class became more clearly differentiated from other Africans in terms of living arrangement and home life. Moreover, the development of community consciousness and the tendency of middle-class blacks to publicly emphasize the distinctions between themselves and other Africans demonstrate that the gap between the African elite and the African masses was cultural as well as material.

Despite these important advances, however, the African middle class still had grievances. In the first instance, the existence of the Land Apportionment Act continued to preclude full security of tenure: even the plushest houses in Marimba Park and Pelandaba were constructed on leased land. The corollary to these continued discriminatory practices was that Africans were barred altogether from living in the most luxurious areas of all, notably the white suburbs. Thus in 1959, when the government of the Federation of Rhodesia and Nyasaland made Jasper Savanhu a junior minister, the first African to attain that rank, it also announced plans to install him in a new house in New Highfield costing £8,000. This sum was well in excess of the value of most houses in the white suburbs, prompting one white liberal publication to comment that Savanhu's residence "will be about as much in place as a mustache on the Mona Lisa."[82] Indeed, white suburbanites felt sufficiently secure from a black invasion of their communities that they did not even bother to include Africans in the restrictive covenants that were aimed at Indians.[83]

For the Zimbabwean African middle class, the politics of constitutional protest had paid dividends, but they were limited, certainly in relation to what was happening elsewhere in Africa by the early 1960s. Agitation couched in the language of the equality of "civilized" people and appealing to British justice and fairness had been instrumental in ushering in the various leasehold schemes, among other things. But this uneasy compromise, which sought to balance the African demand for security of tenure with the settler determination to keep Rhodesia white, was seen by the black middle class as a temporary arrangement; it was no substitute for the ultimate goal of uncircumscribed freehold tenure in property, wherever one could afford it. And this goal, it was eventually concluded, could only be attained through a formal transfer of political power from the white ruling class to the fully emergent African elite. It is to this issue—the issue of the political construction of the African middle class—that we now turn.

The Political Construction of the African Middle Class

PART II

The Political Construction of
the African Middle Class

5

A New Beginning
The Roots of African Politics, 1914–1933

FROM AN ORGANIZATIONAL STANDPOINT, the emerging middle class in colonial Africa first announced its appearance in the realm of politics. Everywhere, protest movements of one kind or another marked the arrival of this social stratum as an articulate, corporate presence in society.[1] In this, as in other respects, Southern Rhodesia was no exception.[2] The two decades between 1914 and 1933, including the pivotal World War I era, were the formative period for the development of middle-class political consciousness and organization. Initially, elite Africans focused on their own class agenda, without much reference to the interests of the colonized workers and peasants. Then, in the mid-1920s, an alternate ideological tendency began to surface, a kind of insurgency within the elite. This emergent political current involved both continuity and discontinuity with the established paradigm. The newer tradition, like the older one, was championed by members of the black petty bourgeoisie, who generally supported the prevailing elite agenda. The insurgent forces represented rupture in that they went beyond the existing program by advocating an all-African political alliance across social and class lines—in short, a coalition of the entire colonized population.

THE SOUTH AFRICAN ANTECEDENTS

The first African protest movements in Southern Rhodesia were organized by black South Africans, a number of whom had assisted the white "pioneers" who established the colony in the 1890s. Other black South Africans subsequently immigrated to Rhodesia in search of land and other economic opportunities, which became increasingly scarce at home after the South African War of 1899–1902 and, especially, the creation of the Union of South Africa in 1910.[3]

In Southern Rhodesia, as in their land of origin, the black South Africans' quest for social mobility included, crucially, an emphasis on political organization of the protest variety.[4] Self-selected and upwardly mobile, the South Africans arrived in Rhodesia with a deep commitment to the modernization project, an embracement of bourgeois notions of progress as yet un-imaginable for the local Africans, who had been colonized much later. The resulting dichotomy formed the basis of a political movement centering on the cultural gap between the immigrant and indigenous African communities, with a corollary emphasis on the values that the black South Africans and the white settlers, many of whom also came from South Africa, shared. Inevi-tably, the contrast was articulated in terms of the usual binary oppositions—civilization and barbarism, Christianity and heathenism.

The Union Native Vigilance Organization, apparently the first modern-izing African political formation in the colony, represented the black South Africans. In 1914, when it seems to have been in existence for some time, the Vigilance Organization petitioned the government to exempt "advanced" Af-ricans from the pass laws—that is, the regulations that controlled the mobility and daily lives of African males in the urban centers and mining districts. In support of their request, the petitioners cited their "loyal service during the Matabele war of 1893, and the Rebellion of 1896," when many black South Africans sided with the white settlers and helped to suppress armed uprisings by indigenous Africans.[5] Thus did the South Africans establish the basis for middle-class black protest in Southern Rhodesia for decades to come: in re-turn for political loyalty to the colonial regime, elite Africans demanded, ide-ally, equality of rights and responsibilities with the white settlers. Alterna-tively, if compelled to operate within a segregationist framework, the black petty bourgeoisie insisted on treatment superior to that accorded the mass of colonized peasants and workers.

Indeed, the Union Native Vigilance Organization, which subsequently changed its name to the Union Bantu Vigilance Association—marking the onset of the names controversy and the identity crisis it denoted—apparently was the first organized body to elaborate an agenda for the African elite. Ever sensitive to the treatment of elite blacks by white society, the Vigilance Asso-ciation complained that the segregated waiting rooms at railway stations were "not designed for the use of civilised people" and suggested that Africans "of a superior and progressive class" should be better accommodated. The group further protested that imprisoned "educated" Africans—many of whom, like their uneducated counterparts, often fell afoul of the pass laws—were pro-vided only a "coarse hempen shirt," the attire worn by all black prisoners. "We natives from the South are accustomed to wear[ing] European clothing such as shirt, coat, trousers, socks and boots," the South Africans objected, re-questing "a differentiation between us and the raw native" in the matter of prison garb, as in other matters. Turning to the racist social conventions of Rhodesian settler society, the black South Africans took umbrage at having to remove their hats—a head gear not normally worn by "raw natives"—in public as a sign of respect to "All white people, of whatever class," some of whom "do not even acknowledge our salute."[6]

As the agitation over prison garb and the removal of hats indicates, the demands of the South African immigrants were both class- and gender-specific. The Union Bantu Vigilance Association, along with the more indigenous black political formations that supplanted it after World War I, was first and foremost a movement of elite males. The men of the African petty bourgeoisie, to be sure, had women-centered grievances. But the aspect of the "woman question" that most exercised the male-dominated black political leadership, whether immigrant or indigenous, was the "demoralization of native girls," that is, the perception that African women were beginning to assume control over their own sexuality and labor power. Thus the Vigilance Association strongly objected to the fact that African women, on reaching twenty-one, the age of majority, could marry under civil law "without their parents' permission, and engage themselves as servants without [parental] permission."[7] The group believed African women, regardless of social standing, should be perpetual minors, forever under the control of their fathers, husbands, or some other male guardian.

INDIGENOUS AND IMMIGRANT ELITES: THE SYNTHESIS

The wistful but apparently elusive quest to regain control over African women's bodies was certainly central to the mission of the Amandebele Patriotic Society. Established in Bulawayo in 1915, the Patriotic Society resulted from a split in another group, the Ilihlo Lomuzi Society, which apparently had been founded the previous year, when it began protesting police raids on the municipal beer hall, sweeps carried out to nab tax defaulters and pass offenders.[8] The Ilihlo Lomuzi Society and its Patriotic Society offshoot apparently were the first political associations to be founded and led, at least in part, by Africans indigenous to Southern Rhodesia, notably elite members of the Ndebele ethnic group, who joined forces with a number of black South Africans.

The Patriotic Society's principal concerns were prostitution, syphilis, and miscegenation, along with the "immoral" and "loose" African women who were blamed for these "social evils." In a rousing flyer announcing its formation, the Patriotic Society, whose alternative name was the Native Movement for the Suppression of Immorality, commanded, "Wake up! Wake up! Wake up! Mandebele." The announcement further proclaimed:

> Your people are in great danger of being wiped out. . . . The Christian law and the law of Msilikasi [the founding monarch of the Ndebele nation] are

being broken down by prostitution. Many of our old and young women are living on mines and [in] Town locations as prostitutes. . . . They have brought disgrace to our nation. The white people are despising us. . . . The judgement of God is upon us. How are we to break down and kill this evil[?] The A.P. Society will lead you to break it down by the help of the Almighty God.[9]

The Amandebele Patriotic Society, later rechristened the Loyal Mandebele Patriotic Society, "which represents a people loyal under the British flag"—an allusion to its support for the imperial power during World War I, which was then in progress[10]—proposed to stamp out prostitution through state repression. But suppressing whoredom would prove to be a daunting task, not least because of the promiscuous way in which elite African men tended to use the term. They deployed the derogative "prostitute" not merely against bona fide sex workers but also against any female resident of an urban center or mining district who, in their view, was not under the direct control of her husband, father, or some other appropriate male guardian.

Although exaggerated, the Loyal Mandebele Patriotic Society's preoccupation with controlling African women as well as its procolonial loyalist orientation were hardly original. Both had been derived from the Union Bantu Vigilance Association.[11] Indeed, the Patriotic Society's very existence denoted a major new development in the rise of the African middle class, namely, the onset of a fusion of the black South African immigrants and an African elite indigenous to Southern Rhodesia. This process, facilitated by missionary education, set the stage for the abatement and ultimate elimination of black South African particularism, social as well as political. Indeed, the prior claim of the black South Africans to social superiority, although articulated in the language of nationality, was really a class position. As such, it was only a matter of time before a critical mass of local Africans, the first products of the mission schools, emerged alongside the South Africans, as they pursued a mutual quest to rise to a higher level in a race-bound colonial order. The Patriotic Society, despite its apparent Ndebele ethnic specificity, was a political expression of this synthesis. Its leaders included individuals associated with the Union Bantu Vigilance Association, which, although formally remaining in existence until the early 1920s, was clearly being eclipsed by the era of World War I.[12]

Significantly, the process of political and social amalgamation commenced in the crucible of a war in which both the immigrant and indigenous elites were anxious to demonstrate their loyalty to imperial Britain. The most conspicuous evidence of elite African fealty during World War I was a fundraising campaign led by the Surprising Singers Association, a choral group conducted by Thomas Maziyane. Like other members of his class, the South African–born Maziyane, who also served as an officeholder in the Loyal Mandebele

Patriotic Society, desired to "encourage and increase the patriotic spirit of the Natives towards helping the sound cause of the British Empire in every way."[13]

Not all Africans, however, agreed that the British cause was worth supporting, at least not to the extent of risking life and limb. Accordingly, there was some resistance among the peasantry, and even among certain chiefs, to the recruitment of soldiers for the Rhodesia Native Regiment, which fought against the Germans in East Africa. The authorities, as they were wont to do, attributed the defiance to outside agitation, namely, enemy propaganda. Some officials pointed an accusing finger at Afrikaner farmers who had settled in Rhodesia and who were sympathetic to renegade Afrikaner military officers back home in South Africa; still resentful of the British from the South African War, these officers had mutinied over their government's decision to side with Perfidious Albion in World War I.[14] Other Rhodesian officials attributed signs of "pro-German" sentiment among Africans, including opposition to conscription, to the nefarious activities of German missionaries, who they believed had "very great facilities for spreading tales amongst the Natives."[15] The authorities were inclined to put stock in such alleged tales, especially after the revolt in Nyasaland in 1915 under the leadership of Baptist minister John Chilembwe, an event they feared could have a disturbing effect on the Rhodesian "native" mind.[16]

The wartime loyalty of the peasantry may have been suspect, but elite Africans, immigrant and indigenous alike, maintained their patriotic spirit until British arms had emerged victorious. Indeed, the integration of the two black elite groups deepened in the post–World War I era, with the South Africans bringing "their relatively sophisticated attitudes and techniques" to the resulting political alliance, as Terence Ranger noted.[17] Those attitudes and techniques were evident in the course of a campaign to establish a single administrative entity in Matabeleland under an Ndebele paramount chief, an initiative spearheaded by Nyamanda—the eldest son and presumed heir of the late King Lobengula, whose domain had been conquered by the colonialists in 1890s. Nyamanda's aims were hardly radical, stopping well short of advocating independence or ethnic secession. Like other paramount chiefs elsewhere in southern Africa, the head of the proposed Ndebele "homeland" would be politically subordinate to the existing colonial regime. Nyamanda's principal objective, rather, was to establish his own hegemony, as the embodiment of the deposed but still politically ambitious Ndebele royal family, over the new African politics then emerging in Matabeleland, as illustrated by the rise of the Loyal Mandebele Patriotic Society, which apparently did not survive the war as an organized body.

Consistent with the pattern of inter-elite political cooperation that had emerged during the war, including in the Patriotic Society, black South Africans were among those supporting Nyamanda's bid for "paramountcy" in Matabeleland. Besides providing crucial technical assistance, the South Africans established the channels for delivering to the British Colonial Office a petition addressed to the king of England, the major document produced by the Ndebele homeland movement.[18] As it happened, though, the imperial authorities in London, with characteristic dismissiveness, pronounced themselves unwilling to interfere in that particular aspect of the Rhodesian "native problem," scuttling Nyamanda's quest for political supremacy among the Ndebele. Triumphant, the Rhodesian authorities announced that they had uncovered the meddling hand of foreign agitation, rejecting the call for an Ndebele homeland as the handiwork of immigrant blacks, in alliance with their compatriots back in South Africa, rather than "a spontaneous production" of Matabeleland's indigenous people.[19]

IN DEFENSE OF THE NONRACIAL FRANCHISE: THE RHODESIA BANTU VOTERS ASSOCIATION

From the dust of Nyamanda's aborted ambitions came a new political project, the Rhodesia Bantu Voters Association (RBVA). Formally established in January 1923, the RBVA was linked to both Nyamanda's homeland movement and the Loyal Mandebele Patriotic Society through a number of black South Africans who played leading roles in all three formations, despite programmatic differences between them. Thus although continuing the loyalist tradition by pledging to "Honour the King" of England, the RBVA formally rejected the outward ethnic orientation of the other two groupings, its constitution mandating a program aimed at the "general uplift of the Bantus irrespective of tribe and status."[20] Consistent with this trans-ethnic and national goal—the first such goal in the history of African political organization in Southern Rhodesia—the founding RBVA executive included representatives from various parts of the country, especially the principal urban centers.

As the name suggests, the RBVA primarily was concerned with securing the franchise, and a number of penumbra rights, for elite Africans. Indeed, defending their right to vote on equal terms with the white settlers remained a cardinal objective of middle-class blacks down to the 1950s. That right had been granted under the proclamation announcing the Reform of 1898, a document that served as a sort of constitution for Southern Rhodesia. Without reference to race, the proclamation offered the vote to all males twenty-one years of age or older who met certain qualifications, namely, personal ownership of immovable property valued at £75 (which, significantly for Africans, excluded both cattle and communally owned land), or an annual income of £50, plus the ability to write one's name, address, and occupation in English.[21]

The Rhodesian settlers, however, strongly objected to a nonracial franchise of any kind, even one determined by wealth requirements that were continually increased to place them beyond the reach of most elite blacks, to say nothing of the mass of Africans, given the racially skewed distribution of income and property. Rejecting the social equality implied by a common franchise and seeking to guarantee perpetual white domination, the colonial regime began a campaign to disfranchise Africans almost as soon as the 1898 proclamation had been issued. As the top colonial administrator stated in 1906: "There is no doubt that [white] public opinion in this Territory is practically unanimous in condemning the grant to natives of any right to the franchise."[22] Despite such attitudes, Africans managed to retain the right to vote, but just barely; as late as 1948 there were only 258 blacks compared with approximately 48,000 whites on the voters roll.[23] The attempt to make blackness qua blackness a voting disqualification failed only because of imperial opposition, one of the few instances in which officials in London used their power of oversight to reject a measure proposed by the Rhodesian government.

Meanwhile, elite Africans vigorously defended the nonracial franchise, which they regarded as the epitome of British justice and fair play, in sum, as vindicating their mantra: equal rights for all civilized men. The RBVA, more than any other organization in the interwar years, eagerly joined the battle to preserve and expand African voting rights. Seeking to increase the number of black voters without challenging the principle of a property-qualified franchise, the RBVA proposed that Africans be allowed to "vote our live stock."[24] This proposal, which sought to remove the barrier excluding cattle as a factor in determining eligibility for the franchise, would have increased the number of eligible voters among a key RBVA constituency, notably, the small group of upwardly mobile black farmers who, unlike the mass of peasants living on communal land in the Reserves, owned property on a freehold basis.[25] The idea of Africans voting their livestock did not, unsurprisingly, appeal to the settler regime. Cynically turning the African elite's own trope against the RBVA, the prime minister, Charles Coghlan, asserted that any dilution of the franchise qualifications would "be at variance with the principle of equal rights for all civilised men and women."[26]

Rebuffed, some RBVA activists in Matabeleland abruptly switched tactics. They turned to the Reserves, areas previously ignored by the RBVA, stirring up resentment over a shortage of land and education, potent issues among the peasantry. The colonial authorities were dismayed by the RBVA's newfound populism, its attempt to conjoin the grievances of elite and mass, town and country. The chief native commissioner vowed to keep in close touch

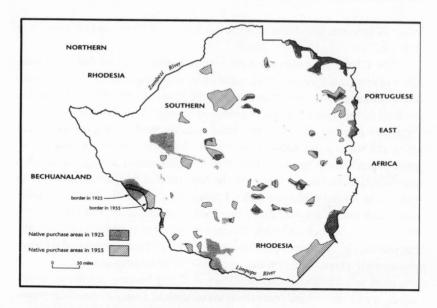

NORTHERN

RHODESIA

Zambezi River

SOUTHERN

PORTUGUESE

EAST

AFRICA

BECHUANALAND

border in 1925

border in 1955

Native purchase areas in 1925

Native purchase areas in 1955

0   50 miles

RHODESIA

Limpopo River

Native Purchase Areas

with its activities, while Prime Minister Coghlan lashed out at Martha Ngano, the RBVA's high-profile South African–born general secretary, the apparent architect of its populist "mass line," and perhaps the preeminent black female political figure in colonial Zimbabwe. Seemingly oblivious to the white-supremacist regime over which he presided, Coghlan railed against "sectional political associations," claiming that whenever a movement is based on race or color, "its potentiality for mischief is undoubtedly increased, in fact I detect the germs of such mischief in the present action of Martha Ngano, whoever she may be."[27]

The authorities need not have worried unduly, for the RBVA's populism was more apparent than real. Its mischief in the Reserves was aimed not so much at championing the grievances of the peasantry as in scaring the colonial regime by raising the specter of an all-African alliance across class lines, a potential cohesion the authorities could forestall by improving the lot of the black elite. This interpretation is supported by the fact that the RBVA's mass appeal, which turned out to be ephemeral, was not accompanied by any formal programmatic changes. Indeed, the association's traditional elite bias was reaffirmed at a conference in 1925, the year of its foray into the Reserves. Among other issues, the conference resolutions emphasized the need for greater investment in education; reaffirmed support for the black free-hold farmers; bemoaned drunkenness at the beer halls, institutions patron-ized largely by urban workers; and attacked miscegenation, "apt to cause what may well be called a white peril," a response to the racist "black peril" hysteria of the time.[28] With the exception of the demand for more and better education, which in any case had been part of the RBVA agenda since its foundation, these issues were largely unrelated to the mundane existence of most African peasants and workers. They were, first and foremost, elite concerns.

Nor did the RBVA's class-specific focus change much over time. Some four years after infuriating his predecessor with its populist appeals, the RBVA contacted the new prime minister, H. U. Moffat, seeking an audience with him. In addition to long-standing issues like education and the plight of the black freehold farmers, the association desired to discuss "special exemptions distinguishing registered voters from other Natives," as well as granting African voters the right to purchase "European" liquor and bear arms, rights then denied all blacks.[29] The RBVA leaders also solicited official support for a newspaper geared toward an African readership, in short, toward the black petty bourgeoisie.[30]

Although remaining faithful to its original elitist mission, the RBVA was beginning to decline by 1930, having suffered two important political setbacks. The first of these was the emergence in 1929 of the Matabele Home Society, an ethnic formation consisting of members of the Ndebele elite who resented what they perceived as black South African domination of the RBVA.[31] The Matabele Home Society directly challenged the RBVA in its regional base, for despite the rhetoric about becoming a national movement, the RBVA's activities largely had been confined to Matabeleland. Still reeling from the rise of the Matabele Home Society, the RBVA experienced a second reversal in 1930 with the death of Martha Ngano, its dynamic chief organizer.

Desperate to revive its flagging fortunes, the RBVA decisively shifted its center of gravity to Gwanda, a Reserve in Matabeleland, although normally the organization would have seen the Reserve as an unlikely venue for investment of the RBVA's diminishing political capital. The circumstances were far from normal, however, because Gwanda was the home of Rhodes Lobengula. A grandson of King Lobengula, the politically ambitious Rhodes had recently returned to Southern Rhodesia after completing his education in South Africa. By attracting the royal scion to its standard, the RBVA hoped to outflank the pro-royalist Matabele Home Society and refute the charge that it was a foreign element in the Rhodesian body politic, lacking organic ties to the colony in general and the Ndebele people in particular. Rhodes, for his part, sought the support of the RBVA in his desire to attain "a position of paramountcy" among the Ndebele, as one colonial official remarked disapprovingly. In attempting to resuscitate the campaign for an Ndebele "homeland" begun a decade earlier by his uncle, Nyamanda, Rhodes thus sided with the more venerable, if wobbling, RBVA against the upstart Matabele Home Society, which would later develop a penchant for meddling in the affairs of the often-contentious Ndebele royal family.[32]

Government officials, fearful of their own propaganda portraying the Ndebele as a warlike people—a "martial race," in the colonial jargon—moved swiftly to sever the ties between Rhodes and the RBVA, using the sanction of the purse. The colonial regime, which had paid for his education, strongly opposed an all-out effort to appoint Rhodes chairman of the RBVA Gwanda branch, threatening to cut off his royal stipend if he joined any political organization, a very powerful disincentive indeed at a time when the global capitalist depression was beginning to descend on Southern Rhodesia. Forced to choose between paramountcy and perquisite, the sybaritic Rhodes elected to jettison his putative allies. The RBVA had lost its high-stakes gamble. The failure to recruit Rhodes into its leadership ranks effectively marked the end of the RBVA as a force in Matabeleland, and certainly in national, politics. It limped on for a few more years, a shadow of its former self, before disappearing altogether after 1933.[33]

THE POLITICS OF ACCOMMODATION: THE SOUTHERN RHODESIA NATIVE ASSOCIATION

The RBVA's failure to break out of its Matabeleland stronghold and realize its national aspirations may be attributed to one overriding factor: a rival formation, the Rhodesia Native Association, already claimed Mashonaland, the colony's other and more populous province, as its base. Founded in 1919, the Rhodesia Native Association, which subsequently became the Southern Rhodesia Native Association (SRNA), represented the same class interests as those of the RBVA. The SRNA's constituency consisted of the African elite in the urban centers of Mashonaland, especially Salisbury, and their rural counterparts in the province's Purchase Areas, as the communities inhabited by the black freehold farmers would become known after the passage of the Land Apportionment Act of 1930, which formalized the system of territorial segregation.[34]

As with the RBVA, the Loyal Mandebele Patriotic Society, and Nyamanda's homeland movement, the SRNA's very existence was further proof of the growing fusion of the black South African elite and the newer indigenous African petty bourgeoisie. Although most of its supporters came from Mashonaland's ethnic Shona majority, the SRNA also commanded the allegiance of many non-Rhodesian Africans resident in the province. These included Eli Nare, the founding president of the SRNA and a former official of the Union Bantu Vigilance Association. Indeed, Rhodesian intelligence reported that the former association was a breakaway from the latter, Nare having been "asked by various natives in Salisbury," presumably indigenous Shona-speakers, to lead a secession from the black South African–dominated Vigilance Association.[35] Nare's two immediate successors as SRNA president, Johannes Mokwile and S. J. Matebese, also hailed from South Africa. It was not until 1928, almost a decade after its foundation, that an indigenous African, Abraham Chirimuta, ascended to the top position in the SRNA.

Although representing the same social forces and denoting similar historical processes, there were significant distinctions between the SRNA on the one hand and other contemporary African political formations, including the RBVA, on the other. Unlike the RBVA, with its foundational national creed, the SRNA initially represented itself as a regional movement, acquiring colony-wide ambitions only later in its existence. The SRNA also was widely seen, and saw itself, as more moderate than the other groups.[36] The SRNA, in the words of one of its top officeholders, had a "policy of trying to keep away from the agitators," a stance much appreciated by the authorities.[37] In a typical comment, the chief native commissioner lauded the SRNA as a "reputable organization," contrasting it to rival associations that "dabble in politics," that is, ones that openly criticized the colonial system.[38] The intelligence services confirmed that the SRNA did "nothing underhand[ed] or against the Government."[39] African critics agreed, deriding the SRNA as a club of " 'good boys' working for the Government to keep the Natives down."[40] As late as 1970 Charles Mzingeli, a noted foe of the SRNA during its heyday of the 1920s and the early 1930s, was still flaying the long-deceased body, claiming that its constitution had been written by government officials, an allegation with some foundation in fact.[41]

Reveling in its collaborationist reputation, the SRNA attempted to transform itself into a colony-wide movement through government fiat. The campaign for national prominence began in 1924, five years after the birth of the SRNA, when Johannes Mokwile assumed the presidency, vowing to erase its regional image and make it "truly representative of Rhodesian Natives" as a whole.[42] Accordingly, Mokwile brazenly recommended to the prime minister that since there was "only one Government," there should also only be one voice for expressing "Native opinion," and that the SRNA, if it had "attained to the consideration of the Government," should be officially recognized as that voice. The authorities politely turned aside the proposal to make the SRNA the sole legitimate representative of Africans in Southern Rhodesia, claiming they were averse to interfere in intra-African affairs "to the extent suggested by J. Mokwile."[43]

Undaunted, the SRNA then requested official assistance to organize branches throughout the colony, with an emphasis on the Reserves. Although admitting that it had "always been amenable to conditions imposed or suggested by the Government," the authorities gently but firmly rejected numerous attempts by the SRNA over several years to expand outside its base in the urban centers and the Purchase Areas. Inhabitants of the Reserves, officials countered, could communicate with the government through their chiefs and headmen, Africans who represented the colonial regime at the village and district levels and who also resented meddling by the SRNA and other formations of city slickers and self-styled civilized blacks, collaborationist or not.[44]

In any case, it is highly unlikely that the SRNA would have made much headway in the Reserves, even without government obstruction. Given its class-specific agenda, as well as its unwillingness to confront the colonial regime on matters of interest to them, the SRNA had little appeal to the land-hungry peasants. Rather, the SRNA's potential constituency in the Reserves consisted largely of the same individuals for whom it spoke in the urban centers and Purchase Areas, that is, teachers, preachers, and others members of the aspiring African middle class whose jobs required them to live in the Reserves or on mission stations, which were generally surrounded by the Reserves.

Despite its deferential attitude toward the government, then, the SRNA conceded nothing to the other, more independent-minded black political formations when it came to championing the cause of elite Africans, rural and urban. The SRNA's agenda included defending the nonracial franchise; petitioning for special rights for African voters, such as exemption from the pass laws and legal access to "European" liquor; ensuring the economic viability of the Purchase Areas; requesting better-quality attire for all "civilized" black prisoners; and expanding education, horizontally as well as vertically, a project crucial to the intergenerational mobility strategies of the black elite. The SRNA also called for an official inquiry into the meager salaries of the "better class" of urban African employees who bore the burden of having to acquire "clothing and other necessities which [their] standard of civilisation demands." To avoid any confusion about the class character of this proposal, the resolution added: "of course we are not advocating that ordinary labourers should receive the same consideration. It would be impossible."[45]

As much as anything, though, the SRNA sought to control African women, an undertaking it pursued more zealously than any movement discussed so far, with the possible exception of the more obscure and short-lived Loyal Mandebele Patriotic Society. The need to clamp down on "loose" and "wayward" women was the most consistent and prominent theme in the SRNA's multi-pronged agenda. "The subject of the womanhood of our people is so important that one would like to awaken your noblest instincts in consideration of it," the SRNA informed the authorities, with uncharacteristic rhetorical flourish.[46] Indeed, no fewer than five of the eight items discussed at the association's 1927 conference centered on the woman question. Among other things, the SRNA wanted legislation to punish adulterous women (but not men) and prohibit women from initiating divorce; to expel alleged prostitutes from the towns and mining centers and require cohabiting couples in those areas to show proof of marriage; to replace male attendants in the women's wards of the segregated black hospitals with female ones; to prohibit the greeting of women "in public by men unknown to them in the most offensive terms," that is, to bar men from making passes at women; and to prevent women from "loitering" in shops, beer halls, and other public places or from gathering outside their homes in "big mobs chatting" with men.[47] The SRNA leaders even wanted to legislate women's fashion, inquiring of the government: "Can any action be taken to make native girls wear longer skirts? The present clothing makes us ashamed."[48]

The SRNA's attempts to control the behavior of African women in both the private and public spheres spoke volumes about the anxieties of the urban-dwelling elite males it represented. The settled family life to which these men aspired, a domestic ideal based on the Victorian model of their missionary mentors, was subverted daily and in ways large and small in the segregated colonial city, reflecting a society in which race was a far more important determinant of class than education, ability, or achievement. Under this system, Africans in the urban centers, elite and proletarian alike, were consigned to the same squalid townships. For elite men, the material and social deprivations of township life—the poor and cramped housing, the lack of privacy, the crowded water stands in the street, the abominably unsanitary conditions— were exacerbated by a serious gender imbalance skewed heavily according to class. Whereas many elite men lived in households with their wives and children, the great majority of township residents were "unattached" male workers, bachelors or married men whose wives and children remained in the countryside, either in Southern Rhodesia or in neighboring colonial territories.[49]

These men, the urban working class, formed the backdrop against which the SRNA elaborated its position on the woman question. The SRNA's attack on "prostitutes" and the concomitant demand that cohabiting couples be legally married were directed at a floating female population in the urban centers (as well as those on the mines and commercial farms),[50] women who had been cut from their moorings in the countryside as a result of land dispossession and the massive out-migration of men. With few prospects in a formal economy dominated by male labor, including the domestic-service sector, the female migrants survived as best they could in the city. They carved out a niche in the informal sector by illicitly selling homemade beer, performing domestic chores for "unattached" men, and making informal living arrangements of various duration with these same men.[51]

The activities of these "loose" women, along with those of their male customers and consorts, provoked the wrath of the SRNA. Such women, the SRNA leaders believed, debased respectable womanhood as embodied by their wives and daughters, and should be sent back to the countryside. Respectable women in search of health care, the SRNA maintained, also needed protection from the prurient gaze of male orderlies, the kind of men who be-friended loose females and bought their beer. As depicted by the SRNA, these male workers spent their free time prowling the streets, loitering in the shops, and drinking themselves into a stupor, all the while leering, ogling, and whis-tling at female passersby, oblivious to the distinction between respectable women and the "loose girls" whose abbreviated hemlines scandalized mod-est men. "Unattached" men, the elite males complained, "do not respect an-other's wife and are unduly familiar with married women."[52] The complain-ants would have agreed with the SRNA that the law should severely punish married women who succumbed to seductive temptations. This, however, was a seemingly superfluous proposal, because such acts of self-defilement were virtually inconceivable to the God-fearing and club-joining wives of elite men —a level of moral rectitude not always matched by their husbands.[53]

The SRNA, in short, painted a picture of an urban township swarm-ing with a dangerous class of Jezebel-like women and their male enablers. These individuals were further represented as posing a clear and present dan-ger to home and hearth, a menace to the bourgeois lifestyle sought by elite men, an important aspect of which was the ability to control the sexuality of their wives. No wonder the male-dominated African middle class fought so long and hard to escape the townships. Among other anxieties, its members dreaded the potentially explosive combination of liquor and libido, even if an actual detonation at home was extremely unlikely.[54]

A RADICAL REPRISE: THE INDUSTRIAL AND COMMERCIAL WORKERS UNION OF AFRICA

The SRNA's distrust of the dangerous class powerfully determined its re-action to a movement that burst onto the Rhodesian political scene in the second half of the 1920s—the Industrial and Commercial Workers Union of Africa (ICU). Founded in Cape Town in 1919, the same year as the SRNA, the ICU was the first African-initiated labor formation in southern Africa, bespeaking a regional and continental renaissance in consciousness and mo-bilization in the aftermath of World War I.[55] Proceeding along the migrant labor trail, the ICU expanded into the urban centers, mining districts, and ru-ral areas of southern Africa, attracting not just laborers but also sharecrop-pers, peasants, and even the more radical sections of the African petty bour-geoisie.[56]

It was this populist phenomenon that formally established a branch in Southern Rhodesia in 1926, although its impact had previously been felt in the colony. There were some significant differences between the leaders of the Rhodesian ICU and their SRNA (and RBVA) counterparts, beginning with life experiences. Whereas most of the SRNA's top men evidently led settled

family lives, whether in the cities or Purchase Areas, a good many of the leading ICU stalwarts were unattached men. Frequently, the Rhodesian ICU activists had done stints of employment in South Africa, perhaps even in Cape
Town, their movement's headquarters and the center of post–World War I
black radicalism in southern Africa. Significantly, too, some of these men
came from Nyasaland, the native country of both the ICU's founder, Clements Kadalie, and a large segment of Southern Rhodesia's working class. By
contrast, the Rhodesia-born leaders of the SRNA were less likely to have lived
abroad, whereas those of South African origin had settled permanently in the
colony, in most cases as family units. Playing to a nascent nativism with an
especially strong anti-Nyasaland bent, the SRNA, hailed by colonial officials
as "purely Rhodesian,"[57] denounced the ICU activists as alien provocateurs.
The SRNA, which forbade its members from joining the rival group on pain
of expulsion, also urged the authorities to ban the ICU for "mislead[ing] the
natives of Southern Rhodesia."[58]

The animus was driven by organizational rivalry and by the SRNA's penchant for taking its cue from the government, which strongly opposed the
ICU, attacking its operatives as "agitators . . . from the Union of South Africa
[who] are endeavouring to import into our Colony the Union atmosphere."[59]
The SRNA leaders, however, were not just being opportunistic in assailing the
ICU; they were genuinely alarmed by its populist appeals, its self-proclaimed
"proletarian" style, and its genuflections to the working class. Consider the illicit female beer brewers, the skokiaan queens, named after the concoction
they made. The SRNA, as we have seen, placed these women at the center of
a web of licentiousness and degeneracy entangling the urban townships. The
ICU, by contrast, offered the women aid and comfort. Thus Charles Mzingeli,
the ICU leader in the SRNA's Salisbury stronghold, having been sent there
from Bulawayo, openly supported illicit beer brewing. As he told an audience
of male workers: "The White people prohibit [beer brewing by the skokiaan
queens]. . . . They [the white people] are Robbers. They arrest you and will not
let the women make a few shillings."[60] Similarly James Mabena, an ICU stalwart in Bulawayo, the movement's Rhodesian headquarters, "considered it reasonable . . . that women [brewers] should be allowed to earn a little money so
as to buy necessities."[61] To the SRNA leaders—who saw the skokiaan queens
as veritable "centres of vice," as a commission appointed by the government
would later put it[62]—such assertions gave political legitimacy to the nefarious
activities of the dangerous class.

The furor of the SRNA and its government patron was not entirely misplaced. The ICU did indeed represent a destabilizing force in Rhodesian politics, departing significantly from the established modes of protest among Africans. Hitherto, the political formations would present their grievances in an
orderly manner: through petitions, deputations, and meetings that adhered to

proper parliamentary decorum. The RBVA, admittedly, had ventured beyond these bounds by appealing to the peasantry, but that was a fleeting exercise, limited in both time and space. The ICU, by contrast, pioneered mass politics in Southern Rhodesia, introducing African urban-dwellers, and less frequently those in the countryside also, to a novel political drama: mass meetings complete with withering critiques of aspects of the colonial regime, if not actual indictments of colonialism as a system. "You are still slaves in Africa—you have no one to represent you in Parliament," Masotsha Ndhlovu, the top ICU leader, announced in a typical broadside delivered at a mass meeting.[63]

Consistent with its self-representation as a union, the ICU took a keen interest in the material and social conditions of urban workers, in sharp contrast to the other political formations. The ICU leaders, who sometimes addressed one another by the proletarian honorific "comrade," offered their working-class audiences a sharp and pithy explication of both the wealth of nations and the theory of surplus value. "The wealth of the country comes from yours and my trousers pockets," one speaker averred. "We do not draw wages. We get 20/-a month, and after we have paid rent what is left?"[64] The ICU did not just denounce substandard wages, however. Among other things, it condemned the neglect of the townships by the white city fathers, assailed police harassment, including incessant checking of passes by officers, and denounced police operations against suspected tax defaulters and pass-law offenders. The ICU, in short, presented itself as a movement seeking to advance the cause of workers both within and outside the workplace. As one speaker gushed: "We are the reformers who can assist you. The I.C.U. stands for all workers. I include the Police who have to patrol the lanes in their bare feet for a few pounds a month."[65] Indeed, at least one African detective—the people who spied on the organization for the government, unwittingly enriching historical research in the process—lost his job because of his membership in the ICU.[66]

Yet for all its militancy and fiery oratory, the ICU's radicalism, or to be more precise, its proletarianism, should not be overstated. Although positioned well to the left on the spectrum, the ICU's rupture with the prevailing black political opinion was anything but complete. Terence Ranger, in his pioneering study of African politics in Southern Rhodesia, told only a partial truth when he described the ICU as a "radical working man's organization, critical of the timidity of the elite."[67] That the ICU sided with the working class and disparaged the petty bourgeoisie for its pusillanimous behavior is beyond question. What has generally been ignored, however, is the extent to which the ICU's agenda converged with that of more full-throttled elite formations like the SRNA and the RBVA.[68] Politically, if not always socially, the ICU represented continuity as much as it did discontinuity with the program of the emerging African middle class.

The ICU, like the other formations, supported the preservation and extension of the qualified nonracial franchise. In the late 1920s, when the Bulawayo municipality ordered the destruction of some of the private homes in the township and banned the construction of new ones, the ICU rushed to the defense of the beleaguered African homeowners, a category that included few workers. Much more vigorously than did the other groups, which took the same position, the ICU championed African entrepreneurship, calling for the replacement of Indian traders in the Bulawayo township with African ones and even making an abortive attempt to open its own business. Education, too, figured prominently on the ICU agenda, and its spokesmen often appeared at the same forums with other (elite) Africans interested in the subject, demanding more schools and better-qualified teachers.

Indeed, but for their South African–inspired rabble-rousing and apparently greater incidence of domestic "unattachment," the leading figures in the ICU may well have been mistaken for full-fledged members of the emerging African middle class. With the noticeable exception of Purchase Area farmers, those who held forth at ICU meetings, that is, clerks, salesmen, and teachers, differed little professionally from the leaders of the SRNA and the RBVA. Academically, the leaders of all three groups appear to have been roughly equal, if facility with the colonial language, as demonstrated in their respective correspondence, is any guide. Ultimately, the ICU distinguished itself from the more elite-bound formations not so much by its proletarianism as its populism, that is, a political agenda that incorporated the grievances and aspirations of all Africans, elite as well as mass.

In accordance with its attempts to build an all-African alliance across class lines, the ICU, although primarily an urban movement, also took an interest in the rural sector, with the peasantry commanding a greater share of its attention over time. In fact, the ICU's rupture with the other formations, and its rejection of certain core principles of Rhodesian settler society, was more thoroughgoing on the agrarian question than it was on the labor question. The ICU, perhaps most crucially, opposed the Purchase Area system. Trumpeted by the colonial regime as a quid pro quo for territorial segregation, the Purchase Areas were embraced not just by "progressive" black farmers but also by urban-dwelling elite Africans, who were prohibited from owning real property in the white city and who therefore sought land elsewhere as a means of social security.[69]

The ICU's opposition to the Purchase Area scheme extended to that most sacrosanct of Rhodesian settler legislations, the Land Apportionment Act, which legally enshrined territorial segregation, of which the Purchase Areas were an integral part. Speaking in the Matabeleland countryside, where the ICU concentrated its rural efforts, Masotsha Ndhlovu blasted the most obvious signs of the enclosure suffered by Africans: "We must have land. This was our country once. Why is it divided by fences?"[70] It is a testament to the perceived effectiveness of its propaganda, although not necessarily to its actual impact, that the chief native commissioner lambasted the ICU for turning Africans against the Purchase Areas. Clearly inflating their powers of persuasion, the official accused ICU emissaries of influencing the Ndebele people more "than anyone else [on the Purchase Area scheme], because they openly advised Natives not to buy land, which they alleged already morally belongs to them. The result has been that, while a large number of plots have been acquired by Natives in various parts of Mashonaland, there is very little demand for land in Matabeleland."[71] Actually, the greater poverty of the Ndebele, who had lost more land to colonial predations than had the Shona-speakers, along with the infertility of the Purchase Areas in Matabeleland compared with those in Mashonaland, were far more important determinants of Ndebele land-purchasing practices than were any promptings by the ICU.[72]

As the exaggerated portrayal of its influence on African cultivators suggests, the colonial regime considered the ICU a real threat, far more so than any other political formation. The ICU, consequently, faced an unprecedented level of surveillance, harassment, and outright persecution, the likes of which would not be seen again for some thirty years, until the rise of mature African nationalism in the late 1950s and early 1960s. According to the chief native commissioner, the ICU had created a "Hyde Park"–type atmosphere in which "contempt and hatred of white men, and government of white men, are sedulously taught."[73] The authorities knew so much about the ICU's activities because few of its meetings, even in the countryside, were free of police surveillance. The police also intercepted the correspondence of ICU activists, a sleuthing expedition joined by some private citizens. Thus under the heading "Typical Native Mentality," a Salisbury weekly published a letter from Charles Mzingeli to Masotsha Ndhlovu, a missive the white editor claimed he had "found."[74]

The authorities did not just gather intelligence on the ICU; they used the information they gathered against it. Government employees, although apparently free to join other political formations (especially the SRNA) without being victimized, were dismissed for belonging to the ICU. The most famous casualty of this policy was Thomas Mazula, the ICU chairman who for three years doggedly, if unsuccessfully, contested his termination as a government clerk, finally taking his case to the Anti-Slavery and Aborigines Protection Society, the London-based reformist group that took an interest in colonial matters.[75] And whereas ICU activists indigenous to Southern Rhodesia and employed by the state could expect dismissal, their counterparts from Nyasaland were branded as foreign agitators and deported. When all else failed, the authorities resorted to judicial repression. In one particularly busy and successful day, prosecutors obtained convictions against three ICU activists—

Mzingeli in Salisbury and Ndhlovu and one Mtelo in Bulawayo—who were found guilty of defaming and slandering colonial officials.[76] Faced with such an onslaught, Ndhlovu consoled himself and his comrades with the thought that they were not alone. Apparently convinced that history would absolve the ICU, Ndhlovu, now an official Zimbabwean hero, his remains resting triumphantly at the National Heroes' Acre burial site, informed an audience: "Reformers are always persecuted. . . . If a man tries to fight for a righteous principle, he is sent to goal."[77]

The colonial regime, however, did more than persecute the ICU. Assuming the reformist mantle, although one quite different from Ndhlovu's, the authorities proposed to distract the ICU's potential audience through social amelioration: by building soccer fields and swimming pools in the townships. As one official put it, the ICU attracted individuals with "spare time on their hands and with no recreation other than idle chatter." Attributing the ICU's appeal to theatrics, the government, this official continued, could reclaim the stage by producing a better show: "One would hear but little of the 'loafer' were recreation provided, and the I.C.U. would have but little chance of attracting a crowd when in competition with a football match."[78] The chosen instrument for seizing control of workers' leisure time from the ICU was the Native Welfare Society. A privately run group that received limited government subsidies, the Native Welfare Society was established in the ICU's Bulawayo redoubt in 1929, around the same time that official ruminations about organized recreation began. Led by government officials, missionaries, businessmen, and assorted other white "friends of the natives," the Native Welfare Society, which advertised itself as "an insurance against 'trouble,'" would later open branches in other urban centers.[79]

As the leadership of the Native Welfare Society attests, the government's battle against the ICU enjoyed wide support in the white settler community. At one point the Bulawayo municipality went so far as to prohibit ICU leaders from holding committee meetings at their city-owned places of residence, only lifting the ban after strong protest by the ICU, including a threat of legal action.[80] The ICU activists in Bulawayo were also denied access to the city-operated beer hall and the missionary-run churches in the township, institutions that opened their doors to less objectionable political formations with business to conduct. As a result the ICU, in a literal demonstration of its outside-agitator status, repaired to the beloved indaba tree, a big tree under which township residents gathered to socialize and pass the time. Yet although charming and useful for reaching the masses—serving as something of the government's dreaded "speakers' corner"—the indaba tree was no substitute for a real building, especially during the rainy and cold seasons. The ICU's inability to find a suitable meeting place no doubt influenced its demand for a community recreation center, a call the city eventually heeded in 1936, af-

ter the ICU had left the political stage, building the facility on the site of
the indaba tree and calling it Stanley Hall, after the then governor, Herbert
Stanley.

THE PROTO-NATIONAL MOMENT: A WIDENING RADICAL CIRCLE

The colonial regime found the ICU all the more threatening because it
doubled as the fountainhead of a wider radical circle, the vanguard of what
might be called a proto-national moment in colonial Zimbabwean history. The
ICU, along with a number of allied organizations with interlocking leader-
ships, shaped and defined this moment. Chronologically, the proto-national
moment lasted from about 1926 to 1933, the crucial period being 1928 to 1931.
Geographically, the proto-national moment was centered in, although by no
means was it confined to, the city of Bulawayo. A major gateway and transportation hub of the regional economy, Bulawayo also served as a kind of underground clearinghouse for ideological commerce between Africans throughout
the southern African subcontinent. Politically, the proto-national moment
stands out as a period of sustained critique of the colonial project, a critique
that, although not formally repudiating foreign rule, seriously questioned the
legitimacy of the racially determined status quo. The denunciation of colonialism was accompanied by a search for countervailing ideas and alternate
modes of organization—political and religious—that would unite Africans in
Southern Rhodesia across the barriers of class, ethnicity, and nationality and
even bring them into a wider pan-African confraternity.

Yet the rise in radical consciousness and mobilization, although deeply
rooted among a determined band of activists, was not generic to the African
elite as a whole. The most prominent members of the African petty bourgeoisie, especially those aligned with the Southern Rhodesia Native Association,
disassociated themselves from the attacks on the colonial regime, with some
of them even abetting the government's repression of the radicals associated
with the proto-national moment. It is precisely this lack of political consensus
among elite blacks that made the moment proto-national rather than national.
A more fully formed African national moment would eventually come to
Southern Rhodesia, but it would come a generation later, and under different
political and social circumstances.

The onset of the proto-national moment may be dated from the formal
arrival of the ICU on Rhodesian soil. This happened in February 1926 when
the South African ICU, regarding Southern Rhodesia as a "legitimate sphere
wherein to extend its activities," appointed Robert Sambo as its agent for the
colony and charged him with establishing a network in Bulawayo, where he
worked, "and in adjacent centres."[81] At the time of his appointment, Sambo, a

Nyasalander who had been in Rhodesia for some seven years, was assistant general secretary of the Southern Rhodesia Native Welfare Association, an organization previously known as the Gwelo Native Welfare Association, after the town in which it was headquartered. Aware that his new position with the ICU would raise the issue of foreign agitation, Sambo preemptively and disingenuously assured the authorities of his loyalty. Using the metaphor of naval warfare, he solemnly pledged not to "sail [his ICU] ship under a false colour" to torpedo the "battle ship" of the Rhodesian state, emphasizing his ties to the Native Welfare Association, which he characterized as a "pure[ly] local organization having nothing to do with outside movements."[82]

Sambo, however, protested too much. The police, who had him under surveillance, knew otherwise. Covertly, his purloined correspondence showed, Sambo denounced the colonial regime as a "great enemy" and solicited external, notably African American, support for the ICU's struggle against "white capitalists" who exploited Africans "to their selfish ends."[83] Despite Sambo's assertion that it was a wholly indigenous movement, the police would also have known that the Native Welfare Association—not to be confused with the previously mentioned and white-controlled Native Welfare Society—was little more than an ICU front. In fact, the Native Welfare Association's founder, Daniel "Fish" Gwebu, was himself a key facilitator of the proto-national moment.

Before establishing the Native Welfare Association, Gwebu had lived and worked in Cape Town, where he cut his teeth politically. In 1924, while employed as a waiter at a Cape Town hotel, he corresponded with the Rhodesian authorities about his plans to return home, seeking their consent to establish a branch of Marcus Garvey's Universal Negro Improvement Association (UNIA), the foremost international black movement of the post–World War I era.[84] When the Rhodesian authorities refused to give their blessings to his UNIA project, Gwebu requested permission to form a branch of the African National Congress of South Africa, but the officials again withheld approval. Gwebu's reason for seeking government endorsement of his proposed political schemes is unclear. Perhaps he wanted to allay the fears of the colonial regime, in deference to its xenophobic concerns about outside agitation. More likely, though, Gwebu sought official consent because he thought it was required. In fact, such a requirement applied only to religious groups seeking to establish educational institutions, not to political organizations.[85]

Whatever his reason for contacting them, Gwebu did not take kindly to the authorities' negative responses. Thinking a ban was in place, he angrily rejected the government's right to veto an African political venture, claiming that he had already recruited some two hundred prospective members of an African National Congress of South Africa cell and emphasizing that they were all "Natives of Rhodesia," as if to forestall the charge of foreign interference. As Gwebu informed the chief native commissioner, he was determined to "org[anize] our people man & women of the Black Race in Africa[;] we must be free man & women here kindly Sir."[86]

Gwebu returned to Southern Rhodesia sometime in 1925, his homecoming apparently hastened by the death of his father, an Ndebele chief, whom he succeeded. Far from dampening his political ardor, however, Gwebu's new position as a cog in the Native Affairs bureaucracy only seemed to strengthen his resolve to liberate the "black race in Africa." The Southern Rhodesia Native Welfare Association, which he formed as a substitute for the UNIA or the African National Congress of South Africa, became a political sanctuary for the ICU's future leadership, including Sambo, who was expelled from the colony in mid-1927, with the fallout from his expulsion reaching as far as the British parliament.[87] Masotsha Ndhlovu, who replaced Sambo as head of the Rhodesian ICU, also was directly linked to Gwebu, having begun his career as a political activist in Southern Rhodesia by joining "the Welfare under Fish Gwebu." Ndhlovu previously worked in Cape Town before returning home "with an ardent nationalist spirit, having got the inspiration from South Africa," just like Gwebu before him.[88]

Gwebu's role as political broker of the proto-national moment did not go unnoticed by the colonial regime. His paymasters in the Native Affairs Department accused him of seeking to make a "cat's-paw . . . [of] law-abiding and well-affected" fellow chiefs, warning that he was "treading a perilous path."[89] Gwebu apparently paid little attention to such admonitions, persisting in his longtime mission to set the African captives free, an offense for which he was at length banished from his ancestral area and forced to resettle elsewhere in the colony. He was, in other words, sent into internal exile.[90]

The proto-national moment, although rooted in the specific circumstances of Rhodesian settler colonialism, was deeply influenced by events taking place throughout the black Atlantic, including South Africa—as the cases of Gwebu, Ndhlovu, and Sambo suggest. In this way, the proto-national moment became something of a pan-African moment as well. Mention has already been made of Sambo's appeal for African American solidarity against Rhodesian racial capitalism as well as Gwebu's interest in the UNIA, which he privileged over the African National Congress of South Africa as a political vehicle when he decided to return home from Cape Town. Actually, the switch from the UNIA to the African National Congress was merely a political ploy used by Gwebu to bypass the disapproval of the Rhodesian authorities. In his mind, the two were interchangeable not just with one another but also with the ICU. During Gwebu's residence in Cape Town, the local branches of all three organizations, which collectively formed his frame of political reference, had been fused into one broad movement under the leadership of the same person—James Thaele, a United States–educated activist and the leading Garveyite in South Africa.[91]

The Rhodesian ICU was associated not just with Garveyism but also with Ethiopianism, the independent African Christian movement that began in South Africa in the late nineteenth century and subsequently spread to other parts of the subcontinent, including Southern Rhodesia. The Ethiopianist formation most deeply involved in the proto-national moment was the African Orthodox Church. Founded in New York in 1921 by a former chaplain-general of the UNIA, the African Orthodox Church projected itself as a religious umbrella for black members of the Anglican and other Catholic-oriented Protestant communions globally. Throughout the pan-African world, the single most important source of news about the emerging African Orthodoxy was the *Negro World,* official organ of the UNIA.[92]

In the late 1920s, an African Orthodox congregation was established in Bulawayo under the leadership John Mansell Mphamba and Dick Dube, ardent Garveyites and ICU activists who took their politics as seriously as they took their religion, if they made a distinction at all. Indeed, Dube readily admitted that his interest in African Orthodoxy was driven by political motives, and he professed little interest in theology as such. Inquiring about correspondence courses offered by the head of the African Orthodox Church in South Africa, Dube noted that his principal concern was in "studying . . . [the] problem of the race . . . so as to [en]able [me] to organize my people under the name [of the UNIA and] African Communities League." As if to demonstrate the organizational permeability that was a hallmark of the proto-national moment, he further asserted that he previously had been in direct contact with the UNIA headquarters in New York, "but it was very hard that time for [the] C.I.D. was troubling us because [it] did not [want the] I.C.U. in this country."[93]

The authorities, who saw the African Orthodox Church and the ICU for the interlocking bodies that they were, harassed the one as much as they did the other. Seeking to cripple the church institutionally, they prevented it from establishing schools and refused to license its ministers as marriage officers, hoping to make it less attractive to those in search of education or desiring to marry by civil (read Christian) rites, that is, the aspiring African elite. As with the ICU, the colonial regime also persecuted the African Orthodox Church through deportation, a treatment meted out to John Mansell Mphamba, the top-ranking church leader.[94] Whereas Sambo—a fellow Nyasalander, ICU activist, and deportee—had masked his opposition to the regime behind feigned expressions of loyalty, Mphamba publicly and lustily denounced colonialism. Assessing the long chain of racial, social, and religious oppression, he found a common link—economic exploitation. As he asserted at an ICU meeting: "First the white man brought the Bible, then he brought guns, then chains, then he built a goal, then he made the native pay tax. Were they told to do this in the Bible? Why does the white man want all this? It is because the white man wants more money. He can make money with machinery, he gets money out of the ground, he makes paper and turns it into money. The white man does not want to give the natives money. Join together and *keep on knocking* —you will win in the end."[95] In a fitting tribute, Mphamba has been immortalized in modern Zimbabwe, albeit in a rather different way from Ndhlovu, his ICU comrade turned national hero. Words from the above speech—"keep on knocking"—now proudly adorn the title of an edited volume that resulted from an oral history project conducted by Zimbabwe's leading labor federation, an undertaking that amounted to a declaration of intellectual independence from the elite-centered and celebratory nationalist historiography favored by the postcolonial dominant class.[96]

Although the most politically daring, the African Orthodox Church was not the only body that gave the proto-national moment an Ethiopianist flavor. The African Methodist Episcopal (AME) Church also formed part of the organizational and ideological smorgasbord that characterized the period. Founded in the early nineteenth century by African Americans protesting racism in white-dominated denominations in the United States, the AME Church entered the South African missionary field in the 1890s, yoked to the local Ethiopianist movement.[97] African Methodism, in turn, arrived in Southern Rhodesia with the black South African immigrants.

By the end of World War I, the Rhodesian AME Church, under the leadership of the Rev. Micah Makgatho, a South African immigrant, had become a source of consternation to the colonial regime, not least because of Makgatho's involvement in Nyamanda's attempt to establish an Ndebele homeland.[98] The onset of the proto-national moment only increased the level of anxiety among the authorities, who could begin to see the outlines of a more radical, ICU-aligned Ethiopianism. To begin with, the watchdogs of colonialism must have been concerned about the activities of Zachariah Makgatho, Micah's son. A former secretary of the Union Bantu Vigilance Association, Zachariah was one of the most remarkable and enduring figures during the formative decades of African politics in Southern Rhodesia, making a smooth transition from the diasporic South African particularism of the Union Bantu Vigilance Association to the more all-inclusive black elite consensus of the post–World War I era. He became an ICU sympathizer soon after the group established its Rhodesian base.[99] More ominously, the apparent death of Micah Makgatho in the period between the collapse of Nyamanda's homeland bid and the arrival of the ICU created what the authorities would have regarded as a dangerous vacuum within the AME Church. As a layman, the populist-oriented Zachariah could not formally replace his father, but succession by a like-minded ordained minister, perhaps in cahoots with the younger Makgatho and others of his ilk, remained a distinct possibility. The evidence suggests that the government deliberately set out to preempt such an outcome. By launching a counterattack on the kind of politically engaged Ethiopianism represented by the Makgatho pair, the authorities hoped to break the emerging radical circle, or at least keep African Methodism out of it.

Hitherto, the colonial regime had not directly interfered in the internal affairs of the AME Church, using instead more conventional measures to contain it. Thus the policy requiring independent African religious movements to obtain special permission to establish schools, a policy that did not apply to white-controlled denominations, had been established specifically with Micah Makgatho in mind. At the same time, the authorities also placed the "strictest surveillance . . . over Maghatho [sic] and his disciples."[100] The government had not, however, attempted to undermine the church from within—until the advent of the proto-national moment.

Before 1927, when the colonial regime embarked on its campaign of subversion, the Rhodesian AME Church existed in an ecclesiastical limbo. Although nominally part of an Episcopal district with headquarters in Cape Town, operationally it remained wholly autonomous, in part because the Rhodesian government prevented AME officials in South Africa from even visiting their putative northern flock. Then, in an about-face, the colonial authorities opened the door for the South African AME Church to enter the mission field in their colony, that is, to take direct control of the existing Rhodesian AME congregations. This was a deft move, one calculated to exploit a political disjunction between the South African and Rhodesian churches. Unlike Micah Makgatho and his hardy band of Rhodesian-based African Methodists, the South African AME Church had mellowed over the years, muting its original liberationist thrust and making peace with the South African government, which returned the favor by offering educational grants, among other concessions.[101] By making the South African–based AME hierarchy responsible for controlling the local church and disciplining its politically unruly members, tasks the colonial state itself had failed to accomplish, the Rhodesian regime hoped to detach African Methodism from the seething cauldron that was the proto-national moment.

For the most part, the AME hierarchy followed the script that had been written for it. Arriving in the proto-national hotbed of Bulawayo, the Rev. Zephaniah Mtshwelo, the minister dispatched from South Africa to neuter African Methodism in Southern Rhodesia, signed a document declaring his personal "loyalty to the Throne and [the] Rhodesian authorities" and agreeing to confine his work to "the advancement of our church, and let the politics of the country alone."[102] Actually, Mtshwelo became very much involved politically, although against the populists who spearheaded the proto-national moment, both within and outside the AME Church, a crusade for which he was lauded by the colonial regime as "a staunch supporter of law and order."[103]

Mtshwelo's opposition to the proto-national moment, which complemented the activities of the Southern Rhodesia Native Association, did not go unchallenged. His principal opponent in the AME Church, it turned out, was none other than Zachariah Makgatho. Backed by fellow church member Thomas Maziyane—the conductor whose Surprising Singers Association had so loyally supported the British during World War I—Makgatho vigorously resisted Mtshwelo's efforts to align African Methodism with the colonial state, thereby vitiating his father's legacy. Mtshwelo, not to be outdone, denounced his detractors as a "bundle of polygamists, bigamists and concubines who are working against the interests of the church daily."[104] Clearly, the official strategy of divide and rule had achieved some success. By fomenting what amounted to an ecclesiastical coup, the authorities provoked internecine warfare within the AME Church, removing some of the sting from Ethiopianism in particular and the proto-national moment in general.

The decline of Ethiopianism, as illustrated by the fissures within the AME Church, mirrored the waning fortunes of the proto-national moment itself. The growing weakness of the ICU, the strongest link in the radical chain, best exemplified the approaching political denouement. The decline and fall of the ICU, a process that had completely run its course by 1933, was due to a variety of factors. Government destabilization played a role, but internal weaknesses and societal constraints were more important. In this connection, Terence Ranger correctly argues that although "effective in terms of exhortation, stimulation, education," the ICU "was not effective in terms of organization."[105] Ultimately, an organizationally ineffective ICU proved unable to withstand the social dislocations attendant on the depression.[106] The dramatic downturn in economic activity resulted in huge job losses, financially crippling the ICU, whose leaders and members became destitute. Under the circumstances, Charles Mzingeli, the ICU's Salisbury representative, abandoned his job as an organizer to open a small restaurant. The depression-induced impoverishment was even less kind to Masotsha Ndhlovu, the once pugnacious ICU helmsman. In desperation, Ndhlovu renounced the moribund ICU, disavowing erstwhile comrades like Mzingeli—the price required for his employment in the Native Affairs Department, an institution he had previously condemned as the chief oppressor of Africans in the colony.[107]

Although perhaps the most humbled, the ICU was not the only protest group that fell victim to hard times; the depression also claimed the political life of the Rhodesia Bantu Voters Association, among others. The Southern Rhodesia Native Association, lodestar of the anti-ICU counterpopulist reaction within African politics, was the only major formation to weather the so-

cial and economic storm, maintaining some semblance of organizational coherence through the 1930s. The SRNA's ability to outlast its rivals resulted
from a propitious combination of factors. First, its collaborationist politics ex-
empted it from the hostility and repression visited on more assertive and
populist groups associated with the proto-national moment. Second, from an
organizational standpoint, the SRNA went into the depression relatively
strong. With a reasonably solid base among sections of the African elite of
Mashonaland, it faced less political competition than either the ICU or the
RBVA, both of which were headquartered in Matabeleland. Finally, it seems
likely that some of the dominant elements in the SRNA, such as clerks and
Purchase Area farmers, may have survived the depression in better financial
shape than the leadership of the other movements. In particular, clerks employed by the government and affiliated with the SRNA would likely have
been favored in any depression-era bureaucratic streamlining, just as they had
been spared victimization during the proto-national moment. With populism
having collapsed as a viable political project, that is, with the end of the proto-
national moment, the SRNA was well placed to transmit the alternative counterpopulist tradition to the new organizational and leadership cohort that
would subsequently emerge, beginning in the mid-1930s.

6

Found and Lost
Toward an African Political Consensus, 1934–1948

THE END OF THE proto-national moment meant that African politics had to be fashioned anew during the depression. In this reformulation, which was powerfully determined by the prior political history, the counterpopulist tendency generally held sway over the populist one. Then came World War II, which ushered in a new militancy among the elite. A parallel process of proletarian radicalization, culminating in a railway strike in the immediate postwar period, set the stage for a new political alliance between the African working and middle classes. The result was a situation not unlike the one then unfolding in other parts of Africa, including the Gold Coast. This alliance, however, was sundered by a general strike in 1948, thereby vitiating the social and ideological bases for the emergence of mature, anticolonial African nationalism.

THE RISE OF THE PREACHER-POLITICIAN

The process of political recuperation necessitated by the collapse of the proto-national moment began modestly enough, the lead being taken by the Southern Rhodesia Native Missionary Conference, which had been established in 1930 as the organized voice of the colony's black Protestant clergy. A segregated poor relation of the white Southern Rhodesia Missionary Conference, the Native Missionary Conference signaled the emergence of a group of clergymen destined to play an increasingly important role in African politics, up to and including the crucial years immediately following the end of World War II. Significantly, a good many of these clerical leaders—men such as Matthew Rusike, Thompson Samkange, and Esau Nemapare—came out of the Wesleyan (British) Methodist Church, and they assumed as prominent a role in the Rhodesian context as did their fellow Wesleyan D. D. T. Jabavu in South Africa during the same period.[1] Indeed, the Native Missionary Conference itself was an outgrowth of the Wesleyan Native Evangelist Convention movement, which began in the mid-1920s.

As a social category, the preacher-cum-politician was a new development in the rise of the African middle class in Southern Rhodesia. Although they were firm believers for the most part, few of the pre-depression political personalities came from the ranks of the Christian ministry; the African Methodist Episcopal Church's Micah Makgatho, whom we met in the previous chapter, was an exception. Even the founders of the proto-national-aligned African Orthodox Church were laymen, whereas some Industrial and Commercial Workers Union of Africa (ICU) activists, notably Masotsha Ndhlovu and Charles Mzingeli, betrayed a kind of rational skepticism by their statements.

As early as 1932, with the proto-national moment on the wane, the Native Missionary Conference had begun to articulate black grievances and aspirations; two years later, it had become the leading political forum for Africans nationally. Like the political formations it superseded, the Native Missionary Conference took up many of the issues favored by the emerging middle class, such as education, the franchise, the Purchase Areas, exemption certificates for "advanced" Africans, the "immorality" caused by the presence of "runaway girls" in the urban townships, and miscegenation. The Native Missionary Conference added some new items to the elite agenda, including a demand for private rooms in the segregated hospitals—an issue that emerged as a key concern of the African elite in the 1930s and one in which the Rev. Matthew Rusike, the Wesleyan Methodist minister, took an especially keen interest. But the Native Missionary Conference, as befitting its claim to national leadership, also sought to represent the interests of the laboring masses, who suffered the most during the depression. Consequently, it formally advocated a minimum wage, "respectfully" pointing out that the wages then prevailing were "grossly insufficient for the monetary needs of men with dependents and does not represent a fair share of the proceeds of their labour."[2]

The Native Missionary Conference's conception of social justice was derived from Anglo-American Protestant "social gospel" ideology,[3] which circulated in southern Africa through the global missionary network and which was largely anathema to trade unionism and political radicalism.[4] Thus despite its intervention on behalf of the working class, the Native Missionary Conference, when judged by the political tendencies inherited from the earlier period, stood closer to the counterpopulist position of the Southern Rhodesia Native Association (SRNA) than it did to the ICU-led populist coalition of the proto-national moment, including the Ethiopianists. Like the SRNA, the Native Missionary Conference presented its claims in deferential rather than defiant language, even as it studiously eschewed the agitational style and active interclass coalition building that were the hallmark of the ICU. The Native Missionary Conference also lacked the radical internationalist and pan-Africanist sensibilities that characterized the proto-national moment. It is a measure of the relative absence of such sensibilities that the most epoch-making political event for black people worldwide during the interwar years, namely, the 1935 Italian invasion of Ethiopia, apparently elicited no organized response in Southern Rhodesia, in sharp contrast to the response from other parts of global Africa, such as West Africa, the transatlantic diaspora, even neighboring South Africa.[5]

A POLITICAL REORGANIZATION: THE SOUTHERN RHODESIA BANTU CONGRESS

The Native Missionary Conference retained its dominant position, more by default than design, until late 1936, when leadership of the African political agenda passed to the newly formed Southern Rhodesia Bantu Congress (SRBC). The SRBC, which would only reach the pinnacle of its influence in the post–World War II era, emerged against the backdrop of a ferocious anti-African political and legal onslaught. Leading the charge was Prime Minister Godfrey Huggins, who had been elected in 1933 on an arch-segregationist platform pledging to make Rhodesia truly white, a goal he maintained had not been pursued with sufficient vigor by previous administrations. At the core of Huggins's ultra-white Rhodesian campaign was a determination to thwart African social mobility, particularly in the urban centers. In partial pursuit of this objective, the prime minister in 1936 proposed the Native Registration Bill, along with two ancillary pieces of legislation, the Native Preachers Bill and the Sedition Bill.

The Native Registration Bill sought to arrest the process of African urbanization by more rigorously controlling migration to the cities and towns, including regulating the activities of the proverbial loose female migrants. The complementary Native Preachers and Sedition Bills, which targeted a new group of African critics, were the most draconian form of censorship to be proposed up to that point. During the proto-national moment, the repressive arms of the colonial state had called for new legislation to deal with the ICU and its allies, but they had been rebuffed by the prime minister and minister of native affairs, H. U. Moffat, who urged stricter enforcement of the existing laws. Now, the less decorous Huggins, believing that white Rhodesia once more was facing subversion, this time by insurgent religious proselytizers, attempted to combat the menace through increased repression.

The proposed laws were directed not at the Ethiopianists, who had so exercised the colonial regime during the proto-national moment, but rather at a diverse and unorthodox body of religious adherents generically known as Zionists, including Pentecostals and followers of Watch Tower, as the Jehovah's Witness movement was called in southern and central Africa. Zionism was quite distinct from Ethiopianism, both theologically and socially.[6] Ethiopianist bodies such as the African Methodist Episcopal Church and the African

Orthodox Church were strictly orthodox in theology, distinguishing themselves from the white denominations more by their insistence on African leadership in African religious affairs than by any doctrinal demarcation. As a general rule, the Ethiopianist leaders were elite Africans who had rejected the racially exclusionary practices of the white missionaries by forming independent churches. Zionism, by comparison, was highly eclectic and heterodox, combining elements of European-derived Christian theology with indigenous forms of spirituality. The Zionist leaders, even when literate, usually in an African rather than the colonial language, occupied a more tenuous position on the social mobility ladder than did their Ethiopianist counterparts.

Although long a part of the Rhodesian religious mosaic, Zionism expanded markedly in the 1930s. Indeed, the end of the proto-national moment, including the decline of Ethiopianism, helped to set the stage for the alternative Zionist drama. On the ecclesiastical stump, the Zionists found a receptive audience during the depression, especially in the countryside. Majestic in their distinctive and often colorful garments, the generally itinerant Zionist evangelists fondly evoked biblical imageries drawn from the major prophets and the apocalyptic Revelation of St. John in the Old and New Testaments, respectively. Many of these unorthodox proselytizers, to be sure, were otherworldly and politically anodyne. Others, however, preached damnation of the unjust white rulers, urging cash-starved peasants to default on their tax obligations to the state, among other acts of defiance, while offering the promise of a new heaven and a new earth, the colonial world turned upside down.[7]

Huggins's Native Preachers and Sedition Bills were directed, first and foremost, at the Zionist challenge. But elite Africans, although not enamored of Zionism, saw the proposed laws as a generalized assault on freedom of speech, religion, and assembly; in short, as "inconsistent with British freedom and with Christian liberty."[8] The African defense of libertarian principles was coordinated by an unlikely group, the Southern Rhodesia Native Association.[9] Although formally remaining in existence, the SRNA had become dormant since the end of the proto-national moment, overshadowed politically by the Native Missionary Conference. Now the Huggins bills offered the SRNA, energized by a number of new and younger leaders, an opportunity to revive itself. The SRNA's opposition to the Huggins bills also marked the first time in its seventeen-year existence that it openly challenged the government on a highly charged political issue.

The most vocal and conspicuous opponent of the Huggins bills was Aaron Jacha, a former government clerk, Purchase Area farmer, brother of the prominent Wesleyan Methodist minister Matthew Rusike, and secretary of the SRNA's Salisbury branch. Jacha attacked the Native Preachers Bill as unnecessary, because the African population, led by "enlightened natives," had consistently rejected movements that showed "antagonism towards European

Administration." He was no less critical of the Sedition Bill, charging that it would empower the government to censor African opinion and ban "native organizations [that protest] certain actions taken by those administering the laws."[10] Jacha, however, reserved his strongest condemnation for the Native Registration Bill, which he regarded as a direct assault on the African elite's quality of life. Although agreeing that there were "undesirable Natives in town" who should be expelled, he argued that these "bad characters should be dealt with under the Vagrancy laws." He found the Native Registration Bill objectionable because it would empower "the police to challenge any Native at sight for his pass, and interfere with decent African women when walking in town."[11]

Eventually, the Native Preachers Bill was withdrawn, not so much because of direct African opposition but because some of the white missionaries who initially advocated the anti-Zionist legislation subsequently disavowed it, apparently out of deference to the elite African critics.[12] Yet the abandonment of the Native Preachers Bill amounted to little more than an empty gesture. As the minister of justice acknowledged, "most of the evils that were aimed at" in that particular legislation were also covered in the Sedition Bill, which, along with the Native Registration Bill, survived the legislative process and became the law of the land.[13]

Meanwhile, mobilization against the increasingly repressive Huggins regime culminated in the formation of the SRBC. Conceived as a broad umbrella movement, the SRBC incorporated a number of existing groupings, the most important of which were the SRNA and the Bantu Community Association of Bulawayo.[14] Formed around 1934 and chaired by the irrepressible Zachariah Makgatho, a holdover from the proto-national moment, the Bantu Community Association sought to fill the political vacuum in the city of Bulawayo created by the fall of the ICU and the Rhodesia Bantu Voters Association.[15] In addition to jointly rejecting the Huggins bills, the SRNA and the Bantu Community Association were united in their opposition to aspects of the government's public health policy in the urban centers, policies that required Africans to undergo compulsory medical examinations as a means of controlling venereal diseases. Although agreeing that the procedures were necessary, elite African males strongly objected to having to undress before all and sundry in a common examination room, demanding the right to personal and private medical consultation. No less intolerable was the fact that "decent women" were sometimes examined in the presence of African male orderlies, a group long suspected of sexual voyeurism by elite African men.[16]

The SRBC, then, was an organized expression of the rising tide of discontent among the black petty bourgeoisie. This, however, was controlled anger. Despite the presence in its ranks of such populist-oriented figures as Zachariah Makgatho, the SRBC was no ICU reconstituted. On the contrary,

4. Members of the Wesleyan (British) Methodist Church synod, 1930s. Standing, left to right: R. W. Ramushu, J. C. Mashingaidze, Esau Nemapare, S. J. Chihota, Matthew Rusike. Sitting, left to right: C. N. Tyeza, O. L. Mocketsi, Herbert Carter, K. M. Gazi. Courtesy of the National Archives of Zimbabwe.

the new formation bore an uncanny resemblance to the SRNA and the Native Missionary Conference, both in terms of program and temperament. The tone was set at the SRBC's inaugural meeting, a conclave chaired by the SRNA's Aaron Jacha. Noting the need for a national coordinating umbrella to act "as a mouthpiece of Africans in general," Jacha emphasized cooperation with the government, despite his own criticisms of the Huggins bills, and he warned the gathering to avoid forming "anything which will be taken as a body of agitators." Such admonitions were, of course, entirely consistent with the SRNA's counterpopulist heritage. As if to drive home the theme of continuity, Jacha suggested naming the new group the Southern Rhodesia Bantu Association,

5. Founding members of the Southern Rhodesia Bantu Congress, which later became the Southern Rhodesia African National Congress. The Congress, founded in 1936, was the first truly colony-wide African political movement. Courtesy of the National Archives of Zimbabwe.

which would simply have replaced "Native" in SRNA with the then more lexically fashionable "Bantu."[17]

In the end, the assembly bucked Jacha and opted for "Congress" over "Association," and so the new body became known as the Southern Rhodesia Bantu Congress. The latter choice apparently was a nod in the direction of regional pan-Africanism. In Southern Rhodesia, as elsewhere on the southern African subcontinent, the African National Congress of South Africa had long stood as a model of political mobilization for colonized Africans. Jacha's own SRNA had previously adopted cultural trappings associated with the South African group, most notably its anthem, "Nkosi Sikelel' iAfrika" (God Bless Africa).

Jacha's nomenclatorial suggestion may have been rejected, but the SRBC scrupulously followed his counsel to avoid the politics of confrontation. Without the provocation of additional repressive legislation, and under the leadership of men drawn largely from the SRNA and the Native Missionary Conference—including Jacha himself, who served as general secretary for its first

6. Leaders of the Native Welfare Society of Bulawayo, 1943. Standing: A. Bulawayo, A. Mangawa, P. Sibanda, A. S. B. Manyoba, R. Edwards, A. E. Sibanda, D. Nasho. Sitting: W. A. Carnegie, A. S. Nleya, J. H. Sobantu, J. S. Lewis. One member is unidentified. Inset: Silas Madeya. Courtesy of the National Archives of Zimbabwe.

nine years—the SRBC maintained a quiescent posture until well into the era of World War II.

WORLD WAR II AND THE RESURGENCE OF AFRICAN MILITANCY

As part of the British Empire, Southern Rhodesia automatically found itself at war with the outbreak of hostilities in Europe in September 1939. The Rhodesian regime contributed directly to the military campaign by providing thousands of troops, most of them African, and by building military bases for use by the British air force. On the economic front, increased production of foodstuffs and industrial goods was matched by rising output in the mining sector, including certain base metals—chrome, titanium, plutonium—demanded by Great Britain and its ally the United States. The result was a mobilization of human power on an unprecedented scale. When the colonized

7. Leaders of the Native Welfare Society, 1945. Standing: F. M. Gambo, A. Makubalo, J. C. Chikoko, Patrick Makoni, F. K. Makwabarara, A. S. Nleya, I. M. Sikabu, J. M. Mesaba. Sitting: Oliver Somkence, C. E. Wyatt, Percy Ibbotson, S. H. Madeya, W. L. Makubalo, W. A. Carnegie, S. L. Lesabe. Courtesy of the National Archives of Zimbabwe.

Africans, especially the peasants, did not voluntarily report to the military recruitment centers, building projects, mines, farms, and other work sites in the requisite numbers, the settler regime reverted to form: it turned to forced labor, which had largely disappeared during the depression.[18]

As in World War I, some officials attributed the peasants' lack of enthusiasm, especially their reluctance to join the military, to anti-British propaganda spread by Afrikaner farmers.[19] The authorities directed most of their ire, however, at what they called loafers in the countryside, many of whom had a habit of heading for the hills, or else the South African or Bechuanaland borders, when recruiters appeared in the villages. "Only a few recruits are coming forward," complained one official; "the local natives have no desire to offer themselves as soldiers," added another.[20] Faced with such widespread resistance, some colonial officials resorted to invectives. The Africans, one of them exclaimed, were "most arrant cowards. . . . One can expect little more from a native people whose mental horizon is extremely restricted."[21] Other officials appealed to the supposed martial instincts of the Ndebele people, noting "a growing shame among the more intelligent section of the male population at the lack of response in Matabeleland in supplying recruits" for the army.[22]

Indeed, there was a disjunction in the African reaction to the war, with the male-dominated petty bourgeoisie showing far greater enthusiasm for the British cause than did the masses, especially the peasants. These elite men— few of whom, not incidentally, were either conscripted or voluntarily joined the army—spearheaded a fund-raising campaign to demonstrate their loyalty to the British Empire, as they had done during World War I. Most of the money, though, actually came from urban workers, who attended the dances, boxing matches, concerts, and other events organized by the elite fundraisers. The fund-raising campaign, asserted choirmaster and intellectual gadfly Charlton Ngcebetsha, was "conclusive proof that [Africans] are perfectly satisfied with the present British democratic regime and that they want no importation whatsoever of Nazi doctrines from the Third Reich."[23] Ngcebetsha was only partially correct. Although Africans in Southern Rhodesia certainly opposed fascism, they enjoyed few democratic liberties under British colonialism and were far from satisfied. It was left to the old populist Zachariah Makgatho, himself a chief promoter of the African voluntary initiative, to offer a fuller and more accurate assessment of the elite position. By contributing to the war funds, Makgatho noted, Africans were demonstrating "their desire not only to play their part in the ultimate overthrow of the Nazi regime but also to present the most convincing case for their liberation from the economic and social disabilities under which they live and labour."[24]

World War II, in fact, fundamentally altered the relationship between colonizer and colonized. In Africa, as elsewhere in the colonial world, wartime propaganda denouncing fascism and extolling the democratic values for which the Allied powers allegedly stood was taken seriously, even literally. And although there was as yet little talk of African self-government and ultimate independence in Southern Rhodesia—in contrast to, say, the British West African territories—colonial Zimbabweans became increasingly assertive during the war and in the immediate postwar years. In 1944, after completing his education in South Africa, Lawrence Vambe, the future journalist and amateur social historian, returned home to find a "profound change in the general outlook of the African people, particularly the educated section. They were more militant."[25]

This militancy was most evident in the rhetoric of the African petty bourgeoisie. In sharp contrast to the official British and Rhodesian views, elite Africans insisted that the Allied promise of a new and more just postwar world order, as envisaged in such celebrated documents as the Atlantic Charter, should apply to colonized peoples.[26] "The African people in this country," one colonial Zimbabwean commented, "have done their best toward the downfall of those grotesque maniacs—Hitler and Mussolini—by supplying cheap labour, by contributions to war funds from their meagre incomes, and by joining for military service. They believe that this war is being waged for the liberation of all men, and that is what they are being told."[27] In return for such sacrifices, elite Africans, citing the Allied pledges, demanded a nonracial meritocracy. "To educate an African well and then close to him all doors of responsible positions is to turn him into a useless agitator," asserted a young Ndabaningi Sithole, still using the language of counterpopulism, although with the significant addition of an implied threat. As an antidote to the politics of agitation, Sithole called for the appointment of Africans to high administrative posts in the schools and in the government bureaucracy, steps he maintained would make the new world order "meaningful" to the colonized people.[28]

Yet despite the increasing militancy, African mobilization lagged far behind African consciousness throughout the war, and few real efforts were made to canalize the discontent. The Southern Rhodesia Bantu Congress, despite its repeated promise to become "the central organization" for all Africans in the colony, had been foundering almost since its inception in 1936.[29] By the era of World War II, some commentators were pronouncing it dead.[30] In 1943, seeking to refute what it claimed were premature obituaries, the SRBC inner circle, led by Aaron Jacha, persuaded the Rev. Thompson Samkange to assume the presidency of the organization.[31] The stolid and sure-footed Samkange, longtime secretary of the Native Missionary Conference and a founding member of the SRBC, was indeed a cornerstone of the emerging African middle class. Even so, he was unable to perform the anticipated resurrection. Until the end of the war, the SRBC remained programmatically vacuous and financially weak, meeting only sporadically and doing little to actually mobilize popular support.

The SRBC's chief political competitor during the war was the African branch of the Southern Rhodesia Labour Party.[32] Formed in 1939 as a segregated auxiliary of the Labour Party, the self-proclaimed champion of white artisans and shopkeepers, the Salisbury-based African branch was led by Charles Mzingeli, the former ICU representative who had been running various small businesses since the end of the proto-national moment. Backed by a small group of loyalists, Mzingeli apparently saw the African branch both as a vehicle to effect his own political rebirth and as an instrument to counter the SRBC. To Mzingeli, the SRBC would have seemed like old wine in a new bottle, a more sober incarnation of the counterpopulist Southern Rhodesia Native Association, his nemesis from the 1920s. Such a view, as shown above, was not without some merit.

The African branch may have succeeded in rescuing Mzingeli from political oblivion. As a vehicle for mobilizing African discontent, however, it was even less effective than the SRBC. At its height in 1944, the African branch had a paid-up membership of just thirty-one, all of them elite Africans, who were the only ones capable of meeting the "relatively high entrance qualification."[33] Mzingeli, whose quasi–trade unionist background predisposed him to

an alliance with the Labour Party, had not anticipated the constraints inherent in such an arrangement, given the politics of race and class in the colonial
setting. Whereas he regarded the African branch as a mechanism for advancing African interests—"and above all to assist in promot[ing] the good tradition of the British Democracy" in Southern Rhodesia—the Labour Party's
white barons hoped to use Mzingeli and his colleagues to control black militancy by keeping Africans from "becoming influenced by those holding more
extreme views."[34] Yet the very idea of Africans operating under the party's
aegis, even in a segregated wing subject to the discipline of the white par-
ent body, was too much for the ultra-diehard racists in the Labour Party. In
1944 these hardliners, demanding a lily-white party, moved to disestablish the
African branch. Although unsuccessful, the attempted expulsion deeply em-
barrassed Mzingeli and shook his faith in interracial class solidarity; it also
sounded the death knell of the African branch.[35]

THE PROLETARIAN INTERVENTION AND THE
RISE OF THE NEW AFRICAN

The elite having failed, it was left to the working class to undertake the
decisive act of African political mobilization during the era of World War II;
this decisive act came in the form of a strike by railway workers in October
1945, amid the ongoing celebration of the defeat of fascism globally.[36] In a
remarkable demonstration of self-organization, African railway workers in
Bulawayo walked off the job to protest abominable living standards that had
been made even worse by stagnant wages and rising inflation, one of the first
in a chain of similar actions by the frustrated proletariat throughout postwar
Africa.[37]

The railway strike in Southern Rhodesia—which quickly spread north-
ward along the line of rail, eventually reaching as far as Broken Hills (now
Kabwe) in Northern Rhodesia—included some ten thousand workers who
had no history of trade-union organization. Indeed, the mutinous workers
acted in open defiance of the legal system, because the Industrial Conciliation
Act of 1934 did not include Africans in the category of employees, condemning them instead to the rightless netherworld of servants who had no legal authority to enter into collective bargaining with their masters.

Given the weak legal and structural position of African labor within the
Rhodesian political economy, the railway strike confounded the colonial officials, including the intelligence services. The walkout also caught the members
of the African petty bourgeoisie unawares, preoccupied as they were with their
own class-specific concerns. Zachariah Makgatho, true to his populist heritage, was one of the few elite Africans who would not have been completely
surprised by the strike, having maintained some contacts with the workers

over the years. Thus in late 1943 Makgatho gave evidence to a government-appointed commission on the plight of urban Africans, representing several self-improvement and ethnic associations with predominantly working-class memberships, some of which would go on to play an important organizing role in the 1945 railway strike. In his testimony, Makgatho focused on the immiserization of the working class—including the plight of an increasing number of women and children[38]—noting specifically that even on "the Railways, where people are given rations, those rations are not enough and they have to go and buy food from their wages."[39]

The resulting strike by these same railway workers was the single most important African-initiated event in the history of Southern Rhodesia since the bloody uprisings of the 1890s. Significantly, the strikers won a number of concessions from their employers, with the result that the walkout was seen as a successful demonstration of African power. The action of the workers, as one historian observed, brought forth "an immediate and far-reaching response from other urban Africans," notably the elite.[40] The 1945 railway strike, in fact, ushered in a new era in the fraught relationship between the black elite and African workers. Up to this point the petty bourgeoisie, as a group, had been deeply estranged from the masses, particularly the working class, socially as well as politically. The ICU, during the proto-national moment, had earned the wrath of a significant section of the middle class, as much for its methods of agitation as for its attempts to bridge the chasm between elites, workers, and peasants. In a kind of posthumous vindication of the ICU's vision, however, the period between the 1945 railway strike and an even bigger general strike in 1948 witnessed a rapprochement, indeed, an evolving political alliance across the social divide between the African middle and working classes. This arrangement, as it happened, sundered before the peasantry could be brought into it.

The olive branch was offered by the elite during the railway strike. The SRBC, in an act of solidarity that belied its foundational status as heir to the counterpopulist mantle, took the lead in raising funds to help support the striking workers. Moving beyond symbolism, the elite leaders formed a new organization, the African Workers Trade Unions of Bulawayo, the first expressly black trade union formed in Southern Rhodesia, not counting the all-inclusive ICU. At the head of the fledgling labor front stood Jasper Savanhu—a scion of Purchase Area farmers, leading African journalist, secretary of the SRBC, and author of a highly acclaimed pamphlet. Appearing just a few months before the strike and bearing the strong imprint of the Atlantic Charter, that canonical wartime document among political activists in the colonies,[41] Savanhu's pamphlet constituted the most systematic public self-expression of elite African aspirations to date.[42]

Consistent with the spirit of his pamphlet, it was a combative Savanhu who ascended to the helm of the Workers Trade Unions. The railway strike "proved that Africans have been reborn," he announced. "The old African of tribalism, conservatism, separatism and selfishness has died away," Savanhu went on, as if entombing the counterpopulist tradition. At the same time, he declared the advent of a political alliance across the social divide: "Africans realise as never before that united they stand and divided they fall." The New Africans, Savanhu continued in a discourse at once observant and transgressive of the race–class divide, realized that the struggle "is not a racial one altogether, but also economic." Consequently, Africans were "welded together by common interests in the fight against economic repression, [that is, a] deprivation of opportunity to work our way up the ladder of success unbridled." This interclass alliance was necessary because the colonized people, irrespective of social standing, had found themselves "in the grip of a ruthless foe — unbridled exploitation by capitalists backed by legalised economic repression," Savanhu thundered, attacking the capital–state nexus in language worthy of the most radical ICU stump speaker. Indeed, Savanhu saw his Workers Trade Unions as the historical successor to the ICU, which, he asserted, had "failed because we were less informed and 'divide and rule' succeeded so well."[43]

Savanhu was not alone in calling for a grand coalition transcending the social divisions among Africans in the post-strike period. Although not encouraging radical labor action, Cephas Hlabangana, president of the supposedly nonpolitical Matabele Home Society, exhorted his fellow elite Africans: "As workers let us rally to the banners of trade unionism."[44] Tennyson Hlabangana — Cephas's younger brother, a fellow college graduate, teacher, and one of the most zealous New Africans — also urged the SRBC to begin organizing workers, because elite blacks were "one and the same with" the colonized proletariat.[45] Tennyson, in fact, was in a fighting mood just around this time. Two months earlier, he had exploded in anger at an advertisement for "European" teachers for African schools, a violation, he asserted, of the government's previous promise to employ, "as much as possible," African teachers in African schools. "If I were a European," Tennyson wrote in spirited defense of nonracial meritocracy and in a tone of moral superiority, "I would sink my head in shame were I to know that my highest and most decisive qualification for a post or my right to earn a comfortable wage was based on the pigmentation of my skin." And he concluded on an apocalyptic note of revolutionary suicide: "Political domination, economic strangulation and social ostracism can only lead the African to a fanatic nationalism in the name of which he may declare in desperation, 'better an end with horror than horror without an end.' "[46]

The reason for this militant rhetoric, this sudden rush to embrace the workers and induct them into a class-transcending New African confraternity, was not difficult to find: the African petty bourgeoisie had become profoundly disillusioned with the status quo. Even before the war ended there was ample evidence that at least in Southern Rhodesia, the postwar settlement would fall well short of the expectations of elite Africans, indeed that little, if anything, would change. The most ominous sign that the new world order would look very much like the old world order came in 1944, when the settler regime renewed its decades-long campaign to disfranchise Africans. From all indications, the Atlantic Charter's promise of universal "social security" would remain but a mocking echo for Africans in Southern Rhodesia.

Under the circumstances, the railway strike was enough to spark a veritable renaissance in organizational revival and formation. The SRBC, now more militantly turned out with a nomenclatorial facelift remaking it into the Southern Rhodesia African National Congress, assumed an increasingly sharp and critical rhetorical pose. The reconstituted National Congress, determined more than ever to become the authoritative voice of the New African, challenged the colonial regime on a wide range of issues, some of which struck at the heart of the system of segregation. Among other measures, the National Congress opposed the renewed attempts to remove Africans from the voter rolls, threatening unprecedented public demonstrations against the proposed disfranchisement; passed a vote of no confidence in the segregated Native Education Department, demanding instead a single education ministry for all races; registered strong opposition to official urban policy, especially the Urban Areas Act of 1946, which intensified the repression codified in the Native Registration Act of 1936; and called for the legal recognition of African trade unions, even raising the possibility of organizing workers itself, as suggested by the Hlabangana brothers.[47]

As the National Congress went about carving out a hegemonic colony-wide role for itself, in rhetoric if not in fact, other groups coalesced around more issue-specific questions; chief among these was the African Voters League, a formation that emerged in the wake of the more radical political environment attendant on the railway strike. Although it took up other issues—such as the Urban Areas Act and the "European" liquor question—the Voters League was primarily concerned with the franchise. And although quintessentially New African, the Voters League had something of a history in that it was a political look-alike of the long defunct Rhodesia Bantu Voters Association, which also had given pride of place to the franchise question during the 1920s. Indeed, the two organizations were directly connected by John Wesley Sojini, a Voters League official and former general secretary of the Rhodesia Bantu Voters Association.

Emerging on the coattails of the railway strike, the Voters League was the most pointed response to the renewed attack on the African franchise. At the end of 1944, after an abortive attempt a decade earlier, Prime Minister Godfrey Huggins floated yet another proposal to remove Africans from the

voter rolls. As a consolation for disfranchisement, two whites would be selected to represent African interests in the Legislative Assembly. Huggins's
latest offensive against the African elite was determined by several factors, including a desire to guarantee his own political survival, which he regarded as
synonymous with the future of white supremacy in Southern Rhodesia. In
this connection, the settler prime minister concluded that Charles Mzingeli's
African branch of the Labour Party posed a threat to his hold on power, at
least in the long run. Huggins worried that the Labour Party, his parliamentary opposition,

> had formed an African Branch of their party and I knew that, except for a
> few dreamers, the idea was to capture the African vote on the common roll,
> the number of which was likely to increase considerably in the next twenty
> years, not to help the Africans but to steer them so that the organised Afri-
> can did not disturb the so called rights of the European Trade Unionists.
> Seeing this danger to the African, having studied the American Negro prob-
> lem, I decided that to protect the African it was essential to take him as far
> as possible outside the European politics.[48]

The agitation against disfranchisement began as soon as Huggins un-
veiled his proposal; it then intensified after the railway strike, culminating in
the formation of the Voters League. The Voters League, like the National
Congress, with which it cooperated, did not object to the idea of special representation for Africans in the Legislative Assembly, as suggested by Huggins. Such representation, however, was appropriate only for the "primitive
masses," not for the emerging African middle class. For elite blacks, the Voters
League firmly "opposed any form of representation in Parliament other than
through the common voters roll." It rejected Huggins's "view that the inauguration of some form of special representation for the primitive masses must
mean denial of the franchise to those Africans who have acquired the necessary qualifications."[49] Operating primarily in the urban centers, the Voters
League kept up a steady barrage of criticism against Huggins's franchise proposals, holding meetings, passing resolutions, and lobbying the government.
The authorities took notice, because a Voters League memorandum figured
as a point of discussion in talks between British imperial and Southern Rhodesian officials in London in 1947. Meanwhile the Voters League, like its National Congress ally, came under police surveillance.[50]

Indeed, the defense of African voting rights became a template for a general political mobilization and, more specifically, for the emerging coalition
between the African middle and working classes. In October 1947 the Voters
League called a meeting in Bulawayo, where an attempt was made to merge
the franchise and labor questions. "A significant feature of this meeting,"
Rhodesian intelligence reported, "was the fact that a suggestion was made
that all native societies functioning at that time should amalgamate with the

Bantu Congress so that the Bantu Congress might become the mouthpiece of all Africans in employment."[51] The government, however, eventually dropped its disfranchisement plan, thereby removing a major source of grievance for the African elite. Subsequently the Voters League, its mission accomplished, disappeared from the political stage.

The National Congress and the Voters League were not the only formations to attempt, albeit awkwardly and inconsistently, to mobilize around the idea of an all-African consensus during the period between the 1945 and 1948 strikes. Also competing to build a multiclass alliance was the Reformed Industrial and Commercial Workers Union of Africa (RICU). Established in April 1946, the RICU was little more than the African branch of the Labour Party under a new guise. Still reeling from the embarrassing expulsion attempt two years earlier, and buoyed by the growing discontent among the colonized people, Charles Mzingeli and his allies decided to strike out on their own politically, even though the African branch formally remained in existence for some time. Indeed, the RICU retained an official posture of proletarian non-racialism, vowing to cooperate with all movements seeking to advance "the well-being of the working class irrespective of colour, race, nationality or creed."[52]

The name of the new organization—Reformed Industrial and Commercial Workers Union of Africa—was anything but accidental. The postwar conjunction of generalized restlessness and growing manifestations of an all-African coalition must have reminded Mzingeli of the proto-national moment, a political drama in which he had been centrally involved. Indeed, Mzingeli represented the RICU as a "revival" of the ICU. But the historical repetition, if it may be so termed, was partly farcical. The RICU represented continuity with the ICU to the extent that it positioned itself as an umbrella movement that incorporated other associations, including trade-specific labor groups (such as professional drivers) and burial societies. Like the ICU, the RICU's claim to be a labor movement was tempered by the elitist orientation of much of its program and leadership; especially noteworthy were the number of building contractors in the RICU, including its nominal president, Daniel Ntuli.

Ultimately, however, the resemblance between the RICU and the ICU was more apparent than real. In sharp contrast to the ICU, which genuinely attempted to become a national movement, admittedly with mixed results, the RICU's field of operation was largely limited to Salisbury. Again the RICU, unlike the ICU, evinced little if any interest in the agrarian question. Lastly the RICU, in accordance with Mzingeli's predilection for constitutionalism— a form of political decorum he apparently learned from his erstwhile Labour Party mentors—generally spurned the politics of agitation that had become synonymous with the ICU during its existence.

The RICU, which emerged amid the ongoing opposition to Huggins's disfranchisement plan, immediately declared in favor of African voting rights. Mzingeli even sent a letter to the British newspaper *The Guardian,* claiming that the Rhodesian regime was about to "put the clock back" on African rights.[53] Yet despite Mzingeli's efforts to internationalize the issue, the RICU played a comparatively minor role in the struggle to preserve the nonracial franchise. Rather, the RICU's big political moment came with the implementation of the Urban Areas Act, when it set out to prove its mettle as a champion of African rights. On this issue, at least, the RICU eclipsed both the Voters League and the National Congress, which also opposed the legislation.[54]

The chief objective of the Urban Areas Act was to better control the African population in the cities and towns, which had increased tremendously during the war.[55] For Africans, the most hated aspect of the legislation was a provision that changed the nature of the relationship between landlord and tenant. Seeking to deny housing to "loafers" and other undesirable urban dwellers, the act made employers responsible for paying their employees' rent; previously, township residents paid the rent directly to the municipalities themselves. Africans of all social strata opposed the new plan, because individuals who found themselves without employment, for however long and for whatever reason, would be subject to eviction. The African petty bourgeoisie, though, had additional reasons for resenting the Urban Areas Act. Besides objecting to the principle of an employer paying their rent, single elite African men were horrified that the law forced them into shared living arrangements with the laboring masses. As one sympathetic white social investigator explained, before the Urban Areas Act,

> a number of civilised or advanced Africans were occupying rooms in Harari township [Salisbury], living one or two persons to a room. These Africans now find themselves forced to live four in a room. Educated and civilised Africans resent the idea of being forced to live four in a small room and what is much more serious, compelled to live with people who are of a different type and who follow different modes of life. Africans are not all of the same type and it is not difficult to imagine the resentment of advanced Africans who have to live cheek by jowl with illiterate and migrant workers.[56]

The African petty bourgeoisie, it seems, set strict social limits on whatever political alliance it may have developed with the working class. A political alliance was one thing, but it did not follow that elite Africans necessarily wanted to live with the working class.

The Urban Areas Act was first implemented in July 1947 in Salisbury, where the RICU had an organizational advantage over the rival National Congress and the Voters League.[57] Within days, the RICU called a meeting that drew a crowd of more than six hundred Africans, as the elite and the masses came together to protest, for both similar and different reasons.[58] A second gathering weeks later attracted an even larger audience, filling the Harari Recreation Hall to capacity and forcing hundreds to remain outside.[59] Mzingeli and his supporters were unable, however, to translate their success in mobilizing the populace against the Urban Areas Act into actual support for the RICU. In 1947, the year of its most spectacular achievements, the RICU had only 150 paid-up members, with the number dropping to 125 the following year, as the government continued to implement the law over strong African objection.[60]

The RICU's modest membership, as well as the existence of two other groups, the National Congress and the Voters League, did not prevent the emergence of yet another political organization. The African Workers Voice Association, founded in early 1947, presented itself as the most energetic defender of the emerging all-African coalition. Led by Benjamin Burombo, a businessman who held the post of organizing secretary, the Workers Voice resulted from a split in the Federation of Bulawayo African Trade Unions, the new name for the African Workers Trade Unions of Bulawayo, which had been created at the time of the railway strike. The Bulawayo-based Workers Voice claimed to be a more radical advocate of the working class than was the African Trade Unions, which the larger-than-life Burombo and his associates accused of being concerned "only with rich men and big business propositions. It is not interested in the common working class." The Workers Voice, by contrast, billed itself as the champion of "the Native in the street—the house-boy, the farm boy, etc."[61]

To prove its proletarian bona fides and outflank the rival African Trade Unions, the Workers Voice took its case directly to the streets of Bulawayo, organizing a series of well-attended meetings. The predominantly working-class audiences at these forums had become increasingly restive since 1945. Heartened by the success of the railway strike and buffeted by stagnant wages and rising inflation, workers in other economic sectors redoubled their efforts to stanch their declining living standards. The Workers Voice gave popular expression to their grievances. Burombo, like Savanhu and the other New Africans, attributed the plight of African workers to racialized economic inequality. "While there was colour-bar in fixing rates of pay and cost of living allowances," Burombo averred, "traders did not make any distinction between an under-paid African and a well paid European[;] hence both Europeans and Africans paid the same prices for the various commodities, [and] the Africans felt the weight of this economic burden more."[62] At meetings attracting as many as three thousand people, Burombo and other Workers Voice leaders made a series of demands on behalf of the working class, including the introduction of hourly and overtime wages, increased opportunities for advancement into skilled positions, sick leave, medical care, and annual paid vacations.[63] The audiences must have appreciated the support: the Workers Voice, according to the police, had "considerable influence among the working class."[64]

The Workers Voice, in its articulation of working-class grievances in popular forums, demonstrated a greater degree of historical continuity and political affinity with the ICU than did Mzingeli's RICU. Indeed, in something of a political coup, the Workers Voice attracted to its standard no less a personage than Masotsha Ndhlovu, the former ICU leader who had been humiliated by the Rhodesian authorities during the depression, when they compelled him to formally repudiate the ICU, then effectively dead, as the price for obtaining employment with the government. In joining the Workers Voice, Ndhlovu thus spurned the RICU, declining a political reunion with Mzingeli, his former protégé.[65] Yet the Workers Voice, although apparently speaking with credibility on behalf of the urban workers, was no more an indubitably working-class organization than was the ICU. The one, like the other, also promoted black capitalism, among other measures designed to benefit the African petty bourgeoisie. The Workers Voice, for instance, lobbied the Bulawayo city council on behalf of African eatinghouse keepers, a category of entrepreneurs that, significantly, included Burombo himself.[66]

THE NATIONAL MOMENT

Between the railway and the general strikes of 1945 and 1948, then, Southern Rhodesia experienced major social turbulence, as evidenced by the widening discontent among the African middle and working classes as well as the increasing number of organizations seeking to give political coherence to that discontent. This period was also characterized by a tentative all-African alliance across the social divide, one that enjoyed the support, to varying degrees, of virtually the entire spectrum of articulated elite opinion. As such, the years between the two strikes were quite different from the proto-national moment of the interwar period, when an ICU-led attempt at a similar political consensus met with stiff resistance from important and organized sections of the African petty bourgeoisie. By contrast, Jasper Savanhu's New African—that is, the colonized elite radicalized by shattered wartime dreams and energized by the railway strike—spearheaded the search for interclass concord from 1945 to 1948.

Indeed, the situation existing in Southern Rhodesia in the period between the two strikes was comparable in many respects to that obtained in other parts of Africa, including the Gold Coast, the bellwether of postwar anticolonial protest.[67] In Southern Rhodesia, as in the Gold Coast, a seething dissatisfaction among members of the major social strata resulted in an organizational renaissance that both reflected and shaped a growing African national consciousness. In the Rhodesian case, this racial and national awareness was the outcome of an ideological breakthrough by the black petty bourgeoisie. Where previously elite blacks tended to be socially specific, pursuing the narrow interests of their own class, in the immediate postwar years they began to see themselves in larger political terms, as part of a wider African nation to which they would provide leadership.

A distinguishing feature of the changes taking place in elite consciousness was an absence of the intra-African social polarization that had defined the proto-national moment. To be sure, the years between the 1945 and 1948 strikes were bedeviled by jockeying for political supremacy by various formations, most famously the National Congress and its allies on the one hand and the RICU on the other. These battles, however, were neither ideological nor strategic. In sharp contrast to the proto-national moment, there was broad agreement on objectives and goals during this period, with each faction claiming that it best represented the African consensus. In sum, a new dispensation had dawned—the national moment.

The national moment was not, however, a nationalist moment. Although a sense of African nationhood began to take hold among Africans in Southern Rhodesia between 1945 and 1948, this nation was not imagined as a sovereign and independent entity. That kind of African *nationalist* consciousness would only come later. Rather the New African, as the living embodiment of the African *national* consciousness, continued to think in terms of protesting European misrule instead of supplanting it with African rule, as in the pre-World War II period. The New Africans' rallying cry, if they had one, would have been "good government now"; it would not have been "self-government," then or later. Tennyson Hlabangana, in his angry outburst warning of a potential "fanatic nationalism in the name of which [Africans] may declare in desperation, 'better an end with horror than horror without an end,'" did not speak for the black petty bourgeoisie as a whole. The older and more unflappable Thompson Samkange, president of the National Congress, the organization that aspired to the status of hegemon of the national moment, had a better reading of the elite political mood. In haunting words that would be echoed some two decades later by Ian Smith, the last and most redoubtable of the alpha-champions of white Rhodesia, Samkange told delegates to the National Congress's annual meeting in 1947: "No sensible African would wish that the Africans take over the Government of this Colony from Europeans, even after a hundred years or even a thousand. Even if it were possible that the Africans form a majority in the House [the Legislative Assembly], which I am positive will not happen till the millennium, experience proved elsewhere that preponderance is not decided by numbers."[68] In Southern Rhodesia, where anticolonial and anti-settler nationalism was still more than a decade away, the national moment would not lead directly to the nationalist moment, as it would in Kwame Nkrumah's Gold Coast.

The national moment, like the proto-national one, had a religious dimension. The leading Ethiopianist formations from the 1920s—the African Orthodox Church and the African Methodist Episcopal Church—entered the depression in a weakened state, emerging from it with small congregations that had largely lost their political moorings. By the era of World War II, then, Ethiopianism, as a religio-political project explicitly allied to the emancipatory strivings of Africans, effectively had collapsed in Southern Rhodesia. Into the resulting vacuum stepped a New African, an exemplar of the national moment—the Rev. Esau Nemapare. In March 1947—at around the same time that Benjamin Burombo left the African Trade Unions to form the Workers Voice—Nemapare broke fellowship with the white missionaries and proceeded to establish a new Ethiopianist denomination, the African Methodist Church.[69] Nemapare, like National Congress president Thompson Samkange, his close personal friend and staunch political ally, was an iconic representative of the African middle class. Indeed, the two Wesleyan Methodist ministers had long been co-workers in the Native Missionary Conference, among other forums.

The ostensible reason for Nemapare's unceremonious departure from his mother church was twofold. First, an agreement between the Wesleyan and Dutch Reform churches to respect the territorial integrity of each other's ecclesiastical domain prevented him from operating in an area in which he had long been interested. Second, Nemapare took strong exception to a Wesleyan report that found him negligent in his administrative and fiduciary responsibilities as a religious and educational supervisor.[70] Yet these were merely "push" factors, for the formation of the African Methodist Church was not simply a reflexive act of rebellion motivated by personal pique or anti-European animus.

Admittedly, Nemapare, like all Ethiopianists, regarded his action as a protest against white religious domination, racial discrimination, and in this case, scapegoating of Africans; hitherto, Nemapare's white missionary superiors had spoken highly of his work.[71] The African Methodist Church, however, also had deeper historical and social antecedents. To begin with, Nemapare had previously exhibited schismatic tendencies.[72] The coming of the national moment created the conditions for him to break with the Wesleyans, making concrete his previous signs of discontent. Seen from this angle, the African Methodist Church represented the culmination of a vision Nemapare had been nurturing for some time, a vision of an African national church that would canalize, at the religious level, the growing African national consciousness. Accordingly, Nemapare cannily went about raising his political profile after the 1945 railway strike, placing himself at the center of a number of debates and struggles, even forming a local branch of the National Congress. He took a particularly active part in the opposition to Huggins's disfranchisement plan.[73] From all indications, therefore, Nemapare saw the African Methodist Church as a complement to the national moment, the religious counterpart to Thompson Samkange's National Congress, even if Samkange, although sympathetic, declined to join his old friend in the African Methodist Church.

Moving beyond the urban centers, the circle of discontent came to encompass the mission schools, the fountainhead of African elite formation. Acts of student defiance were not new; a number of strikes had occurred in the 1920s and 1930s. The nature and scope of the unrest changed dramatically during the national moment, however, when students showed an increased willingness to use the strike weapon. Especially significant was a strike at the Dadaya mission school in July 1947, hard on the heels of Nemapare's Ethiopianist thrust. The Dadaya student strike began as a protest against the whip, that most conspicuous symbol of European rule throughout colonial Africa. Female students, angered at being spanked, responded with a class boycott. The student walkout eventually resulted in a showdown between Garfield Todd, the New Zealand–born missionary who served as principal of Dadaya, and Ndabaningi Sithole, a teacher at the school. Todd, who would go on to become prime minister of Southern Rhodesia, fired Sithole, the future African nationalist theoretician, on charges (seemingly unfounded) of instigating the strike. Sithole's dismissal caused a howl of protest, as the leading black political formations— the National Congress, the Voters League, the RICU—lined up to denounce yet another act of injustice against the African nation and demand an official inquiry. Rhodesian intelligence considered the Dadaya student strike an important link in the chain of events leading up to the momentous general urban strike of 1948.[74]

THE 1948 GENERAL STRIKE AND THE LIMITS OF INTERCLASS ALLIANCE

The 1948 strike, the first such all-sector walkout in Southern Rhodesia, was the acid test of the national moment. The result was a complete failure. If the 1945 railway strike inaugurated the oneness of political purpose between the elite and the working class that defined the national moment, then the 1948 strike brought into sharp relief the limits of this alliance, and indeed tore it asunder. It was one thing to collect funds for workers who, on their own accord, had struck a single, if crucial, sector of the economy; to take the initiative in building a nascent labor movement; and to speak on behalf of the working class—all of which the elite African leaders had done from the time of the railway strike to the eve of the general strike. It was an altogether different

matter for these elite leaders and the organizations they ran to directly challenge capital and the state by backing, much less calling, a general strike that
would bring the booming postwar economy to a grinding halt, even if that is
what the increasingly destitute workers were determined to do.[75]

Thus when, on April 14, 1948, workers in Bulawayo walked off the job, sig-
naling the beginning of the general strike, it was over the strenuous objection
of all the major African organizations, including the National Congress, the
RICU, the African Trade Unions, even the Workers Voice, which had been the
most vocal in airing proletarian grievances during the previous months. Along
with florid rhetoric about a better deal for the "house boy," the Workers Voice
also counseled against the strike weapon and advised limiting the means of
redress to lobbying the authorities and to discussing legal action, just like the
supposedly more moderate African Trade Unions. Benjamin Burombo and
other speakers at Workers Voice meetings, the police attested, "unanimously
condemned" striking.[76]

The elite leaders remained opposed to the strike as a weapon up to the
point that the walkout commenced, and thereafter as well. Four days before
the strike, and with talk of a general withdrawal of labor rife, a conclave of "all
leading African organisations" rejected such a course of action.[77] Then, a day
before the actual walkout, officials of these same organizations, desperate to
avert the impending proletarian revolt, called a mass meeting in Bulawayo.
The exact turnout at this event is uncertain, "but it seemed to the C.I.D. de-
tails who visited the scene that practically every native in Bulawayo was there."
Also there was the entire elite leadership, including the top men in the Workers Voice and African Trade Unions; they were joined by seven whites, "friends
of the natives." The workers, however, were unimpressed by the lineup of dignitaries on the dais. As the police reported:

> The meeting was a complete pandemonium. None of the Europeans were
> given a hearing—[Bulawayo City] Councilor [J. H.] Bailey [a key white sup-
> porter of the Workers Voice] was shouted down with cries of "He is the man
> who has been deceiving us all along." The native leaders got up in succession
> and tried to calm the mob. The mob would not listen but started shouting
> "Sit down we are going on strike tomorrow. . . . " The [African] Executive,
> together with the Europeans then retired and 2 natives named George and
> Maghato[78] mounted the platform urging natives to strike without fail in the
> morning. Thereafter the meeting broke up in complete confusion and dis-
> order and the town natives went streaming back to their places of residence
> shouting "Chia, Chia."[79]

Enoch Dumbutshena, a junior member of the retiring executive, remembered
decades later that the "strike was on, but the leaders were still in conference."[80]

A similar meeting in Salisbury, where Charles Mzingeli's RICU called on

the workers to exercise restraint, produced almost identical results. Lawrence
Vambe, the young journalist and confidant of Mzingeli, recorded the scene in
his marvelous inside account of black Salisbury: "Charles Mzingeli, in his
constitutional approach, tried to put it [the discussion on whether to strike] on
a calm and reasonable level, but he was not only angrily shouted down, he was
seized physically, lifted off his feet and made to give an undertaking that the
strike would go on until the white exploiters had made the concessions demanded by the black people. The meeting went on all day and some of us
[leaders] feared violence might break out at any time."[81] Mzingeli, who denied
having agreed either to call or to support a strike, offered an even less flatter-
ing self-portrait. On the first day of the walkout, he later told an official investigation commission, he attempted to counsel a group of workers, presumably
in the niceties of constitutional conduct. His admonition had scarcely begun,
however, when he was "interrupted by some among the crowd who said they
were on strike and did not want any cowardly business about it."[82] Such "extremists," according to Mzingeli, had joined his organization at the time of
the protests over the Urban Areas Act, but became "disgruntled and resigned
forthwith" when their demands that the RICU lead the impending strike
were rejected.[83]

In sum, the general strike of 1948 took place against the pleadings, even
without the knowledge, of the elite black leadership, the self-styled labor leaders among them included. The evidence here is incontrovertible, flatly contradicting Ngwabi Bhebe, who, in a fanciful hagiographical rendition, has
Benjamin Burombo and his Workers Voice conspiratorially planning and exe-
cuting the strike.[84] On the contrary, Burombo's actual role was that of sub-
verter, not leader, of the 1948 strike. As Mzingeli told the Rev. Arthur Cripps
—the beloved British maverick missionary, Fabian socialist, and confidant of
African leaders—"no influence could have stirred up the workers in all those
industries, but hunger!!!"[85] The workers, to quote Mzingeli again, had learned
from the 1945 railway strike that "the only way to make one's self felt is to
with-hold one's own labour."[86]

The strike began in Bulawayo and subsequently spread to other parts of
the colony, aided by a proletarian underground intelligence network consisting of "Railway transship boys and African railway passengers," according to
the police report.[87] Railway workers, whose grievances had been settled in
1945, were the only major category of urban workers not joining the general
walkout. Yet even before some workers in Salisbury and the smaller urban
centers could join them, the Bulawayo workers—the most militant throughout the national moment and the first to go on strike—prematurely had declared victory and called off the walkout, assured by Burombo that the colonial regime had capitulated. At a mass meeting on the second day of the
strike, Burombo "waved a piece of paper," assuring his audience that it "con-

tained the Government's guarantee that single men in employment should receive £5 a month and married men £7.10," a geometric increase over the then prevailing monthly average of £1.5 to £1.10. The declaration was "greeted with acclamation and there was an immediate return to work on the part of all natives."[88]

But Burombo's announcement, which exceeded even the wildest imagination of the strikers, was too good to be true. The workers, in fact, had been duped. The colonial regime—not to mention the many private employers, including householders smarting from the nonappearance of the usual retinue of personal servants—had made no commitment about wage increases of any kind, and certainly nothing on the magnitude that persuaded the Bulawayo strikers to return to work. The only concession the African leaders, who came forward as mediators once the walkout began, managed to wring from the intransigent government negotiators was an agreement to appoint a commission to look into the question of wages and working conditions, and then only seven days after the strike ended. When the grand deception was revealed, Burombo pleaded miscommunication, claiming he had been misunderstood.

There can be little doubt, however, that the workers accurately received the message Burombo intended to convey. By acting to terminate a walkout he had always opposed, even if it meant hoodwinking the constituency he claimed to represent, Burombo evidently hoped to burnish his image as a forceful leader who could control his followers, thereby outshining the other African notables who also sided with the government and the employers in calling for an immediate end to the strike. That Burombo acted in the objective interests of capital and the state is beyond doubt; the only unanswered question is whether he did so subjectively as well, that is, whether his hoax had been coordinated with the colonial officials. On the one hand, Burombo's subsequent conviction on charges of "persuading" workers to go on strike (the prosecution's witnesses belonged to the rival African Trade Unions), a judgment that was overturned on appeal, seems to refute the hypothesis of a Judas kiss.[89] On the other hand, there was a certain amount of correlation in the immediate aftermath of the strike, with the authorities arranging for Burombo to retract his erroneous announcement on the radio, a medium not usually accessible to African political operatives.

In his retraction broadcast, Burombo asserted that the wage rates mentioned in his earlier speech were the minimum amounts required for basic survival, as determined by surveys. Although regretting the communication mishap, he remained opposed to the strike. "I am sorry that a misunderstanding has occurred," he allowed, "but nevertheless I still repeat to go back to work and I make it quite clear that the conditions you have entered into with your employers remain final until the Government machinery has made its recommendations to you."[90] In other words, the workers should continue with the pre-strike conditions, with only the vague promise of an official investigation, the recommendations of which would not be binding on individual employers. As workers in other centers walked off the job, they too were pressured into calling off the strike under the same terms as their Bulawayo comrades, the walkout having lost its momentum. The working class, in short, had been betrayed by the elite leadership, particularly the leader in whom it had reposed the greatest confidence, namely, Benjamin Burombo.

But then the question immediately arises: How could the workers have so easily fallen prey to the machinations of men for whom, only days earlier, they had shown such disdain, if not outright contempt? The working class, although quite capable of spontaneous self-organization, as demonstrated in both the 1945 and 1948 strikes, had produced no independent structures sufficiently competent to coordinate a national strike. The railway workers had maintained good discipline and effective communication in 1945 because the strike was localized as well as because of the nature of their industry. In 1948, by contrast, the strikers came from different sectors of the economy and were scattered all over the colony. Although effective propaganda agents, the "railway transship boys" who carried news of the strike wherever they went were no substitute for an organized leadership. The African working class in Southern Rhodesia, still recruited from a largely agrarian base, had not yet produced an effective stratum of leaders from among its own ranks, something akin to the artisans of colonial Sierra Leone.[91] Once they decided to walk off the job, therefore, the workers had little choice but to accept as intermediaries the elite leaders who had opposed the strike, with all the potential for double-crossing inherent in such an arrangement. It was thus the structural and ideological weaknesses of the working class that ultimately explain the liquidation of its interests during the 1948 general strike.

The outcome of the strike shattered the political consensus and interclass alliance that was the national moment. The New African, hailed as the vanguard of the African nation at the time of the railway strike, had turned out to be an untrustworthy ally of the working class. Far from being trade unionists in the conventional sense, elite leaders such as Burombo led movements that had a broad sociopolitical agenda, only a part of which concerned workers, and then not necessarily the most important part. As one pioneering study of the phenomenon in various parts of late-colonial Africa put it, these men were "not trade-unionists become politicians so much as political men in the labor movement."[92] Broken and dispirited, the workers abandoned the political men to their own devices after the 1948 strike, thereby thwarting the immediate development of a national anticolonial front comprising all the colonized social forces—elite, workers, and peasants—in short, the development of mature African nationalism. Southern Rhodesia would not, after all, go the way of the Gold Coast.

The elite leadership responded to the collapse of the national moment by seeking greater internal unity. Talk of combining all political formations under one broad umbrella was a recurring theme in the rise of the African middle class. The idea had been broached during the 1920s, but it foundered on irreconcilable differences between the Southern Rhodesia Native Association and the ICU. The formation of the National Congress (in its Bantu Congress incarnation) in 1936 seemed to fulfill a longtime dream for African political amalgamation. Yet that, too, was not to be. The emergence of yet more organizations during the national moment led to renewed calls for unity. The issue assumed special urgency at the beginning of 1947 because of an impending visit by members of the British royal family, for which the elite leaders scrambled to ensure that a welcoming message on behalf of the African population would be delivered by one of their own. Constant bickering, however, made it impossible for the Africans to choose a spokesman from their own ranks, with the result that the "African" welcoming address was read by the chief native commissioner. In the ensuing brouhaha, which went on for months, most observers blamed the RICU's Charles Mzingeli for the embarrassing episode.[93]

Then, two months before the general strike, the warring factions appeared to make peace. In a publicly staged show of reconciliation, the RICU and its National Congress antagonist agreed to bury the hatchet and work together for the good of the African nation. Accordingly, Mzingeli and Bradfield Mnyanda, the National Congress's chief representative in the capital, jointly formed yet another organization, the Salisbury African Vigilance Committee, "to deal with purely local affairs." As part of the compromise, Mzingeli reportedly also consented to "yield" to the National Congress on colony-wide issues.[94]

The search for elite political unity quickened after the disastrous general strike. In July 1948, the National Congress and the RICU resolved to form a single body, thereby making the Salisbury accord national. No sooner had the deal been brokered, however, than Mzingeli abruptly broke ranks, apparently unwilling to consummate a union in which he would not be the undisputed leader, especially if it meant conceding hegemony to the despised National Congress. Instead, Mzingeli declared for unity on his own terms, preemptively announcing the formation of a competing umbrella body, the awkwardly named National Forum of All Progressive Organisations of Southern Rhodesia.[95]

Mzingeli's defection brought forth a great hue and cry, but the RICU leader remained unfazed. Charlton Ngcebetsha, the contrarious public intellectual, declared, with uncharacteristic generosity and politeness, that Mzingeli "would earn our everlasting gratitude" by returning to the African political fold and working with the National Congress. Mzingeli, ever uncharitable, retorted that he did "not want any admiration from" from the likes of Ngce-betsha.[96] The Rev. Esau Nemapare of the newly formed African Methodist Church, appalled by Mzingeli's one-upmanship, offered the view that disunity was the greatest enemy facing Africans. Mzingeli, his astringent pen at the ready, lampooned the Ethiopianist. Nemapare, he sneered, "does not seem to realise that the multiplicity of Churches is just as bad" as the multiplicity of political organizations.[97] Privately, the Rev. Arthur Cripps urged Mzingeli to reach an accommodation with the National Congress in the interest of unity. Mzingeli agreed that unity was "surely to be desired." However,

> I am afraid that I must point out that it is in the interest of the Congress itself and its followers that intelligent African leaders must reject its claim to be the head of all African people in the Colony. . . . I am determined for a showdown with [the] Congress fellows if they dare continue to interfere with [the] progressive opinion of [the] African people. . . . This so-called Congress has done [the] African cause more harm than any other dummy organisation. We cannot therefore close our eyes to [its] bad past record, even for the sake of Unity. . . . I can safely say that the only chance for the Congress today is to dissolve and reform again.[98]

Although refusing to follow Mzingeli's advice and commit political sui-cide, the National Congress, like the other elite-dominated political forma-tions, including the RICU, had lost the sense of purpose they had acquired during the national moment. Conceding that he "had been unable to do a fully effective job" during his turbulent five-year presidency, a dejected Thompson Samkange resigned in the midst of the unity crisis to devote himself to church work and his Purchase Area farm.[99] With Samkange gone, the National Con-gress muddled on to the next major crisis, namely, the struggle over the estab-lishment of the Federation of Rhodesia and Nyasaland. Meanwhile, Burom-bo's African Workers Voice Association, now completely discredited among the working class, pulled out of the urban arena altogether and went in search of greener political pastures in the countryside. As it retooled for its new rural mission, the name of the organization was changed to the *British* African Na-tional Voice Association. As well it might. Despite his role as articulator of proletarian and other African grievances in the period leading up to the 1948 strike, Burombo in the end misled the urban masses, privileging the Brit-ish over the blacks, the whites over the workers, and the colonizer over the colonized.

7

Back toward the Beginning
The Pursuit of Racial Partnership, 1949-1958

THE RUPTURE OF THE emerging interclass alliance during the general strike of 1948 eventually sent the African middle class in search of new political arrangements. The central fact of Southern Rhodesia's political life during 1949-58 was the Federation of Rhodesia and Nyasaland, which was established in 1953. After strongly opposing the idea, the elite African political organizations and activists embraced the federation once it came into being, many of them with great gusto. This about-face was motivated by a promise that the federation would bring major benefits to the African middle class in the form of a "racial partnership" with the white settlers. To many elite Africans, racial partnership seemed like a synonym for the nonracial meritocracy they had long demanded, the very principle on which elite African politics in Southern Rhodesia had been founded. This new arrangement meant that the black middle class would eschew the kind of class-transcending, all-African alliance that had defined the national moment, opting instead for a coalition with the white liberals who were in the vanguard of new racial-partnership ideology. In the end, however, the Federation of Rhodesia and Nyasaland failed to deliver on its promises, dashing the hopes and expectations of the black petty bourgeoisie. By 1958, the foundations of racial partnership had seriously eroded, and indeed were on the verge of collapsing, sending the African elite on yet another political odyssey.

THE SPECTER OF 1948

The general strike of 1948 cast a long shadow over Southern Rhodesia. After exhaustive research and study that lasted some two years and included a report written by an official commission, the colonial regime decided on a strategy to control African working-class militancy. The result was the Subversive Activities Act of 1950, a vaguely worded law empowering the government to prohibit strikes and trade union activity at will and enabling it to punish violators through fines, imprisonment, and deportation. Nor did the authorities seek to conceal the fact that the law was a direct response to the proletarian challenge. Its origin, the minister of justice explained in introducing the repressive measure, "goes back to 1948 ... [when] there was a series of more or less serious native disturbances throughout the Colony known as the Native General Strike."[1]

The Subversive Activities Act, which was modeled on South Africa's Riotous Assemblies and Criminal Amendment Act of 1914, had two main clauses. The first clause banned literature "calculated to stir up hostility and ill-feeling between the various races," whereas the second and perhaps more important one made it an offense to prevent people who "want to go legitimately to their work from so going," a measure aimed at alleged "intimidators," such as those who had led the 1948 walkout.[2] Ominously, the Subversive Activities Act was driven by a new ideological zeal: the onset of the Cold War since the general strike had emboldened the colonial regime to insulate the Africans against the red menace, a move consistent with its long-standing campaign to defend Western civilization. Although admitting that communism had not "taken any hold" on Southern Rhodesia, the minister of justice still considered it "a very real threat." The new law, he asserted, was "the only way to prevent the spread of subversive propaganda and Communistic doctrines amongst the under-privileged section of the community."[3]

The Subversive Activities Act was the most provocative piece of anti-African legislation since the Urban Areas Act of 1946. As it made its way through the legislative process, the bill was sharply criticized by those formations that continued to lay claim to working-class leadership in the wake of the 1948 debacle, namely, the Salisbury-based Reformed Industrial and Commercial Workers Union of Africa (RICU) and the Federation of Bulawayo African Trade Unions. RICU leader Charles Mzingeli and his vice president, Solomon Maviyane, strongly objected to the proposed law, claiming that it "appears to [the African] as a weapon specifically aimed against him and designed to prevent him from advancing by legitimate means."[4] Continuing a long tradition among elite Africans, they challenged the government's civilizationist claims, rejecting the proposition that "discriminatory legislation as applied in this colony is an ideal and accepted precept of Western civilisation."[5] In a similar vein, the African Trade Unions mocked the regime's democratic pretensions, pointing out that the Subversive Activities Bill was motivated by "preferential and discriminatory treatment of citizens of a country that claims to be democratic and to have inherited the British traditions of justice."[6]

Opposition to the Subversive Activities Bill was not, however, universal among elite African political leaders. In sharp contrast to the position taken by the RICU and the African Trade Unions, Stanlake Samkange, general secretary of the Southern Rhodesia African National Congress, issued a statement endorsing the proposed law, in principle if not in detail. A son of the Rev. Thompson Samkange, the former National Congress president, Stanlake had gained his position as part of a sweeping change in the organization's leadership after the 1948 general strike.

Stanlake Samkange urged the government to amend the bill to compel employers to allow the formation of workers' committees (as distinct from trade unions); he also complained that the proposed law gave the authorities powers that were "a little too wide and general." On the whole, however, he accepted the official anticommunist line, arguing that the Subversive Activities Bill was a necessary piece of legislation. In deciding its position, Samkange opined, the National Congress "had to bear in mind that we are first and foremost Rhodesians—secondly Africans, a section of the Rhodesian community. As such we cannot but support the principles of the Bill since it seeks to safeguard the existence of the governmental form of our country. . . . We are therefore as eager as any community in the country to oppose communism."[7]

Samkange, however, had received no mandate from the National Congress's executive for his Rhodesia-first, anticommunist broadside but had acted entirely on his own. At its annual general conference less than two weeks later, the National Congress erupted in furor over its general secretary's unilateral action. The conference disassociated itself from Samkange's statement and indeed declared its opposition to the Subversive Activities Bill. The president, Enoch Dumbutshena, went further. Despite a personal friendship with Samkange, Dumbutshena denounced the general secretary's action as "damaging to the cause of the African people" and resigned in protest.[8]

Never one to pass up an opportunity to rib his longtime National Congress nemesis, a gleeful Charles Mzingeli announced that the criticism of Samkange's action was wholly unjustified. Quoting from its constitution, Mzingeli asserted, tongue in cheek, that the document required the National Congress "to assist Government officials by explaining to the African people that discriminatory laws are not made for the purpose of persecuting them, but for their development." Thus, concluded the RICU leader, in endorsing the Subversive Activities Bill, "Mr. Samkange did just what the [National Congress's] constitution demands."[9] Mzingeli's mischievous blast notwithstanding, the National Congress's repudiation of Samkange's unauthorized statement closed the circle of African opposition to the Subversive Activities Bill. The National Congress had now joined other political formations, notably the RICU and the African Trade Unions, in rejecting the proposed legislation.

No amount of African antagonism, however, would prevent the settler regime from enacting the bill into law. No sooner had this been done than the government, confirming the worst fears of the African critics, invoked the new law in its ongoing campaign against the working class. It issued a decree banning publications of the World Federation of Trade Unions—the European-based, left-leaning union umbrella movement—which the minister of justice denounced as a "Communistic body" with a habit of attacking "the Colonial powers in Africa and their treatment of the African populations." The decree also prohibited the importation of material published by the Pan-African Trade Union Conference, an organization affiliated with the World Federation of Trade Unions.[10] Subsequently Joshua Nkomo, a future trade unionist, was prosecuted under the Subversive Activities Act for bringing into the colony material published by the World Federation of Trade Unions. Although found guilty, he escaped with a light sentence—a reprimand.[11] But the authorities had made their point. They would tolerate no links, however tenuous, between the African working class in Southern Rhodesia and progressive movements abroad, especially if the latter were deemed anticolonial and therefore susceptible to red-baiting.

AMALGAMATION AND ITS DETRACTORS

The Subversive Activities Act came in the midst of an even more vexed struggle then being waged by the African elite, this one centered on opposition to the proposed fusion of Southern Rhodesia, Northern Rhodesia, and Nyasaland. Amalgamation, the term initially used by the advocates of fusion, was not a new idea. The first concrete step toward greater political union took place in 1916 when the British South Africa Company (BSAC), at once the government and largest investor in both colonies, attempted to amalgamate the two Rhodesias. The BSAC administration in Southern Rhodesia regarded amalgamation as a political and economic imperative; it would result in greater bureaucratic efficiency, remove restrictions on interterritorial trade, make it easier to attract the white settlers who were thought to be vital to development, and, not least, facilitate the recruitment of labor. For tactical reasons, however, amalgamation was opposed by the unofficial members of the Southern Rhodesian Legislative Council, that is, those who were voted into office by the predominantly settler electorate, in contrast to the official members, who were appointed by the BSAC. The Southern Rhodesian settlers believed immediate amalgamation with Northern Rhodesia, a less developed colony, would undermine what was then their most pressing political objective —to do away with the BSAC administration and assume control of the government themselves.[12]

On attaining self-government in 1923, the Southern Rhodesian settlers warmed to the idea of amalgamation, largely for the same reasons as had the ousted BSAC, which they regarded as despotic and which simultaneously also lost administrative control of Northern Rhodesia to the British Colonial Office. Then, in 1930, the amalgamation initiative passed from the Southern Rhodesian settlers to their counterparts on the other side of the Zambezi

River. The sudden and urgent demand for amalgamation by the Northern Rhodesian white community resulted directly from a commission that looked into the issue of "closer union" between the British territories in East and central Africa, including Northern Rhodesia.[13] In response to the commission's report, the British imperial authorities declared their willingness to consider closer union, providing the interests of the Africans were given precedence over those of non-Africans, that is, whites and Indians.[14] In Northern Rhodesia, the doctrine of native paramountcy, as the imperial declaration was soon christened, prompted an all-out political white flight. The settlers there demanded amalgamation with their fellow Europeans in Southern Rhodesia, where white rule was unquestioned and the idea of native paramountcy did not arise.

The resulting amalgamationist fever on both sides of the Zambezi did not go unnoticed by the colonized people. An organized body of Northern Rhodesian Africans rejected amalgamation, fearing what it regarded as Southern Rhodesia's more repressive native policy. Instead, the Northern Rhodesian Africans proposed a union with Nyasaland, where the white settler community was far weaker, numerically and politically, than it was in both Northern and Southern Rhodesia, the latter especially. This apparently was the first time such a proposal had been made; hitherto Nyasaland had not been mentioned in connection with the amalgamation of the two Rhodesias.[15]

Meanwhile, Africans in Southern Rhodesia also came out against amalgamation, arguing, like the northern anti-amalgamationists, that Southern Rhodesia would likely dominate the united polity, with negative consequences for the colonized people in all the territories concerned. Thus in 1936 the Southern Rhodesia Native Missionary Conference, then the principal voice of black political opinion in the colony, passed a resolution "respectfully" requesting the government to consult the Africans before making any move toward closer union. But the Native Missionary Conference was not content to leave the colonized people completely at the mercy of the settler regime, for it also urged the British imperial authorities to retain their veto power over legislation that affected Africans.[16] The Rev. Thompson Samkange, the Native Missionary Conference's hard-driving secretary, went even further: he rejected amalgamation outright, citing rampant racial discrimination in Southern Rhodesia.[17] The African hostility to amalgamation, in the Rhodesias as well as in Nyasaland, was forcefully communicated to an imperial commission, which tabled its report in 1939 and which, consequently, rejected the idea of closer union. Peter Kumalo, a noted Southern Rhodesian African activist, lauded the commission's "wise and unanimous decision."[18]

World War II relegated the amalgamation question to the political back burner, although the fire was never fully extinguished. In 1941, for instance, an individual identified only as "an African in S.R.," responding to continued

talk in official circles about it, attacked closer union as a ploy by Southern
Rhodesian capitalists to obtain cheap northern labor: "It is obvious that commercial and industrial heads are in favor of Amalgamation for their eyes are
fixed on the benefit that they would obtain if the two Rhodesias and Nyasaland were joined together. The Africans not being commercially developed do
not see anything beneficial to them as a result of Amalgamation. . . . [Africans
believe] that the capitalists want Amalgamation because besides other benefits for them labour would be cheap."[19] Some three years later the National
Congress, at its annual conference, restated the African antagonism to closer
union. Now under the presidency of Thompson Samkange, a consistent critic
of the idea, the National Congress came out "totally against amalgamation."
This decision so infuriated Charles Olley, the vociferously anti-black mayor
of Salisbury, that he barred delegates attending the conference from using
Recreation Hall, the city-owned meeting place in the African township.[20]

The National Congress's opposition to closer union intensified during the
national moment, the period of renewed African assertiveness in the years
between the railway strike of 1945 and the general strike of 1948. In 1947
Thompson Samkange, in his presidential address to the National Congress's annual conference, again lambasted amalgamation. Sounding a quasi-nationalist,
almost nativistic, note, he declared that from a Southern Rhodesian standpoint, there was no economic imperative to unite with Northern Rhodesia
and Nyasaland. "The resources of the [Southern Rhodesian] Colony are un-
tapped which when fully developed can make us self-sufficient," Samkange
opined. Far from being a Southern Rhodesian initiative, he went on, the amalgamation issue was "being pressed by Northern Rhodesian Europeans, probably a few dissatisfied capitalists," a reference to the powerful South African-
dominated interests that controlled that territory's all-important copper mining
industry.[21]

Thompson Samkange's apportionment of blame was misplaced. Southern Rhodesian capital and state were no less eager for closer union than were
their Northern Rhodesian counterparts. Indeed, by 1947 Southern Rhodesia
once again had become the leader of the amalgamationist lobby, having developed even more powerful economic motives for closer union than it had during the prewar period. Southern Rhodesia's wartime-induced industrial development depended critically on three factors: gaining a share of the foreign
currency earned from Northern Rhodesian copper, getting preferential access
(in relation to South Africa) to Nyasaland's vast labor pool, and creating new
markets in the north.[22]

Concurrently, the British imperial authorities, previously lukewarm, even
hostile, to amalgamation, as evidenced by the 1939 commission on closer union,
began to embrace the idea on both economic and political grounds. A fusion
of the three British possessions would likely mean an expanded market for

British industries, even as it relieved the imperial treasury of the burdens of colonial administration in Nyasaland, the poorest of the three territories. The British, furthermore, had compelling strategic reasons for supporting amalgamation in the post–World War II period. Since the end of the South African War of 1899–1902, successive British governments had sought to contain Afrikaner nationalism. However, the election in 1948 of the National Party, with its apartheid manifesto and its anti-British rhetoric, seemed to doom the policy of containment. Under the circumstances, an amalgamated Rhodesia and Nyasaland, prosperous and pro-British, was seen as a bulwark against potential Afrikaner expansionism on the southern-central African subcontinent.[23]

FROM AMALGAMATION TO FEDERATION

By 1948, then, the British imperial authorities were prepared to give their blessing to a political and administrative union of the Rhodesias and Nyasaland —meaning, concretely, a reconstituted settler-dominated polity largely controlled by Southern Rhodesia. The trouble, of course, was that the leading African political formations in all three territories had long opposed such a scheme. What is more, the anti-amalgamationists believed they had a firm commitment from London that amalgamation would not be imposed over their objections. As late as 1947, the National Congress's Thompson Samkange, referring to the 1939 commission, confidently predicted that "the British Parliament will not go against its pledged word" and force closer union on an unwilling African population.[24] Thus the imperial authorities, although determined to pursue amalgamation in partnership with the settlers, felt compelled to make some gesture that could be construed as a concession to African sentiment. The result was a declaration by the supporters of closer union that they had abandoned the quest for amalgamation and would settle instead for federation.

According to this logic, federation involved a union that offered its component parts greater autonomy, in contrast to amalgamation, which envisioned a more centralized polity. The switch from amalgamation to federation was backed by a propaganda offensive, including advertisements in Southern Rhodesia's African-oriented press—which was circulated in the northern territories—aimed at convincing the opponents of closer union that their antagonists genuinely were interested in a compromise. Yet although little more than a semantic reshuffling, these maneuverings were not entirely without effect. At its 1949 annual conference, the National Congress, still reeling from the previous year's political disaster and the subsequent leadership changes, found itself unable to respond to the new challenge. Despite the robust opposition of previous conferences and leaders to amalgamation, the 1949 conclave could muster no more than a pusillanimous injunction "to await further information, and to see what the constitution contained, regarding the ways and means of Federation."[25]

As with Stanlake Samkange's defense of the Subversive Activities Bill, the National Congress's irresolute stance on federation proved to be out of step with the elite African consensus, even in the changing post-1948 circumstances. Leaping, as always, at the opportunity to taunt his rivals, Charles Mzingeli, his opposition to closer union under any label as firm as ever, blasted the National Congress. "We are fully aware," he averred, that the supposed concession "is not federation but amalgamation through the back door!" Characteristically accusing his opponents of opportunism, Mzingeli continued: "every responsible African in Southern Rhodesia, with the exception of a few seeking better positions, is deadly opposed to the present movement [for] the so-called Federation of the three territories."[26] He did not, however, persist in this divisive rhetoric. For once in his long and not altogether inglorious career as a political operative, Mzingeli suppressed his cantankerous urges long enough to work cooperatively with other African organizations and leaders in the campaign against federation. Indeed, that struggle may well have been his finest hour—rivaled only by the campaign from which he had just emerged, this one for the right of women, mostly the spouses and mates of working-class men, to gain legal residence in Salisbury's African township.[27]

The African opposition to federation, which included the initially wavering National Congress, increased in direct proportion to the pace of negotiations between the British imperial authorities and the settler politicians in the colonies. In his report for the year 1951, the chief native commissioner noted that the "politically-minded" urban African elite, a "comparatively small but very vocal" group, was "almost unanimously opposed to federation." Claiming that the African masses were "passive and apathetic" on the issue, he denounced the activists as "demagogues [who] do not as yet generally represent Native opinion as they claim to do."[28] The following year the chief native commissioner reported that the situation had worsened, with the urban-educated African, that great bane of colonial bureaucrats, supposedly on the verge of insurrection. The vast majority of the African population, the official reiterated, "is happy and contented, is not politically minded, and is prepared to accept the Government's decision on Federation." It was otherwise with the activists, or what the chief native commissioner called "some of the more irresponsible of the urban natives, and I have to report a deterioration of their attitude to the Europeans. . . . [In] recent months, I have sensed a spirit of near insolence by many Africans."[29]

Indeed 1952, the year the imperial authorities and the settler representatives finalized the deal to establish the federation, also marked the high point

of antifederation agitation in Southern Rhodesia and the other two territories. Determined to take their case directly to the center of empire, the opponents of federation called for African inclusion in the official Southern
Rhodesian delegation that was scheduled to hold talks in London with the
imperial government. Among the organizations making this demand were
the National Congress, the British African National Voice Association (now
transformed into a largely rural movement in the wake of its disastrous performance during the 1948 general strike), and the time-honored Southern
Rhodesia Native Association (now called the Southern Rhodesia African Association, out of deference to the most recent nomenclatorial shift in the self-
designation of the colonized elite).

Claiming that the criterion for selection as a delegate was membership in
the Legislative Assembly, an all-white body, the government curtly rejected
the call for African participation in the London talks.[30] There was "no constitutional reason why representatives of African organisations should be allowed to go as observers, any more than delegates from European organisations," the authorities objected. In any case, they asserted, the parliamentary
negotiators would "speak for the people as a whole."[31] With the opposition to
federation reaching fever pitch, however, the elite black leaders were in no
mood to be told that the same government that was determined to impose
closer union on Africans would also represent African interests in the negotiations over the said closer union. As the pressure mounted, the Southern
Rhodesian regime was forced to yield on the principle of direct African representation in the talks, especially in view of the fact that the Northern Rhodesian and Nyasaland delegations would include Africans.

Yet if Africans were going to join their delegation, the Southern Rhodesian authorities were determined that they, and they alone, would select
the African delegates. Thus, without even the pretense of consulting African
organizations, the government peremptorily announced its choices: Jasper
Savanhu and Joshua Nkomo. Savanhu, who had emerged at the time of the
1945 railway strike as an articulate tribune of African grievances and as a
leader of the fledgling trade union movement, had since moved on to become
Southern Rhodesia's top black newspaperman, in the employ of the white-
owned, African-oriented press. The younger and less-seasoned Nkomo was a
social worker with Rhodesia Railways, a job that brought him into direct contact with the strategically important railway workers, a group on whose behalf
Savanhu had once spoken with much eloquence and feeling.

Stung by the regime's contemptuous attitude, the competing African political formations, in an unusual show of unity, banded together to oppose
its handpicked delegates. The leaders of the RICU, the National Congress,
and the African Association fired off a joint telegram to the Fabian Colonial Bureau—the London-based anticolonial lobby and staunch opponent of

federation—denouncing Savanhu and Nkomo as lacking standing among the colony's Africans.[32] When two Africans in Bulawayo attempted to rally support for the beleaguered delegates, the incensed leaders dispatched another telegram to London. This second missive breezily dismissed one of the would-be defenders, E. M. Hikura, as being of unknown personal and political identity, while using a nativist argument to deride the other, Charlton Ngcebetsha, a South African immigrant and veteran activist, as "an alien African not representative of [the] major African organizations" in Southern Rhodesia.[33]

The Southern Rhodesian African delegates, still braving a wave of resentment at home, had a rough time at the London talks. Unlike their Northern Rhodesian and Nyasaland counterparts, who denounced federation as a power grab by the Southern Rhodesian settlers at every turn, Savanhu and Nkomo barely uttered a word, whether within or outside of the conference room.[34] For several weeks, both men remained at the mercy of their government patrons, lacking as they did the international connections of the other African delegates, who were kept fully briefed by London-based supporters, African and British alike. Nkomo admitted as much, albeit decades later. "We did not know our way around London," he wrote in his 1984 autobiography, "we had little money and no idea how to get in touch with the press or the BBC."[35] When they refused to join the Northern Rhodesian and Nyasaland Africans in boycotting the first session of the talks, Savanhu and Nkomo were denounced as "stooges" by an antifederation member of the British parliament. Still politically naive, Nkomo "did not know what a stooge was, but it sounded bad."[36]

Nkomo, however, would prove to be a quick study. Sensing the strong tide of African opinion against any form of closer union, he reversed himself and came out squarely against federation on returning home. Savanhu, his previous radicalism now but a fading memory, refused to follow suit. As editor in chief of African Newspapers, which owned virtually every black-oriented publication of note in the colony, Savanhu had much more to lose, both professionally and personally, than did the more formally educated Nkomo, a university graduate.

The pace of antifederation agitation quickened after the talks in London, when it became clear that, contrary to Thompson Samkange's prediction five years earlier, the British imperial authorities would indeed force closer union on the Africans. As awareness of this fact deepened, the loose alliance that had been mobilizing against federation became more coherent and better organized. The result was the formation of the All-African Convention. An umbrella movement that incorporated the leading antifederation organizations, the All-African Convention was led by Mzingeli as president, with Nkomo as a member of the executive. The group's constitution committed affiliated bodies to a policy of non-cooperation, including refusal to contest the seats re-

8. Jasper Savanhu, a journalist whose political career was launched by the railway workers' strike of 1945, subsequently became a member of parliament of the Federation of Rhodesia and Nyasaland. Courtesy of the National Archives of Zimbabwe.

served for Africans in the federation's parliament.[37] (Six of the thirty-five seats were reserved for Africans, two from each territory.)

In Bulawayo, long a center of black agitation in Southern Rhodesia, anti-federation activities were coordinated by the Supreme Council of Bulawayo African Organisations, a coalition of local groups headed by Nkomo. In its most impressive display of organizational skill, the Supreme Council organized a boycott of the municipal beer halls on March 15, 1953, declared the occasion a national day of prayer, and held a huge rally that was attended by more ten thousand people.[38] Shortly thereafter, African leaders from all three colonies met in Northern Rhodesia to coordinate opposition to federation on an interterritorial basis, an unprecedented demonstration of pan-African political comity. Among other decisions, the leaders agreed to boycott the parliamentary seats reserved for Africans and to send a joint delegation to London to lobby against federation.[39]

Weeks earlier, the opponents of federation in Southern Rhodesia had already taken such a step by dispatching Nkomo back to London. In addition to being more loquacious, he had a different message this time. Making the rounds in London, Nkomo announced that there was "little difference—[only] the franchise—between . . . [South Africa's] apartheid policy and [Southern] Rhodesia's segregation policy," adding that Africans would not support

9. Benjamin Burombo entered politics in the period leading up to the 1948 general strike—an event in which he, like the rest of the elite African leaders, played a less than glorious role. Courtesy of the National Archives of Zimbabwe.

10. Masotha Mike Hove, one-time editor of the *Bantu Mirror* who went on to become a member of parliament of the Federation of Rhodesia and Nyasaland. Courtesy of the National Archives of Zimbabwe.

11. Charles Mzingeli, a
political activist whose career
spanned the decades before and
after World War II,
subsequently became alienated
from the African political
mainstream and ended up
supporting Ian Smith's rebel
regime. Courtesy of *Parade.*

any move toward closer union until the settler regime "had put her house in
order."[40] Nkomo's new refrain earned the critical acclaim of the Fabian Colonial Bureau, which had given him a poor review during his previous visit to
London with the official Southern Rhodesian delegation. "There was some
talk that his fare had been paid by non-Africans," the group's secretary exulted about the second trip, "but even if that were the case, he spoke very forcibly against Federation and I think he did a good job from the African point
of view."[41] In fact, Nkomo's fare had been paid by Africans in Bulawayo, one

of whom extended a loan of £350 toward the trip, a debt that, like any number of similar political accounts, was never settled.[42]

Meanwhile, back in Southern Rhodesia the attack on federation continued unabated. Robert Mugabe, then a teacher in Salisbury, weighed in to answer critics who intimated that opposition to federation was anti-Christian. Federation, Mugabe argued, was nothing less than an attack on the nascent consciousness of an emerging people: "Surely, no educated Africans have yet refused that Christianity—practical Christianity—is 'the soul of civilisation.' But many of us are greatly suspicious, and rightly so, of moves with sinister motives. Federation is such a move. Sir Godfrey Huggins has made it abundantly clear that it is primarily aimed at nipping African nationalism in the bud. Thus Federation becomes an instrument that will be wielded to suppress our self-determination and progress."[43] Ever the articulator of consensus rather than the molder of opinion, Mugabe was merely expressing a view widely shared by African activists.

Thus the opposition of Africans in Southern Rhodesia to closer union, whether defined as amalgamation or federation, was consistent, serious, and credible. That opposition, which eventually became organized on a local, national, and regional basis, began in the 1930s and continued up to the eve of the creation, in September 1953, of the Federation of Rhodesia and Nyasaland, or the Central African Federation, as it was more popularly known. Such a stance refutes the notion that Africans in Southern Rhodesia, in contrast to those in Northern Rhodesia and Nyasaland, offered little resistance to the imposition of federation.[44] If anything, the Southern Rhodesian Africans regarded themselves as being in the forefront of the struggle against the proposed political marriage. For instance, during the transition from amalgamation to federation, Charles Mzingeli, noting the stated willingness of African organizations in Southern Rhodesia and Nyasaland to form a united front against any move toward closer union, accused Northern Rhodesia's African leaders of being "agents of the Federation Machinery. I am sorry to say so. But it is my conviction and [that of] many [other] African leaders" in Southern Rhodesia.[45]

The subsequent emergence of the view that Africans in Southern Rhodesia were less than fervent in their opposition to federation, if not outright collusive in its creation, may be attributed to the different reactions in the three territories to the Central African Federation, once it became a fact of life. Most African activists in Northern Rhodesia, and especially in Nyasaland, remained unreconstructed, bitterly opposing the new polity during its entire ten-year existence. In Southern Rhodesia, by contrast, the bulk of the elite African leadership, including many former opponents of closer union, opted for conciliation and eventually made peace with the Central African Federation, at least for a while.

In Southern Rhodesia, antifederation sentiment began to recede by mid-1953, when it became apparent that closer union was imminent, whether or not the Africans liked it. The major act of surrender came when the All-African Convention formally repudiated non-cooperation, the core of the opposition to federation, effectively inviting its leaders to contest the election. Faced with a fait accompli, the erstwhile exponents of non-cooperation declared the battle against federation lost but vowed to continue the war for African rights from the seat of power, namely, the federal parliament. This imperative became especially pressing after Godfrey Huggins's Federal Party, the dominant political force in the coming federation, drafted Jasper Savanhu and Masotha Mike Hove, editor of the *Bantu Mirror,* Savanhu's old job, to run for the seats reserved for Africans in Southern Rhodesia.[46] The new consensus among the African leadership was well expressed by Solomon Maviyane, now titular president of the RICU. Maviyane argued that "following the imposition of [the] Federation scheme and [the] endorsement of two African candidates for Federal seats by a powerful Federal Party . . . we have no alternative but to work hard to make [the] Federal scheme a success."[47]

Inevitably, the jockeying to determine who would take on the Federal Party candidates resurrected the querulous spirit of the past, as former antifederation allies traded charges of duplicity and bad faith. Nkomo, his eye firmly fixed on the ultimate prize, took out newspaper advertisements outlining his qualifications for the job of parliamentarian.[48] The All-African Convention was sufficiently impressed to endorse him for the African seat in Matabeleland, while giving the nod to Stanlake Samkange for the one in Mashonaland—evidently deciding to round out its slate with university graduates. The apparent decision to run the academically best and brightest against Savanhu and Hove, neither of whom had gone to university, meant bypassing the even less formally educated Mzingeli, president of the All-African Convention and unofficial dean of the engagé autodidacts. A piqued Mzingeli, reverting to verbal pugilism, an art at which he was so adept, denounced the Convention's candidates as men motivated by the perquisites of electoral office.[49]

As it happened, neither the All-African Convention nor its candidates would receive any such bounty. Both Samkange and Nkomo were drubbed at the polls: the one by Savanhu and the other by Hove. The victory of the Federal Party–backed candidates was hardly surprising. All candidates for parliament, including those contesting the seats reserved for Africans, were elected on the common roll, which is to say they were elected by an overwhelmingly white electorate. Indeed, Savanhu and Hove won their seats as part of a landslide victory by the Federal Party, which went on to form the government of the newly created Central African Federation. Huggins, after two decades as prime minister of Southern Rhodesia, ascended to the same post in the federation, an entity he had done more to create than had any other single person. Savanhu, the most articulate voice of the New African during the national moment of 1945–48, had made an even longer and more arduous political journey. Having confronted Huggins on the other side of the divide during the 1945 railway strike, Savanhu now made a full about-face, completing his adventure from adversary to ally by becoming part of the Federal Party's parliamentary majority, albeit from the back benches.

FEDERATION AND RACIAL PARTNERSHIP

The dispirited former opponents of federation, after being routed in the election, could reasonably have been expected, upon regaining their equilibrium, to return to the politics of agitation. No such antifederation regrouping, however, would take place. Instead, the majority of politically engaged Africans were systematically drawn into the ranks of various associations whose avowed objective was to create a more perfect federation, one that would be more hospitable to Africans—the African elite, to be more precise—than was the arrangement envisaged by Huggins and his Federal Party. In short order, the ideology and practice of racial partnership, as the vision of a better deal for the black petty bourgeoisie became known, emerged as the central motif in African politics, until the rise of mature African nationalism in the late 1950s.

The idea of a new racial partnership between Europeans and Africans was first mooted around the time of the transition from amalgamation to federation. It was the centerpiece of the battle for the hearts and minds of elite blacks—the effort to convince them that they had nothing to fear from closer union and indeed would benefit from it. In the course of the referendum to approve Southern Rhodesia's participation in the proposed federation—it was ratified by the legislative bodies in the other two territories—a group of white ultra-diehards, campaigning on a xenophobic platform, had denounced closer union as a dilution of settler power, citing, among other things, the talk about racial partnership. Huggins, however, rejected this interpretation as slanderous and just so much electoral demagoguery. Reassuring the largely European electorate of his unwavering support for settler supremacy, political and otherwise, the prime minister quipped that his idea of partnership between white and black was akin to the partnership between a horse and its rider.

Huggins was as good as his word, governing the Central African Federation in much the same way that he had governed Southern Rhodesia, that is, as a bastion of white power. Not all whites, however, subscribed to the unmitigated horse-and-rider approach to colonial rule. A small minority, mainly postwar white-collar immigrants from Britain, had an alternate vision of racial partnership in which the African elite would be gradually incorporated into the white-dominated civil society. Bitter foes of African nationalism, these white newcomers, who were reviled by "old Rhodesians" as naive do-gooders, signaled a willingness to concede the principle, if not always the practice, of equality to the black petty bourgeoisie. The egalitarian proffer did not, of course, include the black horde, and the unwashed African peasants and workers would remain separate and apart from the imagined multiracial community of "civilized" people.

Ethnocentric and paternalistic to the core, the white liberals took for granted the superiority of Western culture. At the same time, they were willing to concede a measure of equality to Africans who attained European standards. Significantly for elite Africans, especially the younger and better educated among them, these newfangled white liberals rejected the kind of organizational and social segregation that previous white "friends of natives" —organized into such groups as the Welfare Society, the Missionary Conference, and the Labour Party—had practiced. In short, the postwar white liberals advocated, although not without qualification and equivocation, the integration of the African middle class into settler society. As a leading organ of white liberal opinion explained: "We believe that the policy of partnership is the only feasible one if European civilization is to survive in Africa; but it must be a policy of 'equal rights for every civilized man' and the Europeans, if they want to lead, must show that they are worthy to be leaders."[50] White settlers, according to this defense of Western civilization, could best demonstrate their worthiness to lead by putting aside the blanket exclusion of all Africans and by supporting the creation of a nonracial meritocracy in which blackness would not be a permanent and automatic social disability.

Many elite Africans, for their part, embraced the politics of racial partnership as a vindication of the old doctrine of equal rights for all civilized men, the ideological axis of African petty-bourgeois agitation from the outset. Indeed, by 1954 the prospect of racial partnership would have excited these upwardly mobile blacks all the more. Despite the genuine alienation caused by the federation hubbub and the unprecedented, although brief, political alliance between elite and non-elite Africans during the postwar national moment, middle-class African politics never completely lost its class-specific leitmotif. Thus, in a book published in 1954—the first such achievement by an African domiciled in Southern Rhodesia—Bradfield Mnyanda, a leading light in the National Congress, was still advancing the old nonracial civilizationist agenda: "Today, the African people—particularly the educated and the civilised among them—can no longer be treated in this Colony or, for that matter, in any part of South[ern] Africa, on the old 'voetsalk-you-bloody-Kaffir' basis. They demand a place in the sun; and he who thwarts their legitimate aspirations will do so at his own peril. By all means, let us have a 'culture bar' in place of the present colour bar."[51] The Rev. Esau Nemapare, writing around the same time as the South African–born Mnyanda, agreed wholeheartedly. "The trouble," offered Nemapare, a prominent Ethiopianist or African independent churchman, "is that in Southern Rhodesia the social bar, which I fully support, is being taken for the colour bar, which no decent European or African wants."[52] The politics of racial partnership, with its emphasis on race neutrality in human affairs, promised to fight for just the kind of society demanded by the likes of Mnyanda and Nemapare, one based on the culture/social-bar rather than the color-bar principle.

From an organizational standpoint, the leading champions of racial partnership were the Inter-Racial Association of Southern Rhodesia (IRA) and the Capricorn Africa Society (CAS). Both groups began from the assumption that the emergent anticolonial nationalism throughout Africa threatened European civilization on the continent. However, the white liberals in the IRA, the CAS, and allied groups deprecated an apartheid-style solution to the perceived problem, arguing instead that the best antidote to African nationalism was for high-minded and far-sighted whites to take the lead in creating a society founded on the nonracial civilizationist ideal. Some elite Africans, mindful of the bitter fruits of previous exercises in racial cooperation, declared a willingness to support the latest attempt at partnership, but only if it produced concrete results in the form of an end to segregation. This point was forcefully expressed by Ernest Mhlanga, a veteran articulator of black aspirations, who asserted that partnership "must not remain a political platitude . . . when in actual fact there is no such thing in existence and neither will it ever come [about]."[53] The pro-partnership formations vowed to campaign for real changes that would improve the life chances of middle-class Africans.

This was certainly the position of the Inter-Racial Association, which was officially launched in July 1953, having been founded by a group of white professionals and businessmen.[54] Asserting that the time for "talk in vague generalisations" had passed, the IRA vowed to demonstrate, through deeds, that racial partnership was really "different from apartheid."[55] Consistent with the politics of partnership, it loathed African nationalism and apartheid alike. Fearing that "Europeans may become Herrenvolk and Africans 'Black Nationalist,'" the IRA rejected both "extremes," opting instead for a centrist "liberal approach" which judged people on the basis of their individual capacity rather than their group membership. Not surprisingly, it lauded the black elite, arguing that "the emergence of a class of advanced Africans is of the utmost significance," and advocated policies to foster and recognize the development of such a social stratum. Accordingly, the IRA supported African freehold tenure in the urban areas, backed a color-blind qualified franchise, and rejected the migrant labor system in favor of a more stabilized work force, a policy endorsed by the captains of industry who were among the association's key underwriters.[56]

Indeed, the IRA was especially active in the area of industrial relations, and it convened a major conference on the subject that included both white and black trade unionists and employers representing secondary industry and mining. The IRA advocated amending the racially exclusionary Industrial Conciliation Act of 1934 to officially include Africans in the category of workers, enabling them legally to form unions and to bargain collectively with their employers. The call for state recognition of African proletarian rights was not, however, synonymous with endorsement of an autonomous black trade unionism, especially one that might be sympathetic to African nationalism. Rather, the IRA's industrial relations proposals, like virtually all of its major initiatives, were aimed at preserving white privilege on the one hand while checkmating African nationalism on the other—even as it sought, ever so gingerly, to widen opportunities for the black elite, including a growing strata of skilled workers. Toward this end, the IRA supported measures to harmonize the "civilised standard of living of the European [worker] . . . with the legitimate demands and ambitions of the Non-European," a task it proposed to accomplish through the creation of a multiracial "progressive trade union movement" under the control of the white "civilised minority." Failure to recognize the aspirations of "the more intelligent and ambitious African workers," the IRA warned, would inevitably lead to "resurgence of [an] extreme African Nationalism from which, once set in motion there is no retreat."[57]

The IRA, like the other pro-partnership formations, was largely an urban organization, with its headquarters in Salisbury and branches in Bulawayo and other towns. From the beginning, the IRA sought to establish racial balance in the composition of its various bodies. Its founding executive committee consisted of seventeen whites, fourteen blacks, four Indians, and three coloureds; *Concord,* the association's official organ, was jointly edited by four individuals, one from each of the four groups.[58] There were, however, more white than black members. In 1954, a year after its founding, 170 of the association's 270 members were white. Still, the African members included a number of prominent individuals, such as Masotha Mike Hove, Lawrence Vambe, Enoch Dumbutshena, Nathan Shamuyarira, Stanlake Samkange, and Charles Mzingeli, the latter two still general secretaries, respectively, of the National Congress and the RICU, both of which experienced a steep political decline during the era of partnership.[59]

Although active on many fronts and endlessly trumpeting the virtues of integration, the IRA, as a promoter of racial partnership, played second fiddle to the Capricorn Africa Society (CAS). The CAS was founded in 1949 by retired colonel David Stirling, an imposing Scotsman who earned his spurs during World War II by leading a unit that operated behind enemy lines, for which he became known as the Phantom Major of Britain's North African campaign. He immigrated to Southern Rhodesia after the war, working as an irrigation engineer and becoming, politically, an ardent exponent of the federation project. Indeed, the CAS's emergence coincided with the artful move from amalgamation to federation on the part of the supporters of closer union, and some opponents of federation, seeing a direct relationship between the two events, denounced the society as a Trojan horse seeking to "trap" Africans. And while spreading pro-federation propaganda throughout the colony[60] —including, it seems, advertisements in the African-oriented press—the CAS forbade its then small cadre of black supporters from openly campaigning for closer union, lest they "provoke extreme anti-Federation Africans into rash and foolish actions."[61]

With federation now in sight, the CAS, seeking to expand its circle of African supporters, had a rebirth in December 1952: it published a manifesto of its vision and goals, an event that received prominent press coverage within and without the British Empire.[62] Looking beyond the coming Central African Federation, the CAS's declaration envisaged a union of all six British territories between Ethiopia and South Africa, within the Tropic of Capricorn —that is, Kenya, Uganda, and Tanganyika as well as the Rhodesias and Nyasaland. In this imagined Federal Dominion of Capricorn, the CAS proposed an updated version of Lord Lugard's dual mandate.[63] Europeans, it announced, "have two responsibilities in Africa": to develop the continent's resources jointly with its original inhabitants and to help the Africans to improve their standards of living, thereby making possible "a living partnership between the races." Ultimately, the CAS hoped to establish in Capricorn Africa a society "founded on a common citizenship open to all those of any race who have attained the qualifications set at the level necessary to protect Western civilisation standards." In short, the CAS claimed to stand for equal rights for all civilized men, a mantra quoted in its manifesto.[64]

Philosophically, the CAS had much in common with the IRA. They believed alike in the superiority of Western culture and subscribed to the liberal approach to race relations. Overlapping memberships attested to the similarities between the groups: Stanlake Samkange, Nathan Shamuyarira, and Lawrence Vambe, to cite three prominent examples, belonged to both. There were, however, some significant differences. The IRA, despite initial attempts to expand to other parts of the Central African Federation, fundamentally was a Southern Rhodesian formation. By contrast the CAS, although based in Southern Rhodesia, aggressively marketed itself as a "pan-Capricorn" movement, establishing branches in Northern Rhodesia, Kenya, and Tanganyika (Tanzania), among other places.[65] And whereas the IRA cast itself as a practical, down-to-earth movement, the CAS was more idealistic in orientation. One IRA member summarized the differences this way: the CAS offered a "blue-print for a complete New Order which it will try to put across as a whole," whereas the IRA operated "more on a Make-Do-And-Mend principle, seeking gradual improvements."[66]

Whatever their differences, though, the CAS and the IRA were united in their aversion to African nationalism and apartheid, which they regarded as two sides of the same coin. Yet to judge by the focus of their ire, both groups took a far more jaundiced view of African nationalism than they did of apartheid. Indeed David Stirling, the CAS's founder, defended Southern Rhodesia's racist legacy. He did not believe that white "attitude in Southern Rhodesia has been wrong in the past, but only that it is becoming wrong in the present and will be disastrously wrong in the future. Our attitude was understandable when there were only a few educated Africans, but now it is quite untenable."[67] The future of Africa, according to this logic, belonged to those who could appeal to the hearts and minds—the former more so than the latter—of the African elite. And from an ideological standpoint, the African elite faced a choice between racial partnership and African nationalism.

It is hardly surprising, therefore, that the CAS manifesto boldly attacked African nationalism, deriding it as a racist movement aimed at driving the Europeans out of Africa, politically as well as physically. The CAS reproached the British imperial authorities for seeking to combat "African racialist aspirations" through a policy of political devolution and economic development. African nationalism, the CAS countered, appealed to the heart rather than the head, and so could not be appeased by political and economic concessions. As the CAS saw it, Africans' desire to control their own destiny was not a rational impulse but "an emotional force [that] can only be countered by a stronger and more practical spiritual and emotional force."[68] This force was, of course, the CAS and its vision of racial partnership.

Aside from African nationalism, the CAS had another deeply ingrained phobia—Indian immigration. The CAS claimed not to be generically hostile to individuals of South Asian descent, accepting that Indians who were already resident in Africa and who accepted the "Capricorn code of loyalty" should be accorded full citizenship rights. However, it strongly opposed further Indian immigration into Capricorn Africa, claiming such movements would inevitably result in "a tug-of-war between Eastern and Western values with the African as victim." The CAS, in fact, was deeply suspicious of independent India, vowing to "keep a close watch" on its activities in Africa, which Stirling believed aided and abetted "African racialism."[69] In sharp contrast to its position on India and Indian immigration, the CAS strongly supported European immigration, along with Western (including white South African) investment, both of which formed the core of its economic program.[70] The Rhodesian business community, local as well as foreign, returned the favor by generously supporting the CAS, underwriting it at a much higher level than it did the rival IRA.[71]

The CAS's deeper pocket was a major factor in its ability to attract adherents, including African ones, in far greater numbers than did the IRA. Bolstered by a full-time black executive officer, the CAS sponsored a seemingly endless string of political, cultural, and social activities—events at which elite blacks mixed freely with the postwar European immigrants who formed the core of the society's white supporters. At its peak in 1958, the CAS had 2,566 members, 65 percent of them African.[72] This figure would have constituted a considerable segment of the black middle class in Southern Rhodesia, and it marked a significant reversal of fortune for the CAS, which had been anathema to African activists in the years leading up to federation. Charlton Ngcebetsha was typical of those making the turnabout. Formerly an important player in the antifederation movement—despite being initially rebuked by other activists for supporting Joshua Nkomo and Jasper Savanhu when they were appointed to the government delegation for the London talks—Ngcebetsha freely admitted his past dislike of the CAS. By 1955, however, he was singing the group's praise in his solo cyclostyle weekly, expressing "full sympathy" with its principles and announcing that he had joined it "to render much useful service for our people."[73] The people Ngcebetsha had in mind were his fellow petty-bourgeois blacks, not the African masses, who figured little, if at all, in the political calculations of the CAS.

Such calculations included an ostentatious conclave, perhaps the CAS's signature event, that was held on the shores of Lake Nyasa in June 1956, when the society gathered a multiracial throng to discuss ways of making its manifesto real. Dubbed the Salima convention, the meeting was attended by delegates from throughout Capricorn Africa, and it resulted in the formation of "citizenship committees" to educate people on the rights and duties of citizenship in a multiracial society. The Salima process culminated in the foundation of the Rhodesian College of Citizenship, a corporate-funded initiative aimed at institutionalizing the work of the citizenship committees.[74]

Elite Africans were drawn to events like the Salima convention and the partnership ideal more generally for both practical and ideological reasons. The era of racial partnership marked the first time that appreciable numbers of white Rhodesians began to relate to Africans on the basis of something approximating social equality, albeit in a private residential setting, because all the major hotels and clubs rigidly excluded Africans. The "tea parties" and "sundowners" given by white acolytes of partnership—events at which, apparently, Africans were served "European" liquor in contravention of the law[75]— were not just multiracial social occasions; they also were opportunities for elite blacks to initiate and nurture personal, political, and business relationships with the more liberal members of the ruling race. Moreover, visiting dignitaries—politicians, diplomats, businessmen, academics, and foundation officials from Europe, the United States, Asia, and Africa—often could be found at these affairs, increasing the potential of elite colonial Zimbabweans for wider contacts, including invitations to visit and study overseas.

"Old Rhodesians" did not take kindly to such interracial fraternization, and many of them found it nothing short of abominable. The resulting nativistic attacks on the white exponents of partnership reached as far as the Legislative Assembly. The leader of the parliamentary opposition, a diehard segregationist, even offered (unsuccessfully) a motion to censure the race traitors. Blasting the "extremist" CAS and IRA for betraying "European standards" and advocating "complete social integration" of the races, he declared that the white multiracialists were "people who have been raised in other countries where the problem that we have to face does not exist; this problem of colour."[76]

Such assaults, coming from the most swashbuckling traducers of Africans in Rhodesian settler society, would only have drawn more blacks into the ideological orbit of the pro-partnership formations. In particular, the CAS manifesto, with its affirmation of equal treatment based on individual merit, was heartily embraced by many elite Africans, individuals such as John Shoniwa. Shoniwa—who would go on to pursue legal training in Britain, where he was supported by several CAS adherents—spoke for many of his social class in a letter to the editor of the colony's leading white daily:

> I write to your paper as an African who has been brought up from the age of seven by the British [he was educated by Anglican missionaries]. I was sent to one of the leading English speaking universities in South Africa [at Cape Town] and I claim to be as well educated and civilised as the average European. . . . The declaration of the Capricorn Africa Society is perhaps the first document setting out a scheme for Africa's future really to capture the imagination of the African in Southern Rhodesia and is a document of true statesmanship. . . . The principle which is implicit in the declaration is this: the recognition that the individual human being—not a race or a class —is the basic unit of society, the right of that human being to equal opportunity, and his right to all the fruits of citizenship if he is capable of attaining civilised standards. . . . The Society may, if it gets the support of every right thinking person, be heralding the dawn of a new age, not only for Capricorn Africa, but possibly for this vast continent as a whole at the very moment when the worsening of racial conflict seems inevitable. . . . I for one will support the Society to my utmost.[77]

Shoniwa was not alone in his effusiveness for the CAS and the politics of racial partnership. Nathan Shamuyarira affirms that "many articulate Africans were seeking to try out the new multi-racial order." Shamuyarira himself tried it out so much that he "feared to lose contact" with the African masses.[78] The hospitality of the suburban-dwelling white multiracialists, adds Lawrence Vambe, like Shamuyarira a leading African journalist, "tended to corrupt, for one was inclined to forget the thousands of black men and women living in squalor" in the nearby townships.[79]

Joshua Nkomo, one of the few "articulate" Africans with a high public profile who did not formally join any of the multiracial societies, recalled that independent black political mobilization virtually ground to a halt during the era of partnership. "The African leadership sank into apathy," he noted in his autobiography. "It was very difficult to get a lively meeting going."[80] In August 1956, when Chad Chipunza, the CAS's opportunistic executive officer,[81] gave a speech celebrating racial partnership in Bulawayo, Nkomo's putative stronghold, it was a politically forlorn Nkomo who bemoaned the fact that "people like Mr. Chipunza had seen in the Capricorn Africa Society a salvation for the African people."[82] Such was the state of independent African politics that the Rev. Thompson Samkange, who had resigned the leadership of the National Congress after the 1948 strike to make way for new blood—including his now tea-drinking son, Stanlake—began seriously to consider reentering the fray.[83] But there would be no political comeback for Thompson Samkange: he died suddenly, apparently the victim of a heart attack, within a couple of weeks of Chipunza's Bulawayo speech.

Meanwhile, the racial-partnership line remained hegemonic. Even Nkomo, despite his distance from the local pro-partnership formations, was not entirely immune to the multiracial impulse. In 1953, he and his wife were treated to a Swiss excursion by Moral Re-Armament, the pacifist, anticommunist movement that served as a kind of international prop to racial partnership in Southern Rhodesia.[84] Moral Re-Armament developed a considerable following among the black middle class in the 1950s, duplicating and augmenting many of the activities of the CAS and the IRA as well as offering Africans the opportunity to travel abroad, especially to its headquarters in Caux, Switzerland.[85]

Racial partnership reached its zenith in 1958, when elite African participation in the multiracial societies peaked. Subsequently, black membership in both the CAS and the IRA—along with the white-dominated political parties with which they were affiliated, directly or indirectly—declined progressively, reaching a point of virtual nonexistence by the mid-1960s. Partnership, for all the good intentions of its exponents, had failed miserably to deliver the promised nonracial meritocracy to the African middle class. To be sure, there had been a great deal of interracial partying, socializing, and good-timing, courtesy of the white liberals. But although gracious hosts, useful contacts, perhaps even genuine friends, these white liberals were ultimately powerless to remove the racist impediments to African social mobility in Rhodesian settler society.

The era of racial partnership, admittedly, was not altogether devoid of collective improvement for the African petty bourgeoisie. For instance, in 1957 the government changed the Liquor Law, which previously prohibited all Africans from consuming "European" liquor, that is, spirits, wine, and lager beer. Many (though by no means all) elite Africans, who were far more likely than the masses to have a taste for such alcohol or be able to acquire it on the black market, had long protested that the Liquor Law turned otherwise respectable people into criminals. Under the amended law, Africans were allowed to purchase alcoholic beverages (lager beer and wine) at will, although they still needed a special permit to obtain spirits.[86] More importantly, elite blacks welcomed the shift in policy that permitted urban-dwelling Africans to purchase homes on a leasehold basis. Some Africans, however, grumbled that they were still barred from obtaining property on a freehold basis, that is, from owning it outright. In any case, this concession did nothing to alter the system of residential segregation. The suburbs—sites of the best housing—remained lily-white, strictly off-limits to Africans, with the exception of domestic servants, of course.

Indeed, far from satisfying elite African aspirations, half-hearted changes only helped to fuel the revolution of expectations that had been created by the coming of federation and its corollary, racial partnership. From the outset, leading spokesmen for the African middle class had laid out their terms for participating in the promised new dispensation, namely, the systematic elimination of institutionalized racism and the creation of a society that would truly reward talented individuals, regardless of race. Elite Africans, Ernest Mhlanga had warned in 1954, were running short of patience and would no longer settle for mere "political platitude." Four years later, there was a growing chorus of lamentation about dashed hopes, unfulfilled dreams, and thwarted ambitions. Whatever the intentions of the liberal multiracial societies, in the end the Central African Federation remained a partnership of horse and rider, with the partners assuming the familiar roles of subordinate and superordinate. Godfrey Huggins and his Federal Party, it turned out, had kept their promise to the white electorate.

For as long as the federation lasted, it was largely in vain that exponents of partnership pleaded for meaningful and substantive changes. As late as 1957, Stanlake Samkange, speaking as a member of an IRA delegation, earnestly informed Roy Welensky, the Northern Rhodesian settler leader who had succeeded Huggins as federal prime minister the previous year, that the pro-partnership forces "wished to find instances of benefit to Africans which they could put forward as arguments in support of Federation."[87] Few such benefits would be forthcoming. The multiracialists, rather, continued to be stymied by the intransigence of the white settler state and society alike, in Southern Rhodesia and the federation as a whole.

Already in 1954 the federal parliament, controlled by Huggins and Welensky's Federal Party, had rejected a motion by a Northern Rhodesian African member that would have outlawed discrimination in the public services controlled by the federal government, such as the railway and the post office. African civil servants, meanwhile, were excluded from all but the lowest rungs of both the federal and the Southern Rhodesian bureaucracies. The situation was no better outside the state sector, where the color bar remained in full force in hotels, restaurants, theaters, and other public facilities. One notable exception was a Bulawayo restaurant, which permitted African diners, by "special arrangements," to be served in the kitchen. Yet even this demeaning service was at length withdrawn on account of "undue publicity."[88] Jasper Savanhu, despite his loyalty to the ruling Federal Party—he had, among other things, voted against the above-mentioned motion to outlaw racial discrimination— fared no better than other Africans when it came to Rhodesian exclusionary practices. Although subsequently made a junior minister in the federal government, he was only allowed to attend functions in the better hotels "secretly."[89] By 1958, then, more and more elite Africans were coming to the conclusion that racial partnership was simply incapable of satisfying their demand for full inclusion in civil society, in sum, of fulfilling their determination to rise from subjects to citizens, to use Mahmood Mamdani's felicitous phrase.[90]

8

An Aborted Coronation
In Search of the Political Kingdom,
1955–1965

RACIAL PARTNERSHIP'S LOSS would eventually prove to be African national-ism's gain. This, however, was no unilinear process, but a wrenching and com-plicated affair played out over a period of several years. Gradually, and often with a heavy heart, the black multiracialists left the pro-partnership forma-tions and made their way into the ranks of the African nationalist movement, the immediate foundations of which had been laid in 1955 and which emerged fully formed two years later, in 1957.

By the early 1960s the black elite, as a social category, had moved to an African nationalist stance, with its leadership demanding a transfer of politi-cal power from the white minority to the African majority. The end of racial partnership also entailed a change in political strategy, requiring as it did an abandonment of the black elite's coalition with white liberals in favor of a new set of alliances with the mass of African workers and peasants. In the end, however, the anticipated black political coronation was aborted by a violent white backlash, which culminated not just in the repression of African nation-alism but also in a historic white settler rebellion against British colonial rule.

THE REAWAKENED AFRICAN NATIONAL CONSCIOUSNESS

To the extent that racial partnership had been conceived as an antidote to African nationalism—and that indeed was its chief raison d'être—it achieved a good deal of success between 1954 and 1958. During this period, the politics of multiracialism largely superseded the uniracial mobilization that had char-acterized elite African political struggles from the outset, beginning in the era of World War I. Among the most articulate sections of the black middle class, the new brand of multiracialism easily eclipsed the African national con-sciousness that had emerged during the national moment of 1945–48 and, in a more attenuated form, during the most intense period of the struggle against the Federation of Rhodesia and Nyasaland, or more colloquially the Central African Federation, in the early 1950s.

Not all members of the emerging middle class, however, had been smitten by the bug of racial partnership. In 1955, the antipartnership forces in Salisbury coalesced into a new formation—the City Youth League. As the name implies, the Youth League was a movement by and for younger people— membership was limited to Africans between the ages of sixteen and forty— individuals who were too young or too distracted to have been politically engaged before or during World War II. In line with a long tradition of political and ideological cross-fertilization on the southern African subcontinent, the Youth League was modeled on the African National Congress of South Africa's Youth League. Indeed James Chikerema, the founding president of the Southern Rhodesian group, had been associated with its South African archetype during a stint of employment in South Africa.[1]

As in South Africa, so too in Southern Rhodesia: the Youth League, brash and impatient, scorned the newly hegemonic multiracialism in black politics. A determined band consisting largely of salesmen, insurance agents, and shopkeepers, the leaders of the Youth League were, for the most part, socially distinct from those Africans who gravitated to the pro-partnership formations. If Southern Rhodesia had been a normal society for Africans, the Youth Leaguers would have been part of the lower middle class. With most of its members educated only to the upper-primary-school level—a not inconsiderable achievement for Africans, even in the postwar period—the league's numbers included few, if any, of the white-collar professionals and university-educated men who constituted the black membership of the leading pro-partnership formations, namely, the Capricorn Africa Society (CAS) and the Inter-Racial Association of Southern Rhodesia (IRA). Although capable agitators and effective organizers, the Youth Leaguers lacked the cosmopolitan outlook and social graces of the better-educated members of their age cohort, such as multiracial stalwarts Stanlake Samkange and Enoch Dumbutshena, or even older activists like Charles Mzingeli or Esau Nemapare, who also boarded the partnership bandwagon. The Youth Leaguers would not, to use a formulation popularized by Nathan Shamuyarira, himself a model in this regard, have made very good "teatime partners."

The Youth League defined its mission as one of preparing African youth —mostly male—for participation in national affairs. It was not a nationalist movement in the sense of demanding a formal transfer of power to the colonized majority, yet that likely would have been the outcome of its call for universal adult franchise, had it been heeded. Actually, this was the first time that a political movement in Southern Rhodesia had raised such a cry, making universal franchise a centerpiece of its program. Irreverent, the Youth League attacked all and sundry, including the white-owned, African-oriented press, the settler state, and the law prohibiting Africans from participating in the state-run lottery. The Youth League even picketed the lottery headquarters, the first

time (to my knowledge) that an African political movement in Southern Rhodesia had deployed that weapon against an agency of the central colonial administration. Most adamantly, though, the Youth League attacked partnership
and its chief sponsors, the Capricorn Africa Society and the Inter-Racial Association. The Youth Leaguers delighted in excoriating the multiracialists,
white and black alike, dismissing them as impotent "tea-drinkers" who were
powerless to alleviate the oppression of Africans. Rejecting their claim that
they were working to uplift the colonized, the Youth Leaguers accused the
CAS and the IRA of seeking to "control us, suppress us, and keep us down
forever."[2]

Having burst upon the political scene, the Youth League showed its mettle
by gaining control of the Salisbury African Advisory Board, the body that advised the white city fathers who managed the township. The Youth League's
triumph came at the expense of the Reformed Industrial and Commercial
Workers Union of Africa (RICU), whose leader, Charles Mzingeli, had become an executive member of the IRA, earning him a place on the Youth
Leaguers' list of despised tea-drinkers.[3] This was a major rupture in African
politics, for Mzingeli previously served as mentor to a number of the Youth
Leaguers, most prominently George Nyandoro, the group's general secretary.
Upstaged by his erstwhile protégés, an embittered Mzingeli, as prickly and
thin-skinned as ever, became permanently alienated from the community of
African activists. His reputation in tatters as a partisan in the movement for
African liberation, however loosely defined, he persisted in his tea-drinking
ways well after his fellow black multiracialists had given up on partnership,
sadly capping his long political career by collaborating with Ian Smith's regime.[4]

The Youth League's capacity for large-scale mobilization faced its most
crucial test in August 1956, when the authorities announced an increase in bus
fares in Salisbury. With indignation at fever pitch in the impoverished townships, the Youth Leaguers saw an opportunity to demonstrate concretely their
affinity with the suffering masses and to further set themselves apart from the
do-nothing tea-drinkers. They called for a bus boycott on the day the fare increases were scheduled to take effect—another political first. The response
was enthusiastic, with most township residents honoring the passenger strike
and walking to work. The most conspicuous holdouts were a group of young
female hostel residents, who opted to flout the boycott and pay the higher fare.
For their defiance, the women were roughed up and assaulted, and a number
of them were even raped—acts committed by boycott enforcers in the name
of the Youth League.[5]

The sexual violence associated with the bus boycott cannot be divorced
from the Youth League's undisguised masculinist demeanor, which created a
sociopolitical context that had no tolerance for defiance by women. Still, there

is no evidence that the Youth League's leadership actually sanctioned violence, especially sexual violence, as a means of enforcing compliance with its entreaty. Although "women's obedience was highly valued in the nationalist movement," as Teresa Barnes has stated, her additional claim of "the nationalist leaders' virtual sanctioning of the rapes" is insupportable.[6] The Youth League leadership was morally culpable in the rapes. That it actually, or "virtually," approved them has not been proven. On the basis of the available evidence, it is more accurate to posit, as Timothy Scarnecchia has done, that the Youth League, by espousing "a politics which essentially reasserted masculinity in the public domain,"[7] helped to create, as well as maintain, a political climate in which such acts could occur.

Although the rude display of testosterone power lessened the luster, the bus boycott bolstered the Youth League's swaggering claim to be at the forefront of African political struggles. For one day, at least, it had persuaded the greater part of the township's work force to forgo its usual means of transportation, disrupting the smooth functioning of white Salisbury's political economy in the process. Startled by such a successful canalization of popular discontent, the settler regime retreated behind that most convenient of British colonial camouflages: it appointed a commission to study the issue of public transportation in Salisbury, the commission's terms of reference being later extended to Bulawayo, which had not been affected by the fare hike in the capital. In its report, the commission recommended a rollback of the fare increase and a ceiling on bus fares for Africans—all of which would be paid for by a special tax on employers of African labor in the two cities, with the exception of those hiring domestic servants.[8]

Buoyed by its success with the bus boycott, the Youth Leaguers began to think more expansively, formulating plans to move beyond their base in Salisbury into the wider national arena. With a membership estimated at from 700 to 1,300 in 1957, the Youth League far and away had become the most visible African political movement in Southern Rhodesia.[9] Consistent with its new colony-wide aspirations, the organization changed its name to the African National Youth League.[10]

As it happened, the Youth Leaguers were not the only ones then bandying about the idea of forming an African political movement on a national scale. In the first half of 1957, Benjamin Burombo, seeking to revive his rural-based and largely moribund British African National Voice Association, began barnstorming Southern Rhodesia with his latest pet project—African unity, political and otherwise.[11] Predictably, Burombo went fishing among the Youth League, touting his message of African combination at one of its meetings.[12] The Youth Leaguers, however, refused the bait. Burombo's unbridled egoism and his reputation for one-upmanship, established so indelibly during the 1948 strike, evidently had preceded him. The Youth League, instead, decided to cast its own political net, pulling in one of the few quarries available, notably the remnants of the Southern Rhodesia African National Congress.

As with the other African political formations, the era of racial partnership had not been kind to the National Congress. After 1953, virtually its entire leadership defected to the politics of multiracialism. While such ex-congressmen as Stanlake Samkange and Enoch Dumbutshena sipped tea with their newfound friends in the white suburbs, the organization fell apart. By 1956 only one branch of the National Congress remained in existence, in Bulawayo. But with a paid-up membership of just forty, it was hardly a viable political force.[13] Thus when the far more dynamic Youth League came proposing political matrimony, the National Congress's Bulawayo branch responded with alacrity. The branch's entire leadership—including Joshua Nkomo, who since 1952 had been putative president of the national organization—resigned en masse to make way for a different kind of union in African politics.[14] In any case, the national organization had long ceased functioning, and the closing of its file by the colonial intelligence services served as an inglorious epitaph. In the aftermath of the 1948 strike, the RICU's Charles Mzingeli had opined that African political unity in Southern Rhodesia was possible only if the National Congress, his bitter rival, "dissolve and reform again." The National Congress had now done just that.

THE NATIONALIST MOMENT

The political reformulation culminated in the establishment of a new organizational structure—the Southern *Rhodesian* African National Congress (as distinct from the previous Southern *Rhodesia* African National Congress). Significantly, the inaugural meeting of the Reconstituted Congress took place on September 12, 1957, a day of considerable importance to the Southern Rhodesian settlers: it was Occupation Day, a national holiday commemorating the founding of the colony in 1890. By turning its public debut into such a powerful counter-hegemonic symbol, the Reconstituted Congress signaled its determination to reestablish African rule. In so doing, it became the colony's first authentic African nationalist formation. The quest for a color-blind meritocracy under colonialism, or "equal rights for all civilized men"—the dominant motor force of elite African politics for nearly half a century—had come to an end. The struggle for African political power had begun.

The emergence of the Reconstituted Congress thus marked the onset of the nationalist moment, that is, the formal demand for an end to foreign domination at the political level. Anticolonialism, both as an idea and as a movement, arrived late in Southern Rhodesia, compared with its arrival in the other British possessions in Africa. In Southern Rhodesia, the anticolonial impulse—the nationalist moment—had been preceded by two other periods of extraordinary and exceptional political agitation, the proto-national and national moments, as discussed in previous chapters. All three moments—the proto-national, national, and nationalist—stand out by virtue of their exploration of interclass alliances between the black elite, or segments of the black elite, and the African workers and peasants. During the proto-national moment of the interwar period, the search for an all-African political concord had been hampered by a split among the emerging petty bourgeoisie, with a conservative, pro-government faction strongly opposing the strategy and tactics of more radical members of its class.

The national moment, born of frustrations deriving from World War II, saw a much more united black elite pursuing an interclass alliance with the African masses, particularly the urban working class—a moment that, as we have seen, came to an unhappy end with the general strike of 1948. The national moment, like the previous proto-national one, sought not so much to challenge the legitimacy of colonial rule as to demand a fairer shake for the colonized population as a whole—in effect, justice without power. By the late 1950s, however, the African elite, or at least a segment of the African elite assuming the role of political vanguard, had concluded that black power was a sine qua non for black justice. Organizationally, this sentiment found expression in the Reconstituted Congress, the coming of which inaugurated the nationalist moment.

The Reconstituted Congress was more than just the sum total of the Youth League and the Bulawayo branch of the old National Congress, its principal component parts. It was, in the spirit of the nationalist moment, a grand synthesis of the leading tendencies in African politics since the immediate post–World War I era, that is, since the beginning of modernist African politics. The resulting big tent included the Southern Rhodesia African Association, which, until its absorption into the Reconstituted Congress, was the colony's oldest African political formation, having had as many lives as the proverbial cat. The African Association, as discussed previously, was founded in 1919 as the Southern Rhodesia Native Association, a group best known for deferring to the colonial regime. Partly because of its collaborationist politics, the Native Association successfully weathered the depression, a political and economic storm that carried away its more assertive rivals. Then, in 1936, the Native Association became the nucleus for a new unity bloc, the Southern Rhodesia Bantu Congress, as the National Congress initially was called. Finally, in the postwar period the Native Association, now called the African Association to reflect the latest nomenclatorial style, reasserted its organizational autonomy—even though, under the agreement that created the Bantu Congress, it should have long ceased to exist.

With the appearance of the Reconstituted Congress, which had been formed amid yet another campaign for black political unity, the African Association was targeted for subsumption, that is, an unfriendly takeover. Within a couple of weeks after it was formed, partisans of the Reconstituted Congress, led by its secretary general, George Nyandoro, hijacked the annual conference of the African Association and demanded a fusion of the two groups. In concrete terms, this meant that the African Association should disband and join the Reconstituted Congress.[15] And indeed the older group soon disappeared from the political stage, this time for good. There is, admittedly, no record of the African Association actually voting itself out of existence. Still, it seems certain that its sudden disappearance, after a lifespan of some four decades, was directly related to the emergence of the amalgamationist Reconstituted Congress.

At the other end of the political spectrum, the Reconstituted Congress received the more enthusiastic backing of the former top official of the Native Association's most implacable foe in the period leading up to the depression, namely, the Rhodesian section of the Industrial and Commercial Workers Union of Africa (ICU). That individual, Masotha Ndhlovu, had been at the helm of the ICU, defunct since the depression, at the height of its influence. By contrast, Ndhlovu's former ICU protégé, Charles Mzingeli, flatly rejected the Reconstituted Congress, even though he had advocated the creation of a like-minded body as far back as 1948. Unlike the younger tea-drinking intellectuals, who increasingly were being drawn to African nationalism as an ideology if not to the Reconstituted Congress as an organization, Mzingeli remained wedded to the racial partnership philosophy, although his RICU, formed in 1946 in a caricatured "revival" of the ICU and spurned by Ndhlovu, now was little more than a paper organization. It is a striking measure of his fall from political grace that in 1960, when rioting broke out in the Salisbury townships, Mzingeli's shop, an establishment that in better days had doubled as a hub of African agitation, was burned by nationalist sympathizers.

Also refusing to hitch his wagon to the nationalist locomotive was Benjamin Burombo, who declined to join Ndhlovu, formerly a partisan of Burombo's British African National Voice Association, in affiliating with the Reconstituted Congress. Burombo's snub may be attributed to his famous narcissism and self-conceit, that is, to the fact that he had not been called to the leadership of the new group. For unlike Mzingeli, who also was not immune to vainglory, Burombo never took tea and therefore had no personal or political investment in the competing racial partnership ideology. If by this point Mzingeli may be said to have become a tragic figure, then Burombo's trajectory can only be described as farcical. Burombo, of course, had played an important catalytic role in the series of events that had led to the formation of the Reconstituted Congress. Yet when the unity he had so passionately advocated finally materialized, his inflated estimate of his own leadership skills blinded him to that fact. Tilting at windmills to the end, Burombo died in

1958—the year after the birth of the Reconstituted Congress—still pursuing his lonely and futile quest for African political combination, on his own terms and under his own leadership.[16]

Although the Reconstituted Congress was largely their handiwork, the erstwhile Youth Leaguers did not seek to dominate its leadership, contradicting earlier rumors that they planned to "capture all the important positions on the executive."[17] The Youth Leaguers, to their credit, were aware of their limitations. Running a group confined to Salisbury, with consciousness-raising agitprop as its modus operandi, was one thing. Organizing a national movement intent on mobilizing all sectors of the colonial population, and that with the avowed aim of seizing political power from the white settlers, was an altogether different undertaking. To attain this infinitely loftier and more difficult objective, the Youth Leaguers believed it was necessary to win over the African intelligentsia, that is, the very group whose members they had previously derided as useless tea-drinkers. Mindful of their relatively modest educational attainments, despite their proven skills at agitation and propaganda, the Youth Leaguers wanted to tap an intellectual, someone more conversant with the wider world than they were, to head the Reconstituted Congress. According to Lawrence Vambe, then the dean of black journalists in Salisbury and himself quite fond of tea, the Youth Leaguers were determined that the new organization should be led by "someone outside their circle, a person of stature, of good education and, of course, flexibility of mind. Certain names were mentioned: Stanlake Samkange, Enoch Dumbutshena and Herbert Chitepo."[18]

It is unclear if either Dumbutshena or Chitepo, the colony's first African lawyer, was actually offered the presidency of the Reconstituted Congress.[19] Samkange, many years after the fact, denied having been approached.[20] What is certain is that the threesome, inveterate tea-drinkers all, declined even to join the group, let alone to lead it. The attempted brain drain against racial partnership having failed, the Youth Leaguers turned next to Joshua Nkomo. As a non-tea-drinker, figuratively and literally, the teetotaling Nkomo would not have produced the same propaganda windfall for the Reconstituted Congress as would Dumbutshena, Chitepo, or Samkange. Nkomo, however, met one important criterion: he had a bachelor's degree. For the Youth Leaguers had, according to Maurice Nyagumbo, their assertively unintellectual confederate, "made up their minds that the new party had to be led by an African [university] graduate."[21]

Nyagumbo also claims that Nkomo's candidacy for president of the Reconstituted Congress was opposed by certain of his own colleagues from the defunct Bulawayo branch of the National Congress.[22] Although written at a time of intense political rivalry with Nkomo, Nyagumbo's account has a certain ring of credibility. Just months before the organization voted itself out of

existence, some members of the Bulawayo National Congress, including a
number of those attending the inaugural meeting of the Reconstituted Congress, had condemned Nkomo for opposing a resolution barring members from
joining the white-dominated political parties.[23] But with the Youth Leaguers now actively courting the black multiracialists, that same charge—being
soft on racial partnership—paradoxically would redound to Nkomo's benefit. Thus did it come about that Nkomo, ever the shrewd political operative,
was "hijacked into the presidency" of the Reconstituted Congress, as he later
characterized it.[24] Joining Nkomo on the executive were former Youth Leaguers James Chikerema (vice president) and George Nyandoro (general secretary).

In Zimbabwean nationalist historiography, there later emerged the con-
tention that Nkomo's election as president of the Reconstituted Congress was
driven by ethnic imperatives. Thus Nathan Shamuyarira—that noted popular-
izer of the moniker "tea drinking"—asserts that the presidential decision presumed that "Nkomo could bring the support of the Matabele people while
Chikerema and Nyandoro would draw in the Mashona."[25] There is scant contemporary evidence to support this claim. Rather, it is apocryphal, dating
from the splintering of the nationalist movement in the 1960s—a schism that
indeed became defined by ethnic cleavages—and projected back into the
formative period of mature African nationalism in Southern Rhodesia. The
ethnic-imperative argument cannot account for the fact that Samkange and
Chitepo, both native Shona-speakers, apparently were considered for the presidency of the Reconstituted Congress ahead of Nkomo. Nor does the ethnic
interpretation explain the initial rejection of Nkomo by his fellow delegates
from Bulawayo. Ultimately, it was Nkomo's education and temperament—his
ability to meet fellow African intellectuals on an equal level and his reputation
as a "moderate" nationalist capable of weaning them from racial partnership
—not his ethnicity, that clinched his election as president of the Reconstituted Congress.

The same consideration that placed Nkomo at its head, namely, the nationalists' desire to woo the pro-partnership African intelligentsia, can be de-
tected in the drafting of the Reconstituted Congress's statement of principles.
The goal may have been that of African nationalism, but the tone owed much
to the language of racial partnership. Its aim, the group's foundational creed
announced, "is the national unity of all inhabitants of the country in true
partnership regardless of race, colour and creed. It stands for a completely integrated society, equality of opportunity in every sphere and the social, economic and political advancement of all. It regards these objectives as the essential foundation of that partnership between people of all races without
which there can be no peaceful progress in this country. . . . It is not a racial
movement. It is equally opposed to tribalism and racialism."[26] This was not

the rhetoric of the Youth League, with its fiery denunciations of racial partnership as political trickery designed to keep the Africans down and its dismissal of multiracialism as racialism multiplied. It was, rather, the carefully chosen language of an organization bent on political poaching. In its ideological struggles with the forces of racial partnership, the Reconstituted Congress, unlike the Youth League, would eschew an openly confrontational approach. It would court the black multiracialists by couching its appeals in a language familiar to them: the language of racial partnership.

These efforts were not altogether in vain. The most prominent mouthpiece of partnership welcomed the Reconstituted Congress's "moderation," offering unsolicited advice on how to prevent "extremists" from taking it over.[27] At the same time, "moderates" Stanlake Samkange and Enoch Dumbutshena, although refusing any official affiliation with it and continuing to take tea, defended the new group against charges that it would become a fountainhead of "anti-white nationalism."[28] For the Reconstituted Congress, this was a hopeful sign: leading black intellectuals were warming to an African nationalist formation, albeit one that spoke the language of racial partnership.

As the Reconstituted Congress was reaching out to pull them in, the black intellectuals simultaneously were being pushed toward an African nationalist stance by a white backlash against even the meager fruits of that partnership. The single rudest shove took place in 1958. At the beginning of that year, Garfield Todd—prime minister of Southern Rhodesia since 1953, when Huggins relinquished that post to assume leadership of the Central African Federation—was removed from office by his own cabinet on account of his purported pro-African orientation. Todd, the rebellious cabinet ministers charged, was dangerously tinkering with white political domination. As evidence, they pointed to his acceptance of the report of an official commission recommending that certain African professionals, mostly teachers and nurses, many of whose salaries fell below the £240 annual income qualification for the franchise, be given the right to vote.[29] Although barely affecting the racial composition of the electorate, which would have remained overwhelmingly European, the alpha-champions of white Rhodesia, always a loquacious assemblage with a penchant for hyperbole, railed against the proposal as a doomsday scenario, a threat to the future of Western civilization and settler domination between the Zambezi and Limpopo Rivers.

In fact, Todd's white opponents had distorted his record and twisted his intentions.[30] As prime minister, his support for the ideals of racial partnership was tentative and qualified, and one of his chief policy objectives was to stem the rising tide of African nationalism. His proposal to enfranchise African teachers and nurses was thus part of an ongoing attempt to turn the black petty bourgeoisie into political stakeholders, potential bulwarks of the status quo. In any case, Todd, a missionary turned politician, was an unlikely candidate for the task of delivering Southern Rhodesia to the Africans on a sliver platter, as alleged by his white detractors, both within the government and the parliamentary opposition. An unalloyed paternalist, he brooked no nonsense from what he regarded as unruly Africans. In 1947, as principal of the Dadaya mission school, he had dealt harshly with a strike by African students. Accusing him of instigating the unrest, Todd fired Ndabaningi Sithole, his own former star student and rising political luminary who had gone on to become a teacher at the school. Then in 1954 Todd, acting now in his capacity as prime minister, was "highly praised" by the Chamber of Industries for his swift suppression of a strike by African coal miners, including declaring a state of emergency and calling out the troops.[31] Some two years later, Todd again armed himself with emergency powers and rushed to the scene personally to supervise the crushing of yet another strike, this one by African railway workers in Bulawayo who, by his account, had made "unreasonable demands" for wage increases.[32] Even Ian Smith, who eventually rose to the rank of head alpha-champion of white Rhodesia, would compliment Todd for dealing "firmly with black agitation."[33]

Although liberal in his use of the stick, Todd, in contrast to the white ultra-diehards, also saw a need for the carrot. In essence, his policy as head of the government was to apply the one to the African working class (as evidenced by his response to the strikes over which he presided), while offering the other to the black elite (as seen in his proposal to enfranchise teachers and nurses). Accordingly Todd, as prime minister, maintained a dialogue with black intellectuals, some of whom, like Ndabaningi Sithole, with whom he had been reconciled since the Dadaya incident, were his former students.

Certainly the African intellectuals agreed that Todd's removal from office was fatal for racial partnership. Shamuyarira called it the "decisive blow," whereas Vambe was "horrified." As the cabinet crisis unfolded, Dumbutshena announced that "Africans are solidly behind" Todd, warning that without him to "inspire confidence," partnership would be meaningless.[34] Partnership became even more inconsequential after Todd's dismal showing in the snap election following his ouster, when his hastily organized political bloc was completely routed at the polls. Todd himself lost his parliamentary seat. A convincing majority of white voters, spurning any attempt at compromise, swung even farther to the right, with the result that the apartheid-style Dominion Party came within a whisker of toppling the ruling United Federal Party.[35] (The United Federal Party was the outcome of a fusion, in 1957, of the United Rhodesia Party, which governed in Southern Rhodesia, and the Federal Party, which ruled at the federal level. Todd, who had been one of the midwives of the United Federal Party while still prime minister, reappropriated the label of the defunct United Rhodesia Party in his failed attempt at a political comeback.)

The hardening of European attitudes was not limited to Southern Rhodesia; white voters also rejected liberal-oriented parties at the federal level. Thus the Constitution Party, a federation-wide formation sponsored by the Capricorn Africa Society and hailed by the liberal press as a "bold bid for African moderates," that is, elite blacks who had not gone over to a nationalist standpoint, was no more successful at the polls than was Todd's political bloc in Southern Rhodesia.[36] Eventually, the Constitution Party was supplanted by the Central Africa Party, which became the electoral standard bearer of racial partnership in the federation. However, the Central Africa Party's convoluted aims virtually ensured its political irrelevance, even to the so-called African moderates: it sought to gain elite black support, but without "giving way to African extremist demands and without diminishing the material benefits which Europeans enjoy in the Federation."[37] Operationally, indeed rhetorically, the Central Africa Party had little to offer the African middle class. In sum, partnership was dead in all but name.

The demise of partnership did not, however, mean that the black intelligentsia was prepared to declare for African nationalism—that is, in its then existing organizational form. As late as the beginning of 1959, Maurice Nyagumbo notes disdainfully, "there were still some so-called African intellectuals who despised the composition of the leadership of the ANC [the Reconstituted Congress] and condemned the party organizers who, they believed, knew nothing of the political reality of the country."[38] If so, the intellectuals had but one viable option: to wrest control of the nationalist movement from those they regarded as unworthy of leadership. But unfortunately for the intellectuals, the conjunction of political forces was not yet propitious for such a rearrangement.

Meanwhile, the Reconstituted Congress was going from strength to strength. Within a year of its appearance, the nationalist formation came to be regarded as a genuine threat to white rule in Southern Rhodesia. Using funds obtained from the newly independent African and Asian countries, it soon acquired all the trappings of a well-oiled political machine, purchasing motor vehicles and bicycles, staffing and equipping offices, and employing full-time organizers.[39] To boost morale on the ground, the nationalists developed a repertoire of songs, always a powerful instrument of cultural and political mobilization among the oppressed.[40]

By the time of its first anniversary in 1958, the Reconstituted Congress, according to Joshua Nkomo, had 477 branches with a combined membership of 170,000.[41] Included in this number, which is likely exaggerated, was a sprinkling of whites, coloureds, and Indians.[42] Not since the onset of modernist politics among the African elite had the settler regime faced such a persistent and sophisticated African opposition. The Reconstituted Congress even called for the dissolution of the Central African Federation, putting it in line with the Nyasaland and Northern Rhodesian African National Congresses as well as reviving the antifederation tradition in Southern Rhodesia.[43]

All over the colony, supporters of the Reconstituted Congress were on the move. In the urban townships, they seized control of the Advisory Boards and the ratepayers associations. Declaring "social war" on the color bar, nationalists in the cities announced plans for massive demonstrations against segregated public facilities, alarming officials at the highest levels in both the Southern Rhodesian and federal governments.[44] Many of the shock troops for the anticolonial campaigns in the urban centers came from the ranks of the emergent trade unions, which were among the first to join the growing nationalist consensus. It bears emphasizing, however, that this new, pro-nationalist labor movement was quite different from the elite-led formations that claimed to speak for the working class during the national moment of 1945–48. By the time of the nationalist moment a decade late, Southern Rhodesia's proletariat, having become more autonomous of the (now tea-drinking) African middle class, had evolved its own organizational and leadership structures. It was thus a relatively independent labor movement, as T. M. Mothibe has argued, that consciously decided to back the nationalist movement.[45]

The nationalist impact was even more pronounced on the peasantry than on the urban working class. During its year-and-a-half existence, the Reconstituted Congress devoted much of its resources to the Reserves, exploiting widespread opposition to the Land Husbandry Act of 1951. This law, which among other things was intended to refine the system of territorial segregation, resulted in large-scale evictions, destocking, and crop destruction.[46] George Nyandoro, who as the party's general secretary knew something of the matter, called the Land Husbandry Act "the best recruiter [the Reconstituted] Congress ever had."[47] Indeed, the Land Husbandry Act, by accelerating the rate of migration from the countryside, helped to lay the social foundations of mature African nationalism by establishing "a more organic link between urban and rural politics," as Brian Raftopoulos has noted[48] The Reconstituted Congress also demanded a repeal of the Land Apportionment Act of 1930, thereby championing the interests of the peasantry and the urban African middle class in the same breath. Easily the most sacrosanct of Rhodesian settler legislation, the Land Apportionment Act was both the bedrock on which the Land Husbandry Act rested and the segregationist fortress that prevented Africans (meaning, concretely, the black petty bourgeoisie) from purchasing real estate in the cities.

The nationalist investment in the Reserves paid off handsomely. The cauldron of discontent proved most hospitable to organizers like Peter Mtanda, an executive member of the Reconstituted Congress. Regarded by Nyagumbo, himself no faint-hearted slouch,[49] as "the most daring and hardworking nationalist of that period," Mtanda, "Holy Bible in hand," traveled from "village to village and from school to school," preaching the gospel of African nationalism.[50] Indeed, it is generally agreed that a majority of the members of the Reconstituted Congress resided in the countryside. Furthermore, unlike supporters in the cities, who tended to be younger people with some formal education, nationalist supporters in the countryside were more heterogeneous, chronologically and socially. At one point, forty of forty-nine congressmen facing prosecution on politically inspired charges—dubbed a "miniature treason trial," after South Africa's more famous Treason Trial—were agrarian producers.[51]

The authorities, for their part, were especially troubled by the nationalist inroads in the Reserves. In a harbinger of things to come, the chief native commissioner's report for the year 1958 condemned the Reconstituted Congress for introducing into the countryside "a gradual intensification of that soapbox oratory which was so characteristic of weekends in the urban areas." The "violent and lurid speeches" of nationalist agitators, the report thundered, were calculated to incite "unsophisticated peasants," turning them against constituted authority.[52] In particular, Native Affairs bureaucrats, in pursuit of their decades-long drive to sever the politico-cultural interaction between town and country—which indeed was one aim of the Land Husbandry Act, although it had the opposite effect—argued for decisive action against the nationalist onslaught. They would soon get their wish. When the Reconstituted Congress was banned in February 1959, farmers—along with trade unionists —were well represented among the more than five hundred nationalists who were detained.[53] Joshua Nkomo himself attributed the banning primarily to his organization's militant agrarianism.[54] Throughout the countryside, the regime's iron fist sought to crush such "artificial enthusiasms," which the authorities regarded as the result of nationalist carpings.[55] Far from eliminating its social foundations, however, the proscription of the Reconstituted Congress paved the way for an even more exuberant African nationalism, one in which the black intellectuals would play a central role.

NATIONALIZING THE INTELLIGENTSIA; OR, TEATIME PARTNERS NO MORE

The vehicle that conveyed the black intelligentsia from racial partnership to African nationalism was the National Democratic Party (NDP), which was established on January 1, 1960, some ten months after the banning of the Reconstituted Congress. The NDP inherited the Reconstituted Congress's political mantle, along with much of its leadership and following. Indeed, the resemblance between the two organizations was too close for the authorities. One official commented colorfully that the Reconstituted Congress had simply been resurrected under a new name, the NDP being no different from its predecessor in "its political exuberance and racial animosity, with all its accompanying impertinences and its wild disdain of the truth."[56] To the NDP publicity secretary, such comments were ominous forebodings of proscription, and he rejected them as accusations "inspired by malice and . . . chronic bitterness" toward autonomous African political mobilization.[57]

Despite the direct political succession, the NDP was more than just the Reconstituted Congress with a nomenclatorial makeover. To begin with, the new movement was more transparently African nationalist than was its predecessor. Gone was the talk of establishing a "true partnership regardless of race, colour and creed," as the Reconstituted Congress had vowed in its foundational statement. Instead, the NDP unequivocally billed itself as a "political party initiated and led by Africans," one that stood simply for "freedom for the African people of Southern Rhodesia."[58]

The NDP's single-mindedness in attaining political power was well reflected in its agenda, which was far less crowded than was that of the Reconstituted Congress. When it first appeared, the NDP had little to say about the major social and economic issues, including the Land Husbandry Act. One reason for the NDP's initial neglect of the land question is the fact that, unlike the Reconstituted Congress, it was forbidden to hold meetings in the rural areas. Yet, even while it remained a predominantly urban movement dependent on the working class for its organizational and political muscle—and this urban bias would eventually change—the NDP made few serious attempts to address labor issues as such.

Instead of cluttering its political plank with a detailed program of action, the NDP advanced one overriding demand: the transfer of power to the African majority, as represented by the NDP. The slogan "one man, one vote" conveniently summarized this single-mindedness. Consequently, the nonracial qualified franchise—the political linchpin of the equal-rights-for-all-civilized-men worldview, which had made a comeback during the era of racial partnership, as we saw in the previous chapter—was repudiated far more vigorously by the NDP than it had been by the Reconstituted Congress. Nkomo, for one, denounced the qualified franchise as "part of the whiteman's scheme to divide Africans."[59]

In typical nationalist fashion, the NDP's minimalist political agenda elided the issue of class differences among Africans. In this way, the party's elite leadership could avoid making firm commitments to its newfound allies among the colonized masses, implying instead that the Africans would solve whatever internal problems they had once colonialism came to an end. Such artful ambiguity was hardly original to the NDP; it also had been a hallmark of that lodestar of nationalism in late-colonial Africa, namely, Kwame Nkrumah's Convention People's Party. "Seek ye first the political kingdom," Nkrumah exhorted his countrymen in biblical fashion, "and all other things shall be added unto you." Not for nothing did the NDP soon install Robert Mugabe—fresh from an extended residency in Nkrumah's Ghana, where he had acquired a Ghanaian spouse to complement his new political fervor—as its chief propagandist and image-maker, otherwise called publicity secretary.

With more cosmopolitan men like Mugabe at the helm, the NDP also struck a more pan-Africanist pose, both politically and culturally, than had its predecessor. NDP stump speakers—the NDP held meetings more frequently than had the Reconstituted Congress—peppered their remarks with references to events elsewhere in Africa, urging Africans in Southern Rhodesia to follow the lead of other colonial subjects north of the Zambezi, who were rapidly removing the yoke of European political domination.[60]

From a pan-African standpoint, the Congo crisis of 1960 had an especially powerful impact on colonial Zimbabweans (and indeed on the white settlers too). In Southern Rhodesia, as elsewhere in Africa and the African diaspora, anticolonial activists hailed the slain Congolese prime minister Patrice Lumumba as a pan-African martyr who had been sacrificed on the alter of neo-colonialism, a victim of Western puppeteers and their black lackeys.[61] By contrast, Lumumba's murderer and principal rival, Moise Tshombe —who enjoyed the warm support of the Belgian ex-colonialists and the Rhodesian settlers, among others—was derided by the anticolonial activists as the ultimate turncoat, a betrayer of his country's newly won independence. Before long, these two figures, Lumumba and Tshombe, emerged as the embodiment of virtue and villainy, respectively, among African activists in Southern Rhodesia. On the political platform and in letters to the editor, these activists condemned the NDP's African opponents (or perceived opponents) as "Tshombes," while acclaiming the party's leaders as "Lumumbas." A typical broadside contrasted Lumumba, "that great son of Africa [who] shall ever be remembered," with Tshombe, "that cruel, ungrateful, inhuman savage."[62] One particularly zealous NDP militant suggested creating politically segregated townships in the urban centers, one for "Tshombes" or "black Europeans" and the other for "Lumumbas" or "sons of the soil."[63]

The Congo crisis even found a place in the NDP's cultural productions. Party members attending a special congress were regaled by theatrical and musical performances that included a swipe at Tshombe and Congolese president Joseph Kasavubu, who also opposed Lumumba. The lead performer reportedly "sent the audience [roaring] with a Lumumba number in which both Tshombe and Kasavubu denied knowledge of the hero's whereabouts. In the front rows, the NDP leaders beamed."[64]

As the pun suggests, the NDP's militant political pan-Africanism was matched by an assertive cultural nationalism that had been noticeably absent from the Reconstituted Congress. NDP orators had a fondness for the "African personality," and they emphasized the need to decolonize the mind along with the body politic. Predictably, history was invoked as part of the process of cultural and psychological decolonization. NDP meetings constantly featured references to the great African past, from ancient Egypt to Great Zimbabwe, while Africans in Southern Rhodesia became the "children of Mambo, Lobengula and Mtasa," precolonial Zimbabwean rulers. Likewise, the nomenclatorial debate—which had culminated in the adoption of the "Zimbabwe" designation—assumed a more personal form in the age of mature nationalism, with some nationalists abandoning their European names for African ones. For instance, where previously Nkomo had been content with an initial, he now began to use his full middle name, Mqubuko; occasionally, he even dropped the anglicized Joshua. The cultural nationalist pose also extended to fashion. In a departure from the Eurocentric sartorial style traditionally favored by Africans in colonial southern Africa—in contrast to, say, those in West Africa—some colonial Zimbabwean nationalists, including Nkomo, began appearing in African-fashioned attire.[65]

The new political and cultural nuances in Zimbabwean African nationalism were directly attributable to major changes in the social composition of the leadership of the NDP, as compared with that of the Reconstituted Congress. The black intellectuals, now abandoning partnership in droves, began gradually to take command of the African nationalist movement, bringing with them the same panache they had displayed in dealing with their white erstwhile teatime partners. By 1960, one organ of white liberal opinion noted, the black supporters of partnership had concluded that the "time had come to withdraw from all multi-racial activities: to resign from Salisbury's [multi-racial] Capital Club; to resign from the C[entral] A[frica] P[arty]; to refuse invitations to cocktail parties. The time had come for Africans to help themselves."[66] In short, teatime had ended.

Evidence of the re-acquired African agency was everywhere. Nine months after the formation of the NDP, the ranks of the black multiracialists had become so depleted that the Rev. Fred Rea, a white Wesleyan Methodist missionary and leading light in the Capricorn Africa Society, suggested disbanding the group. In a "confidential" letter, Rea told CAS founder David Stirling that the society should "continue its work under another banner, mobilising a new generation and starting off untrammeled by the hang-over of the past."[67] Actually, Stirling had arrived at an even more radical conclusion. "Most of the moderate Africans who never joined [the Reconstituted] Congress and who did not commit their names in support of N.D.P. on its formation have now, almost to a man, joined that organisation," Stirling had written to Lawrence Vambe, one of the few remaining "moderates," a full two months before receiving Rea's letter. "If I was an African," Stirling, the chief apostle of partnership, continued, "I would certainly have joined [the NDP] by now. . . . I can see no alternative to bringing about adequate political reforms other than by Africans everywhere closing ranks within the N.D.P."[68] Partnership, indeed, had died.

There was, in fact, a veritable "revolt of the intellectuals" against racial partnership, as Nathan Shamuyarira characterized it at the time.[69] Inevitably, the rebels turned to African nationalism. In one particularly good day for the nationalists, five prominent intellectuals publicly declared their fealty to the NDP before a crowd of two thousand chanting "freedom now"—Southern Rhodesia's version of the slogan "self-government now," a mantra first popularized in late-colonial Ghana. Those undergoing this ritual induction into African nationalism were Dumbutshena and Chitepo—both of whom, as we have seen, had steadfastly avoided any affiliation with the Reconstituted Congress, despite apparently having been considered for its presidency—along with Ndabaningi Sithole (author of Southern Rhodesia's African nationalist "bible"), Bernard Chidzero (Ph.D.), and Edward Pswaryi (M.D.). Although maintaining his own links with the partnership-aligned Central Africa Party, the eminently respectable and responsible Stanlake Samkange (M.A., later Ph.D.) was moved to assert that the NDP had gained a "respectability which the African National Congress did not have and is shielded from the accusation that it is a party of irresponsible young men who have achieved nothing in life."[70]

Among the NDP's high-achieving recruits was John Shoniwa, then a law student in Britain.[71] Shoniwa, who was numbered among the earliest tea-drinkers, had been nothing if not rapturous in his praise of the Capricorn Africa Society's declaration of principles on its promulgation in 1954. Yet six years later, despite depending partially on white CAS adherents to underwrite his education, Shoniwa would no longer speak with the tongue of partnership, at least not unequivocally.

Shoniwa was hardly unique in his bumpy and somewhat less than fully executed journey from racial partnership to African nationalism. Other Africans who joined the NDP also found it convenient to maintain some association with the multiracial societies. No one exemplified this tendency better than Leopold Takawira. A one-time executive member of the multiracial Central Africa Party, Takawira served as executive officer of the CAS from 1957 to 1960, promoting partnership on a paid, full-time basis. Indeed, Takawira initially seemed to exploit the nationalists' dilemma for the benefit of the multiracial cause. Crusading for partnership even as the leaders of the banned Reconstituted Congress languished in detention, he seemed to dismiss African nationalism as unreflective, in full accordance with the CAS's position. "The Capricorn ideology—to create a common patriotism in Central and East Africa—is now being taken for granted by all thinking people," Takawira reported in August 1959, after returning from a tour of Southern Rhodesia's principal urban centers. Weeks later, Takawira, still itinerating for the CAS, visited the eastern part of colony, where he received "most encouraging support" from Ndabaningi Sithole, among others. "My faith in the Society [CAS] is growing daily," he concluded at the end of this trip.[72]

Takawira's faith in African nationalism would soon begin to grow as well. It was certainly strong enough for him to attend the inaugural meeting of the NDP in January 1960—although as an honored guest, not as a founding member of the party. Still, the CAS executive officer was accorded the privilege of addressing the assembled body. His speech, however, was pure partnership, appealing to a shared sense of chivalry between the men of the black elite and the white ruling class. Pleading with the Southern Rhodesian prime minister not to ban the new organization, which he noted was being founded on nonviolent principles, Takawira declared: "We are gentlemen and we will assume that Sir Edgar [Whitehead] is a gentleman." Takawira's "moderation" was too much for the NDP leaders, who found it prudent to disassociate themselves from his comments.[73] Yet the tiff—if indeed that is what it was, since the whole event may well have been scripted—in no way ruptured the relationship between Takawira and the nationalists. Weeks later, he was made chairman of the NDP branch in Harari, Salisbury's oldest African township, and given a seat on the party's national executive—without, however, relinquishing his position in the CAS and, it seems also, his membership in the Central Africa Party.

To his CAS employers, Takawira portrayed his double-dealing as positively in the best interest of partnership. His status as a top NDP official, he confided to CAS financier Jonathan Lewis in London, "is a good reflection on the Capricorn Africa Society in Southern Rhodesia, as you know that in the past the Society was regarded with suspicion."[74] Earlier Takawira, setting off on a visit to the Northern Rhodesian copperbelt, officially to stump for partnership, had assured Lewis that "My membership in the [NDP] makes me acceptable to the African Nationalists."[75]

Takawira's attempt to be all things to all men, multiracialists and nationalists alike, did not please the CAS power brokers, who suspected they were really subsidizing African nationalism. It now became a matter of how to dismiss Takawira graciously, with as little political fallout as possible. Fred Rea explained the dilemma facing the CAS leadership:

> In a short while we shall have to face the question whether, now that Leo Takawira has chosen to take an active part in the N.D.P. he can continue to hold office as chief executive of C.A.S. Our dilemma is an acute one. It will be difficult to get any worthwhile African successor to Leo. I do not see however how he can fill both offices at once: nor is it at all clear to me that his principles in N.D.P. are compatible with those he represents in C.A.S. It

is impossible for us to send him forth on his most valuable work as a speaker because in the eyes of the Africans he no longer represents C.A.S. but N.D.P. ... If Leo drops out it will probably mean that we lose our African membership. Somebody is very likely to interpret it as a hostile move of discrimination against a patriot.[76]

In August 1960, Takawira provided a perfect justification for his dismissal by failing a litmus test: he joined the rest of the NDP leadership in opposing the National Indaba, the swan song of racial partnership. Organized by the multiracialists, including the CAS, the National Indaba was a last-ditch attempt to reaffirm the validity of the partnership ideal by finding a happy medium between unmitigated white supremacy and an increasingly bold African nationalism. Yet even as the forces of partnership mobilized to make their last great stand, Rea reported, Takawira had marched off in the opposite direction, refusing to support a "project so essentially Capricornian" as the National Indaba. Instead, Rea complained, Takawira had turned the CAS office into an unofficial "N.D.P.H.Q. and Leo has thoughts for nothing but N.D.P."[77] Takawira finally was forced to relinquish his position as CAS executive officer in October 1960, just before the convening of the National Indaba (which proposed, among other things, a new fifty-member parliament with ten seats reserved for Africans).[78] His farewell party doubled as a fundraising event, enabling him to repay various loans to the CAS, including unauthorized ones.[79]

This was not the end of Takawira's relationship with the CAS, however. In late 1960 he fled the colony to avoid arrest, supposedly for making seditious statements. Arriving in Britain, Takawira, using contacts made from his days as a professional exponent of partnership, proceeded to establish an NDP outpost in the CAS's London office. While no doubt raising his stock in the NDP, Takawira's adroit maneuvering provoked the ire of some CAS officials back in Southern Rhodesia, opening a rift between the group's British and Rhodesian branches. In particular, it seemed to the Rhodesian-based Fred Rea, who was then frantically trying to salvage something of partnership, that Takawira once more had bamboozled the CAS into subventing African nationalism. The NDP, Rea protested, was little more than a stalking horse for the CAS's ideological enemies, that is, pan-Africanism and communism. Fearing contagion from the crisis then playing out in the Congo—from which white refugees were flowing into Southern Rhodesia[80]—Rea denounced the NDP's adherence to pan-Africanism as verging on "treasonable activity" and faulted the Zimbabwean African nationalists for becoming a part of "Moscow's game in Africa."[81]

Politically, the Rhodesian and British branches of the CAS seemed to be heading in different directions. As late as 1960, important segments of the society's Rhodesian-based leadership seemed determined to persevere in the foundational policy of containing African nationalism, as evidenced most poignantly by the National Indaba. By contrast, the CAS's British officers, apparently taking their cue from David Stirling himself, eventually came to the conclusion that containment was doomed, and indeed may have failed outright. In practical terms, this softening stance translated into an acceptance, albeit half-heartedly, of African nationalism. Hence the support offered such British-based multiracialists turned nationalists as Leopold Takawira and John Shoniwa. Teatime, that handy metaphor for the movement for nonracial meritocracy under colonialism, had ended. It was now up to the erstwhile white partners to decide whether, and to what extent, they would support its successor, namely, the African-led movement to end colonial rule.

DEFIANCE, DISCORD, AND DOMINION

The NDP spent much of 1960 reorganizing its leadership. Joshua Nkomo, president of the Reconstituted Congress, had been out of the country when that organization was banned. He remained abroad for the next twenty months, making his headquarters in London, and was named director of international relations for the NDP on its formation. Then, toward the end of 1960, he returned home to assume the presidency of the NDP, the third occupant of that office in the party's ten-month existence. (Michael Mawema, the founding president, was followed briefly by Leopold Takawira, before he fled to Britain.)

It was a changed nationalist movement as well as a changed country to which Nkomo returned. Along with political and cultural vibrancy, the intellectuals also brought into the NDP their dissentious ways and, all too often, their outsize ambitions. Too many of the party's highly educated new recruits fancied themselves as natural leaders, deserving of executive posts, or higher, by virtue of their membership cards. The resulting jockeying for position made the NDP a far less disciplined and cohesive organization than the Reconstituted Congress had been.

The tumultuousness in the NDP hierarchy was mirrored in the streets. In July 1960, the arrest of three top NDP leaders led to serious clashes between the police and thousands of the party's supporters in Salisbury.[82] Within days, similar disturbances broke out in Bulawayo. In October 1960, Africans again squared off with the security forces in Salisbury, Bulawayo, and Gwelo. Faced with such convulsions, the government repeatedly called in the army and reserve police units, which resulted in hundreds of arrests, scores of injuries, dozens of deaths, and widespread destruction of property.[83] Collectively, these events amounted to a political and psychological turning point, marking as they did the first time since the uprisings of the 1890s that blood had been shed in open confrontations between the security forces and the colonized people.

It was against this backdrop that a conference was called to review Southern Rhodesia's constitution. The conference, held in London in early 1961 under imperial sponsorship, included the Southern Rhodesian government and various parliamentary and extra-parliamentary opposition groups, including the NDP. Incredibly, the NDP delegation agreed to a new constitutional formula that completely vitiated the nationalist call for universal suffrage—a demand Nkomo, the delegation's leader, had previously termed "the only solution in Southern Rhodesia."[84]

The new constitution called for an expanded parliament with sixty-five seats, fifteen of which would be reserved for Africans. Under this arrangement, the franchise would still be determined by income, but with a new twist. Voters would now be placed on two separate and unequal rolls, called A and B. Parliamentarians holding the fifteen seats reserved for Africans would be elected by those on the B roll, whose members had a lower property qualification for voting than did those on the A roll; parliamentarians holding the other fifty seats would be elected by those on the A roll. Although nominally nonracial, the A roll would actually be dominated by white voters, given the racially skewed distribution of wealth and income. The new constitution also eliminated the reserve clause in the old constitution, which gave the British government the right, which it hardly, if ever, invoked, to veto legislation adversely affecting Africans.

The NDP's acceptance of these terms was tantamount to hoisting the white flag. The new constitution left the great majority of Africans disfranchised. Perhaps a few thousand elite blacks would have qualified for the B roll; very few Africans, however, would have made the A roll. More significantly, perhaps, the new constitution had the real potential to tame African resistance by institutionalizing it in a parliament with a built-in white majority. An African parliamentary bloc, relegated to permanent opposition, would replace the reserve clause—the elimination of which had long been a settler objective, despite its nonuse—as the chief nuisance of whatever white government happened to be in power. Indeed, the new constitution opened the door to full decolonization under white rule, another long-sought settler objective. With the reserve clause gone, settler politicians like Ian Smith would later argue, the British imperial authorities had no good reason to deny a motion by the Rhodesian parliament requesting independence—a request then being successfully made by other colonial legislatures in Africa.

Clearly, the NDP delegation to the constitutional congress had blundered badly, straying far from the party's foundational principles. Believing they had undermined the nationalist cause throughout the Central African Federation as a whole, an indignant Hastings Banda, leader of the Malawi National Congress, then the bellwether of anticolonial agitation in British central Africa, sharply rebuked the colonial Zimbabwean delegates. Apparently speaking in his dual role as medical doctor and political diagnostician, Banda, as he was wont to do, pronounced glumly, "They have no guts, no spine and no back-bone."[85] His diagnosis was shared by many in the NDP, including Leopold Takawira, who was temporarily suspended for his outspokenness. But such silencing could not be enforced, and the ensuing outcry soon forced an abrupt about-face. Not only did the NDP officially disavow the new constitution, but its entire political strategy subsequently came to focus on opposing it.

The NDP's reversal, however, failed to forestall a schism within the nationalist movement, marking the onset of the factionalism that would so rend Zimbabwean African nationalism in the years ahead. The outcome of this first breach was the Zimbabwe National Party. Asserting that the NDP had abandoned the African cause, the Zimbabwe National Party reaffirmed its commitment to trade unionism, pan-Africanism, and especially universal suffrage.[86] The new party's claim to the nationalist mantle received some international recognition, at least initially. In something of a diplomatic coup, Zimbabwe National Party delegates appeared alongside those of the NDP at an African solidarity conference in Ghana.[87]

With factionalism came tribalism, that is, the politicization of ethnicity.[88] Although on the national level activists criticized the Zimbabwe National Party for destroying African unity, the denunciation was especially shrill in Matabeleland, where one critic dubbed the breakaway group the Shona National Party.[89] Evidently concerned about their own leadership prospects, some of the NDP's intellectual recruits—who were heavily Shona-speaking— became dissatisfied with the ethnic composition of the party's hierarchy, complaining of a disproportionate number of individuals from the Ndebele minority. Stanlake Samkange, although still declining to join the nationalist camp and remaining a leader of the pro-partnership Central Africa Party, heard these grumblings by his former teatime partners (politically speaking), and he reported them in his "confidential," subscription-only outlet, *Samkange Newsletter*—a publication patterned on the continent-wide *Africa Confidential,* which also specialized in political intelligence. There was, Samkange confided to his subscribers, "dissatisfaction [within the NDP], particularly amongst the Shona-speaking members, that the party is dominated by the Matabele. This, of course, is not voiced publicly but is definitely spoken about in private."[90] Some observers, particularly in Matabeleland, were inclined to believe that the Zimbabwe National Party had come to publicly vent such private musings. These skeptics rejected the offshoot party's claim to be truer to the nationalist cause than was the NDP, seeing it instead as a fig leaf for advancing Shona particularist aspirations within Zimbabwean African nationalism.

Meanwhile the NDP, seeking to reaffirm its standing as the authoritative voice of Zimbabwean nationalism, took a number of steps to outflank the Zimbabwe National Party. In a move aimed at silencing ethnic gripes in Mashonaland—where, in any case, the Zimbabwe National Party was having difficulty recruiting—more Shona-speakers were brought into the NDP's up-per echelons. Mostly, though, the NDP sought to eclipse the Zimbabwe Na-tional Party by mobilizing mass opposition to the new constitution. When the government decided to hold a referendum on whether to accept the proposed charter, the NDP organized a counter-referendum. The nationalist tally, based on the NDP's original one man/one vote formula, showed almost universal African rejection of the constitution, with 467,189 against and only 584 in fa-vor. In the official referendum, by contrast, registered voters, the overwhelm-ing majority of them white, accepted the document by a margin of 41,949 to 21,848, with much of the white opposition coming from settler diehards who saw any direct African representation in parliament as opening the floodgates to black rule.[91]

The NDP's counter-referendum was something of a dress rehearsal for a wider campaign to delegitimate the colonial regime and make the colony un-governable. In pursuit of this larger goal, the NDP rediscovered the peasantry, a group it had mainly ignored up to this point. With the return of the land question to a position of prominence on the nationalist agenda, the NDP be-gan boldly and openly to agitate the countryside, despite official restrictions on doing so. Throughout the Reserves, nationalist militants clashed repeatedly with the forces of the colonial regime, as represented by the despised Na-tive Affairs Department.[92] The top Native Affairs bureaucrat condemned the NDP for encouraging tax evasion and disregard of the Land Husbandry Act. Unsuspecting peasants, he fulminated, were led to believe that "government had gone" and that NDP membership "license[d] you to plough where you wished, to have as much land or as many cattle as you wished, or to free you from dipping cattle."[93]

"Freedom farming" in the rural areas was complemented by "freedom sitting" in the urban centers. In a campaign modeled on the civil rights move-ment in the United States, with its tactics of civil disobedience and sit-ins, launched several months earlier, the NDP declared war on segregated pub-lic facilities in Bulawayo.[94] "Freedom sitters-in," members of the party's Ac-tion Group, invaded whites-only hotels, restaurants, tearooms, buses, even churches, clashing with segregationists.[95]

Everywhere, in town and country alike, the nationalists attacked the gov-ernment's actions and raised suspicions about its motives. For instance, taking a hard pro-natalist line, as nationalists traditionally had been wont to do, NDP militants condemned various health programs, including vaccinations, on "al-legations of causing sterility."[96] The critique of all things colonial extended to the missionary enterprise, heretofore considered sacrosanct by most elite Af-ricans. Although generally careful not to condemn Christianity itself, lest they alienate potential supporters, some nationalists lashed out at the missionary enterprise as an agency of colonialism. Other anticolonial activists extolled

the virtues of the precolonial indigenous faiths, going as far as opening political rallies by seeking the blessings of the ancestors, especially Nehanda, a (female) leader of the 1896–97 uprising who was hanged for her efforts.[97]

The NDP's nationwide campaigns did much to take the sting out of the
charge, made most prominently by the rival Zimbabwe National Party, that it
had sold out the African cause. Its raison d'être now increasingly in doubt, the
Zimbabwe National Party soon withered away. The colonial regime, however,
would prove to be a more formidable foe. Government authorities, seeking in
their turn to dispatch the NDP, heightened the level of police harassment
against the party. Physical repression of the nationalists was accompanied by
a new and well-funded ideological assault on African nationalism.

This initiative, called Build-A-Nation Campaign, sought to intensify the
existing ethnic divisiveness within the ranks of the nationalists as well as create new ones. For instance, Steve Kock, the campaign's white spinmeister and
tribalist mischief maker in chief, attempted to turn the cultural nationalist expressions that accompanied the rise of the NDP into an ethnic wedge. In an
opinion piece strategically placed in one of the principal African-oriented
weeklies, Kock mocked Joshua Nkomo's newfound appreciation for the precolonial rulers, suggesting that the NDP leader and his fellow Ndebele were
no more scions of the soil than were the colonialists. "It would be interesting
to know which rulers he [Nkomo] refers to," Koch commented. "Mr. Nkomo
is a Matabele and consequently comes from 'immigrant' stock just like Europeans do. I take it, when he speaks of 'our hereditary rulers' Mr. Nkomo refers
to the Mashonas who, alone are the only indigenous 'natives' of this country."[98] The nationalists struck back by physically attacking the black agents of
the Build-A-Nation Campaign and putting out word that they had come to
"sterlize the people."[99]

On the positive side, the Build-A-Nation Campaign endeavored to enroll black voters on the B roll and generally to court elite African "moderates," who, in the view of the authorities, formed a silent majority among the
black petty bourgeoisie.[100] By this point, however, African moderates had become an endangered political species, only half-embraced by the colonial regime on the one hand and assailed by the ever-bolder nationalists on the
other. In a characteristic blast, Dumiso Dabengwa, a fiery NDP youth leader
in Bulawayo, condemned the "so-called African moderates" as "sell-outs."
And Dabengwa, later to become a top strategist in the military insurgency
against white rule, concluded on a menacing note, one that betrayed the biblically based training of the nationalist leadership. "Those who are not with
us are against us," he pronounced.[101] The colonial authorities, who were definitely against the NDP, finally sounded its death knell. In a move Joshua
Nkomo attributed to their desire to advance the Build-A-Nation Campaign,
they banned the party in December 1961.[102]

The nationalists, however, had prepared for the regime's heavy-handedness. Whereas the proscription of the Reconstituted Congress had caught them unawares, resulting in an almost yearlong organizational vacuum, this time around the nationalists had planned more carefully. Just days after being outlawed, the NDP reemerged in a new guise: the Zimbabwe African People's Union (ZAPU). ZAPU inherited the NDP's membership and mass allegiance, along with much of its leadership. Once again, Nkomo was made president of the renamed organization, recalled to nationalist service along with several other top NDP leaders. But with James Chikerema and George Nyandoro added to its executive, the ZAPU leadership also looked somewhat like that of the Reconstituted Congress. Detained on the banning of the Reconstituted Congress, Chikerema and Nyandoro had missed the NDP leadership lineup. The return to the nationalist hierarchy of these two founders of the City Youth League and erstwhile opponents of tea drinking—both Shona-speaking, significantly—strengthened Nkomo in relation to the disaffection-prone intellectuals, nationalist newcomers who were less prominent in ZAPU than they had been in the NDP at the time it was banned.

Generally, ZAPU remained faithful to the NDP's political program, although with some important nuances. In a move that symbolized a deepening of its predecessor's pan-Africanist leanings, ZAPU created the executive post of secretary for pan-African and external affairs (the NDP had a director of international affairs). More significant was ZAPU's increased emphasis on mobilizing women on behalf of the nationalist cause. Although both the Reconstituted Congress and the NDP had women's auxiliaries, ZAPU went further, creating an executive post of secretary for women's affairs, a first in Zimbabwean African nationalism. The new portfolio went to Jane Ngwenya, whose epiphany as a nationalist took place on her way home from church, baby on her back, when she happened on a political meeting being addressed by Benjamin Burombo.[103] Most important of all, perhaps, ZAPU differed from its predecessors—the NDP as well as the Reconstituted Congress, both of which officially eschewed violence as a means of ending colonial rule—in its stated willingness to fight fire with fire by resorting to armed struggle, if the settler regime continued to repress peaceful protest. ZAPU, in any case, enjoyed only a brief legal existence. It, too, was banned in September 1962, the third incarnation of African nationalism to be declared illegal in just over as many years.

AFRICAN NATIONALISM AND SETTLER REPRESSION

By the time of ZAPU's banning, Rhodesian white politics had come to center on a vitriolic debate about how to contain African nationalism. The United Federal Party, in power for close to three decades, albeit under different names, had brought the colony through depression and war, eventually presiding, in the postwar years, over unprecedented white immigration and prosperity for all classes of settlers. To most whites, the African nationalist challenge appeared all the more menacing precisely because of the good times, a veritable golden age of settler colonialism in Southern Rhodesia. When the nationalist challenge did not go away, despite persistent government repression, white ultra-diehards, who had long sniped at the government from the parliamentary opposition, became a real political threat to the United Federal Party. Some of these ultra-diehards, as noted in the previous chapter, had even opposed the Central African Federation, the goose that laid the golden egg of the postwar economic boom, arguing that it would pose a long-term danger to white supremacy. Now, with the nationalists demanding African majority rule, the ultra-diehards declared themselves vindicated. Echoing a mantra the chief native commissioner attributed to the nationalists, the ultra-diehards brayed that government had gone, mocking what they saw as the United Federal Party's impotence in the face of the black peril.

The ultra-diehards vowed to bring government back and to face down African nationalism once and for all. In March 1962, hard on the heels of the banning of the NDP and the emergence of ZAPU, these alpha-champions of white Rhodesia agreed to put aside the tactical and personal differences that had long divided them organizationally. The outcome was the Rhodesia Front, a united bloc of ultra-diehards dedicated to keeping Rhodesia a white-supremacist state, no matter the cost.[104] Subsequently, the United Federal Party government announced elections for December 1962, the anticipation of which had created the urgency for the Rhodesia Front's formation.

Fighting from the "center," the United Federal Party attacked both the African nationalists and the white ultra-diehards as extremists. The ruling party, however, considered the extremism of the nationalists a much greater vice than that of the Rhodesia Front, the official parliamentary opposition. Thus the government increased the repression of the nationalists, outlawing ZAPU in the months leading up to the election, even as it continued to court the African "moderates" through the Build-A-Nation Campaign. Turning to the Rhodesia Front, the United Federal Party invoked the legacy of Godfrey Huggins—its now retired founder and a man of unimpeachable white-supremacist credentials, respected even by the most rabid ultra-diehards[105]— claiming it was best qualified to protect settler prosperity by maintaining investor confidence and checking the African nationalists.[106] The majority of white voters, however, disagreed. Instead, they entrusted the colony's future to the ultra-diehards, giving the Rhodesia Front the mandate to rule.[107]

While the whites fought it out politically, the nationalist leaders remained in detention and restriction, where they had been placed since the banning of ZAPU. Joshua Nkomo, who once again had been out of the country when the nationalist movement was banned, returned at the beginning of 1963 and was promptly placed under restriction by the new Rhodesia Front government. Then, in April 1963, Nkomo and most of the banned ZAPU's executive members broke their restriction orders and fled to Dar es Salaam, apparently with the intention of forming a government in exile. Taken aback by their sudden appearance in his capital, Tanzanian president Julius Nyerere—a man with considerable moral authority in African nationalist circles throughout the continent—advised the uninvited Zimbabweans to return home to lead their people in the struggle.

Nyerere's rebuff sparked a crisis within the Zimbabwean nationalist leadership, bringing to the surface discontent that had been festering for some time.[108] Dissidents, most notably the intellectuals who had joined the nationalist camp with the formation of the NDP, attacked Nkomo's leadership, calling him aloof and disengaged. Noting that he had been out of the country two out of the three times the nationalist movement was banned, they accused Nkomo of being a jet-setting chieftain, a leader who waged the battle for Zimbabwean independence mainly in the international media, and then from the relative safety and comfort of foreign capitals. Nkomo was not, the dissidents claimed, much interested in taking on the settler regime where it mattered most: in the townships and Reserves of Southern Rhodesia. Previously, Nkomo had been likened to the martyred Lumumba and acclaimed as the Moses of Zimbabwe.[109] Now, the dissident intellectuals denounced him as a coward who had led them across the Zambezi, away from the promised land of Zimbabwe and into the political wilderness of Dar es Salaam. Thus emerged the single most divisive issue in Zimbabwean nationalism that would continue well into the post-independence period—Nkomo's leadership.[110]

His stewardship of the movement in jeopardy, Nkomo fled the sharp tongues of his detractors and returned home, determined to give the lie to the charge that he was not a man of the people. Back in Southern Rhodesia, Nkomo and his supporters in the nationalist leadership decisively outflanked the dissidents, rallying the majority of the rank and file to their side, including those in the Shona-speaking stronghold of Salisbury. The Nkomo loyalists— who included the decidedly unintellectual James Chikerema and George Nyandoro—then began making plans to resuscitate ZAPU under a new name, the People's Caretaker Council (PCC). Their nomenclatorial choice was anything but accidental. Upon the founding of the ZAPU, its leaders had quietly agreed that, in the event of it being banned, they would go underground to prepare for guerrilla warfare instead of forming a new, above-board organization.[111] By using the provisional term "caretaker" for their new organization, the Nkomo loyalists, who claimed to uphold nationalist orthodoxy, technically abided by the letter of that agreement.

The dissidents, outmaneuvered politically, dispensed with such fastidious-

12. George Nyandoro (left)
and James Chikerema,
important figures in the rise of
African nationalism in the
1950s. Here they are wearing the
fur hats favored by many
activists during a "cultural
nationalist" phase in the early
1960s. Courtesy of *Parade*.

13. Robert Mugabe (left) and
Ndabaningi Sithole, two leading
African nationalist figures of
the 1960s and beyond. Courtesy
of *Moto.*

ness altogether. Returning from Dar es Salaam, they kept up their attacks on Nkomo and proceeded to organize the nationalist rump—the minority that had not joined the pro-Nkomo camp—into a rival movement, the Zimbabwe African National Union (ZANU). Formed on August 8, 1963, just two days before the official launching of the PCC, ZANU made no pretense of being provisional. It was, in both theory and practice, a permanent organization whose emergence signaled a definitive rupture between Nkomo and his opponents, a rift that turned largely on issues of conflicting personalities. Led by former ZAPU national chairman Ndabaningi Sithole, regarded as a moderate nationalist cut from the same political cloth as Nkomo, ZANU's aims differed little, if at all, from those of ZAPU/PCC. As one of the two NDP delegates to the 1961 constitutional talks—the other was Nkomo—Sithole had, after all, been implicated in the most vexing and divisive issue to face Zimbabwean African nationalism to date. Rather than policy or ideological differences, then, the ZAPU/ZANU schism was driven by personality conflicts that took the form of a second revolt of the intellectuals, this time against Nkomo's leadership.

Although it eventually came to assume strong ethnic overtones, originally the split within the nationalist movement did not correspond to a neat division between the two main ethnic blocs: Shona and Ndebele. ZANU, to be sure, never established a strong base in Matabeleland, remaining a largely Mashonaland movement. For a considerable period of time after the schism, however, ZAPU/PCC retained a commanding national following among members of both major ethnic groups. This fact was demonstrated not just by the presence at Nkomo's side of such iconic Shona-speaking nationalists as James Chikerema and George Nyandoro, but even more poignantly by the outcome of the first fratricidal war between ZAPU/PCC and ZANU. In this showdown, which took place between August 1963 and April 1964 and which was especially fierce in the Salisbury townships, the ZAPU/PCC forces used their superior numbers as well as their superior arms to deadly effect, completely routing the ZANU partisans. Eugene Watson, a British journalist brought in to replace Nathan Shamuyarira as editor of the top Salisbury-based, African-oriented daily, witnessed the mayhem. In his own attempt to follow the mass line, Watson backed ZAPU/PCC editorially over the upstart ZANU. He reported that Nkomo loyalists controlled the townships to such an extent, and with such brute force, that ZANU supporters began "disclaiming that they ever had anything to do with Sithole, or if they had, they had changed their minds and wanted to rejoin the people."[112]

As the nationalists engaged in this orgy of self-destruction, the new Rhodesia Front government watched gleefully from the sidelines, studiously refusing to intervene, perhaps even stoking the fire. Then, in April 1964, having established to its own satisfaction the absurdity of African rule, the regime struck against the nationalists, its repressive capabilities now greatly bolstered by having inherited the bulk of the military and intelligence apparatuses of the Central African Federation, which had been dissolved the previous year.[113] Both ZAPU/PCC and ZANU were banned for good and their leaders clapped in prison, as the regime moved toward its objective of outlawing African nationalism itself.

The war on African nationalism subsequently resulted in the proscription of a trade union movement and a religious formation, which the authorities described as nationalist, and more specifically ZAPU/PCC, fronts. The minister of law and order—a cabinet post apparently unique to Rhodesia and apartheid South Africa—banned the Zimbabwe African Congress of Unions (previously called the Zimbabwe African Confederation of Unions) for "working hand in glove with African nationalism."[114] The minister also outlawed the Zimbabwe Church of Orphans, which was perhaps the most extraordinary Ethiopianist formation to date. The "orphans" in question, it seems likely, were the children (read the entire Zimbabwean nation) of the detained and imprisoned nationalists.

The Rhodesian authorities regarded the Zimbabwe Church of Orphans as a repository of the cultural symbols associated with African nationalism. Men attending church gatherings, the minister of law and order declared in banning the group, generally sported "fur hats and carried carved walking sticks, which have become the 'uniform' " of ZAPU/PCC. One particular gathering, at which fur hats and walking sticks were much in evidence, "followed a pattern of nationalist songs and hymns, together with prayers for Joshua Nkomo and other . . . [ZAPU/PCC] restrictees." The sermon was "nothing more than a subversive political speech interspersed with biblical references . . . [that had been] twisted in such a way as to produce the political meaning" desired by nationalists masquerading as preachers, the minister of law and order objected.[115]

The all-out war on African nationalism, as represented by the actions against ZAPU/PCC, ZANU, and allied groups, coincided with the rise to power of Ian Smith, who was among the most extreme of the settler ultradiehards and the ultimate alpha-champion of white Rhodesia. Indeed, on the very day ZAPU/PCC and ZANU were banned, Smith had become head of the ruling Rhodesia Front, which in turn made him prime minister. His regime did not, Smith later explained, intend to join the "scramble to get out of Africa." Instead, he was determined to end the United Federal Party's "dreadful philosophy of appeasement."[116] Government had definitively returned.

Having, they believed, solved the African nationalist problem, Smith and his colleagues turned next to the settler nationalist problem. Since attaining self-government in 1923, the Rhodesian settlers had been looking forward to ascending to the next and final rung on the British imperial hierarchy—a path previously traversed by the sister "white" dominions of Canada, Australia, New Zealand, and South Africa—that is, outright independence. For decades, these yearnings had led settler politicians to rail against the reserve clause, a measure that was finally eliminated under the constitution of 1961—with the initial approval of the African nationalists, before they changed their minds, as we have seen. Thus, after banning the African nationalist movements, Smith, convinced that the way was now clear constitutionally for such a move, demanded independence from Britain. As justification, he cited the 1961 constitution. Smith also noted that Nyasaland and Northern Rhodesia, the other former Central African Federation territories, had evolved into the independent nation-states of Malawi and Zambia, probably the first and last time he ever advocated "equality" with Africans.[117]

The imperial power, however, balked at Smith's demand. Under pressure from the new African states, the British authorities insisted on delaying independence until Rhodesia (the "Southern" having been dropped when Northern Rhodesia became Zambia) put in place mechanisms for eventual universal franchise, effectively meaning black majority rule.[118] But the Rhodesia Front regime, true to its daredevil reputation, would have none of it. Smith ostentatiously declared that African rule, to him an oxymoron, would not happen in a millennium, and certainly not in his lifetime.[119] He would at length be proven wrong on both counts, although not before he had unleashed unprecedented terror, death, and destruction on the colonized Africans, especially the peasantry.

Meanwhile, Smith and his associates, determined to create a Rhodesian Reich on which the sun of African nationalism would never set, proceeded to dumbfound even some of their own diehard supporters. They boldly staged a white settler rebellion, unilaterally declaring independence in November 1965.[120] In the annals of British settler colonialism, this was the first such revolt by Anglo-Saxon kith and kin since the American Revolution of 1776. Accordingly, the Rhodesian declaration of independence was modeled on that of the United States, with the 1961 constitution as the annexure.[121] These documents, the rebel regime proclaimed, provided ample justification for the Rhodesian settlers' decision to "resolve the political affiliations which have connected them with another people and to assume among other nations the separate and equal status to which they are entitled. . . . We have struck a blow for the preservation of justice, civilization, and Christianity."[122]

If there were any doubts about the return of government after the treatment accorded the African nationalists, they were now laid to rest. The era of classical African nationalism in Rhodesia—the struggle to end colonial rule through peaceful protest, or short of armed struggle, at any rate—dramatically had come to an end. A new era—this one characterized by guerrilla warfare, a brutal counterinsurgency campaign, and international sanctions against the Rhodesia Front regime—had dawned.[123]

More than anything else, the events of 1965 were a rude denial of African middle-class aspirations, politically and otherwise. The Rhodesia Front's assertion that its settler-supremacist, anticolonial rebellion constituted a defense of justice, civilization, and Christianity was especially galling to elite blacks, whose three-generation-long struggle for full citizenship rights had been predicated on these very ideals. Now, finally, after having fully emerged as a social category, one that was conscious of itself and its historic mission, the African petty bourgeoisie was breezily dismissed as an enemy of justice, civilization, and Christianity, its collective will violently negated.

In addition to closing off all avenues to peaceful protest and driving the African nationalists into armed struggle, the settler rebellion finished off whatever residual sentiments of racial partnership had continued to linger after 1960. The African moderate, endangered for half a decade, now became extinct. A peaceful coronation having been aborted, the African nationalists would have to pursue the political kingdom by other means, notably armed struggle.

Conclusion

MONDAY, DECEMBER 31, 1956, was something of a red-letter day in the rise of the African middle class in colonial Zimbabwe. On that New Year's Eve, elite Africans organized a remarkable social event at the Salisbury West School, located in the capital's principal African township. Ostensibly, the occasion was a reception in honor of Samuel Parirenyatwa, the first African in Southern Rhodesia to obtain a medical degree. More broadly, though, the celebration offers a poignant social backdrop to the political events that round out this study. The timing, to begin with, was significant: it took place just eight months before the formation of the Southern Rhodesian African National Congress (the Reconstituted Congress), the colony's first full-scale African nationalist movement. The reception thus brings into sharp sociological relief both the rationale behind the subsequent embrace of African nationalism by elite blacks and, ultimately, the settler rebellion of 1965 that interdicted the nationalist challenge.

Actually, the Parirenyatwa reception was misnamed. Far from being just a celebration of one man's achievement, it was a collective exercise in class glorification, a kind of homecoming of the African petty bourgeoisie as a whole. Indeed this event was perhaps the closest thing yet to a social gathering of the African middle class on a national scale, featuring as it did a who's who among the black elite. In attendance were "men and women from the top class of Africans" in Salisbury and other parts of the colony. The ensuing commotion at Salisbury West School aroused the curiosity of many township residents, as may have been expected. But there was no room at the event for those of lesser social standing; the masses, quite literally, had to make do with the view from the outside—what they were able to see by peering through the school windows.[1]

Viewers within and without witnessed a striking scene. The front row, in particular, commanded attention. In that place of honor sat Parirenyatwa and his family, flanked by no fewer than ten university graduates, all of them magisterially attired "in full academic dress." This was no ordinary party; in fact, it was no party at all. The assembly had not been called to engage in light bantering or to share laughs over drinks. For one, Africans were then prohibited from consuming "European" alcohol; the ban would only be lifted later in the new year, after a decades-long campaign against it. And even though many elite men, especially, were known to partake of the forbidden drink in private, their notions of respectability generally precluded publicly flouting the law, because offenders could be arrested, fined, even imprisoned.[2]

Rather than merriment and glad-handing, the event was given over entirely to speeches, "one after another, from 8:30 to 12 p.m." The opening address was delivered by Herbert Chitepo, a patron of the Salisbury Cultural Club, the elite social group that sponsored the event. Chitepo, like Parirenyatwa, his high school classmate, had been in the vanguard of another professional breakthrough for the colonized middle class. On becoming Southern Rhodesia's first African lawyer some four years earlier, Chitepo had confounded the likes of Native Commissioner J. W. Posselt, who, at the beginning of the century, had opined that "it would be ludicrous to imagine a Mashona holding a University degree, or being called to the Bar."

Striking a familiar note, Chitepo commended Parirenyatwa's parents "for working so hard, in the face of financial and other difficulties, to educate their son." Enoch Dumbutshena, vice president of the Salisbury Cultural Club and notable articulator of elite grievances and aspirations, as we have seen throughout this volume, offered Parirenyatwa's accomplishment as a vindication of African intellectual capability. "He has demonstrated beyond all doubt that we Africans can do what other races can do, if given the opportunity," Dumbutshena exulted. Gideon Mhlanga, the veteran president of the African Teachers Association, agreed wholeheartedly. Parirenyatwa's achievement, he averred, proved that Africans were rising up the social ladder, and he concluded by leading the audience in proclaiming, "Africans, we rise."[3]

Such an exercise in class jubilation may be contrasted with J. H. Sobantu's protest a generation earlier (in chapter 1) that the "civilised native" was not being "given a better chance of rising to a higher level." Now, a self-conscious and self-consciously African, and certainly civilized, middle class, imbued with far greater expectations, was publicly trumpeting its emergence. As befitting its newly acquired maturity and boldness, the black petty bourgeoisie was on the cusp of discovering yet another mission, this one aimed at capturing state power. For despite the progress being celebrated, Southern Rhodesian settler society continued to fetter the full development of the colonized elite—political, social, and economic.

The new charge of the African middle class, along with the internal class contradictions it initially spawned, was prominently displayed at the Parirenyatwa event. Joshua Nkomo, who some eight months later would rise to the presidency of the Reconstituted Congress, marking the onset of a long career in the front ranks of Zimbabwean African nationalism, made "one of the best speeches that night." Determined not to miss so momentous a gathering,

14. Samuel Parirenyatwa dances with an unidentified woman at an Easter dance organized by the Salisbury Social and Cultural Club in 1958. The first African in colonial Zimbabwe to obtain a medical degree, Parirenyatwa later became a political activist. His subsequent death under mysterious circumstances made him one the first martyrs of mature African nationalism. Courtesy of the National Archives of Zimbabwe.

Nkomo had rushed to Salisbury by air, then still a rare and expensive mode of transportation, having read about the reception while on a visit to Northern Rhodesia. As if preparing culturally for his upcoming nationalist mission, he extolled the great African past. Nkomo also urged Parirenyatwa—who, as his deputy, would die some six years later under highly suspicious circumstances, making him perhaps the first martyr of mature African nationalism in Zimbabwe—to study traditional medical practices and medicines to "see whether they cannot be put to some good use."[4]

Nkomo may have made a good speech that night, but it was George Nyandoro who caused the most fireworks. A top official in the City Youth League, the more significant of the two groups that would soon combine to form the Reconstituted Congress, Nyandoro joined Nkomo in imploring Parirenyatwa to "investigate African medicines."[5] Yet Nyandoro, true to form, also struck a discordant note. Having been "introduced as a nationalist," he attacked racial partnership, then still the dominant, although obviously not unchallenged, ideology among the African middle class. With an eye toward the nationalist coalition of elites, peasants, and workers that the Youth League even then was tentatively seeking to forge, Nyandoro announced bluntly, and with perfect obliviousness to the social character of the event he was attending, that he "opposed the creation of class barriers" among Africans. The Youth League, he continued, believed "all Africans are the same. Chitepo, Parirenyatwa, [Stanlake] Samkange [who also was present] . . . should be the same; they should get equal treatment."[6]

These were not, at the time and place, mere innocent comments. Nyandoro, in fact, had lived up to his reputation as a nationalist firebrand. He had

openly flayed the black tea-drinkers, as the Youth Leaguers branded individuals like Chitepo and Samkange, who, they believed, wasted time hobnobbing
with white liberals instead of organizing the African masses. In insisting on
equality for all Africans, regardless of social standing, Nyandoro directly challenged the adherents of racial partnership in the audience. For instead of demanding equal treatment for all the colonized, racial partnership called for an
alliance of the black petty bourgeoisie and the white settlers to the exclusion
of the African masses.

Within four years of the Parirenyatwa event, however, the African middle
class, as a social category, had been all but completely won over to Nyandoro's brand of African nationalism. The elite embrace of African nationalism meant, first and foremost, that the African masses had to be mobilized to
support the campaign against colonialism. This imperative required, in turn,
a repudiation of the black elite's foundational creed of "equal rights for all
civilized men," a formula that had been promoted with particular vigor and
hope during the era of racial partnership. Organizationally, the failure of the
historic quest for nonracial meritocracy would lead to the emergence of the
Reconstituted Congress and its successors. The African middle class increasingly had come to the conclusion that the advancement of its collective interests required taking power from the white settlers. The settlers, for their part,
could not imagine maintaining their privileges without retaining power. Hence
the rebellion of 1965.

The rebellion expressed the Rhodesia Front regime's unrelenting hostility to the black middle class and its ideology of African nationalism. The
United Federal Party, which the Rhodesia Front unseated in the election of
1962, had taken a more nuanced approach to the nationalist challenge. Believing it needed a "measure of African support" to continue governing, the
United Federal Party courted segments of the colonized middle class, the so-
called African moderates.[7] At the same time, the United Federal Party government also launched a policy of repression against the nationalists, even as
it claimed to uphold "British justice in Central Africa." Unimpressed, the
white electorate eventually turned to the Rhodesia Front, which promised a
definitive solution to the nationalist problem. In pursuit of this objective, the
Rhodesia Front regime would institutionalize a system of naked repression,
arrogating to itself all the instruments of the modern police state, including mass murder, assassination, torture, and disinformation. The result was a
hyperauthoritarian state, shorn of all pretensions of legality, one that prosecuted a brutal and terror-filled counterinsurgency against the African nationalists.

In the end, however, the nationalist guerrilla armies prevailed, forcing a
negotiated political surrender on the white settler regime. Accordingly, the
triumphant African nationalists assumed power in 1980, proclaiming the in-

ternationally recognized independent state of Zimbabwe. The structures of power, however, remained largely unreformed. Juridical independence would not, after all, bring with it democratic governance and social justice. The mass of people, now twice dispossessed, would have to assume a new mission. They, too, would seek to rise in the scales of human development.

Notes

INTRODUCTION

1. The name Zimbabwe, of course, only became an official designation with independence in 1980. However, Africans (beginning with members of the middle class) began using the term in the early 1960s, counterpoising it against the name Rhodesia, which they had come to regard as colonial, white, and alien. In this study, I use variously the names Southern Rhodesia, Rhodesia, Zimbabwe, and their derivatives. Zimbabwe is usually used in conjunction with "colonial."

2. I use the terms "middle class," "elite," and, less frequently, "petty bourgeois" interchangeably.

3. Terence Ranger, *Are We Not Also Men? The Samkange Family and African Politics in Zimbabwe, 1920-64* (Portsmouth, N.H.: Heinemann, 1995).

4. Allison K. Shutt, "Purchase Area Farmers and the Middle Class of Southern Rhodesia, c. 1931-1952," *International Journal of African Historical Studies* 30, 3 (1997): 555-581; idem, "Pioneer Farmers and Family Dynasties in Marirangwe Purchase Area, Colonial Zimbabwe, 1931-1947," *African Studies Review* 43, 3 (2000): 59-80. See also Allison K. Shutt, "'We Are the Best Poor Farmers': Purchase Area Farmers and Economic Differentiation in Southern Rhodesia, c. 1925-1980" (Ph.D. dissertation, University of California, Los Angeles, 1995).

5. Shutt, "We Are the Best Poor Farmers."

6. Charles van Onselen, *Chibaro: African Mine Labour in Southern Rhodesia, 1900-1933* (London: Pluto Press, 1976); David Johnson, *World War II and the Scramble for Labour in Colonial Zimbabwe, 1939-1948* (Harare: University of Zimbabwe Publications, 2000).

7. Ranger, *Are We Not Also Men?*

8. Ngwabi Bhebe, *B. Burombo: African Politics in Zimbabwe, 1947-1958* (Harare: College Press, 1989).

9. Elizabeth Schmidt, *Peasants, Traders, and Wives: Shona Women in the History of Zimbabwe, 1870-1939* (Portsmouth, N.H.: Heinemann, 1992); Teresa A. Barnes, *"We Women Worked So Hard": Gender, Urbanization and Social Reproduction in Colonial Harare, Zimbabwe, 1930-1956* (Portsmouth, N.H.: Heinemann, 1999).

10. Carol Summers, *From Civilization to Segregation: Social Ideals and Social Control in Southern Rhodesia, 1890-1934* (Athens: Ohio University Press, 1994); Timothy Burke, *Lifebuoy Men, Lux Women: Commodification, Consumption and*

Cleanliness in Modern Zimbabwe (Durham, N.C., and London: Duke University Press, 1996).

1. RUNNING AGAINST THE WIND

1. NAZ, N3/21/1: Acting Assistant Police Commissioner to Secretary to Administrator, 6 December 1915.

2. *Report of the Chief Native Commissioner for the Year 1916* (Salisbury: Government Printer, 1917), 12.

3. J. F. A. Ajayi, *Christian Missions in Nigeria, 1841–1891: The Making of a New Elite* (Evanston, Ill.: Northwestern University Press, 1969); Norman Etherington, *Preachers, Peasants and Politics in Southeast Africa, 1835–1880: African Christian Communities in Natal, Pondoland and Zululand* (London: Royal Historical Society, 1978).

4. Leroy Vail, ed., *The Creation of Tribalism in Southern Africa* (London: James Currey, 1989); Leroy Vail and Landeg White, *Power and the Praise Poem: Southern African Voices in History* (Charlottesville: University Press of Virginia, 1991).

5. See Kenneth J. King, "African Students in Negro American Colleges: Notes on the Good African," *Phylon* 31, 1 (1970): 16–30; R. Hunt Davis, Jr., "Producing the 'Good African': South Carolina's Penn School as a Guide for African Education in South Africa," in *Independence without Freedom: The Political Economy of Colonial Education in Southern Africa,* ed. Agrippah T. Mugomba and Mougo Nyaggah (Santa Barbara, Calif.: ABC-Clio, 1980), 83–112.

6. *Bantu Mirror,* 20 June 1936.

7. *Report by H. S. Keigwin, Esquire, Native Commissioner, on the Suggested Industrial Development of Natives* (Salisbury: Government Printer, 1920), 3.

8. *Report of the Native Affairs Committee of Enquiry, 1910–11* (Salisbury: Government Printer, 1911), 13.

9. *Report by Keigwin,* 3.

10. NAZ, N3/6/3, South African Native Affairs Commission: Evidence, 103.

11. Ibid., 160.

12. *Report of the Commission Appointed to Enquire into the Matter of Native Education in All Its Bearings in the Colony of Southern Rhodesia* (Salisbury: Government Printer, 1925), 86.

13. Ibid. Rhodesian lore had it that settler women were "more racist" than their menfolk, largely on account of the women's relationships with African domestic servants, who were mostly male. See Jock McCulloch, *Black Peril, White Virtue: Sexual Crime in Southern Rhodesia, 1902–1935* (Bloomington and Indianapolis: Indiana University Press, 2000), 111.

14. The Legislative Council was renamed the Legislative Assembly in 1923, when Southern Rhodesia attained self-government.

15. *Debates of the Legislative Assembly,* 8 April 1931, vol. 10, col. 378.

16. L. H. Gann and M. Gelfand, *Huggins of Rhodesia: The Man and His Country* (London: George Allen and Unwin, 1964), 135.

17. L. H. Gann, *A History of Southern Rhodesia: Early Days to 1934* (New

York: Humanities Press, 1969); James A. Chamunorwa Mutambirwa, *The Rise of Settler Power in Southern Rhodesia (Zimbabwe), 1898–1923* (Rutherford, N.J.: Farleigh Dickinson University Press, 1980); Carol Summers, *From Segregation to Civilization: Social Ideals and Social Control in Southern Rhodesia, 1890–1934* (Athens: Ohio University Press, 1994).

18. Michael O. West, "Indians, India, and Race and Nationalism in British Central Africa," *South Asia Bulletin: Comparative Studies of South Asia, Africa and the Middle East* 14, 2 (1994): 86–103.

19. Ian Phimister, *An Economic and Social History of Zimbabwe, 1890–1948: Capital Accumulation and Class Struggle* (London and New York: Longman, 1988).

20. *Report of the Land Commission, 1925* (Salisbury: Government Printer, 1925).

21. Robin Palmer, *Land and Racial Domination in Rhodesia* (Berkeley and Los Angeles: University of California Press, 1977).

22. Dickson A. Mungazi, *Education and Government Control in Zimbabwe: A Study of the Commissions of Inquiry, 1908–1974* (New York: Praeger, 1990).

23. *Report of Commission into Native Education.*

24. Dickson A. Mungazi, *Colonial Education for Africans: George Stark's Policy in Zimbabwe* (New York: Praeger, 1991); idem, *The Underdevelopment of African Education: A Black Zimbabwean Perspective* (Washington, D.C.: University Press of America, 1982). For the classic statement on underdevelopment in Africa, see Walter Rodney, *How Europe Underdeveloped Africa* (Washington, D.C.: Howard University Press, 1974).

25. *Debates of the Legislative Assembly,* 8 April 1931, vol. 10, cols. 370–371.

26. This decision angered Huggins's more diehard supporters, who abandoned him altogether in 1934 when, after a similar development in South Africa, he engineered the fusion of his Reform Party with the Rhodesia Party to form the United Party. The formation of the United Party marked a return to political hegemony of the "national bourgeoisie," which had suffered a setback with the ouster of the Rhodesia Party the previous year.

27. Gann and Gelfand, *Huggins of Rhodesia.*

28. *Native Mirror,* April 1933. Sobantu's letter was actually sent to the "white" *Bulawayo Chronicle,* which unilaterally forwarded it to the *Mirror.*

29. *Native Mirror,* April 1933.

30. Ibid.

31. Michael O. West, "Pan-Africanism, Capitalism and Racial Uplift: The Rhetoric of African Business Formation in Colonial Zimbabwe," *African Affairs* 92 (1993): 273–274; *Bantu Mirror,* 18 June 1955.

32. NAZ, S235/485: Minutes of the Southern Rhodesia Advisory Board for Native Development, 16–17 December 1932, 7.

33. Lawrence Vambe, *From Rhodesia to Zimbabwe* (Pittsburgh: University of Pittsburgh Press, 1972), 164.

34. *Native Mirror,* July 1931.

35. *Bantu Mirror,* 12 June 1937. When the two got together, they did not discuss "useless things . . . but matters of great importance, such as education, civilisation . . . the future of the African race, etc." See *Bantu Mirror,* 30 October 1937.

36. *Bantu Mirror*, 3 May 1941.

37. *Native Mirror*, October 1935.

38. See, for example, F. M. L. Thompson, *The Rise of Respectable Society: A Social History of Victorian Britain, 1830–1900* (Cambridge, Mass.: Harvard University Press, 1988).

39. NAZ, S138/41: Brown to Native Commissioner, Inyati, 26 February 1931.

40. NAZ, S138/41: Njokweni to Principal, Inyati, 25 February 1931.

41. Just over a year after the Njokweni incident this individual, the principal, the Rev. W. G. Brown, called in the police to put down a strike by students demanding better food, contemptuously dismissing the protesters as "native boys unused to any correction in their homes and [who] come here and have to be practically tamed." A church investigation committee later accused Brown of "bad treatment" of the students and stripped him of much of his authority. He then resigned to become head of a government-run industrial school, which had been established as part of the reorientation of African education. See SOAS, CWM, SA, Incoming 95, Neville Jones File: [Report of Inyati Student Strike] To the Members of the South African District Committee; SOAS, CWM, SA, Incoming 94, W. G. Brown File: Brown to Chirgwin, 29 April 1932; ibid.: Brown to Chirgwin, 21 March 1933.

42. NAZ, S138/41: Chief Native Commissioner to Secretary to Premier (Minister of Native Affairs), 20 March 1931; ibid.: Moffat, A. N. C. Tapson and Complaint from Native, 23 March 1931; ibid.: Chief Native Commissioner to Principal of Inyati, 4 June 1931.

43. *Central African Examiner*, 3 January 1959, 8.

44. UWA, Historical and Literary Papers, Records of the South African Institute of Race Relations, R7 (file 3): Mwamuka to Jones, 30 January 1942.

45. *Bantu Mirror*, 23 January 1937.

46. RHL, Mss Brit Emp S365, FCB 100/2 (item 14): S. D. Maviyane and Charles Mzingeli, Memorandum on the Subversive Activities Bill (Act), 25 September 1950.

47. *Bantu Mirror*, 22 June 1940.

48. *Bantu Mirror*, 4 April 1942.

49. Sterling Stuckey, *Slave Culture: Nationalist Theory and the Foundations of Black America* (New York: Oxford University Press, 1987), 193–244.

50. Richard Elphick, *Kraal and Castle: Khoikhoi and the Founding of White South Africa* (New Haven and London: Yale University Press, 1977), 86 n 47.

51. J. B. Peires, *The House of Phalo: A History of the Xhosa People in the Days of Their Independence* (Berkeley: University of California Press, 1981).

52. André Odendaal, *Black Protest Politics in South Africa to 1912* (Totowa, N.J.: Barnes and Noble Books, 1984), 6; Keletso E. Atkins, *The Moon Is Dead! Give Us Our Money! The Cultural Origins of an African Work Ethic, Natal, South Africa, 1843–1900* (Portsmouth, N.H.: Heinemann, 1993), 95.

53. T. R. H. Davenport, "The Consolidation of a New Society: The Cape Colony," in *The Oxford History of South Africa: South Africa to 1860,* ed. Monica Wilson and Leonard Thompson (New York and Oxford: Oxford University Press, 1969), 1:327.

54. Henry Slater, "The Changing Pattern of Economic Relationships in Ru-

ral Natal, 1838–1914," in *Economy and Society in Pre-Industrial South Africa,* ed. Shula Marks and Anthony Atmore (London: Longman, 1980), 162–163.

55. Atkins, *The Moon Is Dead!* 80.

56. The depersonalization and dehumanization of Africans in British culture, beginning with nomenclature, went back several centuries. As early as the seventeenth century, Peter Linebaugh and Marcus Rediker assert in their masterful history of the Atlantic laboring class, " 'Black Tom' was becoming a London stereotype." See Peter Linebaugh and Marcus Rediker, *The Many-Headed Hydra: Sailors, Slaves, Commoners, and the Hidden History of the Revolutionary Atlantic* (Boston: Beacon Press, 2000), 132.

57. NAZ, ANG 1/1/35: African Teachers Association of Southern Rhodesia: Memorandum on Native Education, 6.

58. *Bantu Mirror,* 30 September 1961.

59. *Bantu Mirror,* 21 March 1953.

60. *Bantu Mirror,* 5 June 1954.

61. *Bantu Mirror,* 23 July 1960.

62. *Bantu Mirror,* 13 August 1960.

63. *Bantu Mirror,* 12 November 1960.

64. For South Africa, see Clifton C. Crais, *White Supremacy and Black Resistance in Pre-Industrial South Africa: The Making of a Colonial Order in the Eastern Cape, 1770–1865* (Cambridge: Cambridge University Press, 1992), 125–133.

65. NAZ, A3/18/21 (55–60), Native Education: A Suggestion.

66. NAZ, S246/782: F. Coe to Secretary, Minister of Native Affairs, 3 March 1931.

67. *Native Mirror,* October 1934.

68. NAZ, S1542/C19, vol. 4 (720–724): Chief Native Commissioner to Secretary to the Prime Minister, 18 December 1934.

69. NAZ, S482/528/39: Louw to Prime Minister, 14 March 1936.

70. NAZ, S482/ 528/39: Acting Secretary for Native Affairs to Secretary to the Prime Minister, 21 March 1936.

71. Many of these black South Africans came from the Eastern Cape, where there was a great proliferation of such "vigilance" associations in the last third of the nineteenth century. See Odendaal, *Black Protest Politics in South Africa.*

72. BIHR, LIN 1/3: Southern Rhodesian Native Missionary Conference, 10–12 June 1936.

73. *Native Mirror,* January 1936.

74. *Bantu Mirror,* 1 July 1944.

75. *Bantu Mirror,* 28 July 1945.

76. *African Weekly,* 7 February 1945.

77. SOAS, MMS General Correspondence, S. Rhodesia, 836/9: Ibbotson to Dodds, 19 July 1944.

78. NAZ, S2791/17/1: [Resolutions of] Southern Rhodesia African National Congress, 12 August 1946, 3.

79. See, for example, Percy Ibbotson, *Report on a Survey of Urban African Conditions in Southern Rhodesia* (Bulwayo: Federation of African Welfare Societies in Southern Rhodesia, 1943).

80. See, for example, *Report of Committee to Investigate the Economic, Social*

and Health Conditions of Africans Employed in Urban Areas (January, 1944); *Report of Commission ... to Investigate the ... Strike amongst the African Employees of the Rhodesia Railways* (Salisbury: Government Stationery Office, 1946).

81. *Debates of the Legislative Assembly,* 12 June 1952, vol. 33, col. 2152.

82. *African Weekly,* 24 December 1947.

83. *Bantu Mirror,* 18 September 1954.

84. *Bantu Mirror,* 16 October 1954.

85. N. M. Shamuyarira, "Green Light for the Word 'African,'" *Concord,* April 1956, 18.

86. D. D. T. Jabavu, "The Origin of 'Nkosi Sikelel' iAfrica,'" *NADA* 26 (1949): 56–57; Alton B. Pollard III, "Rhythms of Resistance: The Role of Freedom Song in South Africa," in *"This Is How We Flow": Rhythm in Black Cultures,* ed. Angela M. S. Nelson (Columbia: University of South Carolina Press, 1999), 98–124 (esp. 100–105); Leslie Bessant, "Songs of Chiweshe and Songs of Zimbabwe," *African Affairs* 93 (1994): 43–73 (see esp. 58–59).

87. NAZ, S2791/17, vol. 1: Minutes of the All Bantu Conference held at Gwelo, 11 November 1936.

88. NAZ, S2584/37: Report on Proceedings of Meeting of Gatooma Branch of the Southern Rhodesia Native Association, 7 November 1936.

89. Ngwabi Bhebe, *Benjamin Burombo: African Politics in Zimbabwe, 1947–1958* (Harare: College Press, 1989), 53.

90. Terence Ranger, *Voices from the Rock: Nature, Culture and History in the Matopos Hills of Zimbabwe* (Harare: Baobab, 1999), 162.

91. See, for example, *Bantu Mirror,* 13 July 1940, 3 January 1942, 8 June 1957.

92. *Samkange Newsletter,* 27 May 1961; *Daily News,* 10 June 1961. Quotation from the latter document.

93. *Bantu Mirror,* 17 June 1961, 24 June 1961, 14 October 1961, 21 October 1961, 4 November 1961.

2. COURTING "MISS EDUCATION"

1. For a broad overview of the origin and development of selected bourgeois societies in western Europe, see Peter Gay, *The Bourgeois Experience: Victoria to Freud,* 5 vols. (New York and Oxford: Oxford University Press, 1984, 1986), vols. 1 and 2; (New York: W. W. Norton, 1993, 1995, 1998), vols. 3–5.

2. *Report of the Commission Appointed to Enquire into the Matter of Native Education in all its Bearings in the Colony of Southern Rhodesia* (Salisbury: Government Printer, 1925), 17–18.

3. *Bantu Mirror,* 12 November 1955.

4. Michael O. West, "Going to America: The Odyssey of Stephen Sithole, an African Evangelical Christian, 1938–53," *Journal of African Travel-Writing* 8/9 (2001): 136–150.

5. Already in 1935, Madeya, then a student at Morgenster Training School, had meditated on the relationship between knowledge and power, concluding that "Knowledge is a latent talent given to us by God for which we must account." Then, in 1957, Madeya strongly attacked artificial birth control, accusing its proponents of choosing hedonism over Christianity. See *Native Mirror,* July 1935;

Michael O. West, "Nationalism, Race, and Gender: The Politics of Family Planning in Zimbabwe, 1957–1990," *Social History of Medicine* 7, 3 (1994): 447–471 (esp. 453–454).

6. *Bantu Mirror,* 26 September 1942.

7. The biblical Nicodemus is described as "a man of the Pharisees" and "a ruler of the Jews" (John 3:1).

8. NAZ, TH10/2/1 (1–6): How I Struggled in Order to Get My Education [undated but probably written in the early 1950s].

9. Ngwabi Bhebe, *Christianity and Traditional Religion in Western Zimbabwe, 1859–1923* (London: Longman, 1979), 27–70; C. J. M. Zvobgo, *A History of Christian Missions in Zimbabwe, 1890–1939* (Gweru: Mambo Press, 1996), 1–21; Norman Atkinson, *Teaching Rhodesians: A History of Educational Policy in Rhodesia* (London: Longman, 1972), 20–38.

10. *Report of the Native Education Inquiry Commission, 1951* (Bulawayo: Rhodesian Printing and Publishing Company, 1952), 3.

11. Carol Summers, *From Civilization to Segregation: Social Ideals and Social Control in Southern Rhodesia, 1890–1934* (Athens: Ohio University Press, 1994).

12. Sybille Küster, *Neither Cultural Imperialism nor Precious Gift of Civilization: African Education in Colonial Zimbabwe, 1890–1962* (Hamburg: LIT, 1994).

13. *Report of the Native Affairs Committee of Enquiry, 1910–11* (Salisbury: Government Printer, 1911), 12–13.

14. *Report of Commission of Native Education,* 63–64.

15. Ibid., 70. The director of native education later reported coming across "boys" who had been educated up to standard V in night schools, no mean achievement. *Report of the Director of Native Education for the Year 1947,* 33.

16. E. K. Mashingaidze, "Government-Mission Co-operation in African Education in Southern Rhodesia up to the late 1920s," *Kenya Historical Review* 4, 2 (1976): 265–281.

17. T. O. Ranger, *The African Voice in Southern Rhodesia, 1898–1930* (Evanston, Ill.: Northwestern University Press, 1970); E. Makambe, *African Protest Movements in Southern Rhodesia before 1930: An Ideological Appreciation of the Socio-Political Roots of Protest Movements* (Pasadena: California Institute of Technology, 1982); Tsuneo Yoshikuni, "Strike Action and Self-Help Associations: Zimbabwean Worker Protest and Culture after World War I," *Journal of Southern African Studies* 15, 3 (1989): 440–468.

18. See, for example, Lawrence Vambe, *An Ill-Fated People: Zimbabwe before and after Rhodes* (Pittsburgh: University of Pittsburgh Press, 1972); Owen Mtangadura, "The Life of an African Boy," *Missionary Magazine* 8, 89 (1957): 124–128.

19. HL, ABC 15.6, Box 2:29, Rhodesia Mission 1886–1955: Judith Smith, Report of Committee on Africa [1900].

20. HL, ABC 15.6, Box 5:43, Rhodesia Mission, 1886–1955: C. C. Fuller, Questionnaire on Industrial Training.

21. SOAS, CWM, Box 59/3: Wilkerson to Thompson, 17 September 1901; James Guveya Kamusikiri, "African Education under the American Methodist Episcopal Church in Rhodesia: Objectives, Strategy and Impact, 1898–1966" (Ph.D. dissertation, University of California, Los Angeles, 1978); John Keith Rennie, "Christianity, Colonialism and the Origins of Nationalism among the Ndau of

Southern Rhodesia, 1890–1935" (Ph.D. dissertation, Northwestern University, 1973).

22. *Report of Commission of Native Education,* 35.

23. *Bantu Mirror,* 1 December 1956. For additional examples of Dumbutshena's writings on education, see *Concord,* April 1956, 13–14; *Central African Examiner,* 9 November 1957, 18; *Central African Examiner,* 26 April 1958, 20.

24. Louis R. Harlan, "Booker T. Washington and the White Man's Burden," *American Historical Review* 71, 2 (1966): 441–467 (see esp. 448).

25. NAZ, N3/6/3: South African Native Affairs Commission: Evidence, 128–129.

26. Ibid., 46.

27. *Report of the Native Affairs Committee,* 12–15.

28. Ibid., 15.

29. Ibid., 13–14, 18.

30. *Debates in the Legislative Council during the Second Session of the Fifth Council,* 7 May 1912, pp. 222–225, cols. 14–21 (quotation on col. 19).

31. Ranger, *African Voice;* Makambe, *African Protest Movements.*

32. *Report by H. S. Keigwin, Esquire, Native Commissioner, on the Suggested Industrial Development of Natives* (Salisbury: Government Printer, 1920), 3.

33. NAZ, A3/18/21 (55–60), Native Education: A Suggestion. Though unsigned, this memo bears Keigwin's unmistakable stamp. See also, H. S. Keigwin, "Native Development," *NADA* 1 (1923): 10–17.

34. NAZ, A3/18/21 (55–60), Native Education: A Suggestion.

35. NAZ, A3/18/21 (9–10): [Memo by Acting Administrator of Meeting on 7 December 1922].

36. *Report of Commission of Native Education.*

37. Ibid., 12, 110 (quotation on 110).

38. *Debates in the Legislative Council during the First Session of the Seventh Council,* 8 June 1920, col. 545.

39. Ibrahim Abdullah, "Rethinking the Freetown Crowd: The Moral Economy of the 1919 Strikes and Riot in Sierra Leone," *Canadian Journal of African Studies* 28, 2 (1994): 197–218.

40. W. E. B. Du Bois, *Black Reconstruction in America, 1860–1880* (New York: Atheneum, 1977; first pub. 1935); Eric Foner, *Reconstruction: America's Unfinished Business, 1863–1877* (New York: Harper and Row, Publishers, 1988); C. Vann Woodward, *Origins of the New South, 1877–1913* (Baton Rouge: Louisiana State University Press, 1971).

41. Michael O. West, "The Tuskegee Model of Development in Africa: Another Dimension of the African/African-American Connection," *Diplomatic History* 16, 3 (1992): 371–387; William H. Watkins, "On Accommodationist Education: Booker T. Washington Goes to Africa," *International Third World Studies Journal and Review* 1, 1 (1989): 137–144.

42. The French followed a more independent policy, but toward the same end: limiting the growth of the educated colonized elite. See Denise Bouche, "Autrefois, notre pays s'appelait la Gaule: Remarques sur l'adaptation de l'enseignement au Sénégal de 1817 á 1960," *Cahiers d'Études Africaines* 8, 29 (1968): 110–122; Peggy R. Sabatier, "'Elite' Education in French West Africa: The Era of

Limits, 1903–1945," *International Journal of African Historical Studies* 11, 2 (1978): 247–266.

43. Edward H. Berman, "American Influence on African Education: The Role of the Phelps-Stokes Fund's Education Commissions," *Comparative Education Review* 15, 2 (1971): 132–145; Thomas Jesse Jones, *Education in Africa: A Study of West, South and Equatorial Africa by the African Education Commission* (New York, 1922); idem, *Education in East Africa: A Study of East, Central and South Africa by the Second African Education Commission* (New York, 1925).

44. Jones, *Education in East Africa*, 230–254; Edwin W. Smith, *Aggrey of Africa: A Study in Black and White* (New York: Richard R. Smith, Inc., 1930), 216–219.

45. HL, ABC 15.6, Box 5:44, Rhodesia Mission 1886–1955: Observations and Recommendations [by East African Commission of the Phelps-Stokes Fund, submitted to Minister of Education, n.d.]; *Report of Commission of Native Education*, 29.

46. Jones, *Education in Africa*, 17.

47. *Education Policy in British Tropical Africa*, Cmd. 2374 (London: His Majesty's Stationery Office, 1925); Kenneth J. King, "Africa and the Southern States of the U.S.A.: Notes on J. H. Oldham and American Negro Education for Africans," *Journal of African History* 10, 4 (1969): 659–677. See also Kenneth James King, *Pan-Africanism and Education: A Study of Race, Philanthropy and Education in the Southern States of America and East Africa* (Oxford: Clarendon Press, 1971).

48. Interview with Rev. Esau T. J. Nemapare, Ngezi Mission, Zimbabwe, 12 July 1993; Michael O. West, "James Aggrey's Impact on Southern Africans," *Southern African Encounter* 3, 1 (1996): 20–23.

49. Smith, *Aggrey of Africa;* Kenneth King, "James E. K. Aggrey: Collaborator, Nationalist, Pan-African," *Canadian Journal of African Studies* 3, 3 (1970): 511–530.

50. *Report of Commission of Native Education*, 46, 76–79.

51. Franklin Parker, *African Development and Education in Southern Rhodesia* (Columbus: Ohio State University Press, 1960), 87–89. Named after the philanthropist Anna T. Jeanes, who funded it, Jeanes teaching initially was instituted as a supplement to industrial education in the southern United States. It was later exported to Africa at the behest of the Phelps-Stokes Fund.

52. Dickson A. Mungazi, *Colonial Education for Africans: George Stark's Policy in Zimbabwe* (New York: Praeger, 1991). See also Dickson A. Mungazi, *The Underdevelopment of African Education: A Black Zimbabwean Perspective* (Washington, D.C.: University Press of America, 1982); Dickson A. Mungazi, *Colonial Policy and Conflict in Zimbabwe: A Study of Cultures in Collision, 1890–1979* (New York: Crane Russak, 1992).

53. *Report of the Native Education Inquiry Commission*, 6.

54. NAZ, S245/1118: Director of Native Education to Secretary for Native Affairs, 27 March 1946. Previously, each missionary society, and even each school, would set its own salary scales according to the availability of funds and teachers.

55. *Native Education: Annual Report by the Director for the Year 1958*, 8; *African Education: Annual Report by the Secretary for the Year 1965*, 5.

56. NAZ, S235/477: Notes on Evidence of Enquiry into Bulawayo Location, 1930, 30; NAZ, ANG1/1/17: Proceedings of the Southern Rhodesia Missionary Conference, June 1936, 11; *Native Mirror,* October 1933, June 1934.

57. *Report of the Director of Native Education for the Year 1953,* 29, 34.

58. *Native Education: Annual Report by the Secretary for the Year 1961,* 12; *African Education: Annual Report by the Secretary for the Year 1965,* 3, 10.

59. *African Education: Annual Report by the Secretary for the Year 1964,* 11.

60. R. C. Bone, "Educational Development in Rhodesia," *Rhodesian Journal of Economics* 2, 4 (1968): 5-27.

61. Grace Todd, "Explosion in Education," *Central African Examiner,* March 1961, 19-20.

62. *Concord,* April 1956, 13-14.

63. See, for example, Michael O. West, "Ndabaningi Sithole, Garfield Todd and the Dadaya School Strike of 1947," *Journal of Southern African Studies* 18, 2 (1992): 297-316.

64. *Report of Committee to Investigate the Economic, Social and Health Conditions of Africans Employed in Urban Areas* (January 1944); *Report of the Native Education Inquiry Commission,* 11-12; *Report of the Director of Native Education for the Year 1954,* 83.

65. Tendayi J. Kumbula, *Education and Social Control in Southern Rhodesia* (Palo Alto, Calif.: R and E Research Associates, 1979); Summers, *From Civilization to Segregation.*

66. *Report of the Director of Native Education for the Year 1949,* 41. See also *Debates of the Legislative Assembly,* 29 October 1943, vol. 23, col. 2654.

67. *Native Education: Annual Report by the Director for the Year 1958,* 8; *Native Education: Annual Report by the Director for the Year 1959,* 3; *Native Education: Annual Report by the Director for the Year 1960,* 13; *Native Education: Annual Report by the Director for the Year 1961,* 3, 11; *African Education: Annual Report of the Secretary for the Year 1962,* 3.

68. *Native Education: Annual Report by the Director for the Year 1959,* 3. At the same time, the Native Education Act also offered African teachers some benefits in that for the first time they were guaranteed uniformity in terms of salaries, conditions of employment, and pensions.

69. Carol Summers, "Demanding Schools: The Umchingwe Project and African Men's Struggle for Education in Southern Rhodesia, 1928-1934," *African Studies Review* 40, 2 (1997): 117-139. On independent educational initiatives in colonial Africa generally, see Terence Ranger, "African Attempts to Control Education in East and Central Africa, 1990-1939," *Past and Present* 32 (1965): 57-85; Harold W. Turner, "African Independent Churches and Education," *Journal of Modern African Studies* 13, 2 (1975): 295-308; S. S. Obidi, "Nationalist's Demands for University Education in Nigeria and Government's Response, 1920-1948," *History of Education* 19, 1 (1990): 55-64.

70. BIHR, LIN1/3: Southern Rhodesia Native Missionary Conference, 10-12 June 1936; *Bantu Mirror,* 27 June 1936. See also Lawrence Vambe, *From Rhodesia to Zimbabwe* (Pittsburgh: University of Pittsburgh Press, 1976), 71-72.

71. *Bantu Mirror,* 19 September 1936.

72. NAZ, ANG 1/1/35: Constitution of the African Teachers Association of Southern Rhodesia, 8.

73. Ranger, "African Attempts," 69–70.

74. NAZ, S138/22: Rhodesia Bantu Voters Association: Annual Conference, 13 July 1925.

75. NAZ, S482/709/39, vol. 1: Rhodesia Bantu Voters Association, 17 July 1929; ibid.: Premier's Private Secretary to Chief Native Commissioner, 5 June 1931.

76. NAZ, S235/477: Notes on Evidence of Enquiry into Bulawayo Location, 1930, 29.

77. NAZ, S85: Evidence of Enquiry into Salisbury Location, 1930, 26, 54, 64, 83.

78. NAZ, S235/477: Notes on Evidence of Enquiry into Bulawayo Location, 1930, 54, 59, 62.

79. NAZ, S235/394: [Bulawayo] Native Affairs Commission Report, 1930, 21–22; NAZ, S86/22/2/177–178: [Salisbury] Native Affairs Commission Report, 1930, 41–42.

80. *Native Mirror,* July 1932.

81. NAZ, S1542/C19, vol. 2 (290): Resolution Passed by the Native Section of the Southern Rhodesia Missionary Conference . . . , Salisbury, 23–25 June 1936; NAZ, S1542/C19, vol. 2: (283–285): Secretary of Native Affairs to Secretary to Prime Minister (Native Affairs), 31 July 1936.

82. *Native Mirror,* January 1934, March 1935, November 1935; *Bantu Mirror,* 5 September 1936; Kamusikiri, "African Education," 153.

83. NAZ, ANG 1/1/35: Constitution of the African Teachers' Association of Southern Rhodesia, 1.

84. In the 1940s, the maximum salary for African teachers with a college degree was £356, whereas the minimum for similarly qualified whites was £385.

85. David Johnson, "Urban Labor, the War, and the Revolt of the Working People in Colonial Zimbabwe (Southern Rhodesia)," *South Asia Bulletin: Comparative Studies of South Asia, Africa and Middle Class* 15, 2 (1995): 72–88; Ngwabi Bhebe, *B. Burombo: African Politics in Zimbabwe, 1947–1958* (Harare: College Press, 1989), 44–88; Ian Phimister, *An Economic and Social History of Zimbabwe, 1890–1948: Capital Accumulation and Class Struggle* (London and New York: Longman, 1988), 219–296; Terence Ranger, *Peasant Consciousness and Guerrilla War in Zimbabwe* (London: James Currey, 1985), 99–136.

86. *Bantu Mirror,* 11 September 1948.

87. NAZ, ANG 1/1/35: African Teachers Association of Southern Rhodesia: Memorandum on Native Education.

88. This certainly was the view of William Madeya of Miss Education fame, who began his essay by recounting how "men like Aggrey [had] won the 'decisive battles' of the world" through knowledge, which they parlayed into power. See *Bantu Mirror,* 26 September 1942.

89. West, "Tuskegee Model of Development"; J. Congress Mbata, "Booker T. Washington and John Tengo Jabavu: A Comparison," *Afro-American Studies* 2, 3 (1971): 181–186; W. Manning Marable, "Booker T. Washington and African Nationalism," *Phylon* 35, 4 (1974): 398–406.

90. Richard Parry, "The 'Durban System' and the Limits of Colonial Power in Salisbury, 1890–1935," in *Liquor and Labor in Southern Africa,* ed. Jonathan Crush and Charles Ambler (Athens: Ohio University Press, 1992), 115–138; Michael O.

West, "Liquor and Libido: 'Joint Drinking' and the Politics of Sexual Control in Colonial Zimbabwe, 1920s–1950s," *Journal of Social History* 30, 3 (1997): 645–667.

91. NAZ, S138/55: Detective/Sergeant of CID to Chief Superintendent of CID, 25 January 1931.

92. *Bantu Mirror*, 29 July 1944.

93. *Native Mirror*, October 1933.

94. *Bantu Mirror*, 11 August 1945.

95. *Bantu Mirror*, 8 September 1945.

96. *Bantu Mirror*, 13 October 1945.

97. *Bantu Mirror*, 17 November 1945, 9 February 1946.

98. *Bantu Mirror*, 4 December 1954.

99. *Bantu Mirror*, 12 March 1949.

100. *Bantu Mirror*, 29 July 1950.

101. NAZ, S1012/28: Federation of African Welfare Societies in Southern Rhodesia: Minutes of the Tenth Annual Conference of African Delegates, 30 September 1950, 5.

102. NAZ, S517: Staff Officer to the Commissioner of Police to Officer Commanding CID Headquarters, 13 July 1949.

103. *Prominent African Personalities of Rhodesia* (Salisbury: Cover Publicity Services, n.d.), 157.

104. NAZ, ANG 1/1/35: African Teachers' Association of Southern Rhodesia: Memorandum on Native Education, 3; *Report of the Native Education Inquiry Commission*, 27.

105. Stanlake Samkange, *Origins of Rhodesia* (London: Heinemann, 1968). In 1970 this book won the Melville J. Herskovits Award, presented annually by the (U.S.) African Studies Association for what is deemed the best new scholarly book on Africa.

106. CHS, Claude Barnett Papers, Box 174, Rhodesia, North and South, 1951–65: Samkange to Barnett, 22 January 1954.

107. *Bantu Mirror*, 6 March 1954.

108. *Bantu Mirror*, 14 February 1953, 7 and 14 November 1953, 17 April 1954, 4 June 1955.

109. *Bantu Mirror*, 7 April 1956, 20 October 1956; *Rhodesia Herald*, 18 February 1956; *Central African Examiner*, 1 March 1958, 10.

110. RAC, RBF, Nyatsime African College, Box 82: Steere to Rockefeller, 15 August 1956.

111. RAC, RBF, Nyatsime African College, Box 82: Rockefeller to Steere, 21 November 1956; ibid.: Steere to Prime Minister, 21 January 1957; ibid.: Steere to Rockefeller, 24 January 1957.

112. RAC, RBF, Nyatsime African College, Box 82: Director of Native Education to Samkange, 23 November 1960.

113. Louis R. Harlan, *Booker T. Washington: The Wizard of Tuskegee, 1901–1915* (New York: Oxford University Press, 1983).

114. RAC, RBF, Nyatsime African College, Box 82: Geren to Hyde, 28 December 1962; ibid.: Foster to Hyde, 9 January 1963; ibid.: Geren to Hyde, 29 January, 1963. Foster, whose trip had been sponsored by the Agency for International Development, prepared a report for the State Department upon returning to the United States.

115. RAC, RBF, Nyatsime African College, Box 82: Samkange to Creel, 7 December 1957.

116. Küster, *Neither Cultural Imperialism*, 175–177; West, "Ndabaningi Sithole, Garfield Todd and the Dadaya School Strike."

117. *Native Education: Annual Report by the Director for the Year 1959*, 3; *Native Education: Annual Report by the Director for the Year 1960*, 13; *Native Education: Annual Report by the Director for the Year 1961*, 3, 11; *African Education: Annual Report by the Secretary for the Year 1962*, 3; *African Education: Annual Report by the Secretary for the Year 1964*, 3; *African Education: Annual Report by the Secretary for the Year 1965*, 3. Student strikes continued after 1965, however. See, for example, A. S. Mlambo, "Student Protest and State Reaction in Colonial Rhodesia: The 1973 Chimukwembe Student Demonstration at the University of Rhodesia," *Journal of Southern African Studies* 21, 3 (1995): 473–490.

118. The close relationship between Christianity, involvement in the cash economy, and elite formation has been noted elsewhere in colonial Africa. See, for example, J. F. A. Ajayi, *Christian Missions in Nigeria, 1841–1891: The Making of a New Elite* (Evanston, Ill.: Northwestern University Press, 1969); Norman Etherington, *Preachers, Peasants and Politics in Southeast Africa, 1835–1880: African Christian Communities in Natal, Pondoland and Zululand* (London: Royal Historical Society, 1978).

119. HL, ABC 15.6, vol. 10, folder 3:14, Mabel Larkins Hack: Hack to Friends, 30 April 1941.

120. Ibid.: Hack to Friends, 1 June 1940.

121. See, for example, Gerald L. Caplan, *The Elites of Barotseland, 1878–1969: A Political History of Zambia's Western Province* (Berkeley and Los Angeles: University of California Press, 1970), 93–94.

122. The state paid for the education of several male descendants of Lobengula, the precolonial Ndebele King. However, the most intellectually promising among them, Nguboyenja, suffered a mental breakdown in the course of pursuing legal studies.

123. *Bantu Mirror*, 18 February 1939.

124. *Bantu Mirror*, 10 January 1948.

125. Ibid.; NAZ, HL1/1/1: Tribute to a Pioneer African Evangelist.

126. *Bantu Mirror*, 24 January 1948.

127. Terence Ranger, *Are We Not Also Men? The Samkange Family and African Politics in Zimbabwe, 1920–64* (Portsmouth, N.H.: Heinemann, 1995).

128. [Joshua] Nkomo, *The Story of My Life* (London: Methuen, 1984), 7–28.

129. Abel Tendekai Muzorewa, *Rise Up and Walk: An Autobiography*, ed. Norman E. Thomas (London: Evans Brothers Ltd., 1978), 3, 21.

130. David Martin and Phyllis Johnson, *The Struggle for Zimbabwe* (New York and London: Monthly Review Press, 1981), 202.

131. *Concord*, April/June 1954, 16–17.

132. Central African Council, *Report of the Commission on Higher Education for Africans in Central Africa* (Salisbury: Central African Council, 1953), 11.

133. Michael Gelfand, *A Non-Racial Island of Learning: A History of the University College of Rhodesia from Its Inception to 1966* (Gwelo: Mambo Press, 1978), 191.

134. UWA, Records of the South African Institute of Race Relations, Kb 6

(file 1): Cripps to Rheinallt-Jones, n.d.; ibid.: Rheinallt-Jones to Cripps, 27 January 1931.

135. See, for example, *Bantu Mirror*, 22 April 1939.

136. *Native Education: Annual Report by the Director for the Year 1959*, 12; *African Education: Annual Report by the Secretary for the Year 1962*, 16.

137. Eshmael Mlambo, *Rhodesia: The Struggle for a Birthright* (London: C. Hurst and Company, 1972), 98. UNISA graduates include Robert Mugabe and Nelson Mandela. See Nelson Mandela, *Long Walk to Freedom: The Autobiography of Nelson Mandela* (Boston: Little, Brown and Company, 1994), 88. Mandela, however, matriculated at UNISA in the 1940s, long before his imprisonment.

138. Nkomo, *Story of my Life*, 29.

139. *Bantu Mirror*, 12 November 1949. See also Ranger, *Are We Not Also Men?* 47–53.

140. An Englishman, Cripps independently operated a school without government assistance, rejecting the conditions attached to official grants. See *Report of Commission of Native Education*, 66–67.

141. NAZ, CR4/1/1 (624–25): Dzwowa to Cripps, 6 January 1947.

142. *Bantu Mirror*, 29 February 1936; *Concord*, April/June 1954, 16–17; Ndabaningi Sithole, *African Nationalism* (Cape Town: Oxford University Press, 1959), 13.

143. Nkomo, *Story of my Life*, 34

144. BIHR, CAS 61: Shoniwa to Lewis, 11 January 1956; ibid.: Shoniwa to Lewis, 10 February 1956; ibid.: Lewis to Shoniwa, 29 March 1956; ibid.: Shoniwa to Lewis, 3 April 1956.

145. Ernestina Shoniwa, who joined her husband in Britain, began pursuing a legal career of her own in 1961, the year she filed for divorce. See BIHR, CAS 97: Lewis to E. Shoniwa, 9 October 1961; ibid.: E. Shoniwa to Lewis, 11 December 1961.

146. BIHR, CAS 61: Lewis to Dye, 17 October 1956.

147. BIHR, CAS 97: Bull to [Lewis], 2 October 1961.

148. Kamusikiri, "African Education," 203–204.

149. *Bantu Mirror*, 17 July 1948, 1 January 1949; Kamusikiri, "African Education," 233.

150. Kamusikiri, "African Education," 264–265; Muzorewa, *Rise Up and Walk*, 47.

151. *Annual Report of the Director of Native Education for the Year 1937*, 19.

152. Sithole, *African Nationalism*, 10.

153. *Report of the Director of Native Education for the Year 1941*, 30.

154. *Report of the Director of Native Education for the Year 1948*, 41–42; *Report of the Director of Native Education for the Year 1949*, 45.

155. NAZ, S482/709/39, vol. 3: Salisbury and District Native Welfare Society: Acting Chairman's Report for the Year Ended October 31st 1944; ibid.: *Native Welfare Bulletin*, November and December 1944.

156. *Report of the Director of Native Education for the Year 1947*, 34; *Report of the Director of Native Education for the Year 1950*, 35.

157. *Report of the Director of Native Education for the Year 1948*, 41; *Report of the Director of Native Education for the Year 1949*, 45; *Report of the Director of Native Education for the Year 1950*, 35; *Report of the Director of Native Education for the Year 1951*, 63; *Report of the Director of Native Education for the Year 1952*, 47.

158. *Report of the Director of Native Education for the Year 1951,* 63; *Report of the Director of Native Education for the Year 1952,* 47.

159. For instance, in 1961 the federal government provided £100 per white pupil, compared to just £5 spent on each African student by the Southern Rhodesian Territorial government. See Todd, "Explosion in Education."

160. Herbert Chitepo, who in 1953 became the first colonial Zimbabwean to be called to the bar, was an advocate, not a barrister or solicitor.

161. NAZ, F209/1689, file 1: Director of Native Education to Secretary for Education, 10 October 1954; ibid., file 3: Deputy Secretary for Education to Registrar, University of Natal, 24 March 1956; ibid., Reply to Mr. Yamba's question No. VII: Tuesday, 6 March [1956].

162. Imanuel Geiss, *The Pan-African Movement: A History of Pan-Africanism in America, Europe and Africa,* trans. Ann Keep (New York: Africana Publishing Co., 1974), 293–304; J. Mutero Chirenje, *Ethiopianism and Afro-Americans in Southern Africa, 1883–1916* (Baton Rouge and London: Louisiana State University Press, 1987), 135–143.

163. *Report of the Native Affairs Committee,* 17.

164. Simbini Mamba Nkomo, identified by the late J. Mutero Chirenje as a colonial Zimbabwean (although others claim he was South African or Mozambican), arrived in the United States in 1910 and graduated from college in 1917. Nkomo died prematurely in the United States in 1925. The next colonial Zimbabwean to study abroad, as far as I can determine, was Stephen Sithole. Sithole, who enrolled at Moody Bible Institute in Chicago in 1946, claimed he walked two thousand miles to Cape Town on the first leg of his journey to the United States. Earlier, in 1931, the secretary to the Southern Rhodesian high commissioner in Britain had reported that there were "two Southern Rhodesian Coloured Students in London." If so, these students must have been "coloured" in the southern African sense of the term, that is, persons of racially mixed descent rather than Bantu-speaking black Africans. See Chirenje, *Ethiopianism and Afro-Americans,* 139; West, "Going to America"; *African Weekly,* 12 February 1947; NAZ, S482/280/39, file 3: Koens to Wright, 8 May 1931.

165. *Final Report of the April/May 1962 Census of Africans in Southern Rhodesia* (Salisbury: Central Statistical Office, 1962), 6, 24.

166. *Bantu Mirror,* 17 January 1948; *African Home News,* 22 May 1954.

167. Gelfand, *A Non-Racial Island of Learning,* 192.

168. There were nearly twenty African doctors in 1960. See, Mlambo, *Rhodesia,* 98.

169. See, for example, Leo Kuper, *An African Bourgeoisie: Race, Class and Politics in South Africa* (New Haven and London: Yale University Press, 1965), 73, 133; St. Clair Drake and Horace R. Cayton, *Black Metropolis: A Study of Negro Life in a Northern City* (New York: Harcourt, Brace and Company, 1945), 515–516.

170. M. B. Lukhero, "The Social Characteristics of an Emergent Elite in Harare," in *The New Elites of Tropical Africa,* ed. C. Lloyd (London: Oxford University Press, 1966), 126–138; Clive Kileff, "Black Suburbanites: An African Elite in Salisbury, Rhodesia," in *Urban Man in Southern Africa,* ed. Clive Kileff and Wade C. Pendleton (Gwelo: Mambo Press, 1975), 81–97.

171. Ranger, *Are We Not Also Men?* 124–158.

172. *Bantu Mirror,* 3 August 1957. See also *Bantu Mirror,* 25 April 1953, 3 October 1953, 6 April 1957, 4 May 1957, 3 August 1957, 4 January 1958.

173. Vambe, *From Rhodesia to Zimbabwe;* Nathan Shamuyarira, *Crisis in Rhodesia* (London: Andre Deutsch, 1965); Ian Hancock, *White Liberals, Moderates and Radicals in Rhodesia, 1953–1980* (New York: St. Martin's Press, 1984).

174. NAZ, F128/L7: Race Affairs: African Advancement, 4.

175. John Pape, "Still Serving Tea: Domestic Workers in Zimbabwe, 1980–1990," *Journal of Southern African Studies* 19, 3 (1993): 387–404; Gay W. Seidman, "Women in Zimbabwe: Postindependence Struggles," *Feminist Studies* 10, 3 (1984): 419–440.

3. THE QUEST FOR BOURGEOIS DOMESTICITY

1. See, for example, Mary Ryan, *Cradle of the Middle Class: The Family in Oneida County, New York, 1790–1865* (Cambridge: Cambridge University Press, 1981); Leonore Davidoff and Catherine Hall, *Family Fortunes: Men and Women of the English Middle Class, 1780–1850* (Chicago and London: University of Chicago Press, 1987).

2. HL, ABC 15.6, Box 2:30, Rhodesia Mission 1886–1955: Smith to Gibson, 31 October 1901.

3. SOAS, CWM: South Africa, Reports 6/1: Hope Fountain Girls' Boarding School: Report for 1920.

4. SOAS, CWM, South Africa, Reports 6/2: Report of Mr. R. McIntosh, Inspector of Schools, of Inspection made of Hope Fountain Girls' Boarding School on 31 July 1922. See also Carol Summers, "If You Can Educate the Native Woman: Debates over the Schooling and Education of Girls and Women in Southern Rhodesia, 1900–1934," *History of Education Quarterly* 36, 4 (1996): 449–471; idem, "Mission Boys, Civilized Men, and Marriage: Educated African Men in the Missions of Southern Rhodesia, 1920–1945," *Journal of Religious History* 23, 1 (1999): 75–91.

5. HL, ABC 15.6, vol. 9, folder 2:5: American Board Mission, East Africa Branch: Report for the Year Ending December 31, 1941, 10.

6. SAA, International Headquarters, Zimbabwe and Malawi, folder 1: Howard Institute and African Educational Problems, 2.

7. NAZ, ANG 1/1/35: Memorandum presented to the Commission of Enquiry on Native Education, August 1951, 5.

8. NAZ, ANG 1/1/17: Proceedings of the Southern Rhodesia Missionary Conference, 4–6 July 1944, 10.

9. NAZ, MS 239/27: Culver to co-workers, 20 April 1956.

10. NAZ, MS 239/27: Suggestions Regarding Home and Family Week; ibid.: Outline for Women's Group—Home and Family Week, 1955; ibid.: Outline for Youth Group—Home and Family Week 1955.

11. The Southern Rhodesia Christian Conference was formed in 1955 as a result of a fusion of the white Southern Rhodesia Missionary Conference and the black Southern Rhodesia African (formerly Bantu, itself a change from Native) Missionary Conference.

12. *Bantu Mirror,* 21 July 1956, 4 August 1956.

13. *Bantu Mirror,* 20 July 1957, 3 August 1957, 18 July 1959.

14. Elizabeth Schmidt, *Peasants, Traders and Wives: Shona Women in the History of Zimbabwe, 1870–1939* (Portsmouth, N.H.: Heinemann, 1992), 151–154. On Wayfaring in South Africa, see Deborah Gaitskell, "Housewives, Maids or Mothers: Some Contradictions of Domesticity for Christian Women in Johannesburg, 1903–39," *Journal of African History* 24, 2 (1983): 241–256.

15. BIHR, LIN 1/1: Address by Sister Muriel Pratten at Wayfarer Meeting, 23 March 1935. The male equivalent of the Wayfarer was called Pathfinder, also a "half-way house" to Scouting.

16. *Native Mirror,* April 1931.

17. NAZ, S179/1208: Address by Mary W. Waters, Organizing Instructress, Native Education Dept., 13 March 1929, 3.

18. Neville Jones, "Training Native Women in Community Service in Southern Rhodesia," *International Review of Missions* 21 (1932): 566–574 (quotation on 569).

19. *Annual Report of the Director of Native Education for the Year 1937,* 19; *Report of the Director of Native Education for the Year 1940,* 19–20.

20. NAZ, S482/709/39, vol. 3: Federation of African Welfare Society in Southern Rhodesia: Minutes of 15th Meeting, 24 June 1944, 4–5.

21. *Report of the Director of Native Education for the Year 1947,* 34.

22. *Report of the Director of Native Education for the Year 1948,* 40–41.

23. *Report of the Director of Native Education for the Year 1949,* 45.

24. *Report of the Director of Native Education for the Year 1954,* 85.

25. *Native Mirror,* April 1934.

26. Barbara A. Moss, "Holding Body and Soul Together: Women, Autonomy and Christianity in Colonial Zimbabwe" (Ph.D. dissertation, Indiana University, 1991), 126–134. See also Farai David Muzorewa, "Through Prayer and Action: The Rukwadzano Women of Rhodesia," in *Themes in the Christian History of Central Africa,* ed. T. O. Ranger and John Weller (Berkeley and Los Angeles: University of California Press, 1975), 256–268; Schmidt, *Peasants, Traders and Wives,* 145–149.

27. SOAS, MMS, Chairman's Correspondence 826/5: Carter to [Mfazi], 23 December 1927; ibid.: Minutes of a Committee . . . to Investigate . . . the Rev Moses Mfazi, 11 January 1928; ibid.: Noble to Noble, 10 March 1928. Quotation from Chairman's Correspondence.

28. Moss, "Holding Body and Soul Together," 126.

29. Ibid., 122–132.

30. On the quest for purity among African Christian women in neighboring South Africa, always a bellwether for Africans in Southern Rhodesia, see Deborah Gaitskell, " 'Wailing for Purity': Prayer Unions, African Mothers and Adolescent Daughters, 1912–1940," in *Industrialisation and Social Change in South Africa: African Class Formation, Culture and Consciousness, 1870–1930,* ed. Shula Marks and Richard Rathbone (London: Longman, 1982), 338–357.

31. NAZ, S482/709/39, vol. 1: [Manyano] Pledge; ibid.: Woman's Conference Dombodema, Plumtree, 21–24 August [1931].

32. *Bantu Mirror,* 25 December 1943.

33. HL, ABC 15:6, vol. 8, folder 1:4: Marsh to Emerson, 2 November 1940; HL, ABC 15.6, vol. 9, folder 2:4: Report of the Women's Work at Mt. Silinda, 1940; ibid.: Report of the Women's Work, 1944. Quotation from 2 November 1940.

34. An African Women's Club operated under the auspices of the Native

Welfare Society, but it seems to have been limited, both in membership and appeal. See *Bantu Mirror,* 29 March 1941.

35. Sita Ranchod-Nilsson, "'Educating Eve': The Women's Club Movement and Political Consciousness among Rural African Women in Southern Rhodesia, 1950–1980," in *African Encounters with Domesticity,* ed. Karen Tranberg Hansen (New Brunswick, N.J.: Rutgers University Press, 1992), 195–217.

36. *African Education: Annual Report by the Secretary for the Year 1965,* 10.

37. *Bantu Mirror,* 21 April 1956, 8 December 1956, 18 April 1959 (quotations from 21 April 1956).

38. *Bantu Mirror,* 25 May 1957.

39. *Bantu Mirror,* 23 April 1955.

40. *Bantu Mirror,* 4 February 1956.

41. *Bantu Mirror,* 13 November 1954, 5 January 1957, 9 November 1957, 5 December 1959.

42. *Bantu Mirror,* 25 May 1957, 10 May 1958 (quotation from 10 May 1958).

43. *Bantu Mirror,* 26 June 1954.

44. *Bantu Mirror,* 8 June 1957; *Central African Examiner,* 10 October 1959, 13.

45. *Report of the Chief Information Officer for the Year 1952,* 66; *Report of the Chief Information Officer for the Year 1953,* 52; *Bantu Mirror,* 24 September 1960.

46. *Report of the Chief Information Officer, Division of Native Affairs, Southern Rhodesia, for the Year 1954,* 60; *Report of the Chief Information Officer: Division of Native Affairs, Southern Rhodesia, for the Year 1955,* 85.

47. *Report of the Chief Information Officer for the Year 1956,* 84–85; *Report of the Chief Information Officer, Division of Native Affairs, Southern Rhodesia, for the Year 1957,* 111. On the rise of a consumer culture in late colonial Zimbabwe, see Timothy Burke, *Lifebuoy Men, Lux Women: Commodification, Consumption and Cleanliness in Modern Zimbabwe* (Durham, N.C., and London: Duke University Press, 1996).

48. *Report of the Commission Appointed to Enquire into the Matter of Native Education in all its Bearings in the Colony of Southern Rhodesia* (Salisbury: Government Printer, 1925), 101.

49. Ranchod-Nilsson, in her study of the Wedza District, asserts that "the FAWC was organized primarily by European women who were the wives of civil servants." However, it seems quite clear that white influence in the organization increased after the settler rebellion of 1965, the period from which most of her evidence is drawn. See Ranchod-Nilsson, "'Educating Eve.'"

50. *Report of the Chief Information Officer, Division of Native Affairs, Southern Rhodesia for the Year 1956,* 84; *Bantu Mirror,* 22 December 1956, 18 April 1959, 23 April 1960, 17 September 1960. White women were asked to act as judges in homemaking contests not because of their greater expertise in this area but because the social distance between them and the African women rendered them impartial in the eyes of the contestants. Whites also were called upon by Africans, and for the same reason, to adjudicate in other situations, such as dancing contests.

51. *Bantu Mirror,* 26 June 1954.

52. *Report of the Chief Information Officer for the Year 1953,* 47; *Bantu Mirror,* 27 June 1953.

53. *Bantu Mirror,* 5 December 1953.

54. NAZ, S1542/A6 (173-181): Report on Employment of Native Female Domestic Labour in European Households in Southern Rhodesia, 27 October 1932; Elizabeth Schmidt, "Race, Sex and Domestic Labor: The Question of African Female Servants in Southern Rhodesia, 1900–1939," in Hansen, *African Encounters with Domesticity*, 221-241; Jock McCulloch, *Black Peril, White Virtue: Sexual Crime in Southern Rhodesia, 1902–1935* (Bloomington and Indianapolis: Indiana University Press, 2000), passim.

55. *Bantu Mirror*, 27 February 1954.

56. *Bantu Mirror*, 5 December 1953, 5 March 1955; *Report of the Chief Information Officer for the Year 1956*, 84. Quotation from the latter document.

57. *Bantu Mirror*, 12 March 1960.

58. *Bantu Mirror*, 6 June 1959.

59. *Bantu Mirror*, 9 April 1960.

60. *Bantu Mirror*, 29 August 1959.

61. Little historical research has been done on middle-class marriage patterns in colonial Africa. One notable exception is Kristin Mann, *Marrying Well: Marriage, Status and Social Change among the Educated Elite in Colonial Lagos* (Cambridge: Cambridge University Press, 1985). The following studies are more sociological in focus: A. K. H. Weinrich, *African Marriage in Zimbabwe and the Impact of Christianity* (Gweru: Mambo Press, 1982); Barbara E. Harrell-Bond, *Modern Marriage in Sierra Leone: A Study of the Professional Group* (The Hague: Mouton and Co., 1975); Christine Oppong, *Middle Class African Marriage: A Family Study of Ghanaian Senior Civil Servants* (London: George Allen and Unwin, 1981); David Parkin and David Nyamwaya, eds., *Transformations of African Marriage* (Manchester: Manchester University Press, 1987).

62. Several centuries after the official adoption of Christianity, many western Europeans, especially members of the upper classes, continued to practice marriage customs that were anathema to the Church, including wife abductions, marrying within the prohibited degrees of kinship, and repudiating and taking new wives. See, for example, Georges Duby, *The Knight, the Lady and the Priest: The Making of Modern Marriage in Medieval France*, trans. Barbara Bray (New York: Pantheon Books, 1983).

63. SOAS, CWM, South Africa, Reports 6/1: W. G. Brown, Shangani Reserve Report for 1921, January 1922.

64. NAZ, A3/18/19 (14 and 25): White to Administrator, 14 May 1915.

65. *Native Mirror*, July 1932.

66. *Native Mirror*, March 1935.

67. *Conference of Superintendents of Natives and Native Commissioners of the Colony of Southern Rhodesia: Verbatim Report of the Proceedings* (Salisbury: Government Printer, 1928), passim.

68. NAZ, A3/18/19 (69–70): Chief Native Commissioner to Secretary, Dept. of Administration, 18 December 1914.

69. NAZ, S1542/M3: Mahachi to Chief Native Commissioner, 14 April 1939; ibid.: Chief Native Commissioner to Mahachi, 18 April 1939.

70. *Conference of Superintendents of Natives and Native Commissioners*, 24.

71. NAZ, A3/18/19 (12): Resolution passed by Southern Rhodesia Missionary Conference: June, 1915.

72. NAZ, A3/18/19 (96–99): Attorney General to Secretary, Dept. of Administrator, 27 June 1913.

73. NAZ, A3/21/55 (16–17): Native Marriages, n.d.

74. *Debates of the Legislative Assembly,* 3 May 1929, vol. 8, cols. 304–308.

75. NAZ, S1542/M3: Chief Native Commissioner to Adjutant, Salvation Army, 17 November 1933.

76. *Native Mirror,* March 1935.

77. NAZ, A3/21/55 (16–17): Native Marriages, n.d.

78. NAZ, A3/21/55 (12–15): Chief Native Commissioner to Secretary, Dept. of Administrator, 21 December 1921.

79. *Conference of Superintendents of Natives,* 71.

80. Adam Kuper, *Wives for Cattle: Bridewealth and Marriage in Southern Africa* (London: Routledge and Kegan Paul, 1982); Parkin and Nyamwaya, *Transformations of African Marriage;* J. L. Comaroff, "Bridewealth and the Control of Ambiguity in a Tswana Chiefdom," in *The Meaning of Marriage Payments,* ed. J. L. Comaroff (London: Academic Press 1980), 161–195; Max Gluckman, "Kinship and Marriage among the Lozi of Northern Rhodesia and the Zulu of Natal," in *African Systems of Kinship and Marriage,* ed. A. R. Radcliffe-Brown and Daryll Forde (London: Oxford University Press, 1950), 166–206.

81. Schmidt, *Peasants, Traders and Wives,* 113–115; Teresa A. Barnes, *"We Women Worked So Hard": Gender, Urbanization and Social Reproduction in Colonial Harare, Zimbabwe, 1930–1956* (Portsmouth, N.H.: Heinemann, 1999), 100–107.

82. SOAS, MSS, Central Africa, Native Committee of Review and Evangelist Convention, Box 631: Native Evangelists' and Teachers' Convention, held at Selukwe, 11 and 12 July 1923, 5.

83. See, for example, BIHR, PE 2: We Are Going to Be Married: Officers' Guide on Christian Marriage, 13; Gilbert Modikai, "Excessive Lobola," *Missionary Magazine,* August 1957, 204–205.

84. *Report of the Native Affairs Committee of Enquiry, 1910–11* (Salisbury: Government Printer, 1911), 4.

85. *Conference of Superintendents of Natives and Native Commissioners,* passim. See also material in NAZ, S138/47, which is too voluminous to cite in full here.

86. In 1951, theology student Abel Muzorewa married the daughter of a "devout Christian widow," paying £25 in cash and two head of cattle as bridewealth, which was rather low for a woman with some education. Four years later Maurice Nyagumbo, then a newly established shopkeeper, considered himself "one of the luckiest people to have paid so little bride-wealth" when he forked out £30 in cash, two head of cattle, and seven goats to his intended father-in-law. Nyagumbo seems to have been lucky indeed. A year later, a fellow Umtali resident had his marriage consideration pegged at £90. The unlucky but eager suitor had only £40, and at last report he was "making desperate attempts to get his [prospective] parents-in-law to reduce their original claim to a more reasonable figure." Earlier, in 1953, another young man in Bulawayo had been forced to abandon plans to marry his sweetheart of five years when he was unable to come up with the sum of £100 demanded by her parents. See Bishop Abel Tendekai Muzorewa, *Rise Up and Walk: An Autobiography,* ed. Norman Thomas (London: Evans Brothers Ltd., 1978), 34–

35; Maurice Nyagumbo, *With the People: An Autobiography from the Zimbabwe Struggle* (London: Allison and Busby, 1980), 90; *Bantu Mirror,* 21 April 1956, 4 July 1953.

87. Two decades earlier, one official had advocated limiting bridewealth as a conservation measure, to prevent overgrazing in the Reserves. This same official also claimed that litigation over bridewealth was tying up the native court system. See NAZ, S138/47: Assistant Native Commissioner, Goromonzi to Chief Native Commissioner, 20 September 1930.

88. *Debates of the Legislative Assembly,* 2 June 1950, vol. 31, cols. 1922–1943 (quotation in col. 1926).

89. *Bantu Mirror,* 17 June 1950, 28 October 1950 (quotations from 17 June).

90. *Debates of the Legislative Assembly,* 19 June 1950, vol. 31, col. 2263. The marriage consideration continued to increase in independent Zimbabwe, prompting a former minister of state for community development and women's affairs to call—unsuccessfully, of course—for the appointment of a commission to fix maximum rates. See *Herald,* 10 March 1986.

91. *Native Mirror,* July 1931.

92. *Native Mirror,* December 1931.

93. *Native Mirror,* October 1931. Chama likely came from Nyasaland.

94. On Titus and the Hlazo family, see T. O. Ranger, *The African Voice in Southern Rhodesia, 1898–1930* (London: Heinemann, 1970), 70–74.

95. *Native Mirror,* October 1931.

96. *Native Mirror,* December 1931.

97. *Native Mirror,* April 1932. Sanehwe's nationality is unclear. She wrote from Ohlange Institute in South Africa's Natal province.

98. *Native Mirror,* April 1932. See also *Native Mirror,* July 1935, for an additional female contribution to the debate on bridewealth.

99. *Bantu Mirror,* 7 November 1953.

100. NAZ, S138/47: Assistant Native Commissioner, Goromonzi to Chief Native Commissioner, 10 February 1932.

101. *Bantu Mirror,* 13 March 1948.

102. *Bantu Mirror,* 5 October 1946.

103. NAZ, S138/47, 1931–32: Native Commissioner, Marandellas to Chief Native Commissioner, 2 March 1932.

104. NAZ, S138/47: Native Commissioner, The Range to Chief Native Commissioner, 7 October 1930; ibid.: Native Commissioner, The Range to Chief Native Commissioner, 20 April 1932 (quotation from 7 October 1930).

105. *Bantu Mirror,* 16 November 1957.

106. *Native Mirror,* October 1933. The following year Malikongwe was dismissed from his position and deported to his native Bechuanaland for being in possession of publications put out by the Communist Party of South Africa.

107. *Native Mirror,* July 1931, October 1931.

108. *Native Mirror,* March 1935.

109. *Bantu Mirror,* 1 February 1947.

110. *Bantu Mirror,* 15 November 1947.

111. *Bantu Mirror,* 12 March 1955.

112. *Bantu Mirror,* 26 January 1957.

113. *Bantu Mirror,* 6 November 1948.

114. *Bantu Mirror,* 11 January 1958.

115. *Bantu Mirror,* 21 May 1960.

116. In Southern Rhodesia, as elsewhere in southern Africa, coloureds—that is, persons of racially mixed descent, constituted a category that was distinct from Africans, socially and legally. See Ibbo Mandaza, *Race, Colour and Class in Southern Africa* (Harare: Sapes Books, 1997).

117. NAZ (Byo), interview with Patrick Makoni, March 22, 1989, by Mark Ncube, 5–6.

118. *Bantu Mirror,* 14 August 1943.

119. On the sociocultural context of elite African socializing generally, see Preben Kaarsholm, "Si Ye Pambili—Which Way Forward? Urban Development, Culture and Politics in Bulawayo," *Journal of Southern African Studies* 21, 2 (1995): 225–245.

120. African women, although not totally absent from these multiracial gatherings, were a rare sight. Naomi's "Home Column" commented on these issues from time to time. See, for example, *Bantu Mirror,* 14 May 1960. On the drinking habits of the African petty bourgeoisie, see Michael O. West, " 'Equal Rights for all Civilized Men': Elite Africans and the Quest for 'European' Liquor in Colonial Zimbabwe, 1924–1961," *International Review of Social History* 37, 3 (1992): 376–397; idem, "Beerhalls and Skokiaan Queens: The State, Female Brewers and Male Drinkers in Colonial Zimbabwe" (manuscript).

121. *Bantu Mirror,* 23 April 1960. This view was not universally accepted. Evangelist (later Rev.) Richard Chibasa, for one, rejected the notion that "there is some tendency of polygamy in the blood of every African [male]. They do not see that it is a miserable and dirty kind of life. It only shows degradation in the nation. Our people who have a bit of knowledge in this new created world should show practical Christianity. But it is disappointing to see some educated men having more than one wife. Surely this is greediness. Greedy people will never enter into the Kingdom of God." See *Bantu Mirror,* 27 July 1940.

122. *Bantu Mirror,* 14 May 1960.

4. THE BEST OF ALL HOMES

1. *Native Mirror,* June 1934.

2. *Report of the Chief Native Commissioner for the Year 1916,* 12; *Report of the Chief Native Commissioner for the Year 1920,* 2. Quotations from the latter document.

3. NAZ (Byo), 23/2/6R, 5777, file 10: Location Superintendent, Bulawayo to Town Clerk, Bulawayo, 26 July 1922.

4. *Report of the Land Commission, 1925* (Salisbury: Government Printer, 1925), 35.

5. See, for example, John R. Stilgoe, *Borderland: Origins of the American Suburb, 1820–1939* (New Haven and London: Yale University Press, 1988).

6. *Debates in the Legislative Council during the Sixth Session of the Sixth Council,* 29 April 1919, cols. 331–332; NAZ, S86/22/2/177–178: Report of the Native Affairs Commission on Its Enquiry into Matters Concerning the Salisbury Native Location, 1931, 15.

7. NAZ, S86/22/2/177–178: Report of the Native Affairs Commission . . . Salisbury, 10.

8. NAZ, S235/394: Report of Native Affairs Commission on Its Enquiry into Matters Concerning the Bulawayo Native Location, 1930, 5; NAZ, S235/477: Notes on Evidence of Enquiry into Bulawayo Location, 29. Despite the complaints, most of the cottages were occupied by members of the emerging black middle class. The 1930 commission report was emphatic on this point, stating that "The poorest type of dwelling tends naturally to be occupied by the poorest tenant." See NAZ, S86/22/2/177–178: Report of the Native Affairs Commission . . . Salisbury, 22.

9. NAZ, S235/477: Notes on Evidence of Enquiry into Bulawayo Location, 62, 26, 72.

10. NAZ, S86/22/2/177–178: Report of the Native Affairs Commission on Its Enquiry into Matters Concerning the Salisbury Native Location, 1931, 15; NAZ, S235/394: Report of Native Affairs Commission on Its Enquiry into Matters Concerning the Bulawayo Native Location, 1930, 20–21; NAZ, S235/439: Report on Gwelo Municipal Location for Natives, 1931; NAZ, S85: [Evidence of Salisbury Native Affairs Commission], 12, 52, 81, 113; NAZ, S235/477: Notes on Evidence of Enquiry into Bulawayo Location, 27–28, 54, 56–57, 62.

11. NAZ, MA15/1/1: Southern Rhodesia Native Association Headquarters, 4 June 1929, 1.

12. NAZ, S86/22/2/177–178: Report of the Native Affairs Commission . . . Salisbury, 5; NAZ, S235/394: Report of Native Affairs Commission . . . Bulawayo, 5–6.

13. *Census of Population, 1946* (Salisbury: Government Printer, 1946), 325. Unlike the white (and Asian and coloured) population, no general census of Africans was taken until the 1950s.

14. NAZ, S86/22/2/177–178: Report of the Native Affairs Commission . . . Salisbury, 4.

15. Ibid., 11; John Burnett, *A Social History of Housing, 1815–1985,* 2d ed. (London and New York: Methuen, 1986), 70–77.

16. NAZ, S235/394: Report of Native Affairs Commission . . . Bulawayo, 4; NAZ, S235/383 (23–24); Location Superintendent, Que Que Sanitary Board to Chief Native Commissioner, 22 December 1924; ibid. (19): Sec., Fort Victoria Sanitary Board to Chief Native Commissioner, 23 December 1924; ibid. (2–3): Secretary, Bindura Village Management Board to Chief Native Commissioner, 5 February 1925; NAZ, S235/439: Report on Gwelo Municipal Location for Natives, 1931, 3; NAZ, S1542/L14: Assistant Native Commissioner, Gatooma to Native Commissioner, Hartley, 7 December 1935.

17. Unlike certain precolonial cities in Nigeria and Morocco, traditional African architecture did not become a standard feature of urban housing in Southern Rhodesia. See Friedrick W. Schwerdtfeger, *Traditional Housing in African Cities: A Comparative Study of Houses in Zaria, Ibadan and Marrakech* (Chichester, U.K.: John Wiley and Sons, 1982).

18. NAZ, S235/394: Report of Native Affairs Commission . . . Bulawayo, 17–18; NAZ, S235/477: Notes on Evidence of Enquiry into Bulawayo Location, 7. Quotation from the first document.

19. NAZ, S235/477: Notes on Evidence of Enquiry into Bulawayo Location, 59.

20. Ibid., 12-13, 27, 82-83, 85-87.

21. Ibid., 85-86.

22. NAZ (Byo), 23/3/7R, 6493: Superintendent of Natives to Town Clerk, Bulawayo, 24 January 1930; ibid.: Acting Town Clerk, Bulawayo to Superintendent of Natives, 31 January 1930; ibid.: Superintendent of Natives to Town Clerk, Bulawayo, 30 September 1930; ibid.: Town Clerk, Bulawayo to Superintendent of Natives, 4 October 1930.

23. W. C. Robertson and Percy Ibbotson, *Report of the Sub-Committee Appointed to Investigate Housing, Wages, and Living Conditions of Africans in Bulawayo District,* September 13, 1939, 4; Percy Ibbotson, *Report of a Survey of Urban African Conditions in Southern Rhodesia, August, 1942—June, 1943* (Bulawayo: Federation of African Welfare Societies in Southern Rhodesia, 1943).

24. Robertson and Ibbotson, *Report of Africans in Bulawayo,* 3.

25. *Bantu Mirror,* 20 November 1937, 4 December 1937, 18 December 1937, 25 December 1937 (quotation from 20 November).

26. NAZ, S1542/L14: Superintendent of Natives, Bulawayo to Chief Native Commissioner, 2 July 1937; ibid.: Secretary for Native Affairs to Secretary to Prime Minister (Native Affairs), 23 July 1937; ibid.: Superintendent of Natives, Bulawayo to Chief Native Commissioner, 30 July 1937; ibid.: Secretary for Native Affairs to Secretary to Prime Minister (Native Affairs), 25 August 1937. Quotation from letter of 30 July1937.

27. Michael O. West, "Liquor and Libido: 'Joint Drinking' and the Politics of Sexual Control in Colonial Zimbabwe, 1920s-1950s," *Journal of Social History* 30, 3 (1997): 645-667.

28. NAZ, S924/G15/2: Superintendent of Natives, Bulawayo to Chief Native Commissioner, 12 August 1933.

29. *Native Mirror,* June 1934.

30. NAZ, Minutes of . . . Joint Advisory Board of the Native Welfare Society of Matabeleland, 12 April 1934, 1-4.

31. NAZ, S1542/V4: Makgatho et al., Bantu Community of Bulawayo to Superintendent of Natives, Bulawayo, 9 January 1935.

32. NAZ, S924/G15/2: Superintendent of Natives to Chief Native Commissioner, 8 January 1935; NAZ, Minutes of . . . Joint Advisory Board of the Native Welfare Society of Matabeleland, 12 April 1934, 1-4. Quotation from the first document.

33. NAZ, S482/551/39: Memorandum: Native Village Settlements, by Assistant Director of Native Lands, 9 January 1934.

34. NAZ, S482/551/39: [Memorandum on Native Village Settlement, 1934?].

35. Ibid.

36. *Debates of the Legislative Assembly,* 21 March 1935, vol. 15, col. 337.

37. *Debates of the Legislative Assembly,* 20 March 1935, vol. 15, cols. 281-294.

38. *Bulawayo Chronicle,* 5 May 1934.

39. *Sunday News* (Bulawayo), 16 July 1933.

40. A. C. Jennings, "Improved Housing for Urban Natives," *Transactions of the Rhodesia Scientific Association* 38 (1941): 129-139.

41. *Bulawayo Chronicle,* 12 October 1935.

42. NAZ, S1542/L14: Acting Superintendent of Natives, Bulawayo to Chief Native Commissioner, 28 July 1936.

43. Ibid; NAZ, S1542/L14: Secretary for Native Affairs to Secretary to Prime Minister (Native Affairs), 3 August 1936.

44. NAZ, S482/551/39: Superintendent Luveve Village Settlement to Native Commissioner, Bulawayo, 5 December 1936.

45. NAZ, S2791/17/1: Resolutions . . . by Bantu Congress, 23 March 1940; *Bantu Mirror,* 27 April 1940; NAZ, S2791/17/1: Resolutions . . . of the Bantu Congress, 12 September 1944; *Bantu Mirror,* 8 November 1947. Quotation from resolutions of 23 March 1940.

46. NAZ, S2791/17/1: [Resolutions of] Southern Rhodesia African National Congress, 12 August 1946, 2.

47. *Report of the Committee to Investigate the Economic, Social and Health Conditions of Africans Employed in Urban Areas* (January 1944); NAZ, S1906: [Howman Committee Evidence], 50.

48. "Social Security: The Native Problem in Southern Rhodesia," May 1945. In the original, "our home" was in boldface. A copy of this document can be found in RHL, Mss Brit Emp S332, Creech Jones 22/6 (216-219).

49. B. J. Mnyanda, *In Search of Truth: A Commentary on Certain Aspects of Southern Rhodesia's Native Policy* (Bombay: Hind Kitabs Ltd., 1954), 12.

50. *Report of the Secretary for Native Affairs and Chief Native Commissioner for Year 1948,* 3. See also the same report for 1950, 2.

51. *Bantu Mirror,* 15 May 1954, 22 May 1954, 29 May 1954, 5 June 1954, 12 June 1954 (quotation in 5 June).

52. *Bantu Mirror,* 24 July 1954.

53. *Report of the Committee to Investigate the Economic, Social and Health Conditions of Africans Employed in Urban Areas.*

54. L. C. Vambe, "An African on Federation," *Concord,* April/June 1954, 41.

55. PRO, CO 1015/11911: "Extract from the Federation of Rhodesia and Nyasaland Newsletter," 1 November 1954.

56. *Debates of the Legislative Assembly,* 2 November 1954, vol. 36, cols. 2127–2129; PRO, CO 1015/11911: "Extract from the Federation of Rhodesia and Nyasaland Newsletter"; *African Home Ownership Scheme of the Southern Rhodesia Government* (Salisbury, April 1957); *Bantu Mirror,* 19 February 1955. The scheme was later expanded to the smaller urban centers of Gwelo, Que Que, Umtali, and Fort Victoria. See *Report of the Secretary for Native Affairs and Chief Native Commissioner for the Year 1958,* 9.

57. *Bantu Mirror,* 12 March 1955.

58. *African Weekly,* 23 February 1955.

59. PRO, CO 1015/1192: Dzwittie et al. to Minister of Native Affairs, 4 March 1955. The letter was jointly written by S. J. Dzwittie (*African Weekly*), G. Mbofana (*Recorder* and *Harvester*), Lawrence Vambe (*African Parade*), and Nathan Shamuyarira (*Bantu Mirror*). Dzwittie, the first African welfare officer in the Bulawayo township, subsequently became a journalist and was transferred to Salisbury, where he edited the *African Weekly* from 1952 to 1955.

60. *Bantu Mirror,* 1 June 1957, 8 June 1957, 9 March 1957.

61. See, for example, *Bantu Mirror,* 14 June 1958, 1 November 1958, 8 November 1958, 29 November 1958, 17 January 1959, 29 August 1959, 26 September 1959, 26 March 1960, 23 July 1960.

62. *Concord,* December 1957, 24.

63. Ibid.

64. *Debates of the Legislative Assembly,* 12 April 1961, vol. 47, cols. 4598–4599. It is unclear exactly how many families were living in the two villages by this time. Additional houses were built after construction of the initial five thousand.

65. *Bantu Mirror,* 29 November 1958.

66. *Bantu Mirror,* 26 March 1960.

67. *Bantu Mirror,* 7 October 1961.

68. *Debates of the Legislative Assembly,* 11 and 18 March 1959, vols. 41 and 42, cols. 2318–2370, 2577–2596 (quotation on col. 2349).

69. *Debates of the Legislative Assembly,* 9 August 1961, vol. 48, cols. 25–40; *Debates of the Legislative Assembly,* 26 August 1964, vol. 57, cols. 1257–1264; *Debates of the Legislative Assembly,* 28 October 1964 and 18 February 1965, vol. 59, cols. 587–606, 1670–1720; *Bantu Mirror,* 24 September 1960.

70. *Bantu Mirror,* 8 March 1958, 15 March 1958, 14 February 1959, 31 October 1959, 21 November 1959, 13 February 1960, 14 May 1960, 24 September 1960, 26 November 1960, 15 July 1961.

71. *Bantu Mirror,* 9 June 1956.

72. *Bantu Mirror,* 23 May 1953.

73. *Bantu Mirror,* 3 September 1955, 15 October 1955,

74. *Bantu Mirror,* 26 October 1957, 31 January 1959, 30 May 1959 (quotation from 30 May 1959).

75. *Bantu Mirror,* 6 December 1958.

76. *Bantu Mirror,* 6 August 1960.

77. *Bantu Mirror,* 19 October 1957, 27 September 1958, 30 May 1959 (quotation from 27 September 1958).

78. *Report on Urban African Budget Survey in Salisbury, 1963/64* (Salisbury: Central Statistical Office, July 1965), 2.

79. *Annual Report of the Director of African Administration for the Year Ending 30th June, 1965,* 28, 8; *Report on Urban African Budget Survey in Salisbury, 1963/64,* 9.

80. E. W. J. Moloney, *The Undefeated* (Sussex, U.K.: Published by E. W. J. Moloney, 1967), 8.

81. Eric Stanley Gargett, "Welfare Services in an African Urban Area" (Ph.D. dissertation, University of London, 1971), 32.

82. *Central African Examiner,* 26 September 1959, 6.

83. Michael O. West, "Indians, India and Race and Nationalism in British Central Africa," *South Asia Bulletin: Comparative Studies in South Asia, Africa and the Middle East* 14, 2 (1994): 93.

5. A NEW BEGINNING

1. For a general overview of the rise of the protest tradition in colonial Africa, see Thomas Hodgkin, *Nationalism in Colonial Africa* (London: Frederick Muller Ltd., 1956); J. Ayodele Langley, *Pan-Africanism and Nationalism in West Africa, 1900–1945: A Study in Ideology and Social Classes* (Oxford: Clarendon Press, 1973); Imanuel Geiss, *The Pan-African Movement: A History of Pan-Africanism in America, Europe and Africa,* trans. Ann Keep (New York: Africana Publishing Co., 1968).

2. T. O. Ranger, *The African Voice in Southern Rhodesia, 1898–1930* (Evanston, Ill.: Northwestern University Press, 1970); E. Makambe, *African Protest Movements in Southern Rhodesia Before 1930: An Ideological Appreciation of the Socio-Political Roots of Protest Movements* (Pasadena: California Institute of Technology, 1982).

3. Caiphas Tizanaye Nziramasanga, "African Immigration to Rhodesia, 1890 to 1945" (Ph.D. dissertation, Oklahoma State University, 1978); Peter Warwick, *Black People and the South African War, 1899–1902* (Cambridge: Cambridge University Press, 1983); Bill Nasson, *Abraham Easu's War: A Black South African War in the Cape, 1899–1902* (Cambridge: Cambridge University Press, 1991); Joyce F. Kirk, *Making a Voice: African Resistance to Segregation in South Africa* (Boulder, Colo.: Westview Press, 1998).

4. André Odendaal, *Black Protest Politics in South Africa to 1912* (Totowa, N.J.: Barnes and Noble Books, 1984).

5. NAZ, N3/7/2 (138–139): Chief Native Commissioner to Secretary to Administrator, 31 March 1914. On the rebellions, see T. O. Ranger, *Revolt in Southern Rhodesia, 1896–97: A Study in African Resistance* (Evanston, Ill.: Northwestern University Press, 1967).

6. NAZ, N3/21/9 (18–20): Superintendent of Natives to Chief Native Commissioner, 19 June 1922; ibid. (15–17): Chief Native Commissioner to Secretary to Administrator, 29 June 1922. Quotation from the first document.

7. NAZ, N3/21/9 (18–20): Superintendent of Natives to Chief Native Commissioner, 19 June 1922.

8. NAZ, N3/7/2 (144–145): Superintendent of Natives to Chief Native Commissioner, 25 March 1914; NAZ, N3/21/1 (30): Superintendent of Natives to Chief Native Commissioner, 15 January 1916.

9. NAZ, N3/21/1 (31): Amandebele Patriotic Society, 15 December 1915; ibid. (9–10): Maziyane, Zembe, and Mahlahla to Administrator, 30 August 1916; ibid. (3–5): Chief Native Commissioner to Secretary to Administrator, 20 September 1916. Quotation from the first document.

10. NAZ, N3/21/1 (8): Maziyane to Superintendent of Natives, 30 August 1916.

11. Makambe, *African Protest Movements.*

12. NAZ, N3/21/9 (26): Chief Native Commissioner to Secretary to Administrator, 18 January 1922; ibid. (18–20): Superintendent of Natives to Chief Native Commissioner, 19 June 1922.

13. *Report of the Chief Native Commissioner for the Year 1919* (Salisbury: Government Printer, 1919), 1; NAZ, N3/32/1 (87–88): Assistant Native Commissioner [district unnamed] to Superintendent of Natives, 12 March 1915; NAZ, N3/21/7 (12): Maziyane to Superintendent of Natives, 16 June 1917; ibid. (6): Assistant Native Commissioner to Superintendent of Natives, 31 July 1917. Quotation from Maziyane's letter.

14. NAZ, N3/32/1 (24–26): Native Commissioner for Fort Rixon to Superintendent of Natives, 22 June 1916; ibid. (17–19): Chief Native Commissioner to Secretary to Administrator, 3 July 1916; ibid. (278): [Memo on] Rumours Re Attitude of Natives, 28 November 1914; ibid. (143–148): Chief Native Commissioner to Secretary to Administrator, 26 April 1915. On the Afrikaner military rebellion, see N. G. Garson, "The Boer Rebellion of 1914," *History Today* 12, 2 (1962): 127–

145; T. R. H. Davenport, "The South African Rebellion, 1914," *English Historical Review* 77, 306 (1963): 53-80.

15. NAZ, N3/32/1 (106-107): Native Commissioner for Hartley to Superintendent of Natives, 20 May 1915.

16. Ibid. (180-183): Detective Sergeant to Superintendent of C.I.D., 23 February 1915. On the Nyasaland revolt, see George Shepperson and Thomas Price, *Independent African: John Chilembwe and the Origins, Setting, and Significance of the Nyasaland Native Rising of 1915* (Edinburgh: Edinburgh University Press, 1958).

17. Ranger, *African Voice*, 51-52.

18. Ibid., 64-87.

19. NAZ, N3/19/4 (83-84): Chief Native Commissioner to Superintendent of Natives, 11 April 1919.

20. NAZ, N3/21/6 (5-9): Constitution of the Rhodesia Bantu Voters Association.

21. Women were given the vote (also on a qualified basis) in Southern Rhodesia in 1919, well before women in any number of other Western industrial countries.

22. NAZ, A11/2/12/3 (79-82): Native Franchise, 18 July 1906.

23. Claire Palley, *The Constitutional History and Law of Southern Rhodesia, 1888-1965: With Special Reference to Imperial Control* (Oxford: Clarendon Press, 1966), 308 n 5. It should be noted, however, that the number of Africans eligible for the franchise had always exceeded those actually on the voters roll.

24. Ranger, *African Voice*, 99-100.

25. Allison K. Shutt has done pioneering work on the freehold farmers in the context of African middle-class formation. See Shutt, " 'We Are the Best Poor Farmers': Purchase Area Farmers and Economic Differentiation in Southern Rhodesia, c. 1925-1980" (Ph.D. dissertation, University of California, Los Angeles, 1995); idem, "Purhase Area Farmers and the Middle Class of Southern Rhodesia, c. 1931-1952," *International Journal of African Historical Studies* 30, 3 (1997): 555-581.

26. NAZ, S482/717/39: Secretary to Premier to Secretary to Governor, 7 June 1924.

27. NAZ, S482/717/39: Chief Native Commissioner to Secretary to Premier, 30 January 1925; ibid.: Premier to Chief Native Commissioner, 4 September 1925.

28. NAZ, S138/22: Rhodesia Bantu Voters Association: Annual Conference, 13 July 1925; ibid.: Assistant Chief Native Commissioner to Secretary to Premier, 3 September 1925. Quotation from the first document. On the "black peril" hysteria, see Jock McCulloch, *Black Peril, White Virtue: Sexual Crime in Southern Rhodesia, 1902-1935* (Bloomington and Indianapolis: Indiana University Press, 2000); John Pape, "Black and White: The 'Perils of Sex' in Colonial Zimbabwe," *Journal of Southern African Studies* 16, 4 (1990): 699-720. On the same phenomenon elsewhere in southern Africa, see Norman Etherington, "Natal's Black Rape Scare of the 1870s," *Journal of Southern African Studies* 15, 1 (1988): 36-53; Charles van Onselen, *Studies in the Social and Economic History of the Witwatersrand, 1886-1914: New Ninevah* (London: Longman, 1982), 2:1-73; Gareth Cornwell, "George Webb Hardy's *The Black Peril* and the Social Meaning of 'Black Peril' in Early Twentieth-Century South Africa," *Journal of Southern African Studies* 22, 3 (1996): 441-453;

Karen Tranberg Hansen, *Distant Companions: Servants and Employers in Zambia, 1900–1985* (Ithaca, N.Y.: Cornell University Press, 1989), passim.

29. On the highly controversial struggle for legal access to "European" liquor, that is, lager beer, wines, and spirits, see Michael O. West, "'Equal Rights for all Civilized Men': Elite Africans and the Quest for 'European' Liquor in Colonial Zimbabwe, 1924–1961," *International Review of Social History* 37, 3 (1992): 376–397.

30. NAZ, S482/709/39, vol. 1: Sojini to Prime Minister, 22 May 1929; ibid.: Rhodesia Bantu Voters Association, 17 July 1929. Quotation from the first document.

31. NAZ, S138/92: Chief Native Commissioner to Superintendent of Natives, 22 January 1931; ibid.: Native Commissioner for Gwanda to Superintendent of Natives, 19 February 1931.

32. R. S. Roberts, "The End of the Ndebele Royal Family," University of Zimbabwe, History Department, Seminar Paper No. 73 (April 1988).

33. NAZ, S138/92: Superintendent of Natives to Chief Native Commissioner, 25 June 1930; ibid.: Superintendent of Natives to Chief Native Commissioner, 4 July 1930; ibid.: Native Commissioner for Gwanda to Superintendent of Natives, 24 July 1930; NAZ, S482/709/39, vol. 1: Secretary to Prime Minister to Chief Native Commissioner, 5 June 1931; NAZ, S138/55: Acting Superintendent of Natives to Chief Native Commissioner, 13 May 1933; NAZ, S235/440 (199–201): Rhodesia Bantu Voters Association, n.d.

34. Robin Palmer, *Land and Racial Domination in Rhodesia* (Berkeley and Los Angeles: University of California Press, 1977); Shutt, "'We Are the Best Poor Farmers.'"

35. NAZ, S2584/37: Detective of B.S.A. Police to Superintendent of C.I.D., 4 March 1927.

36. James R. Hooker, "Welfare Associations and Other Instruments of Accommodation in the Rhodesias between the World Wars," *Comparative Studies in Society and History* 9 (1966): 51–63.

37. NAZ, S2584/37: Chipwaya to Minister of Native Affairs, 28 June 1929.

38. NAZ, N3/21/5 (5): [memorandum by Chief Native Commissioner], 31 August 1923.

39. NAZ, S2584/37: Detective of B.S.A. Police to Superintendent of C.I.D., 4 March 1927.

40. NAZ, S2584/37: Chipwaya to Chief Native Commissioner, 28 June 1929. Chipwaya, a leader of the SRNA, was quoting one its opponents.

41. ICS, Zimbabwe, Trade Unions: Industrial Commercial Union (1): Transcript of an interview with Mr. L. C. Mzingeli, held in Harare Township, 15 September 1970, 2. In 1926, the SRNA president submitted "an amended constitution for Government approval before asking the Association in Salisbury to confirm it." See NAZ, S2584/37: Acting Chief Native Commissioner to Secretary to Premier, 1 September 1926.

42. NAZ, S2584/37: Mokwile to Chief Native Commissioner, 27 November 1924.

43. NAZ, S138/22: Mokwile to Prime Minister, 27 February 1925; ibid.: Chief Native Commissioner to Secretary to Premier, 5 March 1925.

44. NAZ, S2584/37: Native Commissioner for Marandellas to Chief Native Commissioner, 17 May 1926; ibid.: Chief Native Commissioner to Matebese, 29 June 1926; ibid.: Acting Chief Native Commissioner to Secretary to Premier, 1 September 1926; ibid.: Chief Native Commissioner to Secretary to Premier, 10 March 1927. Quotation from the latter document.

45. NAZ, S2584/37: Southern Rhodesia Native Association: Resolution C, Natives as Wage Earners [1928].

46. NAZ, MA15/1/1: Southern Rhodesia Native Association Headquarters, 4 June 1929.

47. NAZ, S2584/37: Southern Rhodesia Native Association: Subjects for Discussion in Conference [1927]; ibid.: Notes of Meeting . . . with Delegation Representing Southern Rhodesia Native Association, 1 June 1927.

48. NAZ, S2584/37: Acting Superintendent of Natives to Chief Native Commissioner, 17 April 1929.

49. Railway workers were more likely to live in family units than other workers, although in private "locations" run by their employers rather than in the municipal townships. See Teresa Barnes, " 'So That a Labourer Could Live with His Family': Overlooked Factors in Social and Economic Strife in Urban Colonial Zimbabwe, 1945-1952," *Journal of Southern African Studies* 21, 1 (1995): 95–113. It was only in the late 1950s that the number of indigenous urban African workers surpassed the number of immigrant ones. See Brian Raftopoulos, "Nationalism and Labour in Salisbury, 1953-1965," *Journal of Southern African Studies* 21, 1 (1995): 79–93.

50. Steven C. Rubert, *A Most Promising Weed: A History of Tobacco Farming and Labor in Colonial Zimbabwe, 1890-1945* (Athens: Ohio University Center for International Studies, 1998).

51. Teresa A. Barnes, "The Fight for Control of African Women's Mobility in Zimbabwe, 1900-1939," *Signs: Journal of Women in Culture and Society,* 17, 3 (1992): 586–608; Elizabeth Schmidt, *Peasants, Traders and Wives: Shona Women in the History of Zimbabwe, 1870-1939* (Portsmouth, N.H.: Heinemann, 1992); Diana Jeater, *Marriage, Perversion, and Power: The Construction of Moral Discourse in Southern Rhodesia, 1894-1930* (Oxford: Clarendon Press, 1993); Michael O. West, "Beerhalls and Skokiaan Queens: The State, Female Brewers and Male Drinkers in Colonial Zimbabwe" (manuscript).

52. NAZ, S235/477: Notes on Evidence of Enquiry into Bulawayo Location, 1930, 82.

53. In 1926, for instance, SRNA president Johannes Mokwile left office in disgrace "when it was found that he was spending the money of the Association and was getting into trouble with women." See NAZ, S2584/37: Detective of B.S.A. Police to Superintendent of C.I.D., 4 March 1927. Writings by elite men centering on the post-World War II era suggest that some of them lived a fast life. See, for example, Nathan Shamuyarira, *Crisis in Rhodesia* (London: Andre Deutsch, 1965); Lawrence Vambe, *From Rhodesia to Zimbabwe* (Pittsburgh: University of Pittsburgh Press, 1976).

54. Michael O. West, "Liquor and Libido: 'Joint Drinking' and the Politics of Sexual Control in Colonial Zimbabwe, 1920s to 1950s," *Journal of Social History* 30, 3 (1997): 645–667.

55. For the South African scene, see Robert A. Hill and Gregory A. Pirio, "'Africa for the Africans': The Garvey Movement in South Africa, 1920–1940," in *The Politics of Race, Class and Nationalism in Twentieth Century South Africa,* ed. Shula Marks and Stanley Trapido (London: Longman, 1987), 209–253; Mary Benson, *The African Patriot: The Story of the African National Congress of South Africa* (Chicago: Encyclopedia Britannia Press, 1964). On Southern Rhodesia, see Tsuneo Yoshikuni, "Strike Action and Self-Help Associations: Zimbabwean Worker Protest and Culture after World War I," *Journal of Southern African Studies* 15, 3 (1989): 440–468.

56. On the origins and development of the ICU, see Clements Kadalie, *My Life and the ICU: The Autobiography of a Black South African Trade Unionist in South Africa,* ed. Stanley Trapido (New York: Humanities Press, 1970; L. Wickins, *The Industrial and Commercial Workers' Union of Africa* (Cape Town: Oxford University Press, 1978); Helen Bradford, *A Taste of Freedom: The ICU in Rural South Africa, 1924–1930* (New Haven: Yale University Press, 1987). On the Rhodesian ICU, see J. R. Hooker, "The African Worker in Southern Rhodesia: Black Aspirations in a White Economy, 1927–36," *Race* 6 (1964): 142–151; Richard Parry, "Culture, Organisation and Class: The African Experience in Salisbury, 1892–1935," in *Sites of Struggle: Essays in Zimbabwe's Urban History,* ed. Brian Raftopoulos and Tsuneo Yoshikuni (Harare: Weaver Press, 1999), 53–94 (esp. 78–88); Ranger, *African Voice,* 148–169.

57. NAZ, N3/21/5 (5): [memorandum by Chief Native Commissioner], 21 August 1923.

58. NAZ, S2584/37: Chipwaya to Prime Minister, n.d.

59. NAZ, S482/815/39: Chief Native Commissioner to Minister of Native Affairs, 2 December 1929.

60. NAZ, S482/815/39: Detective Sergeant to Superintendent of C.I.D., 16 December 1929.

61. NAZ, S235/477: Evidence of Enquiry into Bulawayo Location, 1930, 51.

62. *Report of Committee to Investigate the Economic, Social and Health Conditions of Africans Employed in Urban Areas* (Salisbury, 1944), 6, 15.

63. NAZ, S482/815/39: Detective to Chief Superintendent of C.I.D., 15 December 1929.

64. NAZ, S482/815/39: Acting Superintendent of Natives to Chief Native Commissioner, 23 April 1929.

65. NAZ, S482/815/39: Superintendent of Natives to Chief Native Commissioner, 19 March 1930.

66. NAZ, S482/815/39: Memorandum: Native Detective Mfelesi, n.d.

67. Ranger, *African Voice,* 148.

68. See, however, Parry, "Culture, Organisation and Class."

69. Shutt, "We Are the Best Poor Farmers." For the particular case of the Samkange family, see Terence Ranger, *Are We Not Also Men? The Samkange Family and African Politics in Zimbabwe, 1920–64* (Portsmouth, N.H.: Heinemann, 1995).

70. NAZ, S138/55: Report of Meeting . . . by I.C.U. at . . . Fort Rixon, 20 January 1931. "When the English took possession of lands overseas," Peter Linebaugh and Marcus Rediker have observed, "they did so by building fences and hedges,

the markers of enclosure and private property." See Peter Linebaugh and Marcus Rediker, *The Many-Headed Hydra: Sailors, Slaves, Commoners, and the Hidden History of the Revolutionary Atlantic* (Boston: Beacon Press, 2000), 44.

71. NAZ, S1542/M8A: Chief Native Commissioner to Minister of Native Affairs, 15 November 1933.

72. Terence Ranger, *Peasant Consciousness and Guerrilla War in Zimbabwe: A Comparative Study* (London: James Currey, 1985), 334.

73. NAZ, S482/815/39: Chief Native Commissioner to Minister of Native Affairs, 2 December 1929.

74. NAZ, S1542/C16 (420): Mzingeli to Chief Native Commissioner, 24 August 1933; ibid. (416): Mzingeli to Editor, *Rhodesian Weekly Review,* 12 September 1933.

75. NAZ, S138/41: Complaints of Thomas S. Mazula, 30 May 1929; RHL, Mss Brit Emp S22, ASAPS, G168: Secretary to Governor to Mazula, 3 July 1929; ibid.: Mazula to Harris, February 1932 [no day given]; ibid.: Harris to Mazula, 17 March 1932; ibid.: Ndhlovu to Harris, 4 May 1932. On the anticolonial lobby in Britain generally, see Stephen Howe, *Anticolonialism in British Politics: The Left and the End of Empire, 1918–1964* (Oxford: Clarendon Press, 1993).

76. *Bulawayo Chronicle,* 1 August 1930. Mzingeli was fined £30 or six months' hard labor, whereas Ndhlovu received a sentence of £20 or six weeks' imprisonment and Mtelo £15 or one month's imprisonment. All the defenders were expected to appeal. It is unclear whether the convictions were overturned or the three paid the fines. As far as I can determine, no ICU member actually served time in prison for political offenses.

77. NAZ, S138/55: Report of Meeting . . . by I.C.U. at . . . Fort Rixon, 20 January 1931.

78. NAZ, S482/815/39: Native Commissioner for Salisbury to Chief Native Commissioner, 18 December 1929.

79. *African Welfare: Its Place and Its Purpose in Southern Rhodesia* (Bulawayo: Federation of African Welfare Societies in Southern Rhodesia, 1951); NAZ, S1542/A6 (19–24): [Mashonaland Native Welfare Society], Memorandum upon the Subject of Native Welfare [1935]. Quotation from the latter document.

80. NAZ (Byo), 23/3/7R, 6493: Ndhlovu to Bulawayo Town Council, 21 March 1930; ibid.: Coghlan to Acting Town Clerk, 10 April 1930; ibid.: Acting Town Clerk to Secretary of ICU, 17 April 1930.

81. SA, PM 1/2/328, PM 93/12: Sambo to Governor of Nyasaland, 10 January 1928.

82. NAZ, S1671: Sambo to Chief, I.O., 31 May 1927.

83. NAZ, S1671: Sambo to Ag[g]r[e]y, 17 March 1927. The letter was addressed to James Aggrey, with whom Sambo had a brief encounter during Aggrey's visit to Southern Rhodesia in 1924. Yet even if the police had not intercepted the letter, the overtly procolonial Aggrey—who Sambo, like many others in southern Africa, assumed to be African American—was hardly someone in whom a radical African activist would have wanted to confide, as we saw in chapter 2.

84. On Garveyism in Southern Rhodesia, see Michael O. West, "A Seed Is Sown: The Impact of the Garvey Movement on Zimbabwe in the Interwar Years," *International Journal of African Historical Studies* (forthcoming 2002).

85. The requirement was directed against the independent African church movement, because a church without its own school system would be unattractive to potential adherents, given the close connection between the spiritual and educational projects in the Christian missionary enterprise in colonial Africa.

86. NAZ, S138/92: Gwabau to Chief Native Commissioner, 17 August 1925. Gwebu's name is spelled "Gwabau" in the archival records.

87. *Parliamentary Debates: House of Commons,* 5th series, vol. 208 (London: His Majesty's Stationery Office, 1927), cols. 1725–1726.

88. NAZ (Byo), AOH/2: Mark Ncube, interview with Mafimba Ncube, 9 October 1981 at Ntabazinduna, 25; NAZ (Byo), AOH/1, Masotsha Ndhlovu [interview], 13–14. Quotations from Mafimba Ncube.

89. NAZ, S2584/37: Chief Native Commissioner to Secretary to Premier, 23 August 1927.

90. NAZ (Byo), AOH/2: Mark Ncube, interview with Mafimba Ncube, 9 October 1981 at Ntabazinduna.

91. Hill and Pirio, "Africa for the Africans"; Amanda D. Kemp and Robert Trent Vinson, "'Poking Holes in the Sky': Professor James Thaele, American Negroes, and Modernity in 1920s Segregationist South Africa," *African Studies Review* 43, 1 (2000): 141–159.

92. A. C. Terry-Thompson, *The History of the African Orthodox Church* (New York: privately published, 1956); Randall K. Burkett, *Garveyism as a Religious Movement: The Institutionalization of a Black Civil Religion* (Metuchen, N.J.: Scarecrow Press, 1978).

93. PTL, Box 9: 103: Dube to Editor *African Orthodox Churchman,* 22 April 1929.

94. On the African Orthodox Church in Zimbabwe, see Michael O. West, "Ethiopianism and Colonialism: The African Orthodox Church in Zimbabwe, 1928–1934," in *Christian Missionaries and the State in the Third World,* ed. Holger Bernt Hansen and Michael Twaddle (London: James Currey, 2002), 237–254; idem, "In Search of Ethiopianism: An Historical Investigator's Personal Odyssey in Zimbabwe," *Journal of African Travel-Writing* 1 (1996): 52–63.

95. Quoted in Ian Phimister and Charles van Onselen, "The Labour Movement in Zimbabwe, 1900–1945," in *Keep on Knocking: A History of the Labour Movement in Zimbabwe, 1900–27,* ed. Brian Raftopoulos and Ian Phimister (Harare: Baobab Books, 1997), 1 (emphasis added).

96. Raftopoulos and Phimister, *Keep on Knocking.*

97. J. Mutero Chirenje, *Ethiopianism and Afro-Americans in Southern Africa, 1883–1916* (Baton Rouge: Louisiana State University Press, 1987); James T. Campbell, *Songs of Zion: The African Methodist Episcopal Church in the United States and South Africa* (New York: Oxford University Press, 1995).

98. Terence Ranger, "The Early History of Independency in Southern Rhodesia," in *Proceedings of a Seminar Held in the Centre of African Studies, University of Edinburgh, 10t–12th April 1964,* 52–74.

99. NAZ, S138/92: Superintendent of Natives to Chief Native Commissioner, 9 June 1927.

100. NAZ, N3/5/2–3 (3–4): Chief Native Commissioner to Superintendent of Natives, 29 September 1919.

101. George Shepperson, "Ethiopianism: Past and Present," in *Christianity in Tropical Africa,* ed. C. G. Baeta (Oxford: Oxford University Press, 1968), 249–264.

102. NAZ, S1542/M8A, 1928–33: Statement signed by Mtshwelo, 1 August 1927.

103. NAZ, S482/815/39: Superintendent of Natives to Chief Native Commissioner, 19 March 1930.

104. NAZ, S1542/M8A, 1928–33: Mtshwelo to Sims, 11 March 1933.

105. Ranger, *African Voice,* 165.

106. Ian Phimister, *An Economic and Social History of Zimbabwe, 1890–1948: Capital Accumulation and Class Struggle* (New York and London: Longman, 1988), 171–218.

107. NAZ, S482/815/39: Chief Native Commissioner to Secretary for Department of Justice, 2 January 1935.

6. FOUND AND LOST

1. Catherine Higgs, *The Ghost of Equality: The Public Lives of D. D. T. Jabavu in South Africa, 1885–1959* (Athens: Ohio University Press, 1997). Jabavu visited Southern Rhodesia in 1931 at the invitation of the Native Missionary Conference, which Thompson Samkange served as secretary. Jabavu, characteristically, "urged upon his [audience] the necessity of good feelings between all the races" in southern Africa, lashing out at "hot headed Natives who talked about pushing the Europeans into the sea." See *Native Mirror,* October 1931; NAZ, N3/21/8 (2–6): An Address by Jabavu [summary by W. Gumede]; Terence Ranger, *Are We Not Also Men? The Samkange Family and African Politics in Zimbabwe, 1920–64* (Portsmouth, N.H.: Heinemann, 1995), 18. Quotation from *Native Mirror.*

2. NAZ, ANG1/1/17: Southern Rhodesia Native Missionary Conference, 15–17 June 1932; *Native Mirror,* July 1932, June 1934, October 1934; *Bantu Mirror,* 27 June 1936; NAZ, S1542/C19, vol. 2: Resolutions by Native Section of Southern Rhodesia Missionary Conference, June 23–25, 1936. Quotation from the latter document. On the Rev. Rusike, specifically, see NAZ, S235/485: Minutes of the Southern Rhodesia Advisory Board for Native Development, 16–17 December 1932; *Native Mirror,* April 1935.

3. Paul T. Phillips, *A Kingdom on Earth: Anglo-American Social Christianity, 1880–1940* (College Park: Pennsylvania State University Press, 1996).

4. Hence Max Yergan, an African American missionary to South Africa in the post–World War I era, eventually left the church to become a political radical. See David H. Anthony III, "Max Yergan in South Africa: From Evangelical Pan-Africanist to Revolutionary Socialist," *African Studies Review* 34, 2 (1991): 27–55.

5. See, for example, S. K. B. Asante, *Pan-African Protest: West Africa and the Italo-Ethiopian Crisis, 1934–1941* (London: Longman Group, Ltd., 1977); William R. Scott, *The Sons of Sheba's Race: African-Americans and the Italo-Ethiopian War, 1935–1941* (Bloomington and Indianapolis: Indiana University Press, 1993); Joseph E. Harris, *African-American Reactions to War in Ethiopia, 1936–1941* (Baton Rouge and London: Louisiana State University Press, 1994); Robert G. Weisbord, "British West Indian Reaction to the Italian-Ethiopian War: An Episode in Pan-Africanism," *Caribbean Studies* 10, 1 (1970): 34–41; S. K. B. Asante, "The

Impact of the Italo-Ethiopian Crisis of 1935–36 on the Pan-African Movement in Britain," *Transactions of the Historical Society of Ghana* 8, 2 (1972): 217–227; Patricia G. Clark, "Stretching Out Their Hands: The South African Reaction to Italy's 1935 Invasion of Ethiopia," in *New Trends in Ethiopian Studies: Papers of the 12th International Conference of Ethiopian Studies,* ed. Harold G. Marcus (Lawrenceville, N.J.: Red Sea Press, 1994), 573–597.

6. This classic distinction was first made by Bengt Sundkler, *Bantu Prophets in South Africa,* 2d ed. (London: Oxford University Press, 1961).

7. On Zionism in Zimbabwe, see M. L. Daneel, *Old and New in Southern Shona Independent Churches* (The Hague: Mouton, 1971). See also Karen E. Fields, *Revival and Rebellion in Colonial Central Africa* (Princeton, N.J.: Princeton University Press, 1985); Madziwanyika S. Tsomondo, "Against Alienism: The Response of the Zionist and the Apostolic African Independent 'Christian' Church Movements to European Colonialism in Zimbabwe," *Journal of Southern African Affairs* 4, 1 (1979): 5–28; John Higginson, "Liberating the Captives: Independent Watchtower as an Avatar of Colonial Revolt in Southern Africa and Katanga, 1908–1941," *Journal of Social History* 26, 1 (1992): 55–80; David Maxwell, "Historicizing Christian Independency: The Southern African Pentecostal Movement, c. 1908–60," *Journal of African History* 40 (1999): 243–264.

8. RHL, Mss Brit Emp S332, Creech Jones, Box 22/7 (2): Samkange to Chief Native Commissioner, 28 February 1936.

9. NAZ, S2584/37: Bamingo to Chief Native Commissioner, 26 February 1936; ibid.: Bamingo to Chief Native Commissioner, 25 April 1936; ibid.: Bamingo to Chief Native Commissioner, 19 May 1936; RHL, Mss Brit Emp S332, Creech Jones, Box 22/7 (6–9): Rusike to Cripps, 19 August 1936.

10. RHL, Mss Brit Emp S22, ASAPS, G168: Rusike to Cripps, 31 January 1936. Earlier in his career, Jacha sometimes used the surname Rusike, like his brother Matthew Rusike.

11. *Bantu Mirror,* 21 November 1936.

12. NAZ, S482/111/40: Native Preachers Act, 1936 [unsigned memorandum].

13. *Debates of the Legislative Assembly,* 23 April 1936, vol. 16, col. 1026.

14. NAZ, S2584/37: Bamingo and Jacha to Chief Native Commissioner, 2 November 1936.

15. NAZ, S482/709/39: Bantu Community Association of Bulawayo, n.d.; *Bantu Mirror,* 1 August 1936.

16. NAZ, S1542/V4: Detective Sergeant to Chief Superintendent, C.I.D., 11 October 1936; ibid.: Acting Superintendent of Natives to Chief Native Commissioner, 12 October 1936; *Bantu Mirror,* 17 October 1936.

17. NAZ, S2791/17, vol. 1: Minutes of the Bantu Conference, 11 November 1936.

18. Kenneth Vickery, "The Second World War Revival of Forced Labor in the Rhodesia," *International Journal of African Historical Studies* 22, 3 (1989): 423–437; David Johnson, *World War II and the Scramble for Labour in Colonial Zimbabwe, 1939–1948* (Harare: University of Zimbabwe Publications, 2000). There was a similar return to coercive labor practices elsewhere in Africa. See, for example, David Killingray and Richard Rathbone, eds., *Africa and the Second World War* (London: Macmillan, 1986).

19. NAZ, S1542/I2 (292): Native Commissioner for Matobo to Chief Native Commissioner, 15 July 1940; ibid. (268): Native Commissioner for Marandellas to Chief Native Commissioner, 5 August 1940; ibid. (131–132): Acting Assistant Native Commissioner to Staff Officer, 29 October 1940.

20. Ibid. (78): Superintendent of Natives to Staff Officer, 6 September 1940; ibid. (98): Native Commissioner for Chipinga to Chief Native Commissioner, 13 November 1940.

21. Ibid. (323): Native Commissioner for Mtoko to Chief Native Commissioner, 4 November 1940.

22. Ibid. (288–289): Native Commissioner for Matobo to Chief Native Commissioner, 4 September 1940.

23. *Bantu Mirror,* 18 November 1939.

24. *Bantu Mirror,* 7 August 1943.

25. Lawrence Vambe, *From Rhodesia to Zimbabwe* (Pittsburgh: University of Pittsburgh Press, 1976), 139.

26. Michael O. West, "Great Historical Document or Just Propaganda? The Atlantic Charter and Global Africa in the Era of World War II" (manuscript).

27. *Bantu Mirror,* 20 February 1943.

28. *Bantu Mirror,* 11 March 1944.

29. *Bantu Mirror,* 20 April 1940.

30. *Bantu Mirror,* 6 March 1943, 13 March 1943.

31. Ranger, *Are We Not Also Men?* 90–92.

32. In 1941 the Labour Party split into two factions, with one faction supporting the African Branch and the other opposing it. They reunited in 1944 but soon split again, largely over the racial question. See M. C. Steele, "White Working-Class Disunity: The Southern Rhodesia Labour Party," *Rhodesian History* 1 (1970): 59–81; D. J. Murray, *The Governmental System in Southern Rhodesia* (Oxford: Clarendon Press, 1970), 198–241; Colin Leys, *European Politics in Southern Rhodesia* (Oxford: Clarendon Press, 1959), 178–189.

33. Steele, "White Working-Class Disunity," 66.

34. RHL, Mss Brit Emp S366, FCB 99/1 (76): Mzingeli to Hinden, 11 September 1942; RHL, Mss Brit Emp S365, FCB 100/2 (30–33): Southern Rhodesia Labour Party, 4.

35. RHL, Mss Brit Emp S365, FCB 99/1 (83): Mzingeli to Hinden, 30 April 1944; ibid. (92): Mzingeli to Hinden, 25 September 1944; ibid. (96): Mzingeli to Hinden, 13 August 1945. Explaining the drop in the party's fortunes in 1947, Labour Party president A. A. Draper complained that it was difficult to keep "the socialist cause in front of the people[,] for even many socialists appear to have grown weary of well-doing as their former [electoral] support has fallen away. . . . Life is comparatively easy for most Europeans and the contrast with conditions in England tends to induce apathy even amongst people who have had socialist convictions there." Ibid. (213): Draper to Parker, 9 January 1947.

36. Kenneth Vickery, "The Rhodesia Railways African Strike of 1945, Part I: A Narrative Account," *Journal of Southern African Studies* 24, 3 (1998): 545–560; idem, "The Rhodesia Railways African Strike of 1945, Part II: Cause, Consequence, Significance," *Journal of Southern African Studies* 25, 1 (1999): 49–71; Arthur Turner, "The Growth of Railway Unionism in the Rhodesias, 1944-1955,"

in *The Development of an African Working Class: Studies in Class Formation and Action,* ed. Richard Sandbrook and Robin Cohen (London: Longman, 1975), 73–98; Johnson, *World War II and the Scramble for Labour,* 141–167; Teresa Barnes, " 'So That a Labourer Could Live with His Family': Overlooked Factors in Social and Economic Strife in Urban Colonial Zimbabwe, 1945–1952," *Journal of Southern African Studies* 21, 1 (1995): 95–113.

37. See, for example, Dan O'Meara, "The 1946 African Mine Workers' Strike and the Political Economy of South Africa," *Journal of Commonwealth and Comparative Politics* 12, 2 (1975): 146–173; Frederick Cooper, "The Senegalese General Strike of 1946 and the Labor Question in Post-War French Africa," *Canadian Journal of African Studies* 24, 2 (1990): 165–215; Tiyambe Zeleza, "The Moral Economy of Working Class Struggle: Strikers, the Community and the State in the 1947 Mombassa General Strike," *Africa Development* 20, 3 (1995): 51–87; Ibrahim Abdullah, "The Colonial State and Wage Labor in Postwar Sierra Leone, 1945–1960: Attempts at Remaking the Working Class," *International Labor and Working-Class History* 52 (1997): 87–105.

38. Barnes, "So That a Labourer Could Live with His Family."

39. NAZ, S1906: Evidence [of Committee to Investigate the Economic, Social and Health Conditions of Africans Employed in Urban Areas], 294–295. See also *Report of Committee to Investigate the Economic, Social and Health Conditions of Africans Employed in Urban Areas* (January 1944).

40. Richard Gray, *The Two Nations: Aspects of the Development of Race Relations in the Rhodesias and Nyasaland* (London: Oxford University Press, 1960), 318–319.

41. West, "Great Historical Document or Just Propaganda?"

42. J. Z. Sawanhu, *Social Security: The Native Problem in Southern Rhodesia* (Bulawayo: Rhodesian Printing and Publishing Co., 1945). The pamphlet used the older orthography; hence "Sawanhu" rather than "Savanhu."

43. *Bantu Mirror,* 2 March 1946. The *Bantu Mirror,* which carried very little on the strike, only published Savanhu's speech six months after the fact. The literature on urban workers in colonial Africa is generally mute on the nexus of labor and race. Jeanne Penvenne's work on Maputo is an outstanding exception. See Jeanne Marie Penvenne, *African Workers and Colonial Racism: Mozambican Strategies and Struggle in Lourenco Marques, 1877–1962* (Portsmouth, N.H.: Heinemann, 1995).

44. *Bantu Mirror,* 29 December 1945.

45. *Bantu Mirror,* 16 August 1947.

46. *Bantu Mirror,* 14 June 1947.

47. *Bantu Mirror,* 21 August 1945, 29 September 1945, 1 June 1946, 20 July 1946, 25 January 1947, 5 July 1947, 12 July 1947, 9 August 1947, 16 August 1947, 8 November 1947.

48. NAZ, S482/717/39: Prime Minister to Governor, 7 June 1946.

49. NAZ, S482/717/39: Memorandum and Scheme on African Representation in Southern Rhodesia: Submitted by the African Voters League, 2 December 1946.

50. NAZ, S482/163/41: Ntuli to Prime Minister, 31 May 1947; ibid.: Secretary to Prime Minister to Secretary to African Voters League, 4 June 1947; ibid.: Ntuli

to Secretary to Prime Minister, 6 June 1947; ibid.: Secretary to Prime Minister to Secretary to African Voters League, 19 June 1947; NAZ, S482/717/39: Staff Officer to Commissioner of Police, 16 December 1946; *Bantu Mirror,* 23 March 1946, 6 April 1946, 13 April 1946, 31 August 1946, 14 February 1948, 22 May 1948; *African Weekly,* 7 August 1946, 26 March 1947, 31 December 1947.

51. NAZ, S517: Report by Officer Commanding, C.I.D., on the African Strike . . . April 1948, 28.

52. RHL, Mss Brit Emp S365, FCB 99/2 (71): Charles Mzingeli and Daniel B. Ntuli [Aims of the RICU], 20 September 1947.

53. NAZ, S517: Report by Officer Commanding, C.I.D., on the African Strike . . . April 1948, 25.

54. NAZ, S1561/19, vol. 1: Commission of Enquiry into Native Disturbances, 19 July 1948, A. 4.

55. Although no general census data are available, the number of Africans in formal employment—not counting those in the informal sector and dependents—went from approximately 20,000 to 46,000 in the Salisbury metropolitan area between 1936 and 1946, and from 15,000 to 33,000 in the Bulawayo metropolitan area during the same period. See *Report of the Urban African Affairs Commission, 1958* (Salisbury: Government Printer, 1958), 162.

56. Percy Ibbotson, "Report of an Investigation into the Effect on Africans in Salisbury of the Implementation of the Natives (Urban Areas) Accommodation and Registration Act of 1946" (February 1949), 5.

57. The Urban Areas Act was not implemented in Bulawayo until 1949.

58. *Bantu Mirror,* 12 July 1947.

59. RHL, Mss Brit Emp S332, Creech Jones 22/6 (267): Mzingeli to Cripps, 29 July 1947.

60. RHL, Mss Brit Emp S365, FCB 99/2 (79–88): RICU: Second Annual Conference, September 11–13, 1948, 5.

61. NAZ, S517: Report by Officer Commanding, C.I.D., on the African Strike . . . April 1948, 20; NAZ, S1561/19, vol. 1: [Evidence of] Commission of Inquiry into Native Disturbances, 19.7.48, A.5. Quotations from both sources, respectively.

62. NAZ, RH16/1/3/1 (21): Notes on the Speeches . . . of the African Workers Voice Association, 8 May 1947.

63. *Bantu Mirror,* 3 January 1948, 28 February 1948, 6 March 1948.

64. NAZ, RH16/1/3/1 (21): Notes on the Speeches . . . of the African Workers Voice Association, 8 May 1947.

65. Ndhlovu did, however, send a letter apologizing for his failure to attend the RICU second annual conference in 1948. See RHL, Mss Brit Emp S365, FCB 99/2 (79–88): RICU, Second Annual Conference, 11–13 September 1948.

66. *Bantu Mirror,* 3 January 1948.

67. George Padmore, *The Gold Coast Revolution: The Struggle of an African People from Slavery to Freedom* (London: Dennis Dobson, Ltd., 1953); Kwame Nkrumah, *Ghana: The Autobiography of Kwame Nkrumah* (London: Thomas Nelson and Sons, 1957); Dennis Austin, *Politics in Ghana, 1946–1960* (London and New York: Oxford University Press, 1964).

68. *Bantu Mirror,* 9 August 1947. Smith, who ruled from 1964 to 1980, asserted that Africans would never govern Rhodesia in a thousand years. He sub-

sequently modified his time line for an end to colonialism, saying it would not happen in his lifetime. Both predictions would, of course, be proven wrong.

69. C. J. Zvogbo, "The Revd E. T. J. Nemapare and the African Methodist Church in Southern Rhodesia," *Rhodesian History* 6 (1975): 83–87; Michael O. West, "In Search of Ethiopianism: An Historical Investigator's Personal Odyssey in Zimbabwe," *Journal of African Travel-Writing* 1 (1996): 52–63.

70. SOAS, MSS, Southern Rhodesia, General Correspondence, Box 1265: Carter to Dodds, 28 March 1947; ibid.: Carter to Dodds, 22 May 1947.

71. NAZ, MET 3/2/1/36: Report on Character and Work of Revd Esau T. J. Nemapare, 1934; NAZ, MET 3/2/1/37: Carter to Howarth, 22 April 1947.

72. NAZ, MET 3/2/1/36: Nemapare to Heath, 11 June 1937; SOAS, MSS, Chairman's Correspondence, Southern Rhodesia, 836/5: Dodds to Carter, 24 December 1943; ibid.: Carter to Dodds, 26 January 1944.

73. See, for example, *Bantu Mirror,* 11 August 1945, 1 September 1945, 9 February 1946, 27 April 1946, 19 July 1947; *African Weekly,* 5 September 1945.

74. Michael O. West, "Ndabaningi Sithole, Garfield Todd and the Dadaya School Strike of 1947," *Journal of Southern African Studies* 18, 2 (1992): 297–316. Teresa Barnes has severely castigated my "androcentric" approach to this episode in Zimbabwean history, asserting that I transmuted a rebellion by female students against colonial education into a struggle between two men, both of whom went on to become prominent political leaders. See Teresa A. Barnes, *"We Women Worked So Hard": Gender, Urbanization and Social Reproduction in Colonial Harare, Zimbabwe, 1930–1956* (Portsmouth, N.H.: Heinemann, 1999), 135, 137, 149. The trouble with Barnes's critique, as I see it, is that (as shown in chapter 2) rebellion against colonial education, whether by female or male students, was hardly new. What was new with the Dadaya strike is that an African teacher with a relatively high profile was victimized, which then transformed what would have remained a local event into a national political issue, with the virtually all-male black leadership coming to the defense of one of its own.

75. Johnson, *World War II and the Scramble for Labour,* 141–167; Jon Lunn, "The Meaning of the 1948 General Strike in Colonial Zimbabwe," in *Sites of Struggle: Essays in Zimbabwe's Urban History,* ed. Brian Raftopoulos and Tsuneo Yoshikuni (Harare: Weaver Press, 1999), 163–182.

76. NAZ, RH16/1/3/1 (21): Notes on the Speeches . . . of the African Workers Voice Association, 8 May 1947.

77. RHL, Mss Brit Emp S365, FCB 99/2 (67–68): Mzingeli [memo on strike], 27 April 1948.

78. Although far from certain, it would indeed be a fitting cap to his political career if the Maghato in question were the old populist and Ethiopianist Zachariah Makgatho, who, if he were still alive (he was as late as 1944), would now be a preeminent elder statesman of African politics. From what is known about him, such a break with fellow members of the elite would not altogether have been uncharacteristic of Zachariah.

79. NAZ, S517: Report by Officer Commanding, C.I.D., on the African Strike . . . April 1948, 51.

80. Enoch Dumbutshena, *Zimbabwe Tragedy* (Nairobi: East African Publishing House), 27.

81. Vambe, *From Rhodesia to Zimbabwe,* 243–244.

82. NAZ, S1561/19, vol. 1: [Evidence of] Commission of Inquiry into Native Disturbances, 21 July 1948, F. 1.

83. RHL, Mss Brit Emp S365, FCB 99/2 (74–77): Charles Mzingeli, My Experience during the African Strike in Salisbury, 19–22 April 1948.

84. Ngwabi Bhebe, *B. Burombo: African Politics in Zimbabwe, 1947–1958* (Harare: College Press, 1989). For critiques of Bhebe, see Johnson, *World War II and the Scramble for Labour,* 141–167; Lunn, "Meaning of the 1948 General Strike."

85. RHL, Mss Brit Emp S365, FCB 99/2 (66): Mzingeli to Cripps, 28 April 1948.

86. RHL, Mss Brit Emp S365, FCB 99/2 (67–68): Mzingeli [memo on strike], 27 April 1948.

87. NAZ, S517: Report by Officer Commanding, C.I.D., on the African Strike . . . April 1948, 58.

88. Ibid., 54.

89. *Bantu Mirror,* 13 November 1948.

90. NAZ, S729/2109/G: Broadcast Statement to all Africans—By the Minister of Justice.

91. Ibrahim Abdullah, "Rethinking African Labour and Working-Class History: The Artisan Origins of the Sierra Leonean Working Class," *Social History* 23, 1 (1998): 80–96.

92. Elliot J. Berg and Jeffrey Butler, "Trade Unions," in *Political Parties and National Integration in Tropical Africa,* ed. James S. Coleman and Carl G. Rosberg, Jr. (Berkeley and Los Angeles: University of California Press, 1964), 340–381 (quotation on 362).

93. *Bantu Mirror,* 11 January 1947, 1 February 1947, 22 February 1947, 1 March 1947, 12 April 1947, 7 June 1947, 16 August 1947, 18 October 1947; NAZ, S517: Report by Officer Commanding, C.I.D., on the African Strike . . . April 1948, 17–24.

94. *African Weekly,* 11 February 1948, 18 February 1948. See, also, NAZ, S517: Report by Officer Commanding, C.I.D., on the African Strike . . . April 1948, 15.

95. *Bantu Mirror,* 24 April 1948, 10 July 1948, 17 July 1948; *African Weekly,* 21 July 1948.

96. *Bantu Mirror,* 14 August 1948, 4 September 1948.

97. *Bantu Mirror,* 24 July 1948, 18 September 1948. For additional exchanges on this head, see *Bantu Mirror,* 2 October 1948, 9 October 1948.

98. NAZ, CR4/1/1 (919): Mzingeli to Cripps, 29 August 1948.

99. Ranger, *Are We Not Also Men?* 120.

7. BACK TOWARD THE BEGINNING

1. *Debates of the Legislative Assembly,* 2 June 1950, vol. 31, col. 1903.

2. Ibid.

3. Ibid., cols. 1905–1906.

4. RHL, Mss Brit Emp S365, FCB 99/2 (104–05): Mzingeli and Maviyane to Secretary of Native Affairs, 12 June 1950.

5. RHL, Mss Brit Emp S365, FCB 100/2 (Item 14): RICU Memorandum on the Subversive Activities Bill (Act), 25 September 1950.

6. *Bantu Mirror,* 1 July 1950.

7. Ibid.

8. *Bantu Mirror,* 15 July 1950.

9. *Bantu Mirror,* 19 August 1950.

10. *Debates of the Legislative Assembly,* 9 May 1951, vol. 32, cols. 1199–1200. On African labor and the struggle over international affiliation during the early period of the Cold War, see Frederick Cooper, *Decolonization and African Society: The Labor Question in French and British Africa* (Cambridge: Cambridge University Press, 1996), 432–453; Yvette Richards, "African and African-American Labor Leaders in the Struggle over International Affiliation," *International Journal of African Historical Studies* 31, 2 (1998): 301–334.

11. RHL, Mss Brit Emp S365, FCB 99/4 (8): Cogill to Nicholson, 23 July 1953.

12. L. H. Gann, *A History of Southern Rhodesia: Early Days to 1934* (New York: Humanities Press, 1969); James A. Chamunorwa Mutambirwa, *The Rise of Settler Power in Southern Rhodesia (Zimbabwe), 1898–1923* (Rutherford, N.J.: Farleigh Dickinson University Press, 1980).

13. *Report of the Commission on Closer Union of the Dependencies in East and Central Africa* (London: His Majesty's Stationery Office, 1929).

14. *Statements of Conclusions of His Majesty's Government in the United Kingdom as regards Closer Union in East Africa* (London: His Majesty's Stationery Office, 1930).

15. *Rhodesia-Nyasaland Royal Commission Report* (London: His Majesty's Stationery Office, 1939), 112.

16. NAZ, S1542/C19, vol. 2 (290–291): Resolutions Passed by the Native Section of the Southern Rhodesia Missionary Conference, 23–25 June 1936.

17. *Bantu Mirror,* 16 May 1936.

18. RHL, Mss Brit Emp S22, ASAPS, G169: Kumalo to Harris, 25 August 1939.

19. *Bantu Mirror,* 25 October 1941.

20. *Bantu Mirror,* 23 September 1944.

21. *Bantu Mirror,* 2 August 1947.

22. Ian Phimister, *An Economic and Social History of Zimbabwe, 1890–1948: Capital Accumulation and Class Struggle* (London and New York: Longman), 219–299; A. S. Mlambo, E. S. Pangeti, and I. Phimister, *Zimbabwe: A History of Manufacturing, 1890–1995* (Harare: University of Zimbabwe Publications, 2000), 31–50; William G. Martin, "From NIC to NUC: South Africa's Semiperipheral Regimes," in *Semiperipheral States in the World-Economy,* ed. William G. Martin (New York: Greeenwood Press, 1990), 203–223.

23. J. R. T. Wood, *The Welensky Papers: A History of the Federation of Rhodesia and Nyasaland* (Durban: Graham Publishing, 1983); Ronald Hyam, "The Geopolitical Origins of the Central African Federation: Britain, Rhodesia and South Africa, 1948–1953," *Historical Journal* 30, 1 (1987): 145–172.

24. *Bantu Mirror,* 2 August 1947.

25. NAZ, S517: Staff Officer to Commissioner of Police, 13 July 1949.

26. *Bantu Mirror,* 21 May 1949.

27. Timothy Scarnecchia, "Poor Women and Nationalist Politics: Alliances

and Fissures in the Formation of a Nationalist Political Movement in Salisbury, Rhodesia, 1950–6," *Journal of African History* 27, 2 (1996): 283–310; Teresa A. Barnes, *"We Women Worked So Hard": Gender, Urbanization and Social Reproduction in Colonial Harare, Zimbabwe, 1930–1956* (Portsmouth, N.H.: Heinemann, 1999), 134–144.

28. *Report of the Secretary for Native Affairs, Chief Native Commissioner and Director of Native Development for the Year 1951* (Salisbury: Government Printer, 1952), 2.

29. *Report of the Secretary for Native Affairs, Chief Native Commissioner and Director of Native Development for the Year 1952* (Salisbury: Government Printer, 1953), 3.

30. On attaining self-government in 1923, the name of the legislative body was changed from Legislative Council to Legislative Assembly.

31. RHL, Mss Brit Emp S365, FCB 99/3 (97): Samuriwo to Chief Native Commissioner, 1 March 1952; RHL, Mss Brit Emp S365, FCB 100/2 (97): Secretary for Native Affairs to President of Southern Rhodesia African Association, 25 March 1952. Quotation from the latter document.

32. RHL, Mss Brit Emp S365, FCB 99/3 (71): Jacha, Mzingeli, and Samuriwo to Secretary of Fabian Colonial Bureau, n.d.

33. RHL, Mss Brit Emp S365, FCB 99/3 (80): Joint African Organisations to Secretary of Fabian Colonial Bureau, n.d.

34. RHL, Mss Brit Emp, S365, FCB 99/3 (84): Nicholson to Mzingeli, 7 May 1952.

35. Joshua Nkomo, *The Story of My Life* (London: Methuen, 1984), 53.

36. Ibid.

37. *Bantu Mirror,* 16 May 1953.

38. *Bantu Mirror,* 14 March 1953, 21 March 1953.

39. *Bantu Mirror,* 18 April 1953.

40. *Bantu Mirror,* 14 February 1953.

41. RHL, Mss Brit Emp S365, FCB 99/4 (2): Nicholson to Mzingeli, 24 February 1953.

42. Nkomo, *Story of My Life,* 57.

43. *Bantu Mirror,* 27 June 1953.

44. See, for example, Larry W. Bowman, *Politics in Rhodesia: White Power in an African State* (Cambridge, Mass.: Harvard University Press, 1973), 46; B. Vulindlela Mtshali, *Rhodesia: Background to Conflict* (New York: Hawthorn Books, 1967), 97–98; Terence Ranger, "African Politics in Twentieth-Century Southern Rhodesia," in *Aspects of Central African History,* ed. T. O. Ranger (Evanston, Ill.: Northwestern University Press, 1968), 237.

45. RHL, Mss Brit Emp S365, FCB 99/2 (92): Mzingeli to Hinden, 9 April 1949.

46. The Federal Party was nothing more than the federalization of Huggins's old United Party, which meanwhile had merged with another political bloc, the Rhodesia Party, to form the United Rhodesia Party. Officially, if not operationally, the Federal Party and the United Rhodesia Party remained separate organizational entities, the one ruling over the federation and the other controlling the Southern Rhodesian territorial government.

47. RHL, Mss Brit Emp S365, FCB 99/4 (5): Maviyane to Selwyn-Clarke, 8 February 1954. See also L. C. Vambe, "An African on Federation," *Concord,* April/June 1954, 41; E. Dumbutshena, "Plain Speaking on Current Politics," *Concord,* December 1954, 36-37.

48. *Bantu Mirror,* 24 October 1953, 21 November 1953.

49. *Bantu Mirror,* 31 October 1953.

50. *Central African Examiner,* 20 July 1957.

51. B. J. Mnyanda, *In Search of Truth: A Commentary on Certain Aspects of Southern Rhodesia's Native Policy* (Bombay: Hind Kitabs Ltd., 1954), 6-7.

52. *Bantu Mirror,* 21 August 1954.

53. *Bantu Mirror,* 18 September 1954.

54. There was an existing group in Bulawayo called the Inter-Racial Society of Bulawayo. The secretary of the older formation explained that the new group "has one advantage which we have not; it is said to have money behind it." See RHL, Mss Brit Emp S365, FCB 99/4 (10-11): Cogill to Nicholson, 31 May 1953.

55. "The Inter-Racial Association," *Concord,* April/June 1954, 43.

56. Yale Manuscript Archives, African 14/306: Proposed Inter Racial Association of Southern Rhodesia: Draft Declaration on African Affairs.

57. NAZ, RH16/1/3/3 (6-10): [IRA] Conference on African Trade Unions: Report of General Secretary, July 3-4, 1954; ibid. (11-17): Inter-Racial Association ... Draft Declaration on Industrial Relations. Quotations from the latter document.

58. Ian Hancock, *White Liberals, Moderates and Radicals in Rhodesia, 1953-1980* (New York: St. Martin's Press, 1984), 26; "This Is Concord," *Concord,* April/June 1954, 13.

59. Hancock, *White Liberals,* 26-27, 50; ICS, Zimbabwe, Pressure Group, Inter-Racial Association of Southern Rhodesia: Interracial Association ... (Salisbury Branch), Executive Committee Members 1956/57; NAZ, F163/39/13: Record of Meeting between Federal Prime Minister and Representatives of the Executive of the Inter-Racial Association.

60. NA (US), 745C. 00/3-1452: Consul to State Dept., 25 March 1952; Hancock, *White Liberals,* 31-32.

61. *Bantu Mirror,* 2 May 1953.

62. *The Capricorn Convention: The World Press on the Capricorn Africa Society's Declaration* (London: Newman Neame, 1953).

63. F. D. Lugard, *The Dual Mandate in British Tropical Africa* (Edinburgh and London: William Blackwood and Sons, 1922).

64. *Capricorn Africa* (London: Newman Neame, 1953), 1-2.

65. Bizeck Jube Phiri, "The Capricorn Africa Society Revisited: The Impact of Liberalism in Zambia's Colonial History, 1949-1963," *International Journal of African Historical Studies* 24, 1 (1991): 65-; Tabitha M. J. Kanogo, "Politics of Collaboration or Domination? Case Study of the Capricorn African Society," *Kenya Historical Review* 2, 2 (1974): 127-142; Alistair Ross, "The Capricorn Africa Society and European Reaction to African Nationalism in Tanganyika, 1949-60," *African Affairs* 76, 305 (1977): 519-535.

66. Erica MacQueen, "Salisbury Letter," *Concord,* July 1956, 26.

67. *Capricorn Africa,* 6-7.

68. Ibid., 6.

69. Ibid., 7–8. See also Michael O. West, "Indians, India and Race and Nationalism in British Central Africa," *South Asia Bulletin: Comparative Studies of South Asia, Africa and the Middle East* 14, 2 (1994): 86–103.

70. David Stirling and N.H. Wilson, *A Native Policy for Africa* (London, 1949).

71. Hancock, *White Liberals,* 43–45.

72. Ibid., 42, 46–47.

73. *African Home News,* 13 August 1955.

74. "Capricorn in Concrete," *Central African Examiner,* 5 July 1958, 14.

75. For an elaboration, see Michael O. West, " 'Equal Rights for All Civilized Men': Elite Africans and the Quest for 'European' Liquor in Colonial Zimbabwe, 1924–1961," *International Review of Social History* 37, 3 (1992): 376–397.

76. *Debates of the Legislative Assembly,* 7 August 1957, vol. 40, cols. 653–662 (quotation from col. 656).

77. *Rhodesia Herald,* 10 March 1954.

78. Nathan M. Shamuyarira, *Crisis in Rhodesia* (London: Andre Deutsch, 1965), 16–17.

79. Lawrence Vambe, *From Rhodesia to Zimbabwe* (Pittsburgh: University of Pittsburgh Press, 1976), 259.

80. Nkomo, *Story of My Life,* 68.

81. As a historian of Rhodesian liberalism noted, Chipunza, "a schoolteacher, never, it seems, abandoned his second career of living off what liberal and, later, R[hodesia] F[ront] Whites wanted to hear." See Hancock, *White Liberals,* 27.

82. *Bantu Mirror,* 18 August 1956.

83. Terence Ranger, *Are We Not Also Men? The Samkange Family and African Politics in Zimbabwe, 1920–64* (Portsmouth, N.H.: Heinemann, 1995), 154–155.

84. Nkomo, *Story of My Life,* 62–64; *Bantu Mirror,* 15 August 1953.

85. Vambe, *From Rhodesia,* 200–201; Shamuyarira, *Crisis in Rhodesia,* 18.

86. West, "Equal Rights for All Civilized Men"; idem, "Beerhalls and Skokiaan Queens: The State, Female Brewers and Male Drinkers in Colonial Zimbabwe" (manuscript).

87. NAZ, F163/39/13: Record of Meeting between Federal Prime Minister and . . . Executive of the Inter-Racial Association, 1 February 1957.

88. *Bantu Mirror,* 2 June 1956.

89. "No Room at the Inn," *Central African Examiner,* August 29, 1959, 5–6.

90. Mahmood Mamdani, *Citizen and Subject: Contemporary Africa and the Legacy of Late Colonialism* (Princeton, N.J.: Princeton University Press, 1996).

8. AN ABORTED CORONATION

1. Lawrence Vambe, *From Rhodesia to Zimbabwe* (Pittsburgh: University of Pittsburgh Press, 1976), 276–277.

2. BIHR, CAS 4: Capricorn Information: Some Facts about the Southern Rhodesia African National Youth League, July 1957, 5. See also *Bantu Mirror,* 13 April 1957, 11 May 1957, 25 May 1957; Nathan M. Shamuyarira, *Crisis in Rhodesia* (London: Andre Deutsch, 1965), 40–41.

3. Brian Raftopoulos, "Nationalism and Labour in Salisbury, 1953-1965," *Journal of Southern African Studies* 21, 1 (1995): 79-93.

4. Most conspicuously, perhaps, Mzingeli became a member of the Smith regime's 1967 "constitutional commission," an attempt to legitimate its unilateral declaration of independence. Despite his services, however, Mzingeli (perhaps not altogether unmercifully for posterity) did not even merit a reference in Smith's bizarre political autobiography. See Ian Smith, *The Great Betrayal: The Memoirs of Ian Douglas Smith* (London: Blake, 1997).

5. Maurice Nyagumbo, *With the People: An Autobiography from the Zimbabwe Struggle* (London: Allison and Busby, 1980), 104-105.

6. Teresa A. Barnes, *"We Women Worked So Hard": Gender, Urbanization and Social Reproduction in Colonial Harare, Zimbabwe, 1930-1956* (Portsmouth, N.H.: Heinemann, 1999), 160.

7. Timothy Scarnecchia, "Poor Women and Nationalist Politics: Alliances and Fissures in the Formation of a Nationalist Political Movement in Salisbury, Rhodesia, 1950-6," *Journal of African History* 27, 2 (1996): 283-310, 303.

8. *Report of Commission of Inquiry into Transport Services of Greater Salisbury and Greater Bulawayo* (Salisbury: Government Printer, 1956). Nkomo was appointed to the commission, becoming the first African in Southern Rhodesia to serve on such a body.

9. BIHR, CAS 4: Capricorn Information: Some Facts about the Southern Rhodesia African National Youth League, July 1957, 3-5.

10. An organization also named the African National Youth League had been formed in Bulawayo, apparently in 1952, since it held its first annual conference the following year, opposing federation, among other things. I find no reference to this latter group after 1955. There does not seem, however, to be any connection between it and the later, Salisbury-based Youth League. See *Bantu Mirror,* 20 June 1953, 8 January 1955.

11. *Bantu Mirror,* 20 April 1957, 27 April 1957, 18 May 1957.

12. *Bantu Mirror,* 13 April 1957.

13. *Bantu Mirror,* 8 September 1956.

14. *Bantu Mirror,* 18 May 1957.

15. *Bantu Mirror,* 28 September 1957.

16. For a fuller—and more positive—assessment of Burombo's political career, see Ngwabi Bhebe, *B. Burombo: African Politics in Zimbabwe, 1947-1958* (Harare: College Press, 1989).

17. *Bantu Mirror,* 31 August 1957.

18. Vambe, *From Rhodesia,* 227.

19. Chitepo enjoyed all the benefits of multiracialism—without, however, officially joining any of the pro-partnership formations. See Ian Hancock, *White Liberals, Moderates and Radicals in Rhodesia, 1953-1980* (New York: St. Martin's Press, 1984), 27.

20. *Sunday Mail,* 17 November 1985.

21. Nyagumbo, *With the People,* 107.

22. Ibid., 108.

23. *Bantu Mirror,* 13 April 1957.

24. Joshua Nkomo, *The Story of My Life* (London: Methuen, 1984), 71.

25. Shamuyarira, *Crisis in Rhodesia,* 46.

26. "Southern Rhodesia African National Congress: Statement of Principles, Policy and Program," in *Zimbabwe Independence Movements: Select Documents,* ed. Christopher Nyangoni and Gideon Nyandoro (London: Rex Collins, 1979), 3–20.

27. "Whither Congress?" *Central African Examiner,* 28 September 1957, 7; "Can We Co-operate with Congress," *Central African Examiner,* 21 December 1957, 5–6.

28. Stanlake Samkange, "Congress Leaves a Door Open," *Central African Examiner,* 22 June 1957, 18; Enoch Dumbutshena, "Aims of S. Rhodesia Congress," *Central African Examiner,* 14 September 1957, 14–15.

29. Hancock, *White Liberals,* 64–67.

30. Ruth Weiss with Jane L. Parpart, *Sir Garfield Todd and the Making of Zimbabwe* (London: British Academic Press, 1999); Dickson A. Mungazi, *The Last British Liberals in Africa: Michael Blundell and Garfield Todd* (Westport, Conn.: Praeger, 1999); David Chanaiwa, "The Premiership of Garfield Todd in Rhodesia: Racial Partnership versus Colonial Interests, 1953–1958," *Journal of Southern African Affairs* 1, 1 (1976): 83–94.

31. NA (US), 845C. 062/2-1154: Consul General to State Department, 11 February 1954. See also Ian Phimister, "Lashers and Leviathan: The 1954 Coalminers' Strike in Colonial Zimbabwe," *International Review of Social History* 39, 2 (1994): 165–196.

32. *Debates of the Legislative Assembly,* 5 October 1956, vol. 39, cols. 937–980; "Strike: Looking Back," *Concord,* December 1956, 12–15.

33. Smith, *Great Betrayal,* 35.

34. Shamuyarira, *Crisis in Rhodesia,* 22; Vambe, *From Rhodesia,* 255; *Central African Examiner,* 18 January 1958, 11.

35. Larry W. Bowman, *Politics in Rhodesia: White Power in an African State* (Cambridge, Mass.: Harvard University Press, 1973), 31–33.

36. "Constitution Party: Bold Bid for African Moderates," *Central African Examiner,* 4 January 1958, 21–22.

37. *Central African Examiner,* 25 April 1959, 12.

38. Nyagumbo, *With the People,* 117.

39. For a discussion of some of the global connections of Zimbabwean nationalist movements, see John Day, *International Nationalism: The Extra-Territorial Relations of Southern Rhodesian African Nationalists* (London: Routledge and Kegan Paul, 1967).

40. Leslie Bessant, "Songs of Chiweshe and Songs of Zimbabwe," *African Affairs* 93, 370 (1994): 43–73.

41. Joshua Mqabuko-Nkomo, "Why Congress Was Banned," *Venture,* June 1959, 4–5.

42. "An ABC to the ANC," *Central African Examiner,* 2 August 1958, 10; Shamuyarira, *Crisis in Rhodesia,* 49–53.

43. ICS, Zimbabwe, Political Parties (1), African National Congress: Southern Rhodesia African National Congress, 18 January 1959.

44. NAZ, F120/L91: Southern Rhodesia African National Congress: Social

War on Colour Bar, 5 November 1958; ibid.: Director of FISB to Secretary of External Affairs, 10 October 1958; ibid.: Advisor on Race Relations to Prime Minister, 20 October 1958; *Report of the Secretary for Native Affairs and Chief Native Commissioner for the Year 1958* (Salisbury: Government Printer, 1959), 125.

45. T. H. Mothibe, "Zimbabwe: African Working Class Nationalism, 1957-1963," *Zambezia* 23, 2 (1996): 157-180.

46. Robin Palmer, *Land and Racial Domination in Rhodesia* (Berkeley and Los Angeles: University of California Press, 1977); William R. Duggan, "The Native Land Husbandry Act of 1951 and the Rural African Middle Class of Southern Rhodesia," *African Affairs* 79, 315 (1980): 227-239; Victor Machingaidze, "Agrarian Change from Above: The Southern Rhodesia Native Land Husbandry Act and African Response," *International Journal of African Historical Studies* 24, 3 (1991): 557-588.

47. Quoted in Ngwabi Bhebe, "The Nationalist Struggle, 1957-1962," in *Turmoil and Tenacity: Zimbabwe, 1890-1990,* ed. Canaan S. Banana (Harare: College Press, 1989), 58.

48. Raftopoulos, "Nationalism and Labour in Salisbury," 85.

49. Hot-headed, Nyagumbo repeatedly came close to blows with colonial officials and others he felt disrespected the nationalist movement and its leaders. See Nyagumgo, *With the People,* passim.

50. Nyagumbo, *With the People,* 116. See also *Report of the Secretary for Native Affairs . . . 1958,* 5-6; *Report of the Secretary for Native Affairs and Chief Native Commissioner for the Year 1959* (Salisbury: Government Printer, 1960), 1-2.

51. "An ABC to the ANC."

52. *Report of the Secretary for Native Affairs . . . 1958,* 5.

53. "The Edgarian Settlement," *Dissent,* 22 October 1959, 11; Mothibe, "Zimbabwe." In a move coordinated with the federal authorities, the other two territorial governments simultaneously banned the Nyasaland and Northern Rhodesian African National Congresses.

54. Mqabuko-Nkomo, "Why Congress Was Banned."

55. *Report of the Secretary for Native Affairs . . . 1959,* 1.

56. *Report of the Secretary for Native Affairs and Chief Native Commissioner for the Year 1960* (Salisbury: Government Printer, 1961), 1.

57. N. K. Marondera, letter to the editor, *Dissent,* 18 February 1960, 14-15.

58. "National Democratic Party: State of Appeal," in Nyangoni and Nyandoro, *Zimbabwe Independence Movements,* 21-22.

59. *Bantu Mirror,* 4 November 1961.

60. "African Politics in Southern Rhodesia," *Central African Examiner,* July 30, 1960, 14-15.

61. On the Congo crisis itself, see Crawford Young, *Politics in the Congo: Decolonization and Independence* (Princeton, N.J.: Princeton University Press, 1965). On the response in Africa and the diaspora, see Kwame Nkrumah, *Challenge of the Congo* (New York: International Publishers, 1967); Frantz Fanon, *Toward the African Revolution* (New York: Grove Press, Inc., 1969), 191-197; John Henrik Clarke, *Africans at the Crossroads: Notes for an African World Revolution* (Trenton, N.J.: Africa World Press, Inc., 1991), 115-125; Karl Evanzz, *The Judas Factor: The*

Plot to Kill Malcolm X (New York: Thunder's Mouth Press, 1992), passim; Komozi Woodard, *A Nation within a Nation: Amiri Baraka (Leroi Jones) and Black Power Politics* (Chapel Hill and London: University of North Carolina Press, 1999), 54–59.

62. *Bantu Mirror*, 11 March 1961.

63. *Bantu Mirror*, 2 December 1961. See also *Bantu Mirror*, 18 March 1961, 22 July 1961, 21 October 1961, 28 October 1961, 23 December 1961, 6 January 1962, 27 January 1962.

64. "NDP Congress: Facing Facts and Gaining Time," *Central African Examiner*, April 1961, 7.

65. See, for example, Shamuyarira, *Crisis in Rhodesia*, 62.

66. *Dissent*, 14 January 1960, 15.

67. BIHR, CAS 42: Fred [Rea] to David [Stirling], 19 September 1960.

68. Ibid.: Stirling to Vambe, 13 July 1960.

69. Nathan Shamuyarira, "The Revolt of the Intellectuals," *Central African Examiner*, June 18, 1960, 10–11.

70. "Intellectuals and Respectables Join the National Democratic Party," *Samkange Newsletter*, 27 June 1960, 1–2 (quotation from 1).

71. *Bantu Mirror*, 11 June 1960.

72. BIHR, CAS 52: Executive Officer's Report on His Bulawayo, Gwelo, and Que Que Trip, 16–29 July, 1959; BIHR, CAS 303A: Executive Officer's Tour of the Eastern Districts, 23–30 September, 1959.

73. *Dissent*, 14 January 1960, 13–18 (quotation on 17).

74. BIHR, CAS 47: Takawira to Lewis, 22 April 1960.

75. Ibid.: Takawira to Lewis, 4 March 1960.

76. BIHR, CAS 47: Fred [Rea] to Hughes, 7 June 1960.

77. BIHR, CAS 42: Fred [Rea] to David [Stirling], 30 August 1960.

78. Sithole was the only prominent NDP member to attend the Indaba, as far as I can determine. With the exception of Mzingeli and the headmasters Gideon Mhlanga and Matthew Wakatama, few noted black multiracialists participated. See *Report of the National Convention of Southern Rhodesia, October 31 to November 5, 1960* (Salisbury: National Committee of the National Convention [1960]).

79. BIHR, CAS 52: Leopold [Takawira] to David [Stirling], 8 July 1959; BIHR, CAS 42: Fred [Rea] to David [Stirling], 19 September 1960; BIHR, CAS 35: Rea to Capricorn Friends, 23 September 1960.

80. The Congo crisis shocked Rhodesian whites across the political spectrum. Ian Smith also asserts that it "had a profound effect on our [white] people." See Smith, *Great Betrayal*, 44.

81. BIHR, CAS 35: Fred [Rea] to Jonathan [Lewis], 30 January 1961.

82. The individuals in question were Michael Mawema, the party's president; Sketchley Samkange, its treasurer; and Takawira.

83. "What Happened in the Townships," *Central African Examiner*, July 30, 1960, 10–12; "Blunder in Bulawayo," *Central African Examiner*, August 13, 1960, 6, 13; "Accident and Aftermath," *Central African Examiner*, October 22, 1960, 6–8; "Impressions of Bulawayo," *Dissent*, August 4, 1960, 2–3.

84. Joshua Nkomo, *One Man, One Vote: The Only Solution in Southern Rhodesia* (Cairo: Dar El-Hana Press, 1961). There is considerable disagreement among the nationalists as to what actually took place at the conference. See Nkomo, *Story*

of My Life, 92–97; Shamuyarira, *Crisis in Rhodesia,* 156–169. In addition to Nkomo, the NDP delegation included Sithole, Chitepo, and George Silundika, the latter two as advisors. Of the four United Federal Party African delegates, Mzingeli, still hopelessly committed to partnership, was the only one of note. The only other prominent African at the conference was Walter Kamba, a Central Africa Party delegate.

85. *Bantu Mirror,* 20 May 1961.

86. *Daily News,* 10 June 1961.

87. *Samkange Newsletter,* May 27, 1961, 1–3; *Samkange Newsletter,* June 27, 1961, 1–3.

88. Leroy Vail, ed., *The Creation of Tribalism in Southern Africa* (Berkeley and Los Angeles: University of California Press, 1989).

89. *Bantu Mirror,* 15 July 1961.

90. *Samkange Newsletter,* September 27, 1961, 2.

91. Bowman, *Politics in Rhodesia,* 53–54.

92. "Rural Rumblings," *Central African Examiner,* April 1961, 4 (this organ had now moved from a biweekly to a monthly format).

93. *Report of the Secretary for Native Affairs and Chief Native Commissioner for the Year Ended 1961* (Salisbury: Government Printer, 1963), 1–5 (quotation from 3).

94. William H. Chafe, *Civilities and Civil Rights: Greensboro, North Carolina, and the Black Struggle for Freedom* (New York: Oxford University Press, 1980).

95. *Bantu Mirror,* 19 August 1961, 2 September 1961, 9 September 1961, 7 October 1961.

96. *Report of the Secretary for Native Affairs . . . 1961,* 3. For a larger discussion of this issue, see Michael O. West, "Nationalism, Race and Gender: The Politics of Family Planning in Zimbabwe, 1957–1990," *Social History of Medicine* 7, 3 (1994): 447–471.

97. *Report of the Secretary for Native Affairs . . . 1960,* 2; *Samkange Newsletter,* September 27, 1961, 2; James A. Chamunorwa Mutambirwa, "The Impact of Christianity on Nationalism in Zimbabwe: A Critique of the Sithole Thesis," *Journal of Southern African Affairs* 1, 1 (1976): 69–81.

98. *African Daily News,* 24 April 1962.

99. *Rhodesia Herald,* 31 August 1962; *Sunday Mail,* 23 September 1962.

100. RHL, Mss Afr S1482, Whitehead Papers 1D (4–6): Problems Affecting the Casting of 'B' Roll Votes in the Forthcoming Election; *Bantu Mirror,* 28 October 1961, 9 December 1961.

101. *Bantu Mirror,* 6 May 1961.

102. *Bantu Mirror,* 16 December 1961.

103. Barnes, *"We Women Worked So Hard,"* 152.

104. Smith, *Great Betrayal,* 41–47. On the social base of the Rhodesia Front, see Ian Henderson, "White Populism in Rhodesia," *Comparative Studies in Society and History* 14, 4 (1972): 387–399; Stephen E. C. Hintz, "The Political Transformation of Rhodesia, 1958–1965," *African Studies Review* 15, 2 (1972): 173–183; and Frank Clements's moralizing work, *Rhodesia: A Study of the Deterioration of a White Society* (New York: Frederick A. Praeger, 1969).

105. Ian Smith dubbed him the "old warhorse." See Smith, *Great Betrayal,* 42.

106. Chengetai J. M. Zvogbo, "Southern Rhodesia under Edgar Whitehead, 1958–1962," *Journal of Southern African Affairs* 2, 4, (1977): 481–492.

107. Hancock, *White Liberals,* 93–100; Bowman, *Politics in Rhodesia,* 33.

108. Bhebe, "Nationalist Struggle," 84–91.

109. See, for example, *Bantu Mirror,* 10 June 1961, 22 July 1961, 25 November 1961.

110. Predictably, the participants themselves give conflicting accounts of the schism. See, for example, Nkomo, *Story of My Life,* 107–119; Nyagumbo, *With the People,* 176–184; Shamuyarira, *Crisis in Rhodesia,* 173–177; and Ndabaningi Sithole, *African Nationalism,* 2d ed. (London: Oxford University Press, 1968), 35–36.

111. Shamuyarira, *Crisis in Rhodesia,* 173.

112. Eugene Watson, *Banned: The Story of the African Daily News, Southern Rhodesia, 1964* (London: Hamish Hamilton, 1976), 57.

113. On the build-up of Southern Rhodesian and federal military forces in the years leading up to the settler rebellion, see Patrick Keatley, *The Politics of Partnership* (Baltimore: Penguin Books, 1963), 234–235; Colin Leys, "The Growth of Police Powers and the 1959 Emergencies," in *A New Deal in Central Africa,* ed. Colin Leys and Cranford Pratt (London: Heinemann, 1960), 126–137.

114. *Debates of the Legislative Assembly,* 23 February 1965, vol. 60, col. 12.

115. *Debates of the Legislative Assembly,* 16 September 1965, vol. 62, col. 1863.

116. Smith, *Great Betrayal,* 37–38.

117. From the Rhodesian declaration of independence, as quoted in Smith, *Great Betrayal,* 67–108.

118. Kwame Nkrumah, *Rhodesia File* (London: Panaf, 1976).

119. Paul L. Moorcraft, *A Short Thousand Years: The End of Rhodesia's Rebellion* (Salisbury: Galaxie Press, 1980).

120. Robert C. Good, *U.D.I.: The International Politics of the Rhodesian Rebellion* (Princeton, N.J.: Princeton University Press, 1973).

121. For a discussion of the American impact on the rebel regime generally, see Gerald Horne, *From the Barrel of a Gun: The United States and the War against Zimbabwe, 1965–1980* (Chapel Hill and London: University of North Carolina Press, 2001).

122. Smith, *Great Betrayal,* 103–106.

123. David Martin and Phyllis Johnson, *The Struggle for Zimbabwe: The Chimurenga War* (New York and London: Monthly Review Press, 1981); Norma J. Kriger, *Zimbabwe's Guerilla War: Peasant Voices* (Cambridge: Cambridge University Press, 1992).

CONCLUSION

1. *Bantu Mirror,* 5 January 1957.

2. Michael O. West, "'Equal Rights for All Civilized Men': Elite Africans and the Quest for 'European' Liquor in Colonial Zimbabwe, 1924–1961," *International Review of Social History* 37, 3 (1992): 376–397.

3. *Bantu Mirror,* 5 January 1957.

4. Ibid.

5. As Gloria Waite has incisively demonstrated, however, on coming to power the nationalists sought more to co-opt and control traditional medicine and its practitioners than truly to integrate them into an overall national medical plan. See Gloria Waite, "Traditional Medicine and the Quest for National Identity in Zimbabwe," *Zambezia* 27, 2 (2000): 235-268. See also idem, *A History of Traditional Medicine and Health Care in East-Central Africa* (Lewiston, N.Y.: Edwin Mellen Press, 1992).

6. *Bantu Mirror,* 5 January 1957.

7. RHL, Mss Afr S1482, Whitehead Papers 1, 2G (71-83): United Federal Party and African Support.

Bibliography

ARCHIVAL DEPOSITS

Borthwick Institute of Historical Research (University of York)
Chicago Historical Society
Houghton Library (Harvard University)
Institute of Commonwealth Studies (University of London)
Jesuit Archives (Harare)
Library of Congress (Washington, D.C.)
National Archives (Washington, D.C.)
National Archives of Zimbabwe (Bulawayo)
National Archives of Zimbabwe (Harare)
Pitts Theology Library (Emory University)
Public Record Office (London)
Rhodes House Library (University of Oxford)
Rockefeller Archive Center (North Tarrytown, N.Y.)
Salvation Army Archives, International Headquarters (London)
School of Oriental and African Studies (University of London)
State Archives (Pretoria)
University of the Witwatersrand Archives
Yale Manuscripts and Archives (Yale University)

ANNUAL REPORTS: OFFICIAL DOCUMENTS, SOUTHERN RHODESIA

African Education: Annual Report by the Secretary
Report of the Director of African Administration
Native Education: Annual Report by the Director
Report of the Chief Native Commissioner
Report of the Director of Native Education
Report of the Chief Information Officer

LEGISLATIVE BODIES

Southern Rhodesia. *Debates of the Legislative Assembly.*
————. *Debates in the Legislative Council.*
United Kingdom. *Parliamentary Debates: House of Commons.*

OFFICIAL COMMISSIONS AND OTHER OCCASIONAL GOVERNMENT DOCUMENTS

Southern Rhodesia. *The African Home Ownership Scheme of the Southern Rhodesia Government.* Salisbury, April 1957.

——. *Census of Population, 1946.* Salisbury: Government Printer, 1946.

——. *Conference of Superintendents of Natives and Native Commissioners of the Colony of Southern Rhodesia: Verbatim Report of the Proceedings.* Salisbury: Government Printer, 1928.

——. *Final Report of the April/May 1962 Census of Africans in Southern Rhodesia.* Salisbury: Central Statistical Office, 1962.

——. *Report by H. S. Keigwin, Esquire, Native Commissioner, on the Suggested Industrial Development of Natives.* Salisbury: Government Printer, 1920.

——. *Report of the Commission Appointed to Enquire into the Matter of Native Education in All Its Bearings in the Colony of Southern Rhodesia.* Salisbury: Government Printer, 1925.

——. *Report of the Commission of Inquiry into Transport Services of Greater Salisbury and Greater Bulawayo.* Salisbury: Government Printer, 1956.

——. *Report of the Commission . . . to Investigate the . . . Strike amongst the African Employees of the Rhodesia Railway.* Salisbury: Government Stationery Office, 1946.

——. *Report of the Committee to Investigate the Economic, Social and Health Conditions of Africans Employed in Urban Areas.* January 1944.

——. *Report of the Land Commission, 1925.* Salisbury: Government Printer, 1925.

——. *Report of the Native Affairs Commission on Its Enquiry into Matters Concerning the Bulawayo Native Location.* 1930.

——. *Report of the Native Affairs Commission on its Enquiry into Matters Concerning the Salisbury Native Location.* 1931.

——. *Report of the Native Affairs Committee of Enquiry, 1910–11.* Salisbury: Government Printer, 1911.

——. *Report of the Native Education Inquiry Commission, 1951.* Bulawayo: Rhodesian Printing and Publishing Company, Ltd., 1952.

——. *Report of the Urban African Affairs Commission, 1958.* Salisbury: Government Printer, 1958.

——. *Report on Employment of Native Female Domestic Labour in European Households in Southern Rhodesia.* 27 October 1932.

——. *Report on Gwelo Municipal Location for Natives.* 1931.

——. *Report on Urban African Budget Survey in Salisbury, 1963–64.* Salisbury: Central Statistical Office, July 1965.

United Kingdom. *Education Policy in British Tropical Africa.* Cmd. 2374. London: His Majesty's Stationery Office, 1925.

——. *Report of the Commission on Closer Union of the Dependencies in East and Central Africa.* London: His Majesty's Stationery Office, 1929.

——. *Rhodesia-Nyasaland Royal Commission Report.* London: His Majesty's Stationery Office, 1939.

——. *Statements of Conclusions of His Majesty's Government in the United Kingdom as regards Closer Union in East Africa.* London: His Majesty's Stationery Office, 1930.

UNOFFICIAL PRIMARY DOCUMENTS

Capricorn Africa. London: Newman Neame, 1953.

The Capricorn Convention: The World Press on the Capricorn Africa Society's Declaration. London: Newman Neame, 1953.

Central African Council. *Report of the Commission on Higher Education for Africans in Central Africa.* Salisbury: Central African Council, 1953.

Ibbotson, Percy. *Report of an Investigation into the Effect on Africans in Salisbury of the Implementation of the Natives (Urban Areas) Accommodation and Registration Act of 1946.* February 1949.

———. *Report on a Survey of Urban African Conditions in Southern Rhodesia.* Federation of African Welfare Societies in Southern Rhodesia, Bulawayo, 1943.

Report of the National Convention of Southern Rhodesia, October 31 to November 5, 1960. Salisbury: National Committee of the National Convention, [1960].

Robertson, W. C., and Percy Ibbotson. *Report of the Sub-Committee Appointed to Investigate Housing, Wages, and Living Conditions of Africans in Bulawayo District.* September 13, 1939.

NEWSPAPERS/JOURNALS

African Daily News (Salisbury)
African Home News (Bulawayo)
African Weekly (Salisbury)
Bantu Mirror (Bulawayo)
Bulawayo Chronicle (Bulawayo)
Central African Examiner (Salisbury)
Concord (Salisbury)
Dissent (Salisbury)
Native Mirror (Bulawayo)
Rhodesia Herald (Salisbury)
Samkange Newsletter (Salisbury)
Sunday Mail (Salisbury)

BOOKS, ARTICLES, AND DISSERTATIONS

Abdullah, Ibrahim. "The Colonial State and Wage Labor in Postwar Sierra Leone, 1945–1960: Attempts at Remaking the Working Class." *International Labor and Working-Class History* 52 (1997): 87–105.

———. "Rethinking the Freetown Crowd: The Moral Economy of the 1919 Strikes and Riot in Sierra Leone." *Canadian Journal of African Studies* 28, 2 (1994): 197–218.

Ajayi, J. F. A. *Christian Missions in Nigeria, 1841–1891: The Making of a New Elite.* Evanston, Ill.: Northwestern University Press, 1969.

Anthony III, David H. "Max Yergan in South Africa: From Evangelical Pan-Africanist to Revolutionary Socialist." *African Studies Review* 34, 2 (1991): 27–55.

Asante, S. K. B. "The Impact of the Italo-Ethiopian Crisis of 1935–36 on the Pan-African Movement in Britain." *Transactions of the Historical Society of Ghana* 8, 2 (1972): 217–227.

———. *Pan-African Protest: West Africa and the Italo-Ethiopian Crisis, 1934–1941*. London: Longman Group, 1977.

Atkins, Keletso E. *The Moon Is Dead! Give Us Our Money! The Cultural Origins of an African Work Ethic, Natal, South Africa, 1843–1900*. Portsmouth, N.H.: Heinemann, 1993.

Atkinson, Norman. *Teaching Rhodesians: A History of Educational Policy in Rhodesia*. London: Longman, 1972.

Austin, Dennis. *Politics in Ghana, 1946–1960*. London and New York: Oxford University Press, 1964.

Barnes, Teresa A. "The Fight for Control of African Women's Mobility in Zimbabwe, 1900–1939." *Signs: Journal of Women in Culture and Society* 17, 3 (1992): 586–608.

———. "'So That a Labourer Could Live with His Family': Overlooked Factors in Social and Economic Strife in Urban Colonial Zimbabwe, 1945–1952." *Journal of Southern African Studies* 21, 1 (1995): 95–113.

———. *"We Women Worked So Hard": Gender, Urbanization and Social Reproduction in Colonial Harare, Zimbabwe, 1930–1956*. Portsmouth, N.H.: Heinemann, 1999.

Benson, Mary. *The African Patriot: The Story of the African National Congress of South Africa*. Chicago: Encyclopedia Britannia Press, 1964.

Berg, Elliot J., and Jeffrey Butler. "Trade Unions." In *Political Parties and National Integration in Tropical Africa*, ed. James S. Coleman and Carl G. Rosberg, Jr., 340–381. Berkeley and Los Angeles: University of California Press, 1964.

Berman, Edward H. "American Influence on African Education: The Role of the Phelps-Stokes Fund's Education Commissions." *Comparative Education Review* 15, 2 (1971): 132–145.

Bessant, Leslie. "Songs of Chiweshe and Songs of Zimbabwe." *African Affairs* 93 (1994): 43–73.

Bhebe, Ngwabi. *B. Burombo: African Politics in Zimbabwe, 1947–1958*. Harare: College Press, 1989.

———. *Christianity and Traditional Religion in Western Zimbabwe, 1859–1923*. London: Longman, 1979.

———. "The Nationalist Struggle, 1957–1962." In *Turmoil and Tenacity: Zimbabwe, 1890–1990*, ed. Canaan S. Banana, 50–115. Harare: College Press, 1989.

Bone, R. C. "Educational Development in Rhodesia." *Rhodesian Journal of Economics* 2, 4 (1968): 5–27.

Bouche, Denise. "Autrefois, notre pays s'appelait la Gaule: Remarques sur l'adaptation de l'enseignement au Sénégal de 1817 à 1960." *Cahiers d'Études Africaines* 8, 29 (1968): 110–122.

Bowman, Larry W. *Politics in Rhodesia: White Power in an African State*. Cambridge, Mass.: Harvard University Press, 1973.

Bradford, Helen. *A Taste of Freedom: The ICU in Rural South Africa, 1924–1930*. New Haven: Yale University Press, 1987.

Burke, Timothy. *Lifebuoy Men, Lux Women: Commodification, Consumption and Cleanliness in Modern Zimbabwe*. Durham, N.C., and London: Duke University Press, 1996.

Burkett, Randall K. *Garveyism as a Religious Movement: The Institutionalization of a Black Civil Religion.* Metuchen, N.J.: Scarecrow Press, 1978.

Burnett, John. *A Social History of Housing, 1815–1985.* 2d ed. London and New York: Methuen, 1986.

Campbell, James T. *Songs of Zion: The African Methodist Episcopal Church in the United States and South Africa.* New York: Oxford University Press, 1995.

Caplan, Gerald L. *The Elites of Barotseland, 1878–1969: A Political History of Zambia's Western Province.* Berkeley and Los Angeles: University of California Press, 1970.

Chafe, William H. *Civilities and Civil Rights: Greensboro, North Carolina and the Black Struggle for Freedom.* New York: Oxford University Press, 1980.

Chanaiwa, David. "The Premiership of Garfield Todd in Rhodesia: Racial Partnership versus Colonial Interests, 1953–1958." *Journal of Southern African Affairs* 1, 1 (1976): 83–94.

Chirenje, J. Mutero. *Ethiopianism and Afro-Americans in Southern Africa, 1883–1916.* Baton Rouge and London: Louisiana State University Press, 1987.

Clark, Patricia G. "Stretching Out Their Hands: The South African Reaction to Italy's 1935 Invasion of Ethiopia." In *New Trends in Ethiopian Studies: Papers of the 12th International Conference of Ethiopian Studies,* ed. Harold G. Marcus, 573–597. Lawrenceville, N.J.: Red Sea Press, 1994.

Clarke, John Henrik. *Africans at the Crossroads: Notes for an African World Revolution.* Trenton, N.J.: Africa World Press, 1991.

Clements, Frank. *Rhodesia: A Study of the Deterioration of a White Society.* New York: Frederick A. Praeger, 1969.

Comaroff, J. L. "Bridewealth and the Control of Ambiguity in a Tswana Chiefdom." In *The Meaning of Marriage Payments,* ed. J. L. Comaroff, 161–195. London: Academic Press, 1980.

Cooper, Frederick. *Decolonization and African Society: The Labor Question in French and British Africa.* Cambridge: Cambridge University Press, 1996.

——. "The Senegalese General Strike of 1946 and the Labor Question in Post-War French Africa." *Canadian Journal of African Studies* 24, 2 (1990): 165–215.

Cornwell, Gareth. "George Webb Hardy's *The Black Peril* and the Social Meaning of 'Black Peril' in Early Twentieth-Century South Africa." *Journal of Southern African Studies* 22, 3 (1996): 441–453.

Crais, Clifton C. *White Supremacy and Black Resistance in Pre-Industrial South Africa: The Making of a Colonial Order in the Eastern Cape, 1770–1865.* Cambridge: Cambridge University Press, 1992.

Daneel, M. L. *Old and New in Southern Shona Independent Churches.* The Hague: Mouton, 1971.

Davenport, T. R. H. "The Consolidation of a New Society: The Cape Colony." In *The Oxford History of South Africa,* vol. 1, *South Africa to 1860,* ed. Monica Wilson and Leonard Thompson, 272–333. New York and Oxford: Oxford University Press, 1969.

——. "The South African Rebellion, 1914." *English Historical Review* 77, 306 (1963): 53–80.

Davidoff, Leonore, and Catherine Hall. *Family Fortunes: Men and Women of the English Middle Class, 1780–1850.* Chicago and London: University of Chicago Press, 1987.

Davis, R. Hunt, Jr., "Producing the 'Good African': South Carolina's Penn School as a Guide for African Education in South Africa." In *Independence without Freedom: The Political Economy of Colonial Education in Southern Africa,* ed. Agrippah T. Mugomba and Mougo Nyaggah, 83–112. Santa Barbara, Calif.: ABC–Clio, 1980.

Day, John. *International Nationalism: The Extra-Territorial Relations of Southern Rhodesian African Nationalists.* London: Routledge and Kegan Paul, 1967.

Drake, St. Clair, and Horace R. Cayton. *Black Metropolis: A Study of Negro Life in a Northern City.* New York: Harcourt, Brace and Company, 1945.

Du Bois, W. E. B. *Black Reconstruction in America, 1860–1880.* 1935. Reprint, New York: Atheneum, 1977.

Duby, Georges. *The Knight, the Lady, and the Priest: The Making of Modern Marriage in Medieval France.* Trans. Barbara Bray. New York: Pantheon Books, 1983.

Duggan, William, R. "The Native Land Husbandry Act of 1951 and the Rural African Middle Class of Southern Rhodesia." *African Affairs* 79, 315 (1980): 227–239.

Dumbutshena, Enoch. *Zimbabwe Tragedy.* Nairobi: East African Publishing House, 1975.

Elphick, Richard. *Kraal and Castle: Khoikhoi and the Founding of White South Africa.* New Haven and London: Yale University Press, 1977.

Etherington, Norman. "Natal's Black Rape Scare of the 1870s." *Journal of Southern African Studies* 15, 1 (1988): 36–53.

———. *Preachers, Peasants and Politics in Southeast Africa, 1835–1880: African Christian Communities in Natal, Pondoland and Zululand.* London: Royal Historical Society, 1978.

Evanzz, Karl. *The Judas Factor: The Plot to Kill Malcolm X.* New York: Thunder's Mouth Press, 1992.

Fanon, Frantz. *Toward the African Revolution.* New York: Grove Press, 1969.

Fields, Karen E. *Revival and Rebellion in Colonial Central Africa.* Princeton, N.J.: Princeton University Press, 1985.

Foner, Eric. *Reconstruction: America's Unfinished Business, 1863–1877.* New York: Harper and Row, 1988.

Gaitskell, Deborah. "Housewives, Maids or Mothers: Some Contradictions of Domesticity for Christian Women in Johannesburg, 1903–39." *Journal of African History* 24, 2 (1983): 241–256.

———. "'Wailing for Purity': Prayer Unions, African Mothers and Adolescent Daughters, 1912–1940." In *Industrialisation and Social Change in South Africa: African Class Formation, Culture and Consciousness, 1870–1930,* ed. Shula Marks and Richard Rathbone, 338–357. London: Longman, 1982.

Gann, L. H. *A History of Southern Rhodesia: Early Days to 1934.* New York: Humanities Press, 1969.

Gann, L. H., and M. Gelfand. *Huggins of Rhodesia: The Man and His Country.* London: George Allen and Unwin, 1964.

Gargett, Eric Stanley. "Welfare Services in an African Urban Area." Ph.D. dissertation, University of London, 1971.

Garson, N. G. "The Boer Rebellion of 1914." *History Today* 12, 2 (1962): 127–145.

Gay, Peter. *The Bourgeois Experience: Victoria to Freud.* 5 vols. Vols. 1 and 2, New York and Oxford: Oxford University Press, 1984, 1986; vols. 3–5, New York: W. W. Norton, 1993, 1995, 1998.

Geiss, Imanuel. *The Pan-African Movement: A History of Pan-Africanism in America, Europe and Africa.* Trans. Ann Keep. New York: Africana Publishing Co., 1974.

Gelfand, Michael. *A Non-Racial Island of Learning: A History of the University College of Rhodesia from Its Inception to 1966.* Gwelo: Mambo Press, 1978.

Gluckman, Max. "Kinship and Marriage among the Lozi of Northern Rhodesia and the Zulu of Natal." In *African Systems of Kinship and Marriage,* ed. A. R. Radcliffe-Brown and Daryll Forde, 166–206. London: Oxford University Press, 1950.

Good, Robert C. *U.D.I.: The International Politics of the Rhodesian Rebellion.* Princeton, N.J.: Princeton University Press, 1973.

Gray, Richard. *The Two Nations: Aspects of the Development of Race Relations in the Rhodesias and Nyasaland.* London: Oxford University Press, 1960.

Hancock, Ian. *White Liberals, Moderates, and Radicals in Rhodesia, 1953–1980.* New York: St. Martin's Press, 1984.

Hansen, Karen Tranberg. *Distant Companions: Servants and Employers in Zambia, 1900–1985.* Ithaca, N.Y.: Cornell University Press, 1989.

Harlan, Louis R. "Booker T. Washington and the White Man's Burden." *American Historical Review* 71, 2 (1966): 441–467.

——. *Booker T. Washington: The Wizard of Tuskegee, 1901–1915.* New York: Oxford University Press, 1983.

Harrell-Bond, Barbara E. *Modern Marriage in Sierra Leone: A Study of the Professional Group.* The Hague: Mouton and Co., 1975.

Harris, Joseph E. *African-American Reactions to War in Ethiopia, 1936–1941.* Baton Rouge and London: Louisiana State University Press, 1994.

Henderson, Ian. "White Populism in Rhodesia." *Comparative Studies in Society and History* 14, 4 (1972): 387–399.

Higginson, John. "Liberating the Captives: Independent Watchtower as an Avatar of Colonial Revolt in Southern Africa and Katanga, 1908–1941." *Journal of Social History* 26, 1 (1992): 55–80.

Higgs, Catherine. *The Ghost of Equality: The Public Lives of D. D. T. Jabavu in South Africa, 1885–1959.* Athens: Ohio University Press, 1997.

Hill, Robert A., and Gregory A. Pirio. "'Africa for the Africans': The Garvey Movement in South Africa, 1920–1940." In *The Politics of Race, Class and Nationalism in Twentieth Century South Africa,* ed. Shula Marks and Stanley Trapido, 209–253. London: Longman, 1987.

Hintz, Stephen, E. C. "The Political Transformation of Rhodesia, 1958–1965." *African Studies Review* 15, 2 (1972): 173–183.

Hodgkin, Thomas. *Nationalism in Colonial Africa.* London: Frederick Muller Limited, 1956.

Hooker, J. R. "The African Worker in Southern Rhodesia: Black Aspirations in a White Economy, 1927–36." *Race* 6 (1964): 142–151.

——. "Welfare Associations and Other Instruments of Accommodation in the Rhodesias between the World Wars." *Comparative Studies in Society and History* 9 (1966): 51–63.

Horne, Gerald. *From the Barrel of a Gun: The United States and the War against Zimbabwe, 1965–1980.* Chapel Hill and London: University of North Carolina Press, 2001.

Howe, Stephen. *Anticolonialism in British Politics: The Left and the End of Empire, 1918–1964.* Oxford: Clarendon Press, 1993.

Hyam, Ronald. "The Geopolitical Origins of the Central African Federation: Britain, Rhodesia and South Africa, 1948–1953." *Historical Journal* 30, 1 (1987): 145–172.

Jabavu, D. D. T. "The Origin of 'Nkosi Sikelel' iAfrica,'" *NADA* 26 (1949): 56–57.

Jeater, Diana. *Marriage, Perversion, and Power: The Construction of Moral Discourse in Southern Rhodesia, 1894–1930.* Oxford: Clarendon Press, 1993.

Jennings, A. C. "Improved Housing for Urban Natives." *Transactions of the Rhodesia Scientific Association* 38 (1941): 129–139.

Johnson, David. "Urban Labor, the War, and the Revolt of the Working People in Colonial Zimbabwe (Southern Rhodesia)." *South Asia Bulletin: Comparative Studies of South Asia, Africa and Middle Class* 15, 2 (1995): 72–88.

———. *World War II and the Scramble for Labour in Colonial Zimbabwe, 1939–1948.* Harare: University of Zimbabwe Publications, 2000.

Jones, Thomas Jesse. *Education in Africa: A Study of West, South and Equatorial Africa by the African Education Commission.* New York: Phelps-Stokes Fund, 1922.

———. *Education in East Africa: A Study of East, Central and South Africa by the Second African Education Commission.* New York: Phelps-Stokes Fund, 1925.

Kaarsholm, Preben. "Si Ye Pambili—Which Way Forward? Urban Development, Culture and Politics in Bulawayo." *Journal of Southern African Studies* 21, 2 (1995): 225–245.

Kadalie, Clements. *My Life and the ICU: The Autobiography of a Black South African Trade Unionist in South Africa.* Ed. Stanley Trapido. New York: Humanities Press, 1970.

Kamusikiri, James Guveya. "African Education under the American Methodist Episcopal Church in Rhodesia: Objectives, Strategy and Impact, 1898–1966." Ph.D. dissertation, University of California, Los Angeles, 1978.

Kanoga, Tabitha M. J. "Politics of Collaboration or Domination? Case Study of the Capricorn African Society." *Kenya Historical Review* 2, 2 (1974): 127–142.

Keatley, Patrick. *The Politics of Partnership.* Baltimore: Penguin Books, 1963.

Kemp, Amanda D., and Robert Trent Vinson. "'Poking Holes in the Sky': Professor James Thaele, American Negroes, and Modernity in 1920s Segregationist South Africa." *African Studies Review* 43, 1 (2000): 141–159.

Kileff, Clive. "Black Suburbanites: An African Elite in Salisbury, Rhodesia." In *Urban Man in Southern Africa,* ed. Clive Kileff and Wade C. Pendleton, 81–97. Gwelo: Mambo Press, 1975.

Killingray, David, and Richard Rathbone, eds. *Africa and the Second World War.* London: MacMillan, 1986.

King, Kenneth J. "Africa and the Southern States of the U.S.A.: Notes on J. H. Oldham and American Negro Education for Africans." *Journal of African History* 10, 4 (1969): 659–677.

———. "African Students in Negro American Colleges: Notes on the Good African." *Phylon* 31, 1 (1970): 16–30.

———. "James E. K. Aggrey: Collaborator, Nationalist, Pan-African." *Canadian Journal of African Studies* 3, 3 (1970): 511–530.

———. *Pan-Africanism and Education: A Study of Race, Philanthropy and Education in the Southern States of America and East Africa.* Oxford: Clarendon Press, 1971.

Kirk, Joyce F. *Making a Voice: African Resistance to Segregation in South Africa.* Boulder, Colo.: Westview Press, 1998.

Kriger, Norma J. *Zimbabwe's Guerrilla War: Peasant Voices.* Cambridge: Cambridge University Press, 1992.

Kumbula, Tendayi J. *Education and Social Control in Southern Rhodesia.* Palo Alto, Calif.: R and E Research Associates, 1979.

Kuper, Adam. *Wives for Cattle: Bridewealth and Marriage in Southern Africa.* London: Routledge and Kegan Paul, 1982.

Kuper, Leo. *An African Bourgeoisie: Race, Class and Politics in South Africa.* New Haven and London: Yale University Press, 1965.

Küster, Sybille. *Neither Cultural Imperialism nor Precious Gift of Civilization: African Education in Colonial Zimbabwe, 1890–1962.* Hamburg: LIT, 1994.

Langley, J. Ayodele. *Pan-Africanism and Nationalism in West Africa, 1900–1945: A Study in Ideology and Social Classes.* Oxford: Clarendon Press, 1973.

Leys, Colin. *European Politics in Southern Rhodesia.* Oxford: Clarendon Press, 1959.

——. "The Growth of Police Powers and the 1959 Emergencies." In *A New Deal in Central Africa,* ed. Colin Leys and Cranford Pratt, 126–137. London: Heinemann, 1960.

Linebaugh, Peter, and Marcus Rediker. *The Many-Headed Hydra: Sailors, Slaves, Commoners, and the Hidden History of the Revolutionary Atlantic.* Boston: Beacon Press, 2000.

Lugard, F. D. *The Dual Mandate in British Tropical Africa.* Edinburgh and London: William Blackwood and Sons, 1922.

Lukhero, M. B. "The Social Characteristics of an Emergent Elite in Harare." In *The New Elites of Tropical Africa,* ed. P. C. Lloyd, 126–138. London: Oxford University Press, 1966.

Lunn, Jon. "The Meaning of the 1948 General Strike in Colonial Zimbabwe." In *Sites of Struggle: Essays in Zimbabwe's Urban History,* ed. Brian Raftopoulos and Tsuneo Yoshikuni, 163–182. Harare: Weaver Press, 1999.

Machingaidze, Victor. "Agrarian Change from Above: The Southern Rhodesia Native Land Husbandry Act and African Response." *International Journal of African Historical Studies* 24, 3 (1991): 557–588.

Makambe, E. P. *African Protest Movements in Southern Rhodesia before 1930: An Ideological Appreciation of the Socio-Political Roots of Protest Movements.* Pasadena: California Institute of Technology, 1982.

Mamdani, Mahmood. *Citizen and Subject: Contemporary Africa and the Legacy of Late Colonialism.* Princeton, N.J.: Princeton University Press, 1996.

Mandaza, Ibbo. *Race, Colour and Class in Southern Africa.* Harare: Sapes Books, 1997.

Mandela, Nelson. *Long Walk to Freedom: The Autobiography of Nelson Mandela.* Boston: Little, Brown, 1994.

Mann, Kristin. *Marrying Well: Marriage, Status and Social Change among the Educated Elite in Colonial Lagos.* Cambridge: Cambridge University Press, 1985.

Marable, W. Manning. "Booker T. Washington and African Nationalism." *Phylon* 35, 4 (1974): 398–406.

Martin, David, and Phyllis Johnson. *The Struggle for Zimbabwe.* New York and London: Monthly Review Press, 1981.

Martin, William G. "From NIC to NUC: South Africa's Semiperipheral Regimes." In

Semiperipheral States in the World-Economy, ed. William G. Martin, 203–223. New York: Greeenwood Press, 1990.

Mashingaidze, E. K. "Government-Mission Co-operation in African Education in Southern Rhodesia up to the late 1920s." *Kenya Historical Review* 4, 2 (1976): 265–281.

Maxwell, David. "Historicizing Christian Independency: The Southern African Pentecostal Movement, c. 1908–60." *Journal of African History* 40 (1999): 243–264.

Mbata, J. Congress. "Booker T. Washington and John Tengo Jabavu: A Comparison." *Afro-American Studies* 2, 3 (1971): 181–186.

McCulloch, Jock. *Black Peril, White Virtue: Sexual Crime in Southern Rhodesia, 1902–1935.* Bloomington and Indianapolis: Indiana University Press, 2000.

Mlambo, A. S. "Student Protest and State Reaction in Colonial Rhodesia: The 1973 Chimukwembe Student Demonstration at the University of Rhodesia." *Journal of Southern African Studies* 21, 3 (1995): 473–490.

Mlambo, A. S., E. S. Pangeti, and I. Phimister, *Zimbabwe: A History of Manufacturing, 1890–1995.* Harare: University of Zimbabwe Publications, 2000.

Mlambo, Eshmael. *Rhodesia: The Struggle for a Birthright.* London: C. Hurst and Company, 1972.

Mnyanda, B. J. *In Search of Truth: A Commentary on Certain Aspects of Southern Rhodesia's Native Policy.* Bombay: Hind Kitabs, 1954.

Moloney, E. W. J. *The Undefeated.* Sussex, U.K.: Published by E. W. J. Moloney, 1967.

Moorcraft, Paul L. *A Short Thousand Years: The End of Rhodesia's Rebellion.* Salisbury: Galaxie Press, 1980.

Moss, Barbara A. "Holding Body and Soul Together: Women, Autonomy and Christianity in Colonial Zimbabwe." Ph.D. dissertation, Indiana University, 1991.

Mothibe, T. H. "Zimbabwe: African Working Class Nationalism, 1957–1963." *Zambezia* 23, 2 (1996): 157–180.

Mtshali, B. Vulindlela. *Rhodesia: Background to Conflict.* New York: Hawthorn Books, 1967.

Mungazi, Dickson A. *Colonial Education for Africans: George Stark's Policy in Zimbabwe.* New York: Praeger, 1991.

——. *Colonial Policy and Conflict in Zimbabwe: A Study of Cultures in Collision, 1890–1979.* New York: Crane Russak, 1992.

——. *Education and Government Control in Zimbabwe: A Study of the Commissions of Inquiry, 1908–1974.* New York: Praeger, 1990.

——. *The Last British Liberals in Africa: Michael Blundell and Garfield Todd.* Westport, Conn.: Praeger, 1999.

——. *The Underdevelopment of African Education: A Black Zimbabwean Perspective.* Washington, D.C.: University Press of America, 1982.

Murray, D. J. *The Governmental System in Southern Rhodesia.* Oxford: Clarendon Press, 1970.

Mutambirwa, James A. Chamunorwa. "The Impact of Christianity on Nationalism in Zimbabwe: A Critique of the Sithole Thesis." *Journal of Southern African Affairs* 1, 1 (1976): 69–81.

——. *The Rise of Settler Power in Southern Rhodesia (Zimbabwe), 1898–1923.* Rutherford, N.J.: Farleigh Dickinson University Press, 1980.

Muzorewa, Abel Tendekai. *Rise up and Walk: An Autobiography.* Ed. Norman E. Thomas. London: Evans Brothers Limited, 1978.

Muzorewa, Farai David. "Through Prayer and Action: The Rukwadzano Women of Rhodesia." In *Themes in the Christian History of Central Africa,* ed. T. O. Ranger and John Weller, 256-268. Berkeley and Los Angeles: University of California Press, 1975.

Nasson, Bill. *Abraham Easu's War: A Black South African War in the Cape, 1899-1902.* Cambridge: Cambridge University Press, 1991.

Nkomo, Joshua. *The Story of My Life.* London: Methuen, 1984.

Nkrumah, Kwame. *Challenge of the Congo.* New York: International Publishers, 1967.

——. *Ghana: The Autobiography of Kwame Nkrumah.* London: Thomas Nelson and Sons, Ltd., 1957.

——. *Rhodesia File.* London: Panaf, 1976.

Nyagumbo, Maurice. *With the People: An Autobiography from the Zimbabwe Struggle.* London: Allison and Busby, 1980.

Nyangoni, Christopher, and Gideon Nyandoro, eds. *Zimbabwe Independence Movements: Select Documents.* London: Rex Collins, 1979.

Nziramasanga, Caiphas Tizanaye. "African Immigration to Rhodesia, 1890 to 1945." Ph.D. dissertation, Oklahoma State University, 1978.

Obidi, S. S. "Nationalist's Demands for University Education in Nigeria and Government's Response, 1920-1948." *History of Education* 19, 1 (1990): 55-64.

Odendaal, André. *Black Protest Politics in South Africa to 1912.* Totowa, N.J.: Barnes and Noble Books, 1984.

O'Meara, Dan. "The 1946 African Mine Workers' Strike and the Political Economy of South Africa." *Journal of Commonwealth and Comparative Politics* 12, 2 (1975): 146-173.

Oppong, Christine. *Middle Class African Marriage: A Family Study of Ghanaian Senior Civil Servants.* London: George Allen and Unwin, 1981.

Padmore, George. *The Gold Coast Revolution: The Struggle of an African People from Slavery to Freedom.* London: Dennis Dobson, 1953.

Palley, Claire. *The Constitutional History and Law of Southern Rhodesia, 1888-1965: With Special Reference to Imperial Control.* Oxford: Clarendon Press, 1966.

Palmer, Robin. *Land and Racial Domination in Rhodesia.* Berkeley and Los Angeles: University of California Press, 1977.

Pape, John. "Still Serving Tea: Domestic Workers in Zimbabwe, 1980-1990." *Journal of Southern African Studies* 19, 3 (1993): 387-404.

Parker, Franklin. *African Development and Education in Southern Rhodesia.* Columbus: Ohio State University Press, 1960.

Parkin, David, and David Nyamwaya, eds. *Transformations of African Marriage.* Manchester, U.K.: Manchester University Press, 1987.

Parry, Richard. "Culture, Organisation and Class: The African Experience in Salisbury, 1892-1935." In *Sites of Struggle: Essays in Zimbabwe's Urban History,* ed. Brian Raftopoulos and Tsuneo Yoshikuni, 53-94. Harare: Weaver Press, 1999.

——. "The 'Durban System' and the Limits of Colonial Power in Salisbury, 1890-1935." In *Liquor and Labor in Southern Africa,* ed. Jonathan Crush and Charles Ambler, 115-138. Athens: Ohio University Press, 1992.

Peires, J. B. *The House of Phalo: A History of the Xhosa People in the Days of Their Independence.* Berkeley: University of California Press, 1981.

Penvenne, Jeanne Marie. *African Workers and Colonial Racism: Mozambican Strategies and Struggle in Lourenco Marques, 1877–1962.* Portsmouth, N.H.: Heinemann, 1995.

Phillips, Paul T. *A Kingdom on Earth: Anglo-American Social Christianity, 1880–1940.* College Park: Pennsylvania State University Press, 1996.

Phimister, Ian. *An Economic and Social History of Zimbabwe, 1890–1948: Capital Accumulation and Class Struggle.* London and New York: Longman, 1988.

———. "Lashers and Leviathan: The 1954 Coalminers' Strike in Colonial Zimbabwe." *International Review of Social History* 39, 2 (1994): 165–196.

Phimister, Ian, and Charles van Onselen. "The Labour Movement in Zimbabwe, 1900–1945." In *Keep on Knocking: A History of the Labour Movement in Zimbabwe, 1900–27,* ed. Brian Raftopoulos and Ian Phimister, 1–54. Harare: Baobab Books, 1997.

Phiri, Bizeck Jube. "The Capricorn Africa Society Revisited: The Impact of Liberalism in Zambia's Colonial History, 1949–1963." *International Journal of African Historical Studies* 24, 1 (1991): 65–83.

Pollard III, Alton B. "Rhythms of Resistance: The Role of Freedom Song in South Africa." In *"This Is How We Flow": Rhythm in Black Cultures,* ed. Angela M. S. Nelson, 98–124. Columbia: University of South Carolina Press, 1999.

Prominent African Personalities of Rhodesia. Salisbury: Cover Publicity Services, 1976.

Raftopoulos, Brian. "Nationalism and Labour in Salisbury, 1953–1965." *Journal of Southern African Studies* 21, 1 (1995): 79–93.

Ranchod-Nilsson, Sita. "'Educating Eve': The Women's Club Movement and Political Consciousness among Rural African Women in Southern Rhodesia, 1950–1980." In *African Encounters with Domesticity,* ed. Karen Tranberg Hansen, 195–217. New Brunswick, N.J.: Rutgers University Press, 1992.

Ranger, Terence. "African Attempts to Control Education in East and Central Africa, 1990–1939." *Past and Present* 32 (1965): 57–85.

———. "African Politics in Twentieth-Century Southern Rhodesia." In *Aspects of Central African History,* ed. T. O. Ranger, 210–245. Evanston, Ill.: Northwestern University Press, 1968.

———. *The African Voice in Southern Rhodesia, 1898–1930.* Evanston, Ill.: Northwestern University Press, 1970.

———. *Are We Not Also Men? The Samkange Family and African Politics in Zimbabwe, 1920–64.* Portsmouth, N.H.: Heinemann, 1995.

———. "The Early History of Independency in Southern Rhodesia." In *Proceedings of a Seminar Held in the Centre of African Studies, University of Edinburgh, 10th–12th April 1964,* 52–74. Edinburgh, U.K.: Center of African Studies, 1964.

———. *Peasant Consciousness and Guerrilla War in Zimbabwe.* London: James Currey, 1985.

———. *Revolt in Southern Rhodesia, 1896–97: A Study in African Resistance.* Evanston, Ill.: Northwestern University Press, 1967.

———. *Voices from the Rock: Nature, Culture and History in the Matopos Hills of Zimbabwe.* Harare: Baobab, 1999.

Rennie, John Keith. "Christianity, Colonialism and the Origins of Nationalism among the Ndau of Southern Rhodesia, 1890–1935." Ph.D. dissertation, Northwestern University, 1973.

Richards, Yvette. "African and African-American Labor Leaders in the Struggle over International Affiliation." *International Journal of African Historical Studies* 31, 2 (1998): 301–334.

Rodney, Walter. *How Europe Underdeveloped Africa.* Washington, D.C.: Howard University Press, 1974.

Ross, Alistair. "The Capricorn Africa Society and European Reaction to African Nationalism in Tanganyika, 1949–60." *African Affairs* 76, 305 (1977): 519–535.

Rubert, Steven C. *A Most Promising Weed: A History of Tobacco Farming and Labor in Colonial Zimbabwe, 1890–1945.* Athens: Ohio University Center for International Studies, 1998.

Ryan, Mary P. *Cradle of the Middle Class: The Family in Oneida County, New York, 1790–1865.* Cambridge: Cambridge University Press, 1981.

Sabatier, Peggy R. "'Elite' Education in French West Africa: The Era of Limits, 1903–1945." *International Journal of African Historical Studies* 11, 2 (1978): 247–266.

Samkange, Stanlake. *Origins of Rhodesia.* London: Heinemann, 1968.

Scarnecchia, Timothy. "Poor Women and Nationalist Politics: Alliances and Fissures in the Formation of a Nationalist Political Movement in Salisbury, Rhodesia, 1950–6." *Journal of African History* 27, 2 (1996): 283–310.

Schmidt, Elizabeth. *Peasants, Traders, and Wives: Shona Women in the History of Zimbabwe, 1870–1939.* Portsmouth, N.H.: Heinemann, 1992.

———. "Race, Sex and Domestic Labor: The Question of African Female Servants in Southern Rhodesia, 1900–1939." In *African Encounters with Domesticity,* ed. Karen Tranberg Hansen, 221–241. New Brunswick, N.J.: Rutgers University Press, 1992.

Schwerdtfeger, Friedrick W. *Traditional Housing in African Cities: A Comparative Study of Houses in Zaria, Ibadan and Marrakech.* Chichester, U.K.: John Wiley and Sons, 1982.

Scott, William R. *The Sons of Sheba's Race: African-Americans and the Italo-Ethiopian War, 1935–1941.* Bloomington and Indianapolis: Indiana University Press, 1993.

Seidman, Gay W. "Women in Zimbabwe: Postindependence Struggles." *Feminist Studies* 10, 3 (1984): 419–440.

Shamuyarira, Nathan. *Crisis in Rhodesia.* London: Andre Deutsch, 1965.

Shepperson, George. "Ethiopianism: Past and Present." In *Christianity in Tropical Africa,* ed. C. G. Baeta, 249–264. Oxford: Oxford University Press, 1968.

Shepperson, George, and Thomas Price. *Independent African: John Chilembwe and the Origins, Setting, and Significance of the Nyasaland Native Rising of 1915.* Edinburgh, U.K.: Edinburgh University Press, 1958.

Shutt, Allison K. "Pioneer Farmers and Family Dynasties in Marirangwe Purchase Area, Colonial Zimbabwe, 1931–1947." *African Studies Review* 43, 3 (2000): 59–80.

———. "Purchase Area Farmers and the Middle Class of Southern Rhodesia, c. 1931–1952." *International Journal of African Historical Studies* 30, 3 (1997): 555–581.

———. "'We Are the Best Poor Farmers': Purchase Area Farmers and Economic Differentiation in Southern Rhodesia, c. 1925–1980." Ph.D. dissertation, University of California, Los Angeles, 1995.

Sithole, Ndabaningi. *African Nationalism.* Cape Town: Oxford University Press, 1959.

Slater, Henry. "The Changing Pattern of Economic Relationships in Rural Natal, 1838–1914." In *Economy and Society in Pre-Industrial South Africa,* ed. Shula Marks and Anthony Atmore, 148–170. London: Longman, 1980.

Smith, Edwin W. *Aggrey of Africa: A Study in Black and White.* New York: Richard R. Smith, Inc., 1930.

Smith, Ian. *The Great Betrayal: The Memoirs of Ian Douglas Smith.* London: Blake, 1997.

Steele, M. C. "White Working-Class Disunity: The Southern Rhodesia Labour Party." *Rhodesian History* 1 (1970): 59–81.

Stilgoe, John R. *Borderland: Origins of the American Suburb, 1820–1939.* New Haven and London: Yale University Press, 1988.

Stirling, David, and N. H. Wilson. *A Native Policy for Africa.* London, 1949.

Stuckey, Sterling. *Slave Culture: Nationalist Theory and the Foundations of Black America.* New York: Oxford University Press, 1987.

Summers, Carol. "Demanding Schools: The Umchingwe Project and African Men's Struggle for Education in Southern Rhodesia, 1928–1934." *African Studies Review* 40, 2 (1997): 117–139.

———. *From Civilization to Segregation: Social Ideals and Social Control in Southern Rhodesia, 1890–1934.* Athens: Ohio University Press, 1994.

———. "If You Can Educate the Native Woman: Debates over the Schooling and Education of Girls and Women in Southern Rhodesia, 1900–1934." *History of Education Quarterly* 36, 4 (1996): 449–471.

———. "Mission Boys, Civilized Men, and Marriage: Educated African Men in the Missions of Southern Rhodesia, 1920–1945." *Journal of Religious History* 23, 1 (1999): 75–91.

Sundkler, Bengt. *Bantu Prophets in South Africa.* 2d ed. London: Oxford University Press, 1961.

Terry-Thompson, A. C. *The History of the African Orthodox Church.* New York: privately published, 1956.

Thompson, F. M. L. *The Rise of Respectable Society: A Social History of Victorian Britain, 1830–1900.* Cambridge, Mass.: Harvard University Press, 1988.

Tsomondo, Madziwanyika S. "Against Alienism: The Response of the Zionist and the Apostolic African Independent 'Christian' Church Movements to European Colonialism in Zimbabwe." *Journal of Southern African Affairs* 4, 1 (1979): 5–28.

Turner, Arthur. "The Growth of Railway Unionism in the Rhodesias, 1944–1955." In *The Development of an African Working Class: Studies in Class Formation and Action,* ed. Richard Sandbrook and Robin Cohen, 73–98. London: Longman, 1975.

Turner, Harold W. "African Independent Churches and Education." *Journal of Modern African Studies* 13, 2 (1975): 295–308.

Vail, Leroy, ed. *The Creation of Tribalism in Southern Africa.* London: James Currey, 1989.

Vail, Leroy, and Landeg White. *Power and the Praise Poem: Southern African Voices in History.* Charlottesville: University Press of Virginia, 1991.

Vambe, Lawrence. *From Rhodesia to Zimbabwe.* Pittsburgh: University of Pittsburgh Press, 1972.

———. *An Ill-Fated People: Zimbabwe Before and After Rhodes.* Pittsburgh: University of Pittsburgh Press, 1972.

van Onselen, Charles. *Chibaro: African Mine Labour in Southern Rhodesia, 1900–1933.* London: Pluto Press, 1976.

——. *Studies in the Social and Economic History of the Witwatersrand, 1886–1914.* Vol. 2, *New Ninevah.* London: Longman, 1982.

Vickery, Kenneth P. "The Rhodesia Railways African Strike of 1945, Part I: A Narrative Account." *Journal of Southern African Studies* 24, 3 (1998): 545–560.

——. "The Rhodesia Railways African Strike of 1945, Part II: Cause, Consequence, Significance," *Journal of Southern African Studies* 25, 1 (1999): 49–71.

——. "The Second World War Revival of Forced Labor in the Rhodesia." *International Journal of African Historical Studies* 22, 3 (1989): 423–437.

Waite, Gloria M. *A History of Traditional Medicine and Health Care in East-Central Africa.* Lewiston, N.Y.: Edwin Mellen Press, 1992.

——. "Traditional Medicine and the Quest for National Identity in Zimbabwe." *Zambezia* 27, 2 (2000): 235–268.

Warwick, Peter. *Black People and the South African War, 1899–1902.* Cambridge: Cambridge University Press, 1983.

Watkins, William H. "On Accommodationist Education: Booker T. Washington Goes to Africa." *International Third World Studies Journal and Review* 1, 1 (1989): 137–144.

Watson, Eugene. *Banned: The Story of the African Daily News, Southern Rhodesia, 1964.* London: Hamish Hamilton, 1976.

Weinrich, A. K. H. *African Marriage in Zimbabwe and the Impact of Christianity.* Gweru: Mambo Press, 1982.

Weisbord, Robert G. "British West Indian Reaction to the Italian-Ethiopian War: An Episode in Pan-Africanism." *Caribbean Studies* 10, 1 (1970): 34–41.

Weiss, Ruth, with Jane L. Parpart. *Sir Garfield Todd and the Making of Zimbabwe.* London: British Academic Press, 1999.

West, Michael O. "Beerhalls and Skokiaan Queens: The State, Female Brewers and Male Drinkers in Colonial Zimbabwe" (manuscript).

——. " 'Equal Rights for All Civilized Men': Elite Africans and the Quest for 'European' Liquor in Colonial Zimbabwe, 1924–1961." *International Review of Social History* 37, 3 (1992): 376–397.

——. "Ethiopianism and Colonialism: The African Orthodox Church in Zimbabwe, 1928–1934." In *Christian Missionaries and the State in the Third World,* ed. Holger Bernt Hansen and Michael Twaddle, 237–254. London: James Currey, 2002.

——. "Going to America: The Odyssey of Stephen Sithole, an African Evangelical Christian, 1938–53." *Journal of African Travel-Writing* 8/9 (2001): 136–150.

——. "Great Historical Document or Just Propaganda? The Atlantic Charter and Global Africa in the Era of World War II" (manuscript).

——. "Indians, India, and Race and Nationalism in British Central Africa." *South Asia Bulletin: Comparative Studies of South Asia, Africa and the Middle East,* 14, 2 (1994): 86–103.

——. "In Search of Ethiopianism: An Historical Investigator's Personal Odyssey in Zimbabwe." *Journal of African Travel-Writing* 1 (1996): 52–63.

——. "James Aggrey's Impact on Southern Africans." *Southern African Encounter* 3, 1 (1996): 20–23.

——. "Liquor and Libido: 'Joint Drinking' and the Politics of Sexual Control in Colonial Zimbabwe, 1920s–1950s." *Journal of Social History* 30, 3 (1997): 645–667.

——. "Nationalism, Race, and Gender: The Politics of Family Planning in Zimbabwe, 1957–1990." *Social History of Medicine* 7, 3 (1994): 447–471.

——. "Ndabaningi Sithole, Garfield Todd and the Dadaya School Strike of 1947." *Journal of Southern African Studies* 18, 2 (1992): 297–316.

——. "Pan-Africanism, Capitalism and Racial Uplift: The Rhetoric of African Business Formation in Colonial Zimbabwe." *African Affairs* 92 (1993): 263–283.

——. "A Seed Is Sown: The Impact of the Garvey Movement on Zimbabwe in the Interwar Years." *International Journal of African Historical Studies* (forthcoming 2002).

——. "The Tuskegee Model of Development in Africa: Another Dimension of the African/African-American Connection." *Diplomatic History* 16, 3 (1992): 371–387.

Wickins, P. L. *The Industrial and Commercial Workers' Union of Africa.* Cape Town: Oxford University Press, 1978.

Wood, J. R. T. *The Welensky Papers: A History of the Federation of Rhodesia and Nyasaland.* Durban: Graham Publishing, 1983.

Woodard, Komozi. *A Nation within a Nation: Amiri Baraka (Leroi Jones) and Black Power Politics.* Chapel Hill and London: University of North Carolina Press, 1999.

Woodward, C. Vann. *Origins of the New South, 1877–1913.* Baton Rouge: Louisiana State University Press, 1971.

Yoshikuni, Tsuneo. "Strike Action and Self-Help Associations: Zimbabwean Worker Protest and Culture after World War I." *Journal of Southern African Studies* 15, 3 (1989): 440–468.

Young, Crawford. *Politics in the Congo: Decolonization and Independence* (Princeton, N.J.: Princeton University Press, 1965.

Zeleza, Tiyambe. "The Moral Economy of Working Class Struggle: Strikers, the Community and the State in the 1947 Mombassa General Strike." *Africa Development* 20, 3 (1995): 51–87.

Zvobgo, C. J. M. *A History of Christian Missions in Zimbabwe, 1890–1939.* Gweru: Mambo Press, 1996.

——. "The Revd E. T. J. Nemapare and the African Methodist Church in Southern Rhodesia." *Rhodesian History* 6 (1975): 83–87.

——. "Southern Rhodesia under Edgar Whitehead, 1958–1962." *Journal of Southern African Affairs* 2, 4, (1977): 481–492.

Index

Page numbers in italic type refer to illustrations.

Adams College (South Africa), 62, 64

African Communities League, 143

African Methodist Church, 33, 169–170

African Methodist Episcopal (AME) Church: decline of, 169; government interference in, 145–146; missionaries of, 76; orthodoxy of, 150–151; in proto-national moment, 144–145, 149

African National Congress of Northern Rhodesia, 215, 287n53

African National Congress of Nyasaland, 215, 287n53

African National Congress of South Africa, 32, 34, 141–142, 154, 204

African National Congress of Southern Rhodesia. *See* Southern Rhodesia Bantu Congress (SRBC; later, Southern Rhodesia African National Congress); Southern Rhodesian African National Congress

African National Youth League (earlier, City Youth League): expansion of, 206–207, 208; goals of, 204–205; leadership issues and, 210–211, 228, 238; sexual violence of, 205–206; terminology of, 212. *See also* Southern Rhodesian African National Congress

African National Youth League (formed in Bulawayo), 285n10

African nationalism: agency in, 219–220; coalition for, 66–67; crisis in, 229–230, 232; defiance and confrontation in, 223–228; divisions in, 35, 211, 225–228, 232; educational agenda of, 51–59; emergence of, 5–6, 34–35, 203–207; housing issues and, 112, 115; inklings of, 167–168; intelligentsia's move into, 216–223, 239; nationalist moment in, 207–216; power assumed in 1980, 239–240; racial partnership to counter,
190, 194–197, 203, 212–213; students' grievances linked to, 59; terminology of, 33–34; whites' attempts to counter, 5–6, 223, 227–229, 232–235

African Native Welfare Association (earlier, Gwelo Native Welfare Association), 31

African Newspapers (business), 186

African Orthodox Church, 143–144, 149, 150–151, 169

African Teachers Association (ATA), 28, 34, 54–55, 56–57

African Trade Unions. *See* Federation of Bulawayo African Trade Unions (earlier, African Workers Trade Unions of Bulawayo)

African Universal Benefit Society, 31

African Voters League, 162–164, 165–166, 170

African Weekly (newspaper), 32, 265n59

African Welfare Society (earlier, Native Welfare Society): as counter to ICU, 139–140; financial aid from, 63–64; housing issues and, 105, 107; members of, *156;* name of, 32; women's group under, 257–258n34

African Women's Club, 257–258n34

African Workers Trade Unions of Bulawayo. *See* Federation of Bulawayo African Trade Unions (earlier, African Workers Trade Unions of Bulawayo)

African Workers Voice Association (later, British African National Voice Association), 166–167, 171, 172, 176, 185, 206

Africans: emergence of mission-educated, 43; relocation of, 107–109; rise of "new," 161–170, 174, 192; stereotypes of mission-educated, 39, 41; use of term, 31–32, 33

agency: domestic ideal and, 73–80; nationalism and, 219–220

ethnicity and ethnic tensions, 57, 211, 225–226, 232

Exeter University Law School (U.K.), 62

Fabian Colonial Bureau (U.K.), 185–186, 189
family, 61–62, 68, 70, 135. *See also* marriage
farmers. *See* cattle; Purchase Area system
FAWC. *See* Federation of African Women's Clubs (FAWC)
Federal Party, 191–192, 201–202, 213, 282n46
Federation of African Welfare Societies, 32
Federation of African Women's Clubs (FAWC), 77–81, 258nn49–50
Federation of Bulawayo African Trade Unions (earlier, African Workers Trade Unions of Bulawayo), 160, 161, 166, 171, 173, 178, 179
Federation of Rhodesia and Nyasaland (aka Central African Federation): acceptance of, 191–192; call to end, 214–215; dissolution of, 233, 234; education under, 49, 64–65, 255n159; establishment of, 79, 176, 177; government of, 16–17; ministers of, 50, 118; opposition to/support for, 111, 112, 180–187, 189–191; racial partnership and, 192–202
Federation of Women's Institutes of Southern Rhodesia, 79, 80
Fort Hare, University College, 60, 64
Fort Victoria: housing of, 103
Foster, L. H., 58, 252n114
Fraser, Gibson, 113–114
"freedom now" slogan, 220
freedom sitting: as tactic, 226
freehold tenure: struggle for, 107, 110–118, 194, 201. *See also* Purchase Area system

Gambo, F. M., *156*
Garvey, Marcus, 141, 143
Gatooma: housing of, 103
Gazi, Rev. K. M., *153*
gender: homeownership and, 104–105, 184; in public sphere, 7; South Africans' demands based in, 122–123; urban imbalance in, 133. *See also* domestic ideal
George (speaker), 171
Ghana: African nationalism in, 220
ghettoes. *See* townships and ghettoes; urban areas
girls, African: associations for, 21, 70–71; education of, 24, 69–70, 71–72; social control

of, 123; training of, 41; use of term, 27–28. *See also* women, African
"God Bless Africa" (anthem), 34, 154
Gold Coast: anticolonial protest in, 167, 169
Gombedza, Nicodemus, 36–37
Good Native: use of term, 14, 55
Goromonzi: school at, 49, 63, 64
government (white-settler-run): administrative positions in, 158; anti-African nationalist efforts of, 227–229, 232–235; association as supportive of, 131–134; on bridewealth debate, 85–88, 91, 261n87; churches opposed by, 143–146; domestic ideal fostered by, 71–73; education and, 15–16, 38–39, 40–51, 53–54, 58, 64–65; general strike and, 172–174; housing issues and, 100, 109–118; ICU opposed by, 138–147; on monogamous recidivism, 82–85; reorganization of (1898), 3; terminology of, 27, 28–29, 32–33. *See also* police force; voting system, nonracial; white settlers; *specific agencies and departments*
Great Zimbabwe, 23, 34–35, 219
The Guardian (newspaper), 165
Gwanda Reserve: RBVA in, 128–130; women's associations in, 76
Gwebu, Daniel "Fish," 141–142
Gwelo: housing of, 103; police/NDP clashes in, 223
Gwelo Native Welfare Association. *See* African Native Welfare Association (earlier, Gwelo Native Welfare Association); Southern Rhodesia Native Welfare Association (earlier, Gwelo Native Welfare Association)

Hadfield, F. L., 45, 53
Hampton Institute (U.S.), 45
Harari Choral Society, 94
Harari Recreation Hall (Salisbury), 166
health care: compulsory exams in, 152; ignored in townships, 102–103; male vs. female care in, 133, 134; NDP on, 226; traditional medicines for, 238, 291n5. *See also* diseases
Helping Hand Club, 76
Highfield village (Salisbury), 109–110
Hikura, E. M., 186
Hlabangana, Cephas, 60, 161
Hlabangana, Nsele S., 88, 89, 92
Hlabangana, Rev. Sitjenkwa, 60, 93
Hlabangana, Tennyson, 57, 60, 161, 168

233–235; on self-government, 168, 278–
279n68; on Todd, 213

Sobantu, J. H., 19–20, 21, *155,* 237

"social bar": use of term, 194

social gospel ideology: as influence, 149–150

social mobility: assertion of, 19–25; avenue to,
8; denial of, 1–2, 14–19; intergenerational,
59; opposition to, 3–5, 13, 39, 48, 59, 150;
South Africans' quest for, 121–122; Zionist
leaders in context of, 151. *See also* Christianity; domestic ideal; education; housing;
politics, African

social standing and respectability, 20–25,
30, 66

Sojini, John Wesley, 162

Somkence, Oliver, *156*

South Africa: Afrikaner nationalism and, 183;
AME Church in, 144–146; black political
activism in, 31–32, 121–123, 126, 135, 142–
143; college students in, 60, 61; establishment of Union of, 121; as influence, 25;
Treason Trial in, 216

South African National Council of
Women, 79

South African Native Affairs Commission
reports, 16, 41

South African War of 1899–1902, 121, 125, 183

Southern Rhodesia: constitution of, 224–225,
226, 288–289n84; expropriation in, 3; federation proposal and, 180–183; self-government
of, 17–18; use of term, 241n1. *See also* Federation of Rhodesia and Nyasaland (aka
Central African Federation); Zimbabwe

Southern Rhodesia African Association. *See*
Southern Rhodesia Native Association
(SRNA; earlier, Rhodesia Native Associa-
tion; later, Southern Rhodesia African
Association)

Southern Rhodesia African Literature
Bureau, 77

Southern Rhodesia African National Congress. *See* Southern Rhodesia Bantu Congress (SRBC; later, Southern Rhodesia
African National Congress)

Southern Rhodesia African National Fund,
56–57

Southern Rhodesia Bantu Congress (SRBC;
later, Southern Rhodesia African National
Congress): African nationalism taken up
by, 207; agenda of, 150–151, 153–154; cross-
class alliances and, 163–164; decline of

(WWII), 158; federation proposal and,
182, 183–184, 185–186; formation of, 30,
33–34, 152–153, 175–176; on freehold
tenure, 110; members of, *154;* name of,
32, 153–154; origins of, 56; political accommodation of, 154–155, 168–169; political reorganization and, 150–155; replacement
for, 54; strikes and, 160–162, 170, 171; Subversive Activities Act and, 178–179; Urban
Areas Act and, 165–166. *See also* Southern
Rhodesian African National Congress

Southern Rhodesia Bantu Missionary
Conference (earlier, Southern Rhodesia
Native Missionary Conference): educational agenda and, 52, 54; federation proposal and, 181; housing issues and, 99,
107; Jabavu's speech to, 274n1; merger of,
256n11; on monogamous recidivism, 82, 84,
85; name of, 29, 30; preacher-politicians in,
148–150, 169; SRBC and, 153

Southern Rhodesia Christian Conference,
256n11

Southern Rhodesia Labour Party, 109, 159,
276n32; African branch, 158–159, 163,
276n35

Southern Rhodesia Missionary Conference,
70, 148, 256n11

Southern Rhodesia Native Association
(SRNA; earlier, Rhodesia Native Association; later, Southern Rhodesia African
Association): agenda of, 29, 30, 132–134;
critique of colonialism and, 140–141; on
destocking, 91; educational agenda and, 53;
federation proposal and, 185–186; leadership and membership of, 130–131, 134–135;
libertarian principles defended by, 151–
152; name of, 29; Native Missionary Conference compared to, 149; opposition to,
135–136, 158, 175; persistence of, 147; political accommodation and, 131–132, 135, 146,
269n41; songs of, 34, 154; SRBC and, 152–
153; subsumed into Reconstituted Congress, 208–209

Southern Rhodesia Native Missionary Con-
ference. *See* Southern Rhodesia Bantu
Missionary Conference (earlier, Southern
Rhodesia Native Missionary Conference)

Southern Rhodesia Native Welfare Association (earlier, Gwelo Native Welfare Association), 141–142

Southern Rhodesian African National Con-

102; rejecting blacks in, 18–19; schools as discipline in, 51; SRNA in, 132; weddings in, 93. *See also* housing; townships and ghettoes
Urban Areas Act (1946), 103, 105, 106, 162, 165–166
urbanization, 50–51, 108–109, 150–151
Ushewokunze, Herbert, 65

values, 75, 79, 90, 91, 122. *See also* domestic ideal; education; self-help tradition
Vambe, Lawrence: CAS goals and, 196, 199; on English, 20; on freehold tenure, 112; on general strike, 172; on girls' education, 24; on housing scheme, 265n59; as IRA member, 195; on Todd, 213; on WWII's impact, 157; on Youth League, 210
van Onselen, Charles, 7
Vera, J. Wilson, 113
voting system, nonracial: British authorities on, 234; constitutional changes in, 224–225, 226, 227; defense of, 127–130, 132, 137, 162–165; demand for universal, 5–6, 204–205; NDP approach to, 217, 224; qualifications for, 53, 126–127; recommendations on expanding, 212; white liberals' support for, 194; white opposition to, 4–5, 19, 127, 162–163; women in, 268n21
Vukani M'Afrika Cultural Club, 76

Waite, Gloria, 291n5
Wakatama, Matthew, 63, 64, 288n78
Washington, Booker T., 34, 41, 45, 55–56, 58
Watch Tower, 150
Waters, Mary, 71, 74
Watson, Eugene, 232
Wayfarers (black girls' organization), 21, 70–71
weddings: "white" type of, 92–98. *See also* marriage
Welensky, Roy, 201–202
Wesleyan (British) Methodist Church: housing issues and, 104; preachers of, 33, 60, 148, *153;* territories of, 169; women's group in, 73–75
Wesleyan Methodist Native Evangelists and Teachers Convention, 86, 148
Western Commonage Advisory Board, 113–114
White, John, 82
white liberals: on African nationalism's lead-

ers, 219; racial partnership and, 192–201; voters' rejection of, 214
white settlers: African middle class opposed by, 3–5, 13, 48, 59, 150; on amalgamation, 180–181; containment policy of, 228–229; education of, 48, 54, 64, 255n159; hardening attitudes of, 212–214; housing issues and, 100–101, 107, 111–113, 115, 118; humiliation by, 21–23; interests of, 16–17, 108–109; labor needs of, 1, 18, 42; nonracial voting system opposed by, 4–5, 19, 127, 162–163; political power of, 17–18; preserving privileges of, 195; rebellion of (1965), 5–6, 234–235, 239, 258n49; terminology of, 27–29, 33. *See also* government (white-settler-run); women, white
white supremacy: challenge to, 19–25; education's role in, 66; elaboration of, 14–19; as federation goal, 192; organization to maintain, 229, 239; unintended counters to, 55–56, 251n88. *See also* Huggins, Godfrey; Smith, Ian
Whitehead, Edgar, 221
woman question, 68–69, 123, 132–133
women, African: domestic-oriented associations for, 73–80, 98; housing issues and, 104–105, 108–109, 184; ideal type of, 72–73; male control of, 123–124, 132–134; in nationalist movement, 228; populist organizing of, 128; scholarship on, 8; sexuality of, 91, 106; skills of, 74; social mobility for, 59; terminology for, 27–28; violence against, 205–206; vote for, 268n21; working issues and, 80, 106, 132–134. *See also* bridewealth; domestic ideal; girls, African; skokiaan queens (women beer brewers)
women, white: on education, 16, 38; as leaders in women's associations, 78–80, 258nn49–50; racism of, 242n13
Women's Prayer Union (Wesleyan Methodist Church), 73–74
working class. *See* labor force, African
World Federation of Trade Unions, 179–180
World War I era, 121, 124–126, 134–135
World War II era: differential responses in, 155–159; education impacted by, 48–51, 59; federation proposal in, 181–182; housing issues and, 111–112; political mobilization in, 159–167; self-help ventures during, 56
Wyatt, C. E., *156*

Michael O. West teaches in the Departments of Sociology and Africana Studies at Binghamton University. He is co-editor (with William G. Martin) of *Out of One, Many Africas: Reconstructing the Study and Meaning of Africa.* He has written widely on Zimbabwean and southern African history, and on the African diaspora.